ABOVE
THE
LAW

ABOVE

THE

LAW

by
James Boyd

THE NEW AMERICAN LIBRARY

COPYRIGHT © 1968 BY JAMES BOYD
ALL RIGHTS RESERVED.
NO PART OF THIS BOOK MAY BE REPRODUCED WITHOUT
WRITTEN PERMISSION FROM THE PUBLISHERS.
FIRST PRINTING.
PUBLISHED BY THE NEW AMERICAN LIBRARY, INC.
1301 AVENUE OF THE AMERICAS, NEW YORK, NEW YORK 10019
PUBLISHED SIMULTANEOUSLY IN CANADA BY
GENERAL PUBLISHING COMPANY, LTD.
LIBRARY OF CONGRESS CATALOG CARD NUMBER: 68–17056
PRINTED IN THE UNITED STATES OF AMERICA

ACKNOWLEDGMENT

I wish to acknowledge a deep debt of gratitude to Milton Viorst for his indispensable editorial assistance, his patient guidance, and his unfailing encouragement.

FOREWORD

There is an old taunt that says every great man has his twelve apostles but it's always the Judas Iscariot who writes his biography. That epithet may draw a flutter of renewed life from the publication of this book. For the subject, Senator Thomas J. Dodd, once had the potential for greatness of a kind; assuredly he had his disciples; and I was the closest of them until disaffection caused me to conspire against him.

This, then, is a story of betrayal, or, more precisely, of counter-betrayal. It concerns the inversion of values that spreads in inexorable ripples once a public man sells out his office and confronts his intimates with a choice between loyalty to their chief and loyalty to their own notions of integrity. The choice between sentiment and justice was made. Its effect—the clandestine exposure of Senator Dodd by his most trusted aides—has been widely condemned. Its alternative was generally ignored. Perhaps this was inevitable, for the greater the ambivalence men feel toward larger questions of ethics and honor, the more militantly they demand allegiance to the simpler irrelevancies. Thus, a flock of United States Senators sat unmoved over a fellow Senator's private pocketing of a quarter of a million dollars in political funds, but rose to gusty heights of invective against the four employees who violated "positions of trust" by exposing that transaction. And nearly a dozen syndicated columnists excused Dodd all the way, while demanding punishment, even prosecution, of those who opened his files and turned him in.

This reaction, more suited to the counsels of the underworld than to those of government and press, failed ultimately in its uncertain aims.

It could not salvage Dodd from a measure of disgrace and censure. Nor did it fatally damage his betrayers. However, like any distortion of the public dialogue, it harmed society at large. It blackened the air just enough to divert public attention from the real issues in the Dodd case, enabling the Senate to scuttle the major part of an investigation that might have touched off irresistible demands for Congressional reform. Our gravest disclosures were hidden from view. We were at length driven into recurring unemployment, blacklisted from government service, and officially denounced by the Senate—reprisals that are meaningful not for their harm to us, but for their effect in intimidating other public employees who might one day have followed our lead.

Senator Dodd, though somewhat deflated, still sits in a chair of might, still commands a vast government payroll, still wields the manifold powers of a committee chairman, still heads up Senate investigations into lawbreaking and into the state of our national security, still has a voice in making our laws, choosing our judges, and influencing our foreign policy. The corrosive customs and venerable deceits of the Senate itself, which Dodd so learned to master, remain unchanged.

And so the Dodd story, and that of the political milieu in which he thrived, has yet to be told. I try to tell it here.

I gladly confess that I recall Tom Dodd as a somehow larger and more appealing figure than his critics acknowledge or the record of the recent past shows. For twelve years I followed him, long enough to leave with me some fond memories and a share in his guilt. Had he been only an empty or venal man, his story would be unimportant. It is what he might have become, had the system through which he rose encouraged his strengths instead of his weaknesses, that gives to his fall an element of tragedy and hence a claim to significance. I am conscious of the terrible responsibility for truth that hangs over me, the more so because I am a committed party to the conflict here described. This circumstance has endowed me with both a vantage to utilize and a prejudice to master. It is for others to judge whether I have risen to that opportunity and that obligation. And judgments will not be lacking, for the Dodd affair is a living controversy whose end no one can yet tell.

James P. Boyd
Lakeville, Connecticut
December 11, 1967

ABOVE
THE
LAW

CHAPTER ONE

IN the late-August afternoon our car passed abruptly from the quiet of country roads, through the greenery of a summer colony, into the garish blare of downtown Atlantic City. A confusing array of hotel structures loomed around us, some reflecting the ornate opulence of 1900, others the glassy glitter of our own day. Neon signs blinked everywhere. It was a vast honky-tonk with a vestige of an earlier stateliness. Here and there a ten-gallon hat, white and substantial like an official presence, bobbed above a sea of madras shirts and floral-printed shifts. These and the photographs of L.B.J. nailed to the telephone poles were visible reminders of what we had come for—the Democratic National Convention of 1964.

Amid beach umbrellas, salt-water taffy and carrousels, the Democratic party had gathered to nominate a President and a Vice-President of the United States. We could feel the electricity that circulated, I think, through all those with a part in these events. And we felt like participants ourselves, for we had been summoned to Atlantic City by Senator Thomas Dodd, a man some believed might be the next Vice-President.

Four of us had driven up from Washington that afternoon in a holiday mood. I was the Senator's principal assistant and speechwriter; Marjorie Carpenter was his personal secretary; Doreen Moloney was his stenographer; Michael O'Hare was the office manager and all-around aide-de-camp.

Michael would be the indispensable pivot at Atlantic City. Though he had never been there before, within hours he would know where all the major hotels and headquarters were, how to cadge extra tickets and floor passes, where to apply pressure to get last-minute reservations, where Perle Mesta held court, how to get more telephones installed, and how, in the midst of limitless confusion, to transport an impatient Senator and his ubiquitous family wherever they wanted to go.

Marjorie and Doreen had aesthetic as well as secretarial responsibilities. One blonde and one dark, one speaking with a soft Arkansas drawl, the other with clipped British precision, they were to decorate the Senator's cavernous suite at the Dennis Hotel. Their job was to make guests comfortable, handle phone calls, and from time to time, take dictation. Though complete opposites, both were attractive, and the Senator liked to show them off.

It was my view that I was along just to be on tap—in case some form of lightning struck and a speech was suddenly needed. You couldn't prepare a Vice-Presidential acceptance speech in advance, first because it would seem presumptuous and second because it might be bad luck. I did not expect the lightning, and, happily cut off from my Washington office responsibilities, with no defined role to play at the convention, I looked forward to four days as a relaxed spectator—on the beach in the daytime and among the delegates at night. At *this* convention, there would be nothing of substance for a Senator's aide to do. L.B.J. had already attended to everything. It was only if I became part of the entourage of the Vice-Presidential candidate that demands would be made.

Senator Dodd, I knew, was mildly irritated at my seeming indifference. He wanted me to stay around his suite, to rise with the enthusiasms and commiserate with the despondencies that marked his mercurial temperament. But, after many months of continuous attendance upon him in Washington, I craved relief from this perpetual hammering of the emotions. At every pretext I slipped away to the carnival atmosphere of the boardwalk, where, in the democracy of Bermuda shorts and sports shirts, the great mingled indistinguishably with the lowly.

Dodd was right, of course, in sensing my aloofness. He had an uncanny faculty for knowing what people were thinking, almost before they knew it themselves. After a dozen years during which he was the dominant figure in my life, our relationship had begun to grow stale.

If in years past I had hung upon his every word and sought to antici-
pate his least wish, I now found extended contact with him somewhat
oppressive. His pungent maxims had begun to sound threadbare, his
thundering prejudices no longer warmed me, his strident certitudes
frequently left me in doubt. For years I had been his willing and
unquestioning alter ego, devoting more and more of my being to
building the public image of another man. I had learned to see issues
and events primarily in terms of their impact on Dodd's fortunes, and,
under the tyranny of a thousand news deadlines, I had come to prize
the exploitable phrase above the elusive fact. And now I was nagged
by a recurring sense of insignificance and tastelessness. Was it my
fault, or the Senator's, or was it simply in the nature of things? I did
not know, but I could no longer respond automatically to his every
impulse.

"Jon Newman is always with Ribicoff," Dodd blurted out on the
second night of the Convention to a room full of visitors. "They are
inseparable. They even eat breakfast together. I saw them this morning. But my administrative assistant is never with me any more. I
guess he is not as interested in my welfare."

A glint of anger blazed up in his hazel eyes. But before I could
reply, he broke the awkward silence with a hasty apology.

"I don't mean that," he said. "I know you do more for me than any
man has a right to ask of another, and when there is nothing to do I
don't blame you for not hanging around here."

But the Boss was hurt and I was somehow at fault. At least I felt
troubled, and as I rambled, in stolen hours, along the beach, I would
mull over the genesis of my growing disquiet.

I first met Tom Dodd, then a newly elected Congressman from
Hartford County, in 1953. I was twenty-four years old and had come
to Hartford only a few months before—shortly after graduation from
Boston University—to work for an insurance company. My job left me
some spare time and, through a nephew of Dodd's whom I had met, I
let it be known that I'd like to volunteer for some political work. With
an accessibility that I later learned was characteristic, Dodd asked me
to drop by his home for a visit.

When I arrived for my appointment at 8 P.M., he was not there.
Mrs. Dodd, a friendly and pleasant woman, put me at ease and then
went on about her business, with the practiced air of one who had

long ago accommodated herself to being stuck with her husband's visitors. Hours passed, while two gigantic Labrador dogs, black as coal, eyed me suspiciously. I did not mind waiting. In those days I would have gladly waited all night for a chance to talk with a member of the United States House of Representatives.

At about eleven o'clock, shortly after Mrs. Dodd invited me into the kitchen for a cup of coffee, a commotion at the rear of the house signaled that the Congressman had at last returned. Doors opened and shut, resonant apologies boomed out from a darkened entry, and then Dodd made his appearance, carrying a crate of oranges, which he placed on the floor. The dogs streaked across the room and clambered joyfully upon him, tails lashing to and fro. He beamed at the big animals, grunting affectionately, cuffing and wrestling with them, teasing and mugging at them with obvious pleasure. Only when they were pacified and lay sprawled at his feet on the kitchen floor did he turn to us.

"I had a wonderful evening, Grace. Fine people. Hello, young fellow, sorry to keep you so late. I hope you can stay a while."

He seemed to me a strikingly elegant figure, unusually handsome with piercing eyes under black brows, a classic profile, prematurely silvering hair framed by a black homburg, and cloaklike coat. He was short, but he had large features and a husky build that seemed to increase his stature. Beneath the first impression of elegance radiated a hint of homespun earthiness, a ruddiness of complexion, a contagious warmth that encouraged a feeling of communion.

"Let's sit here in the kitchen for a while. I think I'll have a little snack. I'm famished."

With that modest announcement, hat and coat still on, he rummaged through the refrigerator, came up with a cold leg of lamb, and began to assault it with a primitive vigor. He stood in the middle of the room, declaiming almost unintelligibly about his day's adventures, while wolfing down the cold lamb. Then, butcher knife in hand, he turned to the orange crate, and as my mild surprise turned to wonderment, he cut an orange in half and, with an explosive, rending, sucking sound, bit out the fruit in a voracious swoop that was awesome in its precision. He repeated the process with another and another and another until he had demolished at least eight oranges. Still unsated, he peered inquiringly around the kitchen, spotted a bunch of bananas and devoured three without pause. Then, with special relish, he reduced to crumbs a large chunk of Limburger cheese.

"A fellow gets mighty hungry on the road," he said, refreshingly oblivious to the impact his performance might have on a stranger. Then he escorted me out of the kitchen, now littered from end to end with the remains of his repast.

In his comfortable sitting room, in front of a log fire, sipping a tumbler of Scotch and savoring a long cigar, he easily returned to a suave urbanity. He made me feel immediately at home, entertained me with stories of my native Maine told in a flawless down-East accent, related personal remembrances of Harry Truman, Sam Rayburn, Alben Barkley, and Adlai Stevenson. He drew from me the story of my own life and background, my attitudes and aspirations. However green and awkward I must have appeared, he seemed deeply interested in me. The blazing logs became embers, Mrs. Dodd had long since slipped away, and we talked on. He took me up to the mountaintop: we would work together, we would lay plans "not for a year but for twenty years." He needed young people around him. There were significant things to be done, and I could help him in doing them. And then I noticed it was 2 A.M. I was embarrassed at having imposed upon a hospitable man whose time was important, but he would hear none of it and in the end let me leave only over strong protests, and with an agreement to have lunch the next day.

I arrived home in a state of unutterable elation and could not think of sleeping that night. A great man had offered me a chance to volunteer in a cause that had enthralled me since the days when, as a small child in pajamas, I used to crouch at the top of the stairs listening to my father relating to his friends the glories of Franklin D. Roosevelt, whose portrait hung above our mantel. I calculated that, with a little tightening of the belt, I could give up overtime work and devote all my free hours to Mr. Dodd. An unexpected deliverance from the humdrum and the ordinary seemed miraculously at hand.

Al Smith was once asked what was the most important element in his rise from the sidewalks of New York to the governorship and to a Presidential nomination.

"Just being around," he said.

There is no orderly blueprint for carving out a place in politics and no substitute for just being around. During my first years with Dodd I was his driver, bag-toter, errand boy, and midnight companion. Like many a politician, he liked a retinue, and I was an eager camp follower. I licked envelopes, ran to the cleaners, purchased cigars, carried press releases around to newspaper offices, kept the scrapbook up to date, and occasionally wrote "letters to the editor" extolling the virtues of Thomas J. Dodd. From the scrapbooks, from the recollections of admirers and critics, and from his own reminiscences in occasional moments of reflection, I learned a lot about the man who had become my idol.

Dodd was raised in a devout, middle-class Catholic home in Norwich, Connecticut, the youngest of five children and the only boy. His grandparents were Irish immigrants. His father, a small contractor, was of the stern and dignified Irish strain, rather than the jovial and convivial, and he set the tone of the household. When a new play or musical would arrive in town, Mr. Dodd would preview it alone; only if it passed his rigid censorship would he take Mrs. Dodd to see it. His four daughters all became schoolteachers, as their mother had been. Tom wanted to be a priest and at length entered a seminary in Buffalo, New York. But he found the religious life austere and cheerless, and decided that, as Catholics say, he did not have a vocation. He had an aspiration, however. He wanted to become an actor, but his father refused to entertain such frivolity and determined that the boy was to be a lawyer.

Dodd was educated, during the Depression, at Providence College and Yale Law School. The contrast between these institutions, one a struggling Dominican theological fortress, the other a highly secular and sophisticated breeding ground of agnosticism, was vast and bewildering. Young Dodd labored long to reconcile the absolutism of Saint Thomas Acquinas with the relativism of Professor Harold Laski. He emerged an unshaken Catholic and a militant New Deal Democrat who believed alike in the moral universe of the Scholastics and the welfare state of the Fabians.

In 1932 he began his last year at law school by winning the presidency of the Yale Democratic Club. With classmate Bob Wagner, son of the crusading New York Senator and one day to be mayor of New York, Dodd organized "The Flying Wedge," a group of enthusiastic college debaters whose mission it was to precede the major candidates along their speaking route each night, warming up the crowds, and keeping them occupied until the campaigners arrived. In squalid halls, on rustic platforms, and on courthouse steps, Dodd learned to conquer a natural fear of public speaking. At most stops there were no microphones or loudspeakers, and the audiences in that angry autumn of depression were not the courteous, passive spectators politicians customarily encounter. Dodd learned, in a sort of trial by combat, to project and conserve his voice, to bully hecklers in an authoritative manner, to take quickly the measure of a crowd, divining the touchstone of its reaction and the jugular vein of its discontent. He could, even then, rise above the mere marshaling of clichés to exercise a rude mastery of the dramatic and the inspirational. I have encountered people who, having long since forgotten the names of the major state candidates that year, could describe to me with lighted eye the early orations of young Tom Dodd.

Homer S. Cummings, leader of the Connecticut Democrats and soon to become F.D.R.'s first Attorney General, heard of Dodd and encouraged him to enter public service. Cummings suggested that the F.B.I. would be a good place to start. So, when Dodd graduated from Yale Law School in the spring of 1933, the new Attorney General sent him to J. Edgar Hoover, who was suitably impressed and tendered an offer as a special agent in what had become, in the era of daring bank-robbing gangs, the most glamorous agency in the public service.

As a novice, Dodd was sent to St. Paul where he found himself too restless, ambitious and individualistic to endure Hoover's harsh discipline. He remained in the F.B.I. for only about a year, long enough to play a minor role in the pursuit of John Dillinger. But it was also long enough to put the F.B.I. stamp permanently on his public image.

Dodd resigned when his patron and mentor, Congressman Francis T. Maloney, became a candidate for the United States Senate. Now married, Dodd joined Maloney's campaign staff and, after the Election-Day victory, was rewarded by an appointment as Deputy Director of Connecticut's W.P.A. Soon he became state director of the new and experimental National Youth Administration. By any measure, Dodd's political career was getting off to a good start.

The N.Y.A. post gave Dodd his first chance to run his own shop, and he reveled in it. The program was broadly designed in Washington to help underprivileged youths from families victimized by the Depression. But its practical impact depended upon the vigor and imagination of its state directors. Dodd saw in it a chance for public service and a springboard to public recognition; he made the best of both opportunities. Years later, in our campaign swings across Connecticut, it was commonplace to see people haltingly approach and say, "You don't remember me, Mr. Dodd, but twenty years ago—" and

then go on to say that because of a Dodd N.Y.A. program in Waterbury they had learned a lifetime trade, or that because of a part-time
N.Y.A. job they had been able to finish high school or begin college or
bring home the few extra dollars a week needed to keep their families
afloat and together. At the pinnacle of his career, Dodd would tell
Senate colleagues that, in retrospect, the years of his N.Y.A. stewardship were the most satisfying and rewarding of his life.

In 1938 Dodd became a special assistant to the Attorney General
and volunteered as a charter member of the first Civil Rights Section
of the Justice Department. This new unit was to undertake an experiment—to test the degree to which the Constitution and the supremacy
of Federal law could be invoked to safeguard civil rights. Attorney
Thomas Dodd was a willing guinea pig. There are yellowed clippings
in his scrapbook for 1939 and 1940 that tell tersely of the losing efforts
of a young Federal attorney to defend civil liberties in dusty, sun-
baked county seats of the Deep South. In Georgia, Dodd defended
the legal rights of illiterate laborers to organize; in Arkansas, he successfully prosecuted red-necked sheriffs for the arbitrary arrest and
shakedown of innocent Negroes; in South Carolina, he pursued the
Ku Klux Klan.

As his personal involvement in the plight of impoverished youth
had deepened his commitment to social reform, so his experience in
the Black Belt opened a new dimension of insight and understanding.
He was barely thirty, but he had seen much. He had learned that
courtliness and genteel manners could be a mask which hid the gross-
est cruelty. He had seen widespread pockets of depravity where the
Federal writ did not run. He had felt the shame and frustration of
facing ignorant jurors in stifling courtrooms where due process of law
was a humorous curiosity. And he saw lawlessness elevated by local
hoodlums to a virtue when he, a Federal officer, had to be escorted
across state lines under local police protection for his own safety.

"We won some cases and we lost some, mostly lost," Dodd said a
generation later. "But we started the fight. We staked out the claim to
Constitutional protection of basic rights, and we helped to lay the
foundation for victories that were to be won by other lawyers in other
decades."

*   *   *

Tom Dodd did not take up a gun in World War II. In his middle thirties, with five children and high blood pressure, he could not qualify for military service. But, determined to do his part, he left the field of domestic reform and became a prosecutor. Starting obscurely with the trying of draft dodgers, he later specialized in espionage and war-frauds cases. He passionately pursued German-American Bundists and profiteering businessmen who were selling faulty goods to the Armed Forces. He played a key role in the trial of a Nazi spy ring that ended in the conviction of several Bundists. (He has to this day on the wall of his Senate reception room a newspaper cartoon memorializing his role in this case.) He further enhanced his reputation by a sensational prosecution that began, as he fondly recalls, with a complaint by Marshal Stalin to President Roosevelt at the Teheran Conference that American-made communications wire was frequently found unusable by the Red Army. The President dismissed that complaint as one of Stalin's lesser reflections on the American war effort, but when he later received the same protest from General Eisenhower, he immediately ordered a top-priority investigation by the F.B.I. Dodd later tried and obtained conviction of high officials of the Anaconda Wire and Cable Company, a subsidiary of the Anaconda Copper Company, for calculated war frauds.

Dodd's success in these fields led in 1945 to an offer to join the American delegation to the Nuremberg War Crimes Trial. It posed a serious gamble for Dodd, now aglow with political designs. The post offered him was a minor one that would take him away from his family and from the political scene for a year or two. Already the proposed trials were being denounced as "illegal" by many, including Senator Robert A. Taft, and in the end Dodd's participation might prove to be a personal liability. But he intuitively saw it as a fateful opportunity. The defendants were to be the Nazi elite: Goering, Hess, Ribbentrop, Bormann, Papen, and top members of the German General Staff. They were to be tried jointly by the victorious Allies, the United States, the Soviet Union, the United Kingdom, and France, in pursuance of a wartime pledge that those guilty of war atrocities and crimes against the peace would be brought before an international tribunal. The chief prosecutor for the United States was to be Supreme Court Justice Robert H. Jackson, for whom Dodd had unreserved admiration.

Dodd decided to accept and in the spring of 1945 flew to Nuremberg to find it in ruins, with the stench of dead bodies still in the air. His zest and flair for the proceedings impressed Justice Jackson, who soon promoted him to Executive Trial Counsel, the number-two position in the delegation. For eleven grim months the four-power court performed what Dodd was later to call "an autopsy on history's most horrible catalogue of human crime." The trial, covered in depth by the press of the world, ended in the convictions of all but three of the defendants. Twelve were sentenced to be hanged, three to life imprisonment. Goering escaped the hangman through suicide. A new precedent in international law had been set, hotly contested in the United States and abroad.

The Nuremberg ordeal made a profound impact on Dodd. For twenty years he has maintained silence about the most important aspects of his participation. He has never written about the trial, as have lesser participants, nor in any of the hundreds of voluble recollections of his past did he ever discuss with me anything substantial about it. He did comment on some of the incidentals, such as his legendary drinking bouts with the Russian delegation, but he has been strangely mute about the central events. Nor would he answer serious inquiries from historians seeking to reconstruct the trial. For a time I thought that perhaps he had played an insignificant role there, but in a luncheon conversation in 1964 a correspondent who had covered the Nuremberg proceedings two decades before told me that Dodd was the key figure behind the American effort.

"Tom always pulled things together when they seemed to be falling apart," he said. "He provided the direction and drive."

Whatever the reasons for his uncharacteristic reticence—whether humility, or a reaction to the horrors unearthed there, or remorse over some aspect of a searing experience—Dodd returned from Nuremberg a changed man. Outwardly he had aged; his hair had whitened at thirty-nine. Inwardly he had become an ideological Cold Warrior, his views on public issues dominated by a preoccupation with the Communist menace. His moral indignation, always strong, had been redirected from domestic injustice to international conspiracy.

Dodd was by now an established political presence in Connecticut, though still detached from the mainstream of its politics. Laurels as a spokesman for freedom and a pioneer in international law rested becomingly on his photogenic features. With philosophic smile, flowing silver hair, soft bow tie, and a pipe held in reflective pose, he looked the authentic statesman. Living comfortably with his burgeoning family near the historic green in Lebanon, Connecticut, in a reconstructed old home that antedated the American Revolution, he meditated on the future. Honors descended on him: the United States Medal of Freedom, a Presidential Citation from President Truman, the Czech Order of the White Lion, awarded by the patriot-President Eduard Benes. The Communists also sought to honor his anti-Nazi record, but he spurned an award from the Polish Government, saying that he would no more accept an honor from the Communists than from the Nazis. He did accept scores of speaking engagements from eager audiences throughout Connecticut and beyond. He dabbled in internationalism, becoming president of Connecticut's United World Federalists, but later, to the relief of his advisers, quietly pulled out on the ground that so long as divisive Communism continued to poison international relations, one-worldism was an unrealistic and unattainable dream.

Then he made his decision. Moving to fashionable West Hartford in Hartford County, Connecticut's Democratic powerhouse, he entered private law practice and drew dead aim at the 1948 Democratic gubernatorial nomination. Thus he began what turned out to be a grueling and frustrating decade of political warfare. It was to devour his physical and emotional resources, undermine his financial well-being, and leave an indelible stain on his view of politics and human nature.

Dodd's 1948 bid ended in failure, due in part to his indifference to the powerful state Democratic organization headed by John M. Bailey and, in part, to his inopportune and uncompromising anti-Communism. His major opponent for the Democratic nomination was Chester Bowles, a personable ex-Republican and former isolationist now turned ardent New Dealer and internationalist. Bowles and Dodd contrasted sharply. This was the year of the Wallace Progressives, a third-party leftist movement founded on the contention that the United States should move sharply toward socialism and cease its hostility toward the Soviet Union. Bowles airily dismissed the "Communist menace," domestic and international. He had once equated the communization of Eastern Europe with the conquest and settling of our own West. He offered ambitious proposals for economic growth in Connecticut and held out the olive branch to the Wallaceites, a well-organized and vocal group expected to draw perhaps 100,000 votes away from the Democratic state ticket. Dodd, rejecting advice that he concentrate on Bowles's non-Democratic, non-Connecticut background, threw down the gauntlet on the Communist issue. He condemned Bowles's naïveté and demanded that the Democratic party unequivocally condemn the Wallace movement as a Communist-infiltrated fifth column.

State Chairman John M. Bailey, a benign cynic whose shrewdness and balance gave perceptible strength to an otherwise bland countenance, was to be the deciding factor. Forever chomping a cigar, Bailey was frankly contemptuous of ideological dispute. He believed in organization, in timing, in compromise, and in working unity. He had become the strong man of Democratic politics because he was dispassionately objective, fair, and true to his word. That the Wallace candidacy would make Truman's cause hopeless in Connecticut, he accepted; but he did not accept the same fate for his first concern, the Democratic state ticket. In the end, at the Democratic State Convention in Hartford, he jettisoned Dodd, nominated Bowles, masterminded the agreement of the Progressive party to withdraw its state ticket in favor of Bowles, and offered Dodd the consolation prize of the lieutenant-governorship with a pledge of future support for higher office—a settlement that would spike division and come as close as possible to satisfying the major elements within the Democratic spectrum. But Dodd bolted—both the convention and the party—with the blunt declaration that he would not run on a ticket backed by Communists. Hailed for his courage by exultant Republicans, he burned his bridges behind him and charged into self-imposed exile.

Bailey proved a minor prophet. Harry Truman's gallant stretch drive could not quite salvage Connecticut, which he lost to Dewey by the margin of the votes Henry Wallace took from him; but Bowles, beneficiary of the Wallace vote, squeaked into office, launching the present era of dominance for Connecticut Democrats and for the Bailey organization.

Dodd—barred from party councils, reduced to a modest law practice, scorned by "practical" politicians who extolled the virtue of rolling with the tide—seemed both finished and unlamented. But he was not long without the rags of vindication. The Communist infiltration of the Progressive party was at length ruefully conceded by Wallace himself. People who had never heard of Dodd before had come to admire his stand on principle. His stature rose even as his political isolation deepened.

By the time of the 1950 election campaign, some Connecticut Democratic leaders had begun to have second thoughts about Dodd. Senator Joseph R. McCarthy was rolling across the land in high gear and, with several Democratic scalps on his belt, had invaded Connecticut to paste "soft on Communism" labels on Democratic candidates, principally the prestigious senior Senator Brien McMahon, chairman of the Joint Congressional Committee on Atomic Energy. Dodd was asked to be the sacrificial David and take on McCarthy in a predominantly Catholic state where the Wisconsin Senator enjoyed strong support. Dodd accepted and, in McMahon's behalf, convincingly assaulted McCarthy's demagoguery in a series of withering statewide broadcasts. Senator McMahon won re-election handily, but Governor Bowles and the Democratic state ticket were defeated. Dodd had recovered some lost political ground.

Two years later, in the summer of 1952, McMahon was suddenly stricken with cancer and died shortly after his name was placed in nomination for President at the Democratic National Convention in Chicago. Dodd wished to succeed him, but Congressman Abe Ribicoff, young, attractive and phenomenally popular in Hartford County, was tapped by Bailey to seek McMahon's Senate seat in the November elections. With Ribicoff, a liberal Jew, and incumbent Senator William Benton, a liberal Protestant, heading the ticket, Bailey, who always played the ethnic percentages, decided that he needed a moderate Irish Catholic to balance things. He was magnanimous enough to turn to Dodd, offering him Ribicoff's prized Congressional seat. Dodd was humble enough to accept. In November, Ike swept all before him in Connecticut, bringing down every major Democrat except one. In a curious twist of fate, Dodd emerged the lone survivor, carrying Hartford County by 24,000 votes despite Ike's 5,000 plurality. With McMahon gone, Ribicoff and Benton defeated, Bowles in India as Ambassador, Bailey's organization battered, and himself the victor in Connecticut's key Congressional district, Dodd's political stock, valueless for years, suddenly appeared to be booming.

It was at this time that I first met Tom Dodd. Though barely sworn into Congress, he already felt constrained by its limitations. He looked to the governorship race a year hence and beyond that to the Senate and after that—who could say what might lie in store for him? Though frustrated at being an unimportant junior member of a 435-man body, he made a constructive record. His Nuremberg fame helped him to a first-term appointment to the Foreign Affairs Committee. He worked well with the House Democratic leadership, voted with his party on basic issues, rose above sectionalism by backing the St. Lawrence seaway, supported internationalism, defended the Eisenhower foreign policy in well-publicized instances, fought for civil liberties, and steadily built an image as a statesman—moderate and enlightened, above partisanship and independent of political control.

But he was not to be governor. Bailey, the architect, still looked on Ribicoff as the vehicle for Democratic resurgence and skillfully sewed up his gubernatorial nomination well in advance of the 1954 state convention. There was no primary law in Connecticut then, no appeal from the concensus of a handful of party leaders. Angered that the bosses had denied him the opportunity for an open fight for the nomination, Dodd announced his resignation from politics and went off to Europe in time to miss the convention altogether. But Bailey pursued him. House Democratic Leader John McCormack publicly urged him to reconsider, and Dodd, perhaps playing coy, permitted himself at last to be persuaded. Renominated by acclamation, he won a whopping re-election to Congress by a record margin of 36,000 votes. He led the party ticket and helped Ribicoff to a hairline victory over Republican Governor John Lodge. I remember our victory party in the Dodd home that crisp November night and can still feel the aura of its shining visions of the future.

Dodd had earned his chance and when he sought the 1956 Democratic Senate nomination in a year when party prospects were to be submerged by the second Eisenhower tidal wave, it was his without opposition. Sitting high up in the balcony of Bushnell Memorial Hall, I thrilled with pride as Dodd, surrounded by his wife, Grace, and their six young children, made a fighting acceptance speech that pumped life and hope into a listless, defeatist convention. He had placed a higher value on the nomination than the party leaders who had cynically presented it to him with the caveat that he would have to raise his own campaign money. Before going to Convention Hall that morning he had said to me, "Even if we lose the election, it is a wonderful honor just to be nominated." It was the last time he was to speak of the possibility of defeat.

I took a leave of absence from my regular job at the Aetna Life Insurance Company, moved into the Dodd home and eagerly plunged into our uphill struggle. I had long since been promoted from driving cars and running errands—perhaps because Dodd panicked at my poor driving—and was now occupied with preparing pamphlets, press statements, position papers, and speech drafts. I gave little thought to victory or defeat. To me, merely to take part in a Senate campaign, working for a man such as Tom Dodd, was sufficiently rewarding.

All the political weathervanes that year pointed to a massive Republican win. Without financial help from his party, without newspaper support, and without an optimistic word from anyone, Dodd fought gamely. He carried the Democratic message to every corner of Connecticut, winning the esteem of local party workers who would later remember him as a fighter undaunted by hard times. Pursuing an eighteen-hour-day schedule of personal appearances that began with dawn at railroad commuter stations and endured past midnight in endless tours of factory night shifts, he impressed something of his personality and drive on the state's voters. With the help of Joe Blumenfeld, his law partner and finance man, he somehow raised $100,-000 and spent a great deal more on credit. We distributed half a million Dodd pamphlets, more than I like to remember, by hand. Television and radio, live and spontaneous in those days, was steadily stepped up, even as the polls brought darkening news. When, in October, Adlai Stevenson's aides publicly gave up Connecticut for lost, Dodd fought on. On the afternoon before Election Day, trembling with fatigue, eyes rimmed with dark circles, Dodd startled his despondent staff by adding to his schedule an open-car tour of the state, "to encourage the party workers."

But no personal effort could withstand the Republican deluge of 1956. Eisenhower defeated Stevenson in Connecticut by 305,000 votes, a margin that far exceeded all previous election records. Dodd ran 175,000 votes ahead of Stevenson, but still lost by a substantial margin. As early as seven-thirty on election night his defeat was certain. But though a year's effort lay in ruins, Dodd remained unabashed. On that night of Democratic disaster, he toured TV and radio stations making gracious concession speeches to audiences he knew to be at peak size. And then he went to bed.

The next morning he had to face the consequences of defeat. Deprived of his House seat, physically and financially exhausted, he nevertheless found encouragement in the morning voting statistics, which in almost all of the state's electoral districts showed Dodd leading every other Democrat. He called me to have breakfast at his home, where others of his staff were assembled. The glowing political posters and bright decorations of the previous night's "victory party" looked

mockingly down upon the wreckage. Sitting in pajamas and bathrobe, his ashen face like a death mask, Dodd delivered not an elegy
but a pep talk.

"This is a victory, not a defeat," he said. And he began charting
plans for a 1958 comeback.

During the autumn of 1957 Dodd engaged in a series of critical
discussions with friends and advisers about his political future.
Having shared a defeat with him, I was accorded the privilege of
giving advice. Dodd was now fifty years old. Ten contentious years
had passed since he returned from Nuremberg and vaulted into the
political arena. Into those make-or-break years he had poured out
every resource of mind and body and yet had nothing tangible to
show for it. Something of his old buoyancy was gone, as though some
dark and secret knowledge of man's ways had left a mark on him.
And an occasional flicker in his left eye, a mild tremor at the corner
of his mouth, bore fleeting witness to his long and consuming travail.

But there were intangibles no man could measure. He was favorably known; he was respected by many; he was very popular in pivotal
areas; he had woven a labyrinthine network of personal relationships
in every part of Connecticut. He was still relatively young, handsome,
and vigorous, and adversity had nurtured in him a canny wisdom.
Above all, he remained bold and aggressive among cautious rivals
who carefully counted costs.

The coming year would redeem or confirm all past reverses. It was
to be a Democratic year, given Governor Ribicoff's unquestioned
strength and the favorable political winds blowing from Maine to California. And there was a vulnerable Republican Senator up for re-election.

Dodd turned to me, I think, because the counsel of his senior advisers was too cautious for his mood and personality. They wanted him
to be conciliatory in pressing his cause, to accommodate Chairman
Bailey, and to leave open a safe retreat to his old Congressional seat if
he failed to achieve the main prize, an outcome which they obviously
thought likely. But to me, it was for Dodd now or never, and the new
state primary law seemed almost tailored to Dodd's situation. I urged
a frontal assault on the Senate nomination, an open fight with Bailey if
necessary and a statewide primary if all else failed. This was what he
wanted to hear; it squared with his own instincts that told him his life

was at a crisis point and there must be no pussyfooting. He asked me to draft an unequivocal public statement announcing his candidacy. Released in October, months in advance of the traditional time for such announcements, it was considered a strong statement and it rocked the state's political circles. Dodd claimed the nomination as a right, asserted overwhelming popular support, pledged an uncompromising fight to the finish, including Connecticut's first statewide primary if party politicians in back rooms tried to flout the public will. If the organization was to beat him this time it would have to beat him in the open.

From October to February, while other candidates hesitated and postured, Dodd toiled to build up so much visible strength that there would be no chance for Bailey to generate a consensus behind someone else. He had set himself to a brutal task. Connecticut is a land of contrasts; its western section includes perhaps the richest stretch of suburbia in the world—Greenwich, Westport, Darien, New Canaan, Fairfield, Stamford—the lush retreats of New York City executives and the rich and well-born; its eastern part features blackened mill towns riddled with poverty and unemployment. It is a highly industrial state, yet one that has deep roots in old rural New England. It is the capital of the world's insurance industry, and Hartford has its own caste of Brahmins. It grows the best cigar leaf and produces the mightiest space engines. Its population is more than fifty percent Catholic, with a large segment of old-line Yankee Protestants and a considerable Jewish element. Its industrial areas are a nationality melting pot—Poles, Irish, Italians, Hungarians, Ukrainians, even Portuguese. It has a handful of cities in the 100,000-to-200,000 class and 160 small towns. Dodd set out to woo the one thousand individual delegates, scattered among all these towns, who held his fate in their collective hands. If he lost this one, it was over for him; there would remain only the dreary processing of wills and contracts.

He had no money and no formal organization. His staff consisted of his legal secretary, Mary Flynn, and three unpaid volunteers: Joe Blumenfeld, his law partner, whose task was to raise a limited budget; Ed Sullivan, a grizzled veteran of the political wars who once drove a beer truck and who would be Dodd's contact man; and myself.

Arrayed against him, as yet unannounced, were two nationally known figures, both millionaires. They were Chester Bowles, his old luster as O.P.A. boss and as Governor now polished up by a widely acclaimed performance as ambassador to India; and William Benton, former Senator, McCarthy-slayer, onetime Assistant Secretary of State, founder of Musak, and currently head of *Encyclopaedia Britannica*. Also lined up against Dodd was the labor movement, partial to Bowles, the political machines of almost all of the major cities, whose leaders detested Dodd as a maverick, and the Bailey organization, publicly uncommitted but known to be quietly opposed to Dodd. Outside his own Hartford County, where his personal popularity assured strong delegate backing, Dodd had to collect his delegates one by one, by pressing the flesh in a hundred small towns and in a few cities where local divisions gave him an opening. Unable to compete with his opponents in spending money, Dodd had to compensate with energy. Every night during the severe winter of 1957–58 he was on the trail, hurrying back and forth over country roads, speaking to small groups of from six to sixty. He knew the state. He knew all the catwalks and shortcuts. In every town and village crossroads he knew people *personally* from way back when. These were the people he had to reach if he was to get the nomination.

I remember how, on one wintry March night, with snow falling steadily and roads almost impassable, he rejected common-sense counsels to cancel an appearance before the Norwich Democratic Town Committee. Twice during the trip from Hartford to Norwich our car skidded off the road, but Dodd would not turn back. We arrived late at night at the Wauregan Hotel in downtown Norwich, fearing that a disappointed audience had long since gone home. Instead we found a warm, boisterous reception, a partisan throng twice the size of that which had heard Bowles in this same room on a clear night two weeks earlier. With snow melting on his coat collar, Dodd spoke compellingly of the rigors facing a poor man in politics. When he finished, he received a spirited ovation and the announcement that eleven of the twelve Norwich delegates had committed themselves to Dodd. On our jubilant trip homeward the snow changed to sleet. It was my turn at the wheel and I tried to proceed cautiously, but Dodd kept pressing me to "make time." At the top of a hill, looking down into a yawning valley, I suddenly lost control of the car and it began spinning round and round, down a twisting incline. For what seemed an eternity Dodd and I hung on, suspended in tense silence, listening helplessly to Ed Sullivan banging from side to side in the back seat. Narrowly missing an oncoming car, we plunged headlong into a great snowbank.

"Don't anyone move or speak," said Dodd.

And for a minute we sat in dark silence listening to the sound of our breathing; then his benediction, "Thank God, no one is hurt."

We were pulled out of the snowbank by a passing farmer and resumed our homeward trek at ten miles per hour, our heads craning out the side windows peering into the sleet, trying to see five yards ahead.

Nor could indignity dampen Dodd's thrust any more than the snows. Hearing that a delegate named Bromley in the rural hamlet of Lisbon was still undecided as the convention approached, Dodd drove out to his secluded farm on a hot Saturday afternoon in June. He found Bromley near the barn, standing on top of a huge manure pile, pitchfork in hand.

"I'm Tom Dodd and I would like to have your support."

No response from Bromley, only a disdainful look. Dodd started clambering up the manure pile.

"I'm an ordinary, independent man, just like yourself," he continued, "and if I can't get the help of independent people living in the country, the city machines will beat me."

Now near the top of the pile, looking a little ludicrous in his panama hat and dark suit, Dodd made his pitch to the taciturn Bromley, who continued to ignore him with fine detachment. The perspiring candidate at length descended with as much aplomb as possible, brushed himself off and looked up for some last sign of acknowledgment.

Bromley lowered his pitchfork, looked down inscrutably at Dodd, and said, "I don't know. I could be for you, maybe. Course, I don't know anything about you, but up to now you're the only one who's asked me."

With that he resumed his labors, and Dodd departed, wondering if he had wasted a precious afternoon.

The nomination drive was now in its decisive stage. Dodd was here, there, everywhere, cajoling, entreating, bluffing, threatening, twenty hours a day. He waited impatiently for people to awake in the morning so he could get in a dozen phone calls before hitting the road. He grimaced at roadside telephone booths when sleepy voices at the other end signified that it was already past midnight and he'd have to stop calling till morning.

The long struggle, fought with total intensity, took its toll. Under the physical demands and mental pressures of the campaign, he was leaning more and more on alcohol as a prop. The involuntary tremors in his face were now a little more noticeable. Near-exhaustion had faded his ruddy complexion.

The opposition spread stories that Dodd was a chronic drunk. The charge that he had received a $50,000 payoff for sponsoring foreign aid to Guatemala while a House member was being circulated among key delegates. Rumors that impending bankruptcy would soon force his withdrawal were carefully planted.

In unguarded moments, on post-midnight rides, after hearing that an old friend had defected or that an old foe had denounced him afresh, he would reflect on the high price that politics exacts. He would speak of valued friendships that had cracked under the clash of ambitions, and of forced alliances with those he disliked and who disliked him. He would lament the thousands of nights over the past quarter century that he had been away from his family, nights when a daughter was having a birthday party or a son was in a school play, hours he had squandered trying to impress querulous strangers—that could not now be reclaimed. He would speak of a life devoted to debate, argument, and recrimination, and of the hot contentions that had from time immemorial quickened the heart, jumped the blood pressure, and toughened the sensibilities. He would see again the long procession of nameless halls and dreary banquet rooms in cheap hotels where he had "sung for his supper," the mornings given to Communion breakfasts and the evenings to wakes, the preposterous antics of the Moose, the Elks, the Eagles, and the Lions that had to be looked on with an approving face. He would reflect on the innumerable trifles he had had to endure for the rare moment of genuine achievement; and the endless nervous waiting, hat in hand, while political hacks, crude, militant, and callously self-seeking, in caucuses, back rooms, and convention suites, decided *his* life and *his* future—and that of his family.

"Why does any man take up politics?" he would say. "Why does any man stay in it?"

And then we would finally arrive at his West Hartford home and, taking advantage of his reflective mood, Ed and I would try to get away to catch a few hours of sleep. But no. The reluctant politician would suddenly revive.

"Come on in for a little talk, boys, please. It's only one o'clock. I have something very important I want to discuss with you." And we knew we were trapped for another session of counting up delegates.

Once inside, after turning on at least a dozen lamps, as if to point out that it was not late at all, he would bring out the dog-eared "lists," mimeographed sheets containing the names of all the 894 delegates. And we would go over them for hours, name by name, each of us giving our latest report on the situation in every town. By now Dodd knew the background of each delegate, his business, his friends, his grievances, his political designs, how to appeal to him.

"This Kelly here is not a bad fellow, Ed. He should be for me. One of my sisters went to school with him. I heard the other day that Bowles turned him down for some minor appointment when he was Governor. Get Frank to talk to him and tell him I'd like to drop by and see him. Sometimes all these fellows want is a little attention. Let's get on this first thing in the morning—without fail."

For several days our count had showed fifty-one percent of the delegates for Dodd on the first ballot. If we could just hold on. Only when the last doubtful delegate was discussed would Dodd nod off to sleep in his chair. And then we would stealthily retreat, fearful of reawakening him.

By convention time in late June, Dodd could not be denied. His adversaries had been outflanked and overwhelmed. His gathering strength and the authentic ring of his primary threats had created a situation that Chairman Bailey and Governor Ribicoff could no longer control without a general bloodletting, so they judiciously had stepped aside and pledged neutrality. And he overcame Bowles and Benton because, at bottom, he had more appeal for rank-and-file Connecticut people and politicians, and he had worked longer and harder to get that appeal across.

He had made at all times a total commitment, while his opponents at critical moments played it safe, holding on to their options. He went over the top on the first ballot on a sweltering June morning, stunning his opposition with a tremendous show of strength in Hartford County, holding his own in the rest of the state, and clinching the nomination in quaint Litchfield County. When Bromley of the manure pile solemnly voted for "Tom Dodd," I put my charts away. It was all over but the counting.

In November, following a campaign that seemed anticlimactic, Dodd defeated incumbent Senator William Purtell by a wide margin, aided by the unprecedented landslide victory of his running mate, Governor Ribicoff, whose pulling power swept Democrats into office in places where a Democrat had not won in a hundred years. The new Senator-elect left for the Caribbean on a long vacation, and I went to Washington, wide-eyed and self-important, to make arrangements for his assumption of office.

On the opening day of the Eighty-sixth Congress in January, 1959, Dodd was sworn in by Vice-President Nixon and took his place on the Senate floor for the first time, while a privileged group of friends and family watched with proprietary gratification from the Senate gallery. After the ceremony, the Senator, Joe Blumenfeld, and I talked of old battles as we walked through echoing halls in the Senate Office Building to take possession of his suite. Inside the high-ceilinged, marbled room with antique fireplace and mahogany doors, which was to be the Senator's personal office, we paused before the great desk, square and forbidding, and the high-backed leather chair that seemed the symbols of the prize that had come after so long a quest.

"You sit in the chair first, Joe," said Dodd.

And after Joe tried it out it was my turn. Then we laughed and applauded as the Senator self-consciously took his place. As the day of his nomination victory had been one of triumphant exaltation, so this was one of almost euphoric anticipation. The ugly, dark things were behind; ahead were the shining battles for civil rights, social reform, economic progress, the defense of freedom, and perhaps a place in history.

Seven weeks after he entered the Senate, Tom Dodd broke the tradition that new Senators should remain silent by delivering a challenge to American policy makers to stand firm in the face of Soviet pressure on Berlin. The speech, which I drafted, attacked the views of two of his most prominent colleagues, Mike Mansfield of Montana and William Fulbright of Arkansas, both of whom advocated more flexible policies designed to avert a major confrontation with the Kremlin.

> The Communists have remained intransigent in their unjust position for 14 years [Dodd said]. Must we therefore retreat from our just position?
>
> Is our Berlin policy too rigid and inflexible? I think not. There is no peculiar virtue in the concept of flexibility. To me, flexibility implies compromise and concession. When applied to funda-

mental principles, right principles, flexibility is not only without virtue; it becomes a vice.

In the debate that followed, senior Senators were impressed with the skill and force with which the newcomer defended his ground. Dodd's maiden speech made front-page headlines, reaped a harvest of editorial garlands, and was the subject of an approving lead article by *Time* Magazine, which credited him with having initiated the most important Senate debate in a decade. That episode set the tone for Dodd's first term—bold, vigorous, controversial, and independent.

Reputed to be a "Johnson man," Dodd showed his independence in 1960 by breaking a near-solid front of Democratic opposition to President Eisenhower's nomination of former Atomic Energy Commission Chairman Lewis L. Strauss as Secretary of Commerce. He not only refused to vote with the leadership, but insisted on taking the Senate floor on the night of the decisive vote to make a bristling defense of Strauss. In one of the most dramatic of modern Senate roll calls, Majority Leader Lyndon Johnson, the master parliamentary strategist, produced a one-vote margin against Strauss. Dodd had staked a lot on a losing cause. But he had shown that he was his own man. He gained stature by demonstrating that he was not afraid to break party ranks or to antagonize the most powerful elements in the Senate.

By this time, Dodd, as acting chairman of the Internal Security Subcommittee, had begun to attract notice, not all favorable, for his investigations into subversion. Drew Pearson called him a "bargain-basement McCarthy." The British critic Kenneth Tynan labeled him a witch-hunter and complained vaguely of star-chamber proceedings. Though conservative columnists lauded him as the leading anti-Communist in the Senate, Dodd, in his relations with his liberal friends, was on a hot seat and he knew it. He was painfully conscious of the ghosts of Joe McCarthy, William E. Jenner, and J. Parnell Thomas lurking in the wings, where they could be summoned forth to discredit his own efforts. But Dodd took the position that he would neither be scared off nor repeat the irresponsible grotesquerie of the past.

Early in 1961, Dodd learned that the Commerce Department of the new Kennedy Administration had approved for shipment to the Soviet Union forty-five precision machines capable of producing miniature ball bearings for space and military rocketry. Dodd had been watching this transaction for some time and had quietly requested the advice of a dozen technical experts. Their unanimous opinion, which

Dodd incorporated into a report, was that these machines, unavailable anywhere else in the world, would provide the Soviets with a major breakthrough in military and space technology. Dodd did not turn to the press; he took his report to President Kennedy, who read it on the spot and ordered the shipment canceled.

With similar discretion, Dodd tackled Communist infiltration of the Committee for a Sane Nuclear Policy, an influential organization opposed to American weapons programs. Dodd disagreed with SANE, but was determined to provoke no charges of Red-baiting. Having acquired evidence that the New York chapter, as well as some others, was dominated by Communists, he refrained from taking public action that could have damaged the reputations of prominent Americans of unquestioned patriotism. Instead, Dodd chose to work with SANE's national leadership, headed by Norman Cousins, editor of the *Saturday Review*, to persuade the Committee to weed out its subversive elements. After closed Senate hearings in which twenty-two New York members, including nine local chairmen, took the Fifth Amendment on questions related to Communist-party membership, SANE revoked the New York charter and organized a new group. So fair was Dodd's inquiry that Cousins later said, "Tom Dodd could have seriously damaged SANE and made political capital out of the investigation. Instead he confined himself to a few specific cases and maintained absolute respect for the rights of the individuals concerned."

To be sure, Dodd occasionally surrendered to frustration and indulged in shooting from the hip. When the American Broadcasting Company put on a television program featuring Alger Hiss and a group of British leftists who attacked Richard Nixon in particular and the United States in general, Dodd blasted newsman-producer Howard K. Smith and demanded a Federal Communications Commission investigation of the program, and those responsible for it. And he indignantly pursued the antics of the aging pacifists Cyrus Eaton and Linus Pauling, calling Eaton "an evil old man" and dragging Pauling before the Senate Internal Security Subcommittee for sharp questioning. But on the whole Dodd's investigations were considered fair and responsible. The veteran civil-libertarian Paul Douglas rose on the Senate floor one day to pay this tribute: "Although Tom Dodd is a vigorous anti-Communist, I know personally that he has many times stood up for those unfairly accused by the far right."

But it was as a crusader against conditions that breed crime and juvenile delinquency that Dodd became most favorably known, especially within the liberal community. In this pursuit, he showed a willingness to take on such important interests as the drug industry, the powerful lobby composed of arms manufacturers and gun users, even the mighty TV networks. Over and over again he conducted highly publicized hearings that pointed up the need for tighter reins on each of these groups.

"Because of inadequate control over drug manufacturers, pharmacists, and even doctors," he charged, "more than half of the deadly drug pills and habit-forming goofballs produced in America are sold illegally, mostly to juveniles."

"Because of insanity in our gun laws," he insisted, "any halfwit, junkie, criminal, or ten-year-old child can obtain a pistol or a machine gun by merely filling out a postcard."

And he accused the eminent leaders of the television empires of "consciously peddling filth, crime, violence, and depravity every night to millions of impressionable children—to make a buck."

It did not seem to bother Dodd that the legislation he recommended in these fields ran into a stone wall. He conveyed the impression that he was prepared for a long siege. He stepped up his speaking program around the country, lined up articles in mass periodicals, and ordered more investigations, more hearings, and more public exposure. *Reader's Digest,* with its circulation of twelve million, canonized Dodd "the Crusader from Connecticut." Network chiefs, corporate barons, and influential lobbyists began to fear him and to court him.

Dodd had thus come far in his first term. As the Democratic National Convention raced toward a climax at Atlantic City in August, 1964, his name remained among the few still being mentioned for the Vice-Presidential nomination.

The first days of the convention were occupied with tedious formalities, and Dodd, who never took part in such things, spent them unhurriedly, in beach robe and slippers, cordially receiving friends and newspapermen in his Dennis Hotel suite. Across the street, the Humphrey headquarters was in a frenzy of activity. I would see Senator Humphrey on occasion hurrying through hotel corridors to a waiting limousine. He never forgot to flash his contagious smile and to gesture at admiring well-wishers who thronged the hallways and sidewalks. On the third day of the convention, Humphrey received a call from the White House requesting him to go to the Atlantic City airport, where a chartered plane was waiting to fly him to Washington. At last the call had come—after many months of agonized wondering and waiting upon the mysterious impulses of The Man. In thirty minutes a plane would deliver him to Andrews Air Force Base, just outside Washington, and a limousine would whisk him over Washington's baking arteries to the cool green of the White House lawn. There, presumably, would be the laying on of hands. He would be the Vice-President, the heir-apparent, and perhaps, one day, President himself. But at the threshold of his expected triumph Humphrey received a final jolt. The Man had yet another unsettling card to deal. The plane of destiny was to carry two passengers, not one, and at the ramp Humphrey found himself staring quizzically into the familiar countenance of Senator Thomas J. Dodd of Connecticut.

"Has the President asked you yet, Tom?" Humphrey said.

"No. Has he asked you yet, Hubert?"

"No."

They boarded in sympathetic silence and sat on opposite sides of the aisle. Humphrey, supremely in control of himself, immediately went to sleep, exhibiting the saving gift that sustains men driven almost beyond the limits of human endurance. Dodd sat silently, staring ahead with unseeing eyes, pondering the strange turn in his fortunes.

There were some in the country who thought Senator Dodd a logical running mate for Johnson and were not surprised when the news of the Dodd-Humphrey flight to Washington flashed over radio and television. After all, wasn't the silver-haired Senator with the striking profile a long-time friend of the President? Four years before at Los Angeles, almost alone among Northeastern Democrats he had fought for Johnson over John F. Kennedy and had placed Johnson's name in nomination with blazing platform oratory. They made an enthusiastic case for Dodd.

A responsible investigator, an internationalist with an impeccably liberal voting record, he had gained prominence through his exposure of social abuses. Dodd, they said, was known for his anti-Communism without being sullied by McCarthyism. Though a hard-liner in the Cold War, he was flexible enough to have been a key figure behind the ratification of the nuclear-test-ban treaty. A northern, industrial-state Irish Catholic, he could give balance to a ticket headed by a Southern Protestant.

Liberal on the politically sacred issues, Dodd—by his anti-Communism, his fight against crime, his F.B.I. background—had acquired a vocal conservative following, and his supporters argued that with Goldwater already the G.O.P. nominee the Democrats had the liberals sewed up and should make some appeal to the center and the right. Dodd, they said, could do it. The Connecticut Senator had an undoubted appeal in the South, and through him, perhaps, Johnson could make a needed gesture toward his old power base without alienating support in the North.

Word of Dodd's sudden trip to the White House reached me in our staff quarters at Ocean City only minutes before live TV coverage showed him boarding the plane. The word came from Doreen Moloney in the Dodd suite at the Dennis. Her normally controlled voice quavered with excitement.

"Mr. Boyd, the Senator is on his way to see the President. He may be offered the Vice-Presidential nomination. He wants you to hurry here immediately and bring any material you may need to draft a speech."

I was astonished and could feel a geyser of mixed feelings surge through me, pounding in my head. Vice-President? To a President with a record of heart trouble? I didn't believe it. I could not so badly misjudge a situation I was so close to. Or could I? Maybe he's going to make the nomination speech for Humphrey, I thought. Marjorie, Michael, and I scrambled around gathering up pencils and pads and rushed for the car. In a subdued silence, keeping for a time our thoughts to ourselves, we drove swiftly through the pleasant resort communities that separate Ocean City from Atlantic City.

At the White House, Dodd was admitted to the President's office first, while Humphrey waited and wondered. The President, tanned and exuberant, hugely enjoying his role as puppeteer and prestidigitator, welcomed Dodd warmly, showing him all about the oval office, garrulously discussing trifles.

"Tom," he said at last, "a lot of people are saying that you would make a good Vice-Presidential candidate."

Dodd had presaged the President's remarks. On the plane, while Humphrey slept, he had decided that he would not be offered the nomination and that, at the first courteous reference the President might make about his Vice-Presidential qualifications, he would at once disavow any aspirations.

"Mr. President," Dodd retorted, "I'm not a candidate for Vice-President, believe me. As W. C. Fields used to say, include me out."

After a half hour of discussion and an inspection of the latest public-opinion polls, Dodd left and Humphrey was ushered in. When the Senator from Minnesota emerged from the President's office he had the look of one who had been anointed. The President, the Vice-Presidential designate, and Senator Dodd then flew to Atlantic City together. On the plane, the President and his running mate relaxed in shirtsleeves, discussing the coming campaign. Dodd, dignified and proper, in a dark, well-tailored suit, was solemn and silent, keeping his thoughts to himself. At the Atlantic City Airport, NBC's Nancy Dickerson asked the President why he had summoned Dodd to the White House.

Before a vast TV audience, the President repaid in full all due-notes owed to Dodd.

He said that Dodd was a friend of long standing and one of those whose qualifications merited serious consideration for the Vice-Presidency, and that his record in the Senate bore this out. Dodd took himself out of consideration at once, Johnson said, calling Dodd an outstanding American and a great Senator whose advice he valued highly.

Then the Presidential party was rushed to Convention Hall, where twenty thousand Americans, perhaps the only group in the country who did not know of the President's decision, were patiently assembled. Johnson himself, in a classic demonstration of overkill, took the platform to announce Humphrey's nomination and thus complete the picture of his total mastery of the convention that had rejected him four years before.

In the midst of this novel rite of investiture, Dodd quietly slipped out of Convention Hall and returned to his hotel suite. Unless he was the center of attention, conventions bored him. He did not enjoy watching other people perform. Manifestly pleased with the day's events, he greeted his family and staff warmly, as they crowded around him. Then he asked me to come into his room alone.

"Well," he said, beaming, "the President was very nice, very complimentary, if I may say so, but I cleared the air right at the start by saying, 'Mr. President, include me out.' I told him that I didn't fancy myself as Presidential material and that the only job I want is the one I have. He made it clear, of course, that I could have a Cabinet post if I wanted one; we talked particularly about the Attorney-Generalship. Very friendly, Jim, very. We stand high in his book."

He began to change his clothes, for he had not forgotten that Perle Mesta's party had already started.

"Some of those people out there are disappointed," he said, motioning toward the sitting room, now jammed with friends and supporters. "They thought I was going to be Vice-President, but you know I had never even considered it, don't you, Jim. It was never in the cards."

I kept a judicious silence.

"I'm not Presidential material, and I've never fooled myself. If he offered it to me, I would have run a mile. The Senate is my cup of tea. There are only two jobs that I would leave the Senate for—F.B.I. director and the head of the Central Intelligence Agency, and I may very well wind up in one place or the other. Naturally, I would want to take you with me. We've got great things ahead of us."

He was now ready for the party and obviously looking forward to it. There was good reason for his elation. The recognition long denied him was now his. The day's events had solidified Dodd's image as friend and trusted confidant of the President. Voters, contributors, and the press could not but be mightily impressed. In Connecticut, people were already saying, "When the President narrowed his search down to two men, Tom Dodd was one of them. He could have been the Vice-President, but he preferred to stay in the Senate."

Ahead of Tom Dodd lay the greatest Senate election victory in the state's history, and a second term, during which growing seniority would steadily augment his personal power and influence. Also ahead lay a contest for political dominance within his state's Democratic party in which he held some trump cards, including the President's friendship. The jewel Connecticut, which he so loved and coveted, should soon be in his pocket.

As I watched and listened, the old affection warmed me once again. His combination of frankness and ambiguity, humility and arrogance, was often bewildering, but there was at times a childlike joy in him, an infectious optimism, a camaraderie he could inspire which swept away misgivings. He was durable. His foibles and his strengths could be depended upon. He was alive where so many were vegetating; he had braggadocio in a sea of mealymouthed timidity; he was an original in a world of imitations. I had worked for Tom Dodd for twelve years and I still found that, at his best, there was something admirable about him.

CHAPTER TWO

I T seemed almost sacrilegious to hurry heedlessly by the solemn splendors of Capitol Hill each morning on the way to my office—past the spray of the fountains, the rustle of stately trees, the broad expanse of green lawn glistening in the dew of morning; surely the august Capitol, with its majestic dome, should compel at least a hushed acknowledgment. But apprehensions over so much to be done and so little time to do it would hasten my steps across the crowded intersection at Constitution and Delaware Avenues and through the marbled halls of the old Senate Office Building, past doors emblazoned with eminent names—Symington, Mansfield, Douglas—to the door near the end of the hall bearing the shield of Connecticut and the name "Mr. Dodd."

Seldom did I approach that door without a presentiment that inside something was amiss. Invariably it was confirmed by the taut announcement from my secretary that "the Senator has been trying to reach you for twenty minutes," which at this early hour could mean only that somewhere in my broad domain of accountability there had been a slip. Almost every morning, Dodd telephoned from home, before office hours began, and even before returning his call I knew well the roster of complaints. A letter from the town chairman of Ledyard had not been answered, he would say; an undeserving Congressman had announced word of a government contract for which Dodd should have been given credit; his sister-in-law had phoned the night

before to say that his name was not mentioned in the local papers as
often as Senator Ribicoff's and "a lot of people are talking about it";
the Congressional Record for yesterday quoted him as having said
something outlandish that he hadn't said at all—or that at least should
have been edited out; Senator Jackson had received a writeup in the
New York Times for a suggestion that *he* had asked *me* to work up
months ago; his schedule was so crowded it must have been put together by a lunatic—he would just have to cancel that hearing this
morning, and why wasn't someone trying to ease his burdens once in a
while? What did he have a staff for?

It never mattered, for the moment, that the answering letter had
been sent to Ledyard the week before; that some types of contract
announcements are by common agreement reserved for Congressmen;
that there was a thick pile of Connecticut newsclippings on his desk,
covering his activities for the past five days; that he had personally
edited the previous day's remarks for the Record; that his suggestion
of months before had been quite the opposite of Senator Jackson's;
that his schedule for the day was blank except for the hearing.

Some unrelated incident had set him off—a morning phenomenon
which I long ago had come to attribute to his body chemistry. Gerry
Zeiller, our able but irreverent executive secretary, contended that
compulsive ill-temper was an occupational disease of Senators.

"They're all half-nutty," he would say. "It's the job; it eats them
up."

Whatever the cause of the Senator's frustration, venting it upon the
staff generally brought him relief, and though he had mumbled darkly
about a confrontation later in the morning, doubtless he would be
mollified and agreeable by the time he arrived at the office.

The Dodd office was overwhelmed with activity in the late summer
of 1964, straining under a double burden. A tired, testy Senate, wrestling in day and night sessions with the remaining "must" items of its
legislative program, alternately galloped and staggered toward adjournment, beneath the spurs of Lyndon Johnson. And the Dodd re-
election campaign, managed from Washington until we could close up
shop and open our Hartford headquarters, encroached relentlessly
upon our energies. The Republican candidate, John Lodge, had been
campaigning for weeks, and Dodd, though disdainful of Lodge, was
not happy about it.

I had come to wear many hats since the comparatively uncompli-
cated campaigns of old: administrative assistant in charge of the

Washington office, legislative aide, speechwriter and editor, press secretary, buffer between the Senator and his many committees and, for
the ninety days preceding election, minister of propaganda. On any
morning matters of urgency cluttered my desk, competing for immediate attention—a speech on civil rights to be completed before noon;
memos to be dictated on the three votes scheduled on the Senate floor
in the afternoon; a bulky report on our three-year television inquiry,
which had waited three weeks for editing; a troublesome breakdown
in the legislative mail section; a suggested press release, hopefully pre-
dicting passage of our drug control bill; a staff vacancy to be filled; an
overdue position paper on five basic issues, to be circulated
throughout Connecticut by the League of Women Voters; a presentation to the Senator of what was included in the $100,000 campaign
advertising package we had approved the previous day; and the inevitable, usually meritorious, staff requests for time off.

In the large room to my right, crowded with file cabinets, typists,
and student interns, the embattled Zeiller, resourceful and loquacious,
dealt effectively with the mounting problems of Connecticut munici-
palities and industries. He was always on the phone, entreating and
intriguing for urban renewal funds for New Britain, sewers for Waterbury, a new stadium for Bridgeport, highways for Groton, defense
contracts and government loans for beneficiaries of all descriptions.
Once he had scrounged Air Force transportation from Naples, Italy,
to Niantic, Connecticut, for a constituent's corpse.

Behind Zeiller, partitioned from view, was our foreign affairs section, headed by balding, moustached, and indefatigable Dave Martin,
a short man with a sonorous voice and a conspiratorial look. Here, a
dozen last-ditch battles to save the Free World were constantly in
progress. Black ambassadors from Africa, refugees from Cuba,
bearded bishops of the Eastern Rite, aristocratic pretenders from
Czarist days, and emissaries from the Congo paraded spookily
through David's office and spilled over into the reception room, giving
it the look of a U.N. vestibule.

To my left, in the center of our five-room suite, was the Senator's
office, well-shielded from unwelcome intrusions. Adjoining was what
we called the outer office—the nerve center of the Senator's tangled
existence—where Marjorie Carpenter and Michael O'Hare assisted
him through his hour-by-hour tribulations.

Michael, alternately grave and comical, with expressive blue eyes
and sensitive face, was chauffeur, manservant, handyman, travel

agent, bookkeeper, custodian, and office manager. Three years before, while an impoverished sociology student at Catholic University, he had applied for a part-time job keeping the Senator's books. Now he managed all financial affairs, personal and official, and was the Senator's omnipresent shadow.

Marjorie, a comely, green-eyed Arkansas blonde of twenty-six, occupied the critical post of the Senator's personal secretary. She was in continual communication with him, a ceaseless challenge requiring unfailing tact, diplomacy, and conciseness. Any awkwardness or uncoated directness in interpreting the staff and the public to the Senator—or the Senator to them—could have explosive effects both within the office and beyond. That eleven personal secretaries had preceded Marjorie in the first three years of Dodd's term was an index of the challenge facing her.

Marjorie guarded his door and his private phone, scheduled his appointments, booked his speaking tours, and answered his personal mail. Bright and perceptive, possessed of a solid background as a schoolteacher and legal secretary, along with the physical stamina to endure twelve-hour days and six-day weeks, Marjorie had inaugurated a three-year era of stability and competence that was gratefully welcomed throughout the Dodd realm. To the professional life of a Senator who instinctively nurtured confusion and cherished procrastination, she brought a measure of order and decision. Dodd affectionately called her "Miss Marjorie," and on occasion admitted grudgingly that over his sometimes vexed and turbulent affairs she had diffused a scent of magnolia.

The reception room was the Senator's showcase. There, in semicaptivity, an audience of visitors forever waited, surrounded by the emblems of Dodd's triumphs. Covering almost all the wall space were plaques, trophies, framed testimonials, and blown-up cartoons, all testifying to the importance of Thomas J. Dodd. The standard ornament was an engraved metal tablet set on handsome dark wood, memorializing the esteem felt for Senator Dodd by the Los Angeles Junior Chamber of Commerce or the New Haven N.A.A.C.P. The most imaginative was a trophy from which flew twelve miniature flags, from the Assembly of Captive European Nations. Many of our callers were duly impressed, but one visiting law professor, I remember, volunteered the observation: "This is the waiting room of a very insecure man."

Throughout the Dodd offices, a bevy of smartly dressed typists, re-

ceptionists, and file clerks worked away busily. Many were highly efficient; all were pretty—a circumstance that derived in part from one of
the Senator's personnel directives: "I want young, attractive people
around me," he would say to me. "It sets the tone of the place. I don't
want to look around my offices and see rows of hedgehogs with slow
heads and fat behinds."

Not all the Senator's personnel policies were so felicitous. The working staff on which I depended suffered from recurring morale problems arising from a double standard the Senator employed. In reality,
Dodd maintained not one staff but three.

The first was made up of political cronies who were being rewarded
for past services. Some of them were never seen in the Washington
office; others took up valuable space, hanging out in the room to the
rear of the reception room, where they endlessly engaged in grave
conferences. None contributed, nor knew how to contribute, to the
work.

A second "staff" was composed of a motley group who had no old
claims on the Senator, but whom he supported, via the public payroll,
for various reasons of personal advantage or generosity: a chronic
school dropout who happened to be the son of a TV executive; a
giggly daughter of an old schoolmate of Mrs. Dodd's who unfortunately could not type or take dictation; a down-on-her-luck associate
of the old N.Y.A. days with a drinking problem; the son-in-law of a
radio commentator who regularly devoted broadcasts to Senator
Dodd's statesmanship; a housewife in Hartford who never entered an
office but who was married to an important politician in the North
End. And there were others. The Senator nourished this curious
menagerie with tender indulgence. To them he was El Benefactor;
of them nothing was required except loyalty.

But toward the third group—the working staff—he directed a sharp
and critical eye. What he excused in the drones he compensated by
extracting from the workers. He had at least one of the traits of a great
administrator. He could, through an artful blend of inspiration and
intimidation—compliment and censure—keep his principal aides totally occupied seventy hours a week, producing far beyond normal
capacity. But, though he paid these key workers very well indeed, the
clear injustice of the double standard inevitably dulled their allegiance and let loose a poison of discontent. A few years before, after a
newspaper exposé of Congressional payroll padding, the Senate had
modified its rules to require the public disclosure of all staff positions

and salaries. An inquisitive clerk could now easily look up the facts and ascertain his relationship on the payroll to any other staff member. That caused no end of trouble for me in trying to administer the Dodd office. I could not effectively discipline a stenographer for taking the morning off when she could point to one of the "protected ones" who had not done a day's work in years, and who received a salary substantially higher than hers.

More than one employee pointed out to me, as if I had not known it long before, that more than $100,000 annually was being used to pay people who performed no identifiable Senate duties. Since Dodd's protegés consumed some four-fifths of the salary allotment for his office staff, he had to expropriate on a large scale the salary allowance of the Juvenile Delinquency Subcommittee, of which he was chairman, and, to a lesser extent, the allowance of the Internal Security Subcommittee, of which he was vice-chairman. Most of his working staff, in fact, was listed on the roster of one or the other of his subcommittees.

Counting the allotment of his two subcommittees and his personal staff allowance, Dodd disposed of a payroll of $300,000 annually, for which he was accountable to no one. The obvious inequities irritated not only Dodd's office employees but also the subcommittee staff members, who officially work for the entire Senate and, in practice, are called upon for services by all Senators who belong to the subcommittee. I recall complaining once to Carl Perian, the highly professional staff director of the Delinquency Subcommittee, that his staff had been too slow in preparing for hearings. Perian retorted, trying to control his exasperation, that of twenty-one people on the subcommittee payroll, all but eight had been assigned to Dodd's personal staff and that of those remaining, three were incompetents pressed on him by the Senator. One was a mentally disturbed young man, the son of a friend of the Senator's, who collected submachine guns and insisted on carrying a revolver at all times.

For a long time, I could and did make up excuses to myself and to others. Wasn't it accepted, as a practical matter, that a Senator could manipulate his personal and committee staffs as he saw fit? Didn't Dodd have to repay in some manner those who had helped him to get elected in the first place? Wasn't the blame really chargeable to society as a whole, which was so casual about the electoral process that officeholders, unless rich, had to forage to pay off their campaign bills? I told myself that the public tolerated these practices as part of a system it found quite acceptable. But, whatever the rationalization, one could not demand high standards of staff performance amid visible misuse of the public trust. Each day I could sense an ebbing of the morale of those on whom I depended most, and I could do little about it for I felt demoralized myself. Was this a small weakness, an ethical blind spot, in an otherwise great and perceptive man? Or was it playing according to the rules of the old, unvarnished spoils game, a game we had been taught to believe was now largely extinct?

Nor was it only the Senator's ethics or the public's neglect that were called into question. I could not ignore forever the fact that I had become part of an operation I could no longer wholly respect.

The Senator's morning arrival was usually a colorful, sometimes a comic, spectacle. From Dodd's home in Georgetown, Michael would, just as the Boss was about to leave, phone in a fifteen-minute alert. Suddenly the word "he's on the way" flashed through the office suite and around to the committee rooms. Idlers were recalled from the coffee shop. Cluttered desk tops, a pet peeve of the Senator's, would be cleared, paraphernalia jammed into drawers and hidden in file cabinets. Overdue statements, letters, memos, and briefing papers would be rushed to completion.

Dodd always entered through the outer office, avoiding the reception room where visitors with appointments waited impatiently. Invariably he was followed by a procession of bearers—Michael, one or two sons, a house guest—carrying valises, a Val-pac, suits to be pressed, a large box filled with shoes to be shined, a clock to be repaired, a pair of antique revolvers to be mounted. That season the Senator was wearing a Charlie-Chan-type Panama hat and, under its wide brim, his mood was written on his face—sometimes smoldering irritability, sometimes beaming joviality, sometimes a hazy euphoria, sometimes cool hostility. He would personally supervise the unloading and disposition of his goods. By nature vague and remote in his instructions on important matters, his directions concerning daily trivia were remarkably precise. The suits were to be pressed but not cleaned, and returned by one o'clock; the various pairs of shoes were to be shined in particular hues; the clock was to be dismantled and reassembled just so; the pistols were to be mounted in exact attitudes on a particular type of wood.

Pausing automatically in front of Marjorie's desk, he would leaf through his in-box and remove items that caught his eye, primarily staff memos requiring answers. Those he did not wish to answer he would ignore. To others he would snap out a reply on the spot.

No, I will not have breakfast with Secretary Rusk in his offices. Let him come over here. I'm all through being an errand boy for the State Department.

Yes, yes. I'll not only vote for the Proxmire amendment, I think I should speak on it. Tell Jim that I agree and to work something up for me.

Now this takes the prize for jackass performances! [He was starting into orbit.] I've told David a hundred times to stop bombarding me with these damned Ukrainians, Guianians, Kurds, Arabs, and Orientals. But he keeps at it, setting up appointments, wasting my time. Doesn't he know I have a state to take care of and a campaign to run? Every time I peek into my reception room it looks like there's a ring of assassins sitting out there. Think of it! If a bona fide constituent ever manages to find his way to my office, he'll be frightened away! People are talking about this. [Then, to Marjorie, a plaintive plea for understanding.] Help me, will you please. You know how to handle these things. I can't do everything myself around here.

Waving off assistance, he would gather up his papers, two valises, pipe, and tobacco pouch and march into his office, leaving behind him a heavy silence.

The office into which Dodd entered was the focus of his existence. From his arrival at ten in the morning, he would often remain without leaving until nine at night. Comfortable, in a slightly elevated swivel chair, he would direct his activities on many fronts, hatch his projects, plan his investigations, receive his courtiers, and let soar his imagination. Here, life was ordered exactly to suit him. His unpredictable flashes of irascibility toward subordinates had the desired effect that he was never for a moment forgotten or taken for granted. All eyes and ears were bent in his direction. Anticipating his needs and fancies was with us a continuous preoccupation. By pressing the right button, he could have a want or a whim attended, produce a staff member or a boon companion, set in motion a furious march of events, or suspend all action or intrusion.

The interior of Dodd's office was his personal creation. He had meticulously orchestrated the lighting, color, decor, temperature, and all the minutiae of furnishing and ornamentation. From this room he had banished the glare and noise, perhaps even some of the tension of the old Senate Office Building. He had removed the fluorescent tubes that hung with their ugly trappings from the high ceiling and replaced them with a variety of dim little lamps that suffused a soothing half-light. He had silenced the omnipresent buzzers that, with a penetrating doomsday drone, forever summoned Senators to votes and quorum calls; he preferred to receive such notices in the soft accents of his secretaries. Long ago, the heavy government-issue desk had been replaced with a delicately curved eighteenth-century Italian model of beautifully veined olivewood. Behind it, to left and right, stood the flags of the United States and Connecticut. The chairs and long divan were of a rich and fragrant red leather. The carpeting was green. Portraits of Cicero, Socrates, Jefferson, and the young Lincoln, along with a huge painting of Sir Thomas More, set the philosophic tone. On the wall nearest his desk hung several of the many pictures of his family, as well as his beloved North Stonington home. Scale models of old sailing ships and lithographs of Connecticut scenes established the New England flavor, while carved images from the Congo and models of Connecticut-built space rockets proclaimed the diversity of the Senator's concerns. In vain, Dodd had tried, after Bobby Baker fell from grace, to acquire the enormous glass chandelier that hung in the office of the Secretary for the Majority. He was more successful, however, in filling the handsome shelves he had had constructed at the rear of his office. From the Library of Congress, Dodd had ordered "twelve yards of books." On arrival, they turned out to be old volumes printed in Russian, but on the shelves they went, adding an exotic touch to the potpourri of culture that already existed.

The total effect was the subject of much office debate. Gerry Zeiller cracked that it looked like the waiting room of a funeral parlor. Visitors would be somewhat taken aback at the dimness after the glare of the adjoining rooms. I found the office soothing, quiet, and comfortable, and I liked to work there when the Senator was out of town. But however much opinions varied, there was no mistaking the Senator's pride in his office. Aides were instructed to show it to visitors from Connecticut in his absence, and he even had a plan for immortalizing it which, from time to time, he enthusiastically revived. On the side of a hill at his North Stonington farm he had found a cave. With a good deal of deepening and leveling, he said, the cave could be transformed into what the Germans call a "rath," or cave-house. Here he would re-create an exact replica of his office for his enjoyment after he retired.

Everything was to be preserved just as it was in Washington and, to make certain, his office was photographed from every conceivable angle, all its contents were carefully catalogued, and precise drawings were made, scaled to measurements. Needless to say, the staff made puns about "the rath of Dodd," but the Senator pressed determinedly forward.

A minute or two after his arrival each morning, Senator Dodd would call me in to discuss the matter that loomed largest for the day. The irritation evident in his early-morning phone calls had usually vanished. We were now partners, solving common problems.

"Jim, I'm terribly concerned about the makeup of my campaign committee. It has a list of Irish names about a foot long. I've cautioned Ed about this time and again—but, you know, Ed's failing these days. Moriarity, O'Connor, McNamara, Fitzpatrick, Sullivan, McCue—why it's God-awful! What I need is a Winterbottom—an old Yankee name. We've had Winterbottoms in all our campaigns. You remember that, don't you? Who have we got?"

"Well, sir, there's a Democratic town chairman up in Goshen who wants to help, name of Sherman Kimberley. I'm sure we can get him."

"Kimberley—Sherman Kimberley—why, that's just about right. First class! We'll put him right up top on the letterhead. Sherman Kimberley. Yes. Get Ed on this right away; I want to make a public announcement today. Try and think of an Italian, too. How are you coming on the television report?"

His quick shift caught me, while still congratulating myself over Kimberley, with my guard down.

"Well—it's coming along. I'm not quite through editing it yet."

"Then let's get cracking! I want it printed and out in a week at the most. You fellows act like you're writing for the archives. Let's get these things done in the here and now. Lodge is knocking my block off every day about spending a lot of committee money and not issuing any reports."

I resisted the temptation to point out that Dodd had himself held up the television report for three years, and took a more diplomatic tack.

"We're getting out the gun report this week, Mr. Dodd, and I've prepared an answer to Lodge showing that your subcommittee has released nine reports in the last four years."

"Well, that's all right I guess, but the best answer is another report.

Let's not answer this dandy, just bury him under with reports. Anything else? Then have Dave come in, and ask Marjorie to start putting through my calls, will you?"

My first audience of the day was over.

During six years of increasing power and prestige, Senator Dodd had changed in ways difficult to define. At fifty-seven he was a bit heavier, a little slower, his complexion slightly pinker, his hair considerably thinner. His mien, though still distinguished, reflected more and more the inroads of inner turmoil and physical abuse. The facial tremors were now more pronounced. The once blazing eyes were at times strangely clouded. He no longer quoted Lincoln's maxim: "After the age of forty, every man is responsible for his own face." Success had stripped away much that was admirable, traits that had seemed ingrained but had turned out, I found, to be circumstantial and tactical. The Tom Dodd of my early recollections—humble, poor, tough, democratic, idealistic, generous-hearted, relentlessly energetic, whose inspirational charisma had drawn people to him—had receded slowly into the background, supplanted by a formidable Peer of the Realm, who, insecure in the possession of rank, chronically overindulged in its perquisites and superficialities.

Woe betide the lolling elevator operator, inattentive waiter, brusque sales clerk, clumsy manicurist, complacent cop, or unresponsive committee witness who happened into the path of the senior Senator from Connecticut. A public tongue-lashing was his normal way of letting them know with whom they were dealing. Sometimes such an outburst could be exhilarating, when administered, for example, to an opinionated female pacifist or a presumptuous lobbyist or a pretentious bureaucrat, for no one was immune. But more often it was disturbing, even ugly. Now and then the Senator would complain that his closest staff people continually begged off, on some pretext or other, from his invitations to dinner. It was true, and it was, as he suspected, a mute expression of disapproval. He could be a highly entertaining and interesting host, but the probability of a scene chilled the prospect of an evening with him; excuses were made and others took our places.

Since coming to the Senate, Dodd had elevated personal convenience to a science. Staff members now did for him what in former days he had done for himself.

Most Senators drive their own cars, but Senator Dodd was always chauffeured about.

If he was in his Washington home and wanted to call someone in Hartford, Chicago, or Phoenix, he would simply dial his private line, and Marjorie would call Hartford, Chicago, and Phoenix and have each of the intended communicants call Dodd at his home. If he was in a hotel room in Los Angeles and wanted to call Joe Doakes in San Francisco, he would dial across the continent to Washington, and have Marjorie, to her embarrassment, call Mr. Doakes in San Francisco to ask him to call Senator Dodd in Los Angeles. A simple phone call took on the dimensions of a national undertaking, but the arrangement saved Dodd time and bother.

If he had a plane to catch, he would wait in his office until a few minutes before departure time, while tension mounted for everyone but him. His ticket, of course, had already been picked up by Michael, and his bags taken to the airport. At last, Michael would be summoned and, the staff having received assurances that the plane was to leave exactly on schedule, Dodd would be rushed to National Airport while Marjorie called ahead to have the plane held. By special dispensation, Dodd's car would be admitted to a spot very near the plane and, unruffled, he would leisurely go up the ramp just as anxious attendants were making ready to roll it away. Dodd insisted on being met at airports, and if staff members were not available, police officers would do. Whenever he flew to Connecticut for weekend holidays at his country home, he would arrange for state police officers to meet his plane, even though they must forego their normal responsibilities to drive him home. When he was traveling cross-country, United States Immigration officers and, on occasion, F.B.I. agents, were pressed into service as chauffeurs at various stops.

Senate aides looked after his clothing, arranged for the payment of his bills, kept his checkbook and his accounts, purchased his gifts to his family on birthdays and anniversaries, sometimes wrote his letters to his children, supervised workmen and repairmen in his home, instructed his servants, entertained his friends, awakened him in the morning, delivered him to his door late at night, and smoothed his path through all the annoyances and obstacles that bedevil the lives of ordinary mortals.

He had so organized his staff as to relieve him of most of the burdens of office. A thousand letters arrived each week and were answered without his seeing them. Hundreds of speeches, a dozen magazine articles, and two books were written in his name by aides. It was my responsibility to brief him on all votes just before he would cast his "aye" or "nay"; subjects that had taken hours of study frequently had to be presented to him in minutes or even seconds, and I am not aware that he ever completely read through a single bill or committee report.

The Congressional Record presents each day a verbatim account of all that is said on the floor of the Senate and House, and thousands of copies are sent out to newspapers, schools, businesses, and subscribers. On most days the Record carried statements on various issues made by Mr. Dodd of Connecticut. But only rarely did he actually appear on the floor to make the speeches attributed to him. They were handed in typed form to Bobby Baker, or his successor, who saw to it that they appeared in the Record just as if they had been delivered with all the verve of a Webster or a Barkley. Robert Lucas, editor of the *Hartford Times,* once wrote to Dodd complimenting him on his speeches and inquiring if he did the writing himself—a sticky question from an important man that was promptly laid on Dodd's desk for personal answer. But it came right back to me. I was assigned the task of ghosting a letter from Dodd to Lucas which denied that Dodd ever used ghosts. The Senator did contribute one editorial change, striking the word "almost" from a line that originally read: "Therefore, the writing is almost always entirely my own."

Dodd never completely solved the problem of farming out his personal appearances but he worked at that too. For a time, Tom, Jr., was sent out quite regularly as a stand-in, as was Carl Perian. With the campaign on, I was getting assignments to substitute for him in debates with Governor Lodge. But his favorite device was the telephoned speech. About an hour before he was scheduled to appear in Norwalk or New Haven or Meriden, Marjorie would phone his hosts with the news that some grave event upon which the public weal depended had detained the Senator in Washington, but that he was making arrangements to broadcast his speech live, direct to the hall, via a private circuit and amplifying equipment provided by the telephone company. A huge, blown-up photo of the Senator would be dispatched from his Hartford office and placed on the platform, and at the appointed moment the voice of the Honorable Thomas J. Dodd, larger than life, came booming out of the amplifier. All he had to do was sit in his Washington office and read. Of course, there was an element of inconvenience in having to wait in his office, so we arranged for him to broadcast from wherever he happened to be. One night, unknown to several hundred Connecticut listeners who had been told that important action on the Senate floor was preventing him from being with them in person, the familiar voice behind the smiling photograph originated from the living room of Thomas G. Corcoran, the Washington lobbyist, Dodd's host that night at dinner.

Dodd's faculty for shedding the drudgery of his Senate post was at times fascinating and ingenious, but I began to see that it was also corrosive. The line between the obligations and the superfluities of office is often a thin one, and in time Dodd came to avoid the one as readily as the other. Constituents who had carefully made appointments and traveled to Washington to see him on government problems were increasingly shunted to staff members. Committee meetings, homework on issues, even votes on the Senate floor were ignored.

The substantive work of the Senate is done in committee, but Dodd found this work tedious and its unpublicized anonymity unrewarding. He would appear at the nationally televised sessions of his Juvenile Delinquency Subcommittee, where he dominated the cameras and called the shots, but only rarely would he attend the working meetings of the major committees he had once coveted and won appointment to—Foreign Relations, Judiciary, Aeronautics and Space Sciences. Protracted "weekend" holidays and frequent vacation trips caused him to miss more and more roll-call votes, and his voting percentage fell down into the 70's and 60's.

One day Senator Everett Dirksen, miffed by criticism from Dodd, rose on the Senate floor and threatened to reveal Dodd's record of absenteeism. This caused a temporary spurt in his attendance, but it did not last long.

"I'm not going to sit around day after day listening to a bunch of performers who love to hear themselves talk, and that's that," he would say in justification. It fell to his staff, however, to fabricate excuses for disappointed constituents, irate Senators, and inquiring newsmen. Most of the time, the explanations seemed to be believed, but we knew the truth and it rankled.

Edward Lockett, a Washington writer hired to ghost a book on Communism for Dodd, called me one day in a state of agitation. Weeks had passed, he said, in which he had failed to get to see the Senator for specific instructions as to what he wanted in his book. "The Senator's secretary keeps referring me to you, which is all right with me," he said, "but after all it is *the Senator's* book. Tell me something, Mr. Boyd, does Senator Dodd really exist?"

He existed all right, but he had his own ideas about how he should operate. He liked the staff system and pushed it to an extreme degree. His drinks were mixed, his cigars lit, his reports agonized over, his letters signed, his lesser decisions made, his words written, his disputes meditated—all by others. Thus was his time and energy freed for the great endeavors which he assured us were continuously underway.

The Tom Dodd who triumphed in Connecticut in 1958 was known and admired as a man of modest means and humble ways who, through a natural empathy with the rank and file, had beaten the millionaires and the bosses. Matthew M. Moriarity, a devoted friend of Dodd's, could remember the Senator's early years in public life as a time of poverty, and of hardship for Grace Dodd, so often left alone with a growing family.

"His home was always very meagerly and modestly furnished . . . his table was frugal," said Moriarity. He recalled how Grace used to drive the children to church and on shopping trips in an old $40 delivery truck, "she would put her baby in the front seat and the four children in the back on a blanket and then joyously go off, happy as a lark. A man's not very prosperous when his wife does that."

Dodd, broodingly conscious of what he considered past privations, had long been determined to make compensation—to himself and to his family. And though the humble Dodd image lived on in Connecticut—it was now only an image. The Dodds currently lived in what, to me at least, seemed the grand manner.

They resided in a $90,000 townhouse, serviced by a maid and a handyman, in the Georgetown neighborhood of Averell Harriman, G. Mennen Williams, Hugh Auchincloss, and Edward Kennedy. Gradually, Dodd transformed what had once been an old, abandoned farm in North Stonington, Connecticut, into a summer estate—200 wooded acres, a private road, a stable, a guesthouse, a tastefully renovated main house with a rich interior of stone and wood. Hundreds of feet of green lawn had been reclaimed from the surrounding forest, and there was an artificial lake, stocked with fish, a hunting preserve, and even a man-made waterfall that murmured restfully through summer nights. It was just a coincidence, insisted Dodd, that the paved highway leading through secluded countryside to the Dodd acres ended abruptly at the entrance to his property, where it became a country dirt road. To his estate he gave a suitable name—Laurel Glen—which he emblazoned on his stationery and used as his official mailing address.

Unlike his more pedestrian Senate colleagues, Dodd dressed fashionably in smartly tailored blue, gray, and brown suits of European cut. He had at least twenty hats, and his shoes were of the latest Italian style. A gold watch chain, descending from coat lapel to breast pocket, had become a Dodd trademark, and, to lend added distinction, he was now experimenting with a little puff of white hair at the back of his neck.

He loved expensive cigars and choice liquors. The cheap Blackstone Panetellas I used to get for him at drugstores in the old days had long since given way to more exotic brands, of varying hues, lengths, and aromas, that filled the walnut humidor on his desk. His tab at Schneider's Liquor Store sometimes ran into the hundreds of dollars. The frugal eater of Moriarity's recollections now dined formally and was a habitué of the finest restaurants in Washington and New York. Luxurious apartments were regularly available to him in New York and Miami. He vacationed frequently in the opulent retreats of the wealthy—Miami Beach, Fort Lauderdale, Palm Beach, the Virgin Islands, and Montego Bay. He traveled abroad at least twice a year, sometimes more. He was, in fact, continually on the move and had begun to travel in the fashion of an authentic tycoon. Wealthy friends and interested corporations had placed at his disposal what amounted to a fleet of sumptuous aircraft, which he summoned and dismissed at his convenience.

The $40 delivery truck was just a quaint memory now. A new Oldsmobile was presented to the Dodds each year by one admirer; another furnished a Lincoln Continental for intermittent use around the "farm." And there were cars for the older boys. Grace Dodd, no longer tied down by penury and a young brood, graciously partook of the new life. She was close to Lady Bird and was "in" with Perle Mesta. Rich new friends gave lavish parties in her and her husband's honor. The President attended her thirtieth wedding anniversary celebration. Resplendent in mink and jewels, Mrs. Dodd enjoyed the social evenings in the mansions along Embassy Row. And she accompanied her husband on his periodic trips to Europe, Asia, Africa, and Latin America.

If Tom Dodd had once been forced by circumstance to neglect his children, he now indulged their wants. All were being educated in, or had recently graduated from, expensive private schools. They shared in the executive planes, the resort life, the Washington social whirl that prominence had brought to their father. Like offspring of the wealthy, they were given vacations abroad, charge accounts at country club and clothing store, extravagant gifts, such as a $5,000 present to son Jeremy. Dodd continued to support his older sons long after they passed the normal age of dependency. And when his younger daughter married, the proud father staged a wedding that rivaled in pomp and elegance the costliest of society nuptials.

Even Dodd's Senate facilities were placed at his children's disposal. The office staff was sometimes literally bogged down in chores for the Dodd family, making their travel arrangements, typing their school papers, helping them obtain a voter registration or a driver's license, procuring their library books, theater and football tickets, even insurance policies. Sometimes this involved more than trivia. Keeping young Jeremy out of a term in the Army became a major staff project. A dozen draft deferment requests were processed for Jeremy, an inveterate school dropout. When at length he graduated from Mexico City College at the age of twenty-five, Dodd had the staff arrange for his son to be accepted in an Army program whereby volunteers serve six months on active duty and then sign up for several years' service as one-night-a-week soldiers in the Army Reserves. Jeremy, however, was not required to serve the six months. His father got him out in five. And when the Monday night soldiering proved irksome to Jeremy, it was arranged for him to be transferred to the less demanding Connecticut National Guard, an organization whose commanding officers are chosen by state politicians and are therefore amenable to political pressures. Jeremy was shortly thereafter honorably discharged from the National Guard, his military obligations legally satisfied.

Dodd's private phone book, appointments schedule, and personal correspondence file now burgeoned with names I had never encountered in my early years with him—Julius Klein, lobbyist for West German interests; Tom Frouge, an urban developer; John Kluge, President of Metromedia, Inc.; Patrick Frawley, head of Schick Safety Razor Co.; Tom O'Neil, Board Chairman of General Tire; Edgar Parser, a diamond merchant; Lazarus Heyman, a Connecticut financier; Sidney Zagri, counsel for the Teamsters' Union; and many others.

All were wealthy and all had an unaccountable urge to press favors upon Tom Dodd which came in many shapes and guises. Cash gifts, interest-free loans, the use of automobiles and airplanes, imported champagnes, carpeting, jewelry, a stereo, a television set, carved chests, silks, clocks, *objets d'art*—accumulated in Dodd's two homes and various bank accounts.

"Generous-hearted friends," explained the Senator, with no trace of apology.

He was enjoying it all, not only the substance of power and wealth, but the eccentricities it permitted. He had a pet poodle, Beauregard, on whom he lavished attention. In the summer of 1964 he decided to send "Beau" from Washington to Connecticut for a summer vacation, and picked the United Aircraft Corporation's executive plane as a suitable mode of transportation. While the poodle was being primped and boxed for his trip by the office staff, the UAC's thirty-two passenger Convair simmered for half an hour on the sun-baked runway at National Airport's Page Terminal, its frustrated cargo of top company officials unaware they were waiting for the arrival of a dog. At length the plane was ordered to clear the runway and the beribboned Beau arrived a minute too late for the take-off. The Senator's pet made his trip via Allegheny Airlines, his transportation officially charged to "campaign travel expenses for Senator Dodd and staff."

And Dodd now humored an old fondness for bizarre costumes. On occasion he appeared on the sober streets of North Stonington decked out in a ten-gallon hat, red bandana, and riding breeches. But more often he indulged his sartorial peculiarities in the more sophisticated environs of Georgetown. There he could be seen on afternoon walks— a black beret slanted across his white head, a paisley cravat blossoming under open shirt collar, a multi-colored tweed sport jacket, shoes with thick crepe soles, and a stout walking stick with crooked handle —looking much like an exiled artist or the actor he once wanted to be.

Such an apparition, had it been seen in certain parts of Connecticut, would surely have confused the accepted picture of plain Tom Dodd, now being freshly polished by the Senator, perhaps tongue-in-cheek, for his campaign against a made-to-order opponent—John Lodge— the scion of a great aristocratic family.

✽　　✽　　✽

At about five o'clock each afternoon when he was in Washington, the Senator concluded his official activities. What some of us called "the hour of the sycophants" was then at hand. If there were callers still in the waiting room, Marjorie or Michael would have to invent some pretext for sending them away gently, perhaps to return another day. Phone calls placed a short time before now produced the Senator's evening favorites: a thin, rhetorical legislative assistant from another Senate office who had known Dodd in the old Justice Department days; a balding, bespectacled technician from Bridgeport whom Dodd had placed in a sinecure in the Space Agency; a watery-eyed, white-faced lawyer from Kansas City who had come to Washington for a weekend and stayed on interminably; and, to fill out the group, an old political retainer, summoned from his perch behind the partition at the rear of the reception room.

His court assembled, the Senator would direct Michael to get out the Scotch, and for the next few hours, Michael would serve as bartender. To admiring listeners the Senator, assured of unflagging sympathy, would unfold his problems, relate his triumphs, and vent his indignations. They would sit patiently while he read aloud long sections of a speech he planned to deliver the following day. They would nod in solemn agreement at his analyses of the folly of Administration foreign policy, frown as he exposed the perfidy of his rivals, and roar exaggeratedly at his latest jokes—which could be funny indeed, for Dodd was an accomplished mimic and raconteur. In turn, he would listen in mock gravity to their advice and catch up on Capitol Hill gossip, at which some of his evening cabinet were quite adept.

There were to be no interruptions to these councils. When a Senator stopped by twice in the same evening, Marjorie extended her regrets, over peals of laughter that could be heard from behind the door, that an important conference prevented Dodd from seeing him. Even calls from Mrs. Dodd were not permitted to intrude.

"Tell her I just left, Miss Marjorie."

"But Senator, I told her that half an hour ago; you should be home by now."

"Well—say I had to attend a meeting; tell her I called and said to go on alone and I'll meet her in the lobby. And have Mike come in."

Then, in explanation to his friends—"That Grace, she's a wonderful person, but I don't see why she insists on dragging me to these musicals. I can't carry a tune, you know. Taking me to a concert is like sprucing up a baboon in evening clothes and taking him to the art gallery. Michael! Don't look so dour. You look like an undertaker to-night. Let's freshen up these drinks."

Dodd needed the ego-boosting of these sessions. In his station he could command entrée to the most interesting company in Washington, but the companionship of equals irritated him, and that of superiors, which he found unendurable, provoked his foulest moods. It was the uncritical esteem of underlings that gratified him most. He basked in the adulation he received. Inevitably, I would be called into the office to report on some matter that engaged the Senator's curiosity. While trying to conjure up a plausible excuse for extricating myself, I would hear again the familiar dialogue. The details might differ from night to night, but the tone was constant. From the thin legislative assistant—"Tom, you are still remembered as the best trial lawyer in the history of the Justice Department. I know; I had to replace you, and it wasn't easy." From the political hanger-on—"You're a great Senator, Tom, greater than Frank Maloney, greater than Brien Mc-Mahon." And from the Kansas City lawyer, assurances that out in the Midwest, Thomas J. Dodd was looked upon as one of the statesmen of our time. "Or of any time," chimed in Bridgeport. At length, the Senator would become surfeited with praise and bored with the blandness of his troupe. He would wait for an opening, then mount a venomous attack that would banish the smiles from everyone's face.

"What do you mean 'your sexual conquests,' you snip," he taunted the rhetorical one. "Why look at you, look at you. You're a wraith of a man—all head and no body. You're a little man, a musty, dusty, mushy, reedy, seedy, little man. You're a woodpecker of a man. Don't insult me by telling me about your bedroom acrobatics."

His irritation thus relieved, he would restore the euphoria. "Just trying to get a rise out of you, John. I'll bet you're really something. It reminds me—"

At the first sign of his returning humor, the grins would reappear and the deliberations would resume. The cigar smoke thickened, enveloping the room in an acrid haze; the hosannas were sung again. Nine o'clock came and went. Mrs. Dodd and the concert retreated further and further from his mind. In the other offices, key staff members wearily remained at their desks. "Mike!" At the Senator's call Michael mechanically entered the throne room to do the honors once more; through the half-opened door I could hear the thin one repeating, "I still say, Tom, and I'll go on saying it—you were the greatest courtroom lawyer in the history of the department."

❀   ❀   ❀

Many a staffer who worked the Senate side of Capitol Hill during
the Kennedy-Johnson Administration fondly remembers the old Carroll Arms. Its cocktail lounge was the closest watering place to the two
Senate Office Buildings but, beyond this happenstance, it had a dis-
tinctive flavor that made it unofficial headquarters for many off-duty
Hill people. By merely crossing the street, a harried Senate assistant
could magically escape the world of jangling anxieties and retreat into
a cool, carpeted oasis where all was dark and subdued. One entered
through a large scarlet door and descended a plush burgundy stairway
into a world illuminated only by little red globes on the tables. From
five P.M. on any working day the Carroll Arms would be filled with a
gregarious mélange of unwinding aides, martini-drinking secretaries,
salty waitresses, hospitable lobbyists, and an occasional Senator.
There was a restful conviviality about the place, a sympathetic, soothing spirit. If you were looking for diversion, you could join one of the
larger tables where a place would be cheerfully made; if you wished
privacy, you found a small table in the back where you could converse
in assured intimacy.

To me, it was a place to go at night. For a long time I had led a
rootless personal existence. My wife and I had been separated since
1963, following a gradual inner estrangement. We remained cordial
and had agreed upon an amicable divorce, to be granted after the
long period of voluntary separation required under Maryland law.

This I knew represented a serious failure in life for which I bore
heavy responsibility, and it had caused me to make a critical reassess-
ment of all my relationships. For years I had devoted almost all my
time and energy to my work, ignoring other, more basic obligations.
In the office I had been something of a martinet. Introverted by nature, wholly absorbed in trying to master a bewildering complexity of
responsibilities for which I had had no real preparation, convinced
that authority and familiarity did not mix, I had long remained aloof
from the staff. But in the past year and a half I had slowly come to
realize the hollowness of this attitude, and had formed friendships
with several staff people whose off-duty company I learned to value.
And that had led to much more. The relationship thus begun between
Marjorie and me was growing into one of deep personal attachment.
The hours away from the office had taken on new importance, and I
waited impatiently for the Senator's night councils to break up.

The inner core of Senator Dodd's staff customarily met at the Carroll Arms after work. Our conversation was generally shop talk. There had been a time when we met in contagious excitement, to relate the achievements and exchange the humor of the day. But the swapping of confidences, in which we all had innocently engaged at first, soon took on a seriousness none of us had anticipated. We found that by pooling information we were learning things that, sealed off in our separate compartments, we had not known before.

Each of us specialized in a different phase of the Senator's complex operations.

The Tom Dodd I knew was primarily the public man. My dealings with him generally pertained to policies, speeches, committee work, and votes. I could cite his views on any issue and was a walking encyclopedia of his public career, but I knew little of the other Tom Dodds.

Marjorie witnessed a different side of him—his hour-to-hour demeanor when not on public display, his family affairs, the details of his personal relationships.

Doreen took his private dictation.

Michael was the first and the last of us to see the Senator each day; he knew where much of his money came from and where it went, though he didn't know the why's.

Gerry Zeiller knew for whom the Senator did favors, but he did not know what the Senator might have received in return.

Dave Martin knew the inside story of his security probes and accompanied him on his trips abroad, seeing still another dimension of the man, but there his familiarity ended.

Carl Perian, the staff director of the Juvenile Delinquency Subcommittee, knew Dodd as a committee chairman, involved in investigations of powerful interests, but Carl was totally divorced from Dodd's other pursuits.

In New York and Hartford were men with whom we had little contact who knew their separate phases of the Senator's affairs—his campaign fund-raising, his business deals, his labor alliances. But in these areas, too, our information was broadening, for the re-election campaign tended to fuse together the Senator's disparate dominions.

It would frequently be nine or ten o'clock, after the Senator had left the office, when Marjorie, Michael, and I arrived at the Carroll Arms. Sometimes, Gerry or Doreen or Dave or Carl would be there and, if so, we would join them; otherwise, we would thread our way through the darkened room to a small corner table at the rear. Too tired to want dinner, we would order drinks and munch on the peanuts and chips that were furnished by the house. Then we would start to chat, and almost unconsciously slip into our nightly exercise—comparing notes. By late September of 1964 we had begun to form serious suspicions about our boss and, with self-destructive fascination, we pried into the foundations of the house we ourselves had labored to build.

I well remember the shaft of disappointment I felt upon discovering that there might be more than mere mismanagement or irresponsibility behind Senator Dodd's manipulations of his public payroll. For years, George Gildea, an uneducated and inarticulate septuagenarian, had been carried on the payroll of the Juvenile Delinquency Subcommittee, at $7,500 a year, as a professional staff member, though he performed no staff duties. I now learned that Gildea had loaned the Senator $23,000 which, after several years, remained unpaid. Another absentee staff member whose presence on the payroll had seemed unaccountable was Al Morano, a former Republican Congressman, now a business consultant in Greenwich, Connecticut. Morano, it turned out, had made three loans to the Senator amounting to $15,000.

At our nightly conferences the mystery behind the Senator's new affluence began to dissolve. The down payment on his home in Georgetown, I learned, was made possible by a $25,000 loan, interest-free and without fixed terms of repayment, from Mathew Manes, a New York lawyer. I knew Manes slightly. He was an able, attractive, and likeable man. But I knew also that his interest in Dodd was not entirely personal, for Dodd had successfully boosted Manes for a highly-sought-after Presidential appointment to the Board of Directors of the General Aniline Corporation, a German firm taken over by our government during World War II. When President Johnson reappointed him to a second term, he called Dodd so that Dodd could be the one to inform Manes, and thus underline his crucial role in the appointment. I learned, too, that the timing of Dodd's payments for the massive renovation of his country retreat, which over the years exceeded $50,000, coincided remarkably with his receipt of the proceeds from various political fund-raising dinners.

Other elements were fitted into the emerging pattern. The luxurious suite at the Essex House which Dodd had used as his own on more than forty occasions when visiting New York was maintained by Julius Klein, a lobbyist and registered foreign agent for West German interests, whose activities had been investigated by the Foreign Relations

Committee, on which Dodd served. Similarly, the vacation hideaways at the Seaview Hotel in Miami Beach and at the Colony Hotel on Montego Bay, Jamaica, were furnished free of charge to Dodd by people who had business interests that stood to profit from the Senator's interventions.

The origins of Dodd's free air service were, I thought, significant. The cost of chartered plane flights, even on aircraft less elegant than those which transported Dodd and his family, was astronomical. We found that the standard charge for even a short charter flight, say round trip between Washington and Hartford, was $524.20 (plus $15 an hour layover charge). Dodd took such trips on a weekly basis, sometimes oftener. The saving to him, therefore, was many thousands of dollars each year, and the motives of those who footed such bills became a matter of concern. Chief among them was McKesson & Robbins, Inc., a New Jersey drug manufacturer then involved in a protracted investigation by one of Dodd's subcommittees. Other benefactors were Avco, Kaman Aircraft, United Aircraft Corporation, Aerojet, and Travelers Insurance Company—all firms which either sought Dodd's help as a Senator in smoothing their path to government contracts, or stood to gain from his action, or inaction, as a legislator and investigator.

The vacation trips to far-away resort capitals, it turned out, were often taken at government expense, under the guise of committee business. As the chairman of the Senate Juvenile Delinquency Subcommittee and acting chairman of the Senate Subcommittee on Internal Security, Dodd had access to government travel funds, over the use of which he was, practically speaking, the sole judge. He could travel almost anywhere in the world without having to render to anyone an accounting of the purpose or achievements of his trips.

At the expense of the Internal Security Subcommittee, Dodd took numerous trips to Florida, ostensibly to interview witnesses in connection with subcommittee hearings. In view of his refusal to walk across the hall to attend his committee hearings in Washington, these forays to Florida seemed rather dubious to me, but there was no one in our circle at the Carroll Arms who knew exactly what went on in Florida.

We did, however, learn the details of other trips. In April 1961, the Senator flew to San Juan, Puerto Rico, with Mrs. Dodd and two Juvenile Delinquency Subcommittee aides, presumably to study juvenile conditions there. After spending a couple of hours with the staff on the morning after their arrival, the Senator took off with Mrs. Dodd on a trip to St. Thomas in the Virgin Islands. Four days after leaving San Juan, they returned from St. Thomas, and on the next morning they checked out of the Caribe Hilton and flew back to Washington. For his expenses on this excursion, Dodd billed the government $495.25.

In February 1962, the Senator and Mrs. Dodd, accompanied by Judge and Mrs. Irving Kaufman, spent ten days vacationing in California as guests of the Beverly Hills millionaire, Alfred Hart. On the day before his return, he called Washington to have Carl Perian produce two members of the Los Angeles Police Department, who were to go to a room he engaged at the Beverly Hills Hotel for a two-hour interview. On the basis of this contrived interview, Dodd charged the taxpayers $452.65 for the air-travel expense of his California vacation.

Other illusions were dispelled. For years I had regarded Dodd's strenuous nationwide schedule of anti-Communist speech-making as an earnest of his dedication to the things he held important. Now, however, I learned of other motives. Dodd was paid as much as $1,500 and $2,000, plus expenses, by well-heeled right-wing groups for single appearances at their "crusades," "alerts," and "seminars." Unless he received a fee, I found, he would not address these affairs. Over a five-year period he took in more than $50,000 as income from anti-Communist speeches, radio broadcasts, and articles. I could not abandon my belief that Dodd was sincere in his cold war philosophy, but I had to concede that, at the least, he was willing to exploit it for personal profit.

And it became apparent that, behind the costly gifts that deluged Dodd, lurked more than the "generous hearts" of his friends. The stereo had come from John Lane, Washington representative of Westinghouse, a firm which was for years entangled in the investigation into price-rigging by one of Dodd's Senate subcommittees. The television set and the imported champagnes and other gifts came from executives of an independent television network who, whatever their friendly feelings toward Dodd, apparently had hopes of remaining free of involvement in Dodd's investigation into television programming. Some of the loaned automobiles were from David Dunbar, who headed a moving and wrecking firm that Dodd's office had aided in obtaining lucrative government contracts. The ornate Dodd silverware had been replated gratis by the International Silver Company, at whose behest Dodd had urged changes in the Treasury Department's silver policy, which determined the availability of silver for industrial use. Some of the jewelry which Mrs. Dodd wore so tastefully was the gift of a diamond merchant named Edgar Parser, who, with Dodd's help, was seeking appointment as ambassador to Luxembourg. The carpeting came from the friend of a man Dodd helped to obtain a Presidential pardon for an income-tax conviction. A stranger named Eddie Perkins turned up in Dodd's office one day and co-signed a $5,000 note for the Senator. Later, Dodd helped Perkins with a zoning dispute involving a Federal agency. And so it went.

Coincidences? I hoped so, though there seemed far too much of a pattern. But I could not bring myself to believe that Dodd was involved in out-and-out dishonesty either.

It had taken months for this story to unfold—in a disorderly, haphazard, speculative manner—and it would be months yet before the scattered parts added up to a recognizable whole. What had started as a game had turned into a preoccupation, then an almost compulsive pursuit, the fruit of which was already bitter. No longer could we feel the pride of old in the work that filled our days. We had begun to realize that the possession of knowledge such as ours entailed alarming responsibilities. But we were by no means sure what they were, or ready to pay their price, or even aware of what that price was.

Marjorie was the first to suggest that the Senator's conduct was immoral and perhaps illegal. Her daily exposure to it was both broader and more intimate than ours. Moreover, she viewed him from a different perspective than Michael or myself; our ethnic and political backgrounds somewhat inured us to the peculiarities of temperamental Irishmen and the moral ambiguities of politicians. And, unlike us, her judgments were not influenced by financial dependence, complicated by past allegiance or rationalized by career expectations. More than a year before, out of personal disenchantment, she had quit the Senator and obtained a position with the House Small Business Committee. He pursued her with offers to return and pledges of an improved office regime. In the six weeks following Marjorie's departure he fired two personal secretaries who had succeeded her and, seeing the old chaos returning, I joined in urging Marjorie to come back. In the end she did, out of a sympathy for the Senator, which he knew well how to elicit, and because she missed her old associates. Now she wanted to leave again. With difficulty, I had persuaded her to stay for three more months, by invoking our personal attachment and the Hill tradition that one simply does not leave a Senator during a campaign. But the implications of staying on troubled her.

"For a long time I've known he was deceitful and irresponsible and selfish," she said. "Now I'm convinced he's dishonest, too. I can't prove it, but I feel it. People have come into the office and given him huge contributions—two thousand, five thousand—in *cash*. If these contributions were legitimate, they wouldn't be in cash. I just know he's stashing it away and won't spend it on the campaign at all. And we have a responsibility in this. We're helping him to fool the people, day by day, and we can't go on justifying it to ourselves forever."

Her directness was vexing; it pricked a sensitive spot. Back in Atlantic City, during the brief hour when the Vice-Presidency seemed to hang terrifyingly before us, we had agreed that we had a duty somehow to inform Lyndon Johnson of the reasons why Dodd must not be placed a heartbeat away from the Presidency. Our anxiety proved needless; our pact was never put to the test. But the ethical questions which that moment helped bring to a head persisted, as did the potential consequences. I could see the sum effort of all my adult years unraveling, and I urged caution. Michael, by nature tight-lipped and conservative, felt the same. Marjorie, the most audacious of us, consented reluctantly to go along. That we were part of something that had become sour and disillusioning, we all agreed; that it was downright crooked, we could not really know and, in varying degrees, found hard to believe. Congressional ethics is an undefined and obscure area of human behavior. The point at which a Senator's small deceits, profiteering, misuse of public facilities, and acceptance of favors become culpable dishonesty is hard to know morally, and harder still to know legally. After all, it was frequently pointed out that the great Daniel Webster had openly accepted annual retainers from interests he supported on the Senate floor. Here we were, amateurishly poking into the brambles which august Senate committees and Executive commissions studiously avoided. Prudence and justice bade us go slow, even in thought.

There were laws, we knew, governing the solicitation, reporting, and use of political contributions. That was something reasonably solid and measurable. We believed that if the cash Marjorie spoke of was not accounted for, if there were any pocketing or misreporting of political contributions, it would be a criminal matter, requiring of us some kind of protest and confrontation, though we could not then visualize the shape it would take. We had been running an adding-machine tape on all contributions that had come into the Washington office since early summer; the total now stood at $135,000, with the peak of the fund-raising season still ahead. We decided to continue this check, as much out of curiosity as suspicion; but beyond that we would give the Senator the benefit of the doubt, hoping that the eventual official reports on contributions and expenditures would prove our doubts groundless.

There was, too, another perspective. Dodd was in the midst of a campaign, in a position most vulnerable to rumors and accusations. He stood at the head of a state ticket that embraced the fortunes of hundreds of lesser Democrats. His voting record as a Senator was, by our standards, good. He was known to be a friend of the President, who was already in some trouble over his friends. Anything that impugned Dodd's honesty would have wide repercussions. What we already knew beyond chance of error had withered our desires to stay with him, but there seemed insufficient reason to bring on a holocaust or start something that could not be honestly judged in the sensationalized atmosphere of a political campaign. When the election was over, we could quietly leave Tom Dodd, hopefully on friendly terms, and seek new careers. In the meantime, we would try to do our jobs as before. That stopgap solution, with all its uncertainties, had one happy virtue—it was the easiest path and it postponed hazardous decisions into the indefinite future.

It was always midnight before our conversations broke up. Later, when alone, I would rehash the considerations that were leading me to a crisis I had not sought and for which I was unprepared. Memories of the earlier years with Tom Dodd, years of comradeship and common striving, were much on my mind. The old ties, the old affections, seemed real and binding, whereas abstract matters of ethics looked so unreal. They were confusing, frothy intrusions upon the certainties and the realities, twisting everything out of its proper proportion.

The Tom Dodd I remembered from a decade before was not a man to be involved casually in immorality, even of the borderline variety. He had always been a staunch moral absolutist. Right and wrong are clearly demarcated, he insisted, and could always be identified. When his son Nicholas was taught in catechism class that it was a less serious sin for a poor man than a rich man to steal $10, Dodd complained to me indignantly that the spurious doctrines of the relativists had invaded even the Catholic schools. He could see a moral issue in almost

every dispute and was exasperatingly pedantic about it. He had publicly stated many times: "Every major question facing this country, at
home and abroad, is at bottom a moral question."

He had always impressed me as a religious man. He went to Mass
on all the required days and many that were not required. He con-
fessed regularly. He participated in annual retreats, corresponded
with a variety of clergymen, and had a drawerful of honorary degrees
from Catholic colleges. In his valises, he always carried prayer books
and rosary beads—and he was not ostentatious or hypocritical about
his religious observances. He was a faithful husband and an indulgent,
if irascible, father. His tax returns were prepared and audited by outside accountants. His affairs were once so aboveboard that until two
years before he always had me open his personal mail. Was it likely
that this man could be a fraud? Having fought so long for the public
interest, was it believable that Dodd could now be using his office for
personal gain?

Perhaps, I thought, I should go to him and talk it out. I owed that to
him, at least. But I knew his nature would not permit it. Where personal criticism was involved, Dodd was unapproachable. Of subordinates he demanded absolute, unqualified fealty; any questioning of his
actions he treated as gross disloyalty. He had a highly conspiratorial
mind and often suspected plots. I had more than once heard him accuse secretaries of deliberately concealing phone messages and of hiding mail. Once he had peremptorily fired a young law student, without explanation, on the report of an informant that the young man
had been seen pausing in front of the Senator's in-box and perusing
the topmost letter. On the next day, all the locks were changed.

Were I to go to him with inquiries about his conduct in areas in
which I had no concern, whether innocent or guilty he would start a
general purge. Nothing would have been accomplished, and innocent
people would have been injured. An unbridgeable gulf would open
between the Senator and me, and a relationship which still meant a
good deal to me would have been destroyed. I decided that there was
nothing to do but wait, hoping, for his sake and my own, that our
twelve-year association would not come to an ignominious end.

On the way home after the interludes at the Carroll Arms, I usually
stopped at Union Station to pick up the bulldog edition of the following morning's *Washington Post*. It gave me a jump on the new day. At
that hour the streets and avenues leading to nearby Capitol Plaza

were always deserted. Floodlights bathed the great Dome in a white mystical light. It was this scene that I had first encountered when, aglow with excitement, I arrived in Washington six years before. It had remained unchanged and unchangeable, an ironic contrast to my own chaotic relationships, which had so badly splintered and would perhaps never be repaired.

CHAPTER THREE

FROM a distance, Hartford has the look of a reborn Camelot, the vaulting glitter of its modern center framed by an ancient skyline of high spires and golden domes. And on the brilliant afternoon of September 28, 1964, it seemed indeed the scene of a monarchic festival. The streets and squares, festooned with bunting, overflowed with a vast multitude. Men and women of every size, shape and color were squeezed everywhere, shoulder to shoulder. Armed with their cameras and transistor radios, waving placards aloft, wearing a collective face of pleasurable expectancy, they made up a host both demonstrative and amiable. The President was coming.

With supersonic seven-league boots, L.B.J. was covering, in the Bunyanesque style he relishes, all New England on that one day. He had set the tone on alighting from Air Force One at Rentschler Field in East Hartford. Breaking away from his protective escort, he barged massively into the excited throngs that pressed forward to touch him and to glimpse from close up his formidable, beaming, sun-creased face. "I touched him! I touched his hand!" exclaimed an enraptured young woman, holding her fingers up, almost in disbelief. The contagion spread electronically along the announced route. The President's entrance into Hartford was a triumph, astonishing for the size and enthusiasm of the crowds that engulfed him at each intersection. He delighted his admirers with bull-horn homilies. Again and again, he reached his long arms into the ecstatic swarms that surged about his car, all but overwhelming the grim-faced Secret Service men. Already, the bodyguard who was "riding shotgun" on the front bumper had had his jacket ripped off and his trousers torn. Nine times the milling thousands stopped the Presidential motorcade in downtown Hartford, and each time they were rewarded with impromptu orations from the big-eared, grinning giant whose patriarchal affection seemed generous enough to encompass them all.

Beside the animated President, Senator Thomas Dodd sat woodenly, a stiff waving of his arm the only accompaniment to the gyrations of his Chief. Once, the President handed him the bull horn, admonishing him to "talk it up, Tom," but Dodd gave up after a few ineffectual stabs. Something about the scene challenged his sense of dignity; he was no longer the crowd hawker of his college days. And he was a little uneasy. He had followed John Kennedy through the Naugatuck Valley in 1960, and the experience had lingered with him. At two A.M., the narrow main streets of those valley towns were choked almost impassably with vociferous crowds that pressed in frantically upon Kennedy's car. Dodd later told me of his alarm, and an anxious look came into his eyes. "Kennedy started this mob stuff," he said. "He eggs them on by reaching for their hands. You can't fool like that with crowds. Some day these monkeyshines will lead to a disaster, and remember that I foretold it." Perhaps he suffered from the same foreboding as he sat beside Kennedy's successor.

From the portico of the Hartford Times Building, Lyndon Johnson looked out upon the one hundred and fifty thousand people who had waited three hours to see him—almost as many people as the entire population of Hartford. Sixty-five thousand wildly cheering admirers packed the square below him. It was the greatest assemblage ever seen in the Connecticut capital, greater than that which had turned out for F.D.R., for Eisenhower, for Kennedy. When told that the crowd set an all time record, Mr. Johnson insisted that it be announced immediately. "And they say I have no crowd appeal," he jibed happily to Dodd. The Senator, in contrast, still seemed ill at ease. When he approached a battery of microphones to introduce the President to an audience grown impatient with preliminaries, he was off his usual form. The old tremor, which invariably recurred in times of anxiety, had stiffened his upper lip and faintly impeded his speech. Dodd was conscious that before Hartford's multitudes he was a flop— but he was powerless to do anything about it.

The President, enjoying himself hugely, teased up the rising ovation by mugging and waving his arms. For a few minutes he lost the crowd by the flat reading of a lusterless text but, sensing the drop in spirit, he put aside his papers and plunged into arm-waving Texas-style homiletics that struck an immediate rapport. Thundering cheers now answered his every sally. "I assumed the Presidency in an hour of national tragedy," he said. "It came on me unawares. I had no time to prepare for it, no time to plan what I wanted to do. But suddenly I was your President, and I had to do the best I could. And so I set to work. I tried to pick up the bits and pieces that John Kennedy had left behind. When I was through, I sent fifty-nine recommendations to the Congress, fifty-nine. The reporters who cover the White House predicted that I'd be lucky to get two passed. You know how many we passed? Fifty-nine! But there's so much more to be done!" His audience was solidly with him.

"Go on and make a change if you want, a change in November," he taunted confidently.

"No! No! No!" rose the expected remonstrance.

He lauded Dodd, though not so flamboyantly as he had when, addressing a $100-a-plate breakfast in Hartford, he closed by saying: "I know that Senator Dodd has independent views on some issues. I respect him for it. But I hope there is no Democrat so doctrinaire, or no Republican so small, that he will not put country above politics and patriotism above party and cast his vote to keep Tom Dodd in the United States Senate!" But that was a year before, when Johnson was Vice-President and Dodd still saw him every day, prowling the halls of the Capitol. As befits a President, Johnson was now a bit less fulsome in his endorsements. Dodd's re-election was essential to the nation and to the Great Society, he said forcefully, and Dodd was proud to receive such praise.

The shadows were already beginning to lengthen in Hartford when the President brought forward Lady Bird, who spoke with the gracious authority of a natural orator about the beauties of Connecticut, which she said had been conveyed to her long before by the charm and warmth of her dear friend, Grace Dodd. Then the President returned to the microphones. "I'm sorry, folks. We love bein' with you, but I tell you we must leave now," he said, to a rumble of disappointment. "If you want me to carry on, if you want to push forward the things that John F. Kennedy started and that I have tried to continue, then give me what help you can and I'll appreciate it. Good-bye now, and God bless you all."

As Johnson finished, a mighty roar of approval rolled up, then trailed away, then suddenly swelled again as the President returned to the platform to wave once more. Recurring cheers followed his slowly moving motorcade out of Hartford. Ahead of him, waiting voters were already massed in New Hampshire, Maine, and Vermont, in places that had never seen a President. Consciously the master of time and distance, he would, on his way back, make a three A.M. visit to Ted Kennedy, lying injured in a Boston hospital.

An hour after the President was gone, a contrasting quiet, like the aftermath of a tornado, hung heavily over the Hartford streets. Isolated pictures of Goldwater, Miller, and Lodge, propped up in store windows, looked melancholy and forlorn. The people had spoken with a finality so monumental that misinterpretation was impossible. Senator Dodd had ridden in many a caravan and he understood that voice. Six weeks before, his rural Connecticut instincts and his professional pessimism had influenced him to make gloomy forecasts that Goldwater and Lodge might be tough, but now he conceded that the Connecticut campaign was already won on its opening day. Oh, he would run hard, as always; he wanted his vote to be up close to Johnson's and ahead of the Connecticut Congressmen. But the old fears need not clutch at the heart this time—and he could hold the spending way down.

Holding the campaign spending down was to be one major objective in 1964. Raising four times as much money as we had ever raised before was to be another. Of the three advertising budgets proposed by our public relations firm, the Randall Company of Hartford, Dodd chose the smallest. The campaign payroll was held to an absolute minimum. There were to be no expense accounts or restaurant tabs for aides, as in previous races. There would be no handouts to local town chairmen to finance get-out-the-vote drives on Election Day. Nor were there to be regional field headquarters, such as we had maintained at the Roger Smith Hotel in Stamford during our 1956 "invasion" of heavily Republican Fairfield County. "No frills," said the candidate. But he was preoccupied as never before with raising money. Though the late adjournment of Congress had reduced the formal phase of our campaign to five weeks, his schedule was studded with fund-raising events that again and again crowded out vote-getting appearances. The contrast between the massive fund-raising effort and the tight lid on expenditures soon became obvious—particularly to those who recalled the Senator's free-spending ways in our threadbare days of old.

By my reckoning, we entered the final weeks before election with a war chest undreamed of in previous races. Starting almost three years before, the Senator had milked Connecticut sources almost dry and had foraged far beyond, staging fund-raising affairs in New York and Washington and even in California, where coteries of well-heeled anti-Communists and government-oriented businessmen could be tapped. He was uncharacteristically tight-lipped and deprecatory about the results, a departure from former times when he would gleefully keep me posted on every $200 contribution. But the Senator was unable to impose the same reticence on the sponsors and organizers of his events; they wanted their accomplishments known and touted about. From their conversations and correspondence, I learned that a dinner in Hartford in November 1961, addressed by Vice-President Johnson, had netted $55,000; a reception in Washington in September 1963, had raised $13,000; a series of affairs throughout Connecticut on October 26, 1963, all of them headlined by Johnson, brought in another $47,000—so that at least $115,000 was in the coffers before the formal campaign period even began. By mid-October 1964, the estimates made by Majorie and me, based on acknowledgment letters, showed that coast-to-coast solicitations had brought in an additional $185,000, raising the Dodd war chest to $300,000 as we entered the homestretch, with promotions that figured to produce another $100,000 still to come. Yet the Senator persisted in predictions of imminent bankruptcy. He contended that he couldn't possibly meet present commitments, amounting to scarcely $100,000, and speculated darkly about cutting back on newspaper ads and television time. Sensing our incredulity, he talked of old political debts that must be satisfied.

There were, to be sure, some obligations held over from earlier races, but not many. Our big 1956 deficit had been absorbed by our '58 campaign and the deficit from '58 was only $19,000—according to our former financial wizard, Joe Blumenfeld, who now wore the robes of a Federal judge. There had been political expenses in non-election years, of course, such as travel and entertainment of constituents. But I knew that for most of his term Dodd had meticulously deducted all such items from his income tax, and therefore, they could not be reimbursed to him out of political-dinner funds. Even if he had changed that tax policy in the past year, with all the free travel and accommodations he received such expenses could not amount to more than six or eight thousand dollars. And, unlike many Senators, Dodd did not have to pay routine office bills out of his pocket. Due to Mike's resourcefulness in foraging office supplies, Dodd actually made a profit on his Senate stationery allowance. So at the most, no more than $30,000 of his $300,000 war chest could have been properly charged to pre-1964 expenses. Where, then, was the money going?

The one man who knew, besides the Senator, was Ed Sullivan, a genial, mild-spoken Irishman who had long ago grown gray in political harness. It was Ed who collected, stored, disbursed, and kept records on the Dodd campaign money. It was also Ed who handled Dodd's personal financial dealings, from the selling of real estate to the negotiation of new loans. His age was an office mystery, but I guessed it at about seventy. His blue eyes bespoke amiability; his florid complexion betrayed conviviality. Though a devout Catholic and solid family man, Ed saw no essential conflict between piety and political trimming. He thought that financial affluence should flow from political power and was frank to voice his determination that Dodd should emerge from the Senate a wealthy man.

Ed bore the marks of a long life as a local politician. Patronage, favors, franchises, and government largesse represented to him the essence of involvement in public affairs. Yet, there was about the man a certain gravelly grace that somehow raised him above the meanness of ward and precinct. I never heard him say an unkind word about anyone. For himself, he was neither ambitious nor predatory. He saw the world in a perpetually optimistic hue, and the Senator as its leading protagonist. Devoted to Dodd, he basked contentedly in the reflected glow of being his Connecticut satrap. Ed was nominally in charge of our Hartford field office, but he did little that fell within the true realm of a Senate aide. He worked incessantly at raising money. In a large shoe box, he kept a card file, constantly growing, of every individual and firm aided by the Senator's Washington office, and he saw to it that they were invited and reinvited to tangibly express their appreciation. Beyond that, he was a mine of political lore, old and new, on which the Senator doted, and he was Dodd's ever-available, ever-agreeable Connecticut companion. From time to time the two of them would disappear on mysterious odysseys, during which we in Washington would lose contact with them, to hear a day or two later that a phenomenal fog had rolled in along the coast, grounding planes, barring travel, and somehow interdicting communication with the outside world. Whatever they did on these expeditions, Dodd somehow seemed to return refreshed, which left no doubt in our minds that he and Ed had not been distressed by their isolation from everyday responsibilities.

I had always found Ed to be garrulous and open, to me at least, for I was a charter member of the Dodd organization. It was from Ed that I had learned the results of the $100-dollar-a-plate fetes in 1961 and 1963. But lately he had become closemouthed. Whenever the conversation chanced upon the state of our finances, he would turn vague and noncommittal. And so I strained to recall our past discussions.

Two comments of Ed's, oft repeated, now seemed keys to the riddle. "Tom spends money like it's going out of style," he would say. We had all made a similar assessment. Then, in recent years, he had added a new observation. "When our next campaign is over, if we handle it right, Tom's financial worries will be over for a long, long time to come." Unintentionally, he seemed to be dropping a clue to what was transpiring.

In campaign and out, Dodd was obviously living far beyond his visible income. With his fashionable townhouse, his country retreat, his spendthrift ways, a houseful of adult sons whom he continued to support, an appetite for luxury, travel, and conspicuous consumption which he disdained to discipline, he was chronically in debt. On his Washington books alone stood a personal indebtedness, not counting mortgages, of $60,000—most of it in the form of notes of several thousand dollars each. Beyond that, I knew that he owed to friends, on a handshake basis, another forty to fifty thousand. Occasionally one of them would talk to me of their investment in the Senator. Sanford Bomstein, a Washington restaurateur, used to joke about "the $5,000 Club," composed of associates whom the Senator had touched for that amount. By 1963, Dodd faced a major financial crisis. His credit, it appeared, was at last exhausted and, unable to borrow money on his own collateral, he had undertaken a desperate search for co-signers on additional notes. One possible salvation was to divert campaign funds to private use, and the wide disparity between the sums coming into the campaign treasury and those expended seemed to indicate that the course at which Ed had hinted was now being followed.

We had seen one notable example of the practice a year before, on the occasion of the wedding of the Senator's daughter Martha. The wedding took place in October 1963, at a time when Dodd was particularly pressed, not only by private creditors but by the Internal Revenue Service which was demanding, on the threat of opening the Senator's books, immediate payment of more than $12,000 in back taxes. Dodd, nevertheless, put on an extravagant wedding, followed by a sumptuous reception at the exclusive Hartford Club, where he entertained several hundred guests with a twelve-piece orchestra, pheasant under glass, free-flowing champagne, and an open bar. Michael, anxiously guarding the Senator's near-empty checking account, figured the cost at no less than $6,000. Others put it much higher. The engraved invitations had been charged to Dodd's Senate stationery account and were payed for by the taxpayers. But from where was the six thousand to come?

Dodd had to make some explanation to Michael, his bookkeeper, and approached him shortly after the wedding. "A wonderful thing happened, Mike," he said. "I was plagued over how I could possibly meet these wedding bills when Grace came to me and told me not to worry. She said she had saved up enough out of her grocery money to pay for the wedding. So it's all taken care of." Aside from the general absurdity of this story, it was Michael, not Mrs. Dodd, who paid most of the grocery bills, as well as all the other household expenses. But another explanation *was* credible. Two weeks after the wedding the same Hartford Club was to be the scene of a hundred-dollar-a-plate breakfast for Dodd's forthcoming re-election drive. Most of the tickets had already been sold. That was the likely source of payment for the wedding, which was made in cash and never showed up on the Senator's meticulous books. Later, Marjorie noticed on the Senator's desk a bill from Ed Sullivan for the canopy used at the church. Attached was a note reading: "Shall I pay this out of the Hartford Account?" (which contained only the proceeds from the political fund-raising affairs). I did not learn Dodd's answer, but to me the question itself was evidence enough that the campaign fund was the source of the wedding money.

That episode loomed large in our minds a year later, with only a few weeks to go before Election Day. Perhaps the Senator had only *borrowed* from his campaign account; perhaps he had honorable intentions for the huge surplus that was now accumulating. It would, after all, be prudent for him to build up large reserves against the need for a last-minute saturation drive if the tide seemed to turn. Or he could have been planning to announce a surplus to be used, under proper accounting procedures, for political expenses in the years ahead. As far as we knew, Dodd had not yet taken the irrevocable step of diverting campaign funds for personal use. No proof whatever existed that he planned a betrayal of the public trust.

Upon the adjournment of Congress on October 3, 1964, Senator Dodd took five staff members to Hartford for his campaign—Marjorie, Doreen, Michael, David, and me. He had rented for two months a comfortable, well-furnished, three-story colonial house on Brace Road in West Hartford, a central location from which he could reach the most distant points in the state in less than two hours of driving. By Senatorial fiat, we all lived there together—the Senator, his wife and sons, and the staff, to say nothing of the daughters and in-laws who would show up periodically to create housing crises. The staff, of course, would have preferred to stay at a hotel, but the Boss insisted that we all live in one place so that we could function better as a "team" and so that he could easily reach any of us whenever he wished. For months he had been speaking in fond anticipation of this familial arrangement. I suspect that he had always unconsciously resented the hours at night and on Sundays that we devoted to our own pursuits, for he invariably found ways of interrupting them, and would be violently angered if he could not reach us, though by morning he would normally have forgotten what was so urgent. Now, under the justification of campaign mobilization, we were constantly at his disposal, amenable to his needs and whims at all times.

It was a pleasant and gracious house, ideally appointed for a large family. On the first floor was a spacious living room where we all gathered twice weekly to watch the Senator on television and where we staged impromptu parties when the staff found itself alone in the house. Filling out the downstairs were two sitting rooms, used for evening conferences, a dining room which was not used at all, and a large, bright kitchen where Mrs. Dodd and her sons clustered in bathrobes each morning for breakfast.

Except for David Martin who bunked in an attic loft, we all slept on the second floor, in a state of tenuous but, in the main, triumphant rectitude. Michael and I shared a room. Marjorie and Doreen shared another, separated from ours by a connecting bath that we rationed out each morning, ten minutes per person, an arrangement not without its indecorums and surprise encounters. Across the hall were the young men of the Dodd family—Tom Jr., twenty-nine, Jeremy, twenty-five, and sometimes Christopher, twenty, a sophomore at Providence College. Senator and Mrs. Dodd occupied the master bedroom. In the morning, Dodd's deep voice, alternately querulous, alarmed, agitated, outraged, gratified, martyred, and philosophical, echoed throughout the floor and served as our faithful alarm clock.

During the day the staff worked not in the house but in three overcrowded rooms on the second floor of a bedraggled building that stood on lower Main Street in downtown Hartford. Outside, bums and winos, displaced from their traditional haunt a few blocks away by the bulldozer and wrecking ball of the Hartford Redevelopment Agency, hung around in uncertainty. They seemed unsettled in their new locale and uncomfortable in the shadow of the immaculate edifices across the street—the Hartford Public Library and the new Federal Office Building, where Dodd also had a suite.

Michael installed an arsenal of rented equipment in our makeshift offices, and I set up an abbreviated version of our Washington operation. We worked amid the distracting clatter of a United Press International news ticker, which kept us current on all news developments, and the click of a two-way teletype machine that connected us to the city rooms of the major newspapers and to our Washington office. A cross-referenced index-card system, along with the help of the Washington staff, enabled us to convert all that the Senator had said or done on any issue over the past six years into instant campaign ammunition. From this long assembly line an uninterrupted stream of press releases, speeches, TV and radio scripts, material for newspaper ads and radio spots flowed to the news centers of the state. With the Senator on the road all the time there was little opportunity to check out texts with him until late at night; consequently the press releases would be in the mail and the scripts already cleared with our advertising agency before he had a chance to read them. But there were no flaps. Years of close collaboration minimized the dangers of slipups, and not once did he complain of being stuck with bad lines or an incorrect position.

I did the writing. Doreen bore the main secretarial burden. Michael, directing a battery of volunteers, handled distribution to the press and still managed to render personal services to the Senator and his family. Marjorie drew the task which, as I knew from past campaigns, was the thorniest: she arranged the Senator's hour-to-hour schedule, a daily amalgam of speaking engagements, civic luncheons, fund-raising meetings, and private appointments with financial and political nabobs. Putting such a schedule together for each day necessitated a continuing process of painstaking mediation between a harassed candidate who refused to be imposed on and the arrogant, self-important "chairmen" and contributors who forever were demanding a piece of his time. Two temporary secretaries aided Marjorie and Doreen. David Martin came and went mysteriously, a Machiavellian glint in his eyes. He was in charge of wooing Connecticut's many Eastern European ethnic groups, which presumably supported the Senator's hard line anti-Communism (except for the pragmatic and numerous Poles, who seemed to favor trade and aid for Poland much more than ideological dispute). In those overheated, poorly lighted rooms, we put in a remorseless, twelve-to-fourteen-hour daily grind that more than once reduced the girls, seasoned veterans of pressure and overwork, to furious tears.

Compared with other political headquarters I had seen in the past —a lot of people sitting around doing a lot of talking, drinking a lot of coffee, but accomplishing very little—our operation was highly efficient. Of course, we were not volunteers; we were professionals, paid by the United States Senate, and had worked together for years. Besides us, six other campaign workers were on the Senate payroll— George Gildea, Ed Sullivan, Jim Gartland, Al Morano, Mary Hamil, and Beverly Curry—and had been occupied for many months with political activities, essentially fund-raising. I wondered if Lodge would find out about this and make an issue of it, for the combined salaries of these eleven Senate employees, prorated to include only that period of time devoted strictly to the election, amounted to a hidden contribution of $50,000 from the United States Government to the Dodd-for-Senate Committee. He didn't.

At nine or ten o'clock each night, we would return to the house on Brace Road. In one or another of the dimly-lit rooms, we would wait for the Senator and the start of our evening business session which, however late the hour, he would insist on conducting. At such times the unreality of our daily existence intruded upon us. Everywhere in the house were pictures of people we had never seen and mementoes of places and events of which we knew nothing. They reflected the long continuity and strong family ties of its rightful habitants, emphasizing by contrast, the motley nature and transient connection of the crew which now wandered through its many rooms, totally and furiously engaged in a cause in which they had ceased to believe. The lack of privacy, the sense of confinement, the overwork, the absence of diversion, the feeling that the Senator had forced us upon his family, and the reverse, all bored in relentlessly at night, causing fretful and feverish hours of tossing on unfamiliar, army-sized beds, systematically posted throughout the second floor, as though in some phantasmal barracks.

Tom Dodd was at his peak in a campaign. However much his excesses, his self-indulgence, his fetish for convenience, his retreats from reality, might hobble him in less demanding times, in an election race he rose to the challenge. A sharp, natural instinct for what people were thinking, refined by three decades in politics, gave him a sure grasp of the mood and tone of the times. If, as in the past, circumstance dealt him the role of the underdog or the giant-killer, he well knew how to assume a slashing, aggressive posture and mount a stupendous offense. But this time he was the established front runner. Everything was going his way and only a gigantic blunder could endanger his victory. So his bearing was calm, urbane, even benevolent. There were to be no attacks on the opposition, no mention of his opponent.

In 1964, Dodd was favored not only by Connecticut's aversion to Barry Goldwater, but also by the Republicans' selection of an inept Senatorial candidate. At the Republican National Convention, John Lodge, after backing Governor Scranton, had been quick to endorse Goldwater. But when his Republican fellow candidates in neighboring New York and Massachusetts abandoned Goldwater, Lodge floundered about, neither disowning nor embracing him. In the end he tried to ignore him, which was impossible. Thus he appeared disingenuous from the start. He was always off balance and could never find the solid footing from which to launch a telling assault on Dodd. Nor did this handsome, graying patrician, who had in the past easily ascended to the posts of congressman, governor, and ambassador, have any stomach for rough and tumble in-fighting with Tom Dodd. So Dodd was free to call the shots and establish the tenor of the campaign.

The plan of Dodd's campaign was essentially the plan of his six years in office: to plant a foot in each major ideological camp, to make an appeal to all basic attitudes of the political spectrum. To right-wingers, conservative businessmen, religious fundamentalists, ethnic patriots, Dodd fostered the image of the peerless anti-Communist whose zeal was grounded in a moral absolutism that challenged much of the reigning liberal thought. To liberals, internationalists, organized labor, the underprivileged, racial minorities, Democrats, he put forth his record of flawless support for the progressive measures of the Kennedy-Johnson Administration, his initiative in promoting the nuclear-test-ban treaty, his leadership in behalf of civil rights, his life-long credentials as a faithful party member. To independents, a group larger than either party in Connecticut, Dodd exploited his non-parti-sanship, his liberalism on some issues and his conservatism on others, his refusal to accept a label or to wear the collar of any faction. And to the many voters who cared little about politics, there was the all-purpose picture of the crime buster, the crusading investigator, the father of six children, the silver-haired statesman who looked so much like a senator that, as the newsmen said, he ought to play one in the movies.

The strategy was simple in concept, but delicate in execution. There was always the risk of getting lines entangled, of looking like a fumbling charlatan. There were so many doctrinaire groups, on left and right, who ceaselessly watched, like jealous lovers, for departures from their own orthodoxy. To carry it off required a strong reputation for political integrity, a high degree of artistry, and a measure of luck. Dodd had all three.

He did not have to *pretend* to be both liberal and conservative; he was naturally fragmented. On fundamental issues he never diluted his domestic liberalism to appease the conservatives; he would not only vote for the welfare state, he would make floor speeches for it. Nor would he turn lukewarm in his global anti-Communism to mollify the liberals. He was a visceral advocate of both positions. And he was, as well, an organization lone wolf, who had as much, or as little, in common with Republicans as with Democrats. He felt real communion with neither and, though on organizational matters he deferred to his position as a Democrat, he was authentically independent on issues. He had publicly branded political platforms a bad farce. He had denounced even-handedly, in the same Senate speech, the Majority Leader and the Minority Leader for lack of leadership.

Tom Dodd's hidden strength lay in the art of timing, private fence-mending, in the selection of battlegrounds. The plaques in his Washington reception room attested to his success in pleasing diverse groups, each of whom seemed to regard his advocacy of their particular cause as the basic Tom Dodd. Each seemed satisfied to dismiss his

aberrations on lesser issues as unfortunate but not crucial manifesta-
tions of the naïveté of a man whose honesty and courage must be
admired, if not always his judgment.

Years of cultivating opposed schools of thought were now paying
dividends. Johnson-Dodd billboards and Goldwater-Dodd bumper
stickers abounded. Dodd's candidacy was supported in Connecticut
by the conservative Young Americans for Freedom and the liberal
Americans for Democratic Action. Journalistic support came to him
from William Buckley, John Chamberlain, and Fulton Lewis, Jr., on
one side, and Norman Cousins and Roscoe Drummond on the other.
The two largest sources of contributions to the Dodd campaign were
conservative businessmen and the AFL-CIO. Patrick Frawley ($10,-
000) and Benjamin Gilbert ($5,000) led the list of individual donors;
Frawley was nationally known as a supporter of the Republican right,
Gilbert shared the distinctions of being the largest Connecticut contributor to both Dodd and Goldwater. Organized labor started off
with a $5,000 check from its Committee on Political Education
(COPE), and by the time the individual AFL-CIO unions had made
their contributions, the take from labor exceeded $50,000. Two pres-
tige committees, sporting impressive letterheads, solicited funds and
published newspaper advertisements in Dodd's behalf. One committee
was composed of prominent liberals (Elmo Roper, Eugene Rostow,
Norman Cousins); the other was made up, for the most part, of
equally well-known conservatives (Mrs. Kermit Roosevelt, Admiral
Radford, Taylor Caldwell). The degree to which Dodd was jointly
supported by right and left was unprecedented in the country, and so
deftly had this support been put together that its inherent contradictions were almost entirely overlooked by the press.

Only a part of the Senator's campaign effort was devoted to the
public platform and the mass media. He reveled in behind-the-scenes
intrigue and was something of a virtuoso at it. His handling of the
Teamsters' Union illustrates this talent, and reveals what I regarded as
his accelerating retreat from conviction.

In 1957, before he entered the Senate, Dodd had represented thirteen rank-and-file union members in a lawsuit that sought to depose
Teamsters' president James Hoffa on grounds that he had been
elected under conditions that were a travesty of the democratic process. Personally, it was not a case to which Dodd was indifferent; he
despised Hoffa and what he represented. The suit, tried before Judge

F. Dickinson Letts in the Federal District Court of the District of Columbia, ended in Hoffa's temporary displacement. A Board of Monitors was appointed by the court to oversee union affairs until honest elections could be properly held. When they were held, Hoffa was overwhelmingly re-elected, but that was scarcely the fault of Dodd, who had put his prestige on the line as a Hoffa foe. Dodd's bold participation in the case engendered much of the hostility he encountered from labor the following year, during his struggle for the Senate nomination. Nevertheless, he continued to pursue the Teamsters' boss. In the Senate, he castigated Hoffa bitterly and pushed legislation designed to break his stranglehold over Teamsters' affairs. Once, when Washington representatives of the union visited Dodd during a routine lobbying canvass, he stormily ordered them out of his office. Opposition to Hoffa led him to vote for a labor "reform" bill that was so hostile to labor as to bring down on Dodd's head a storm of protest from honest trade unionists throughout Connecticut.

But by 1964, Dodd's relations with Hoffa had improved dramatically, even as the embattled union czar was being rocked by a series of federal indictments and convictions. After listening to denunciations of Hoffa for years, I was surprised when Dodd began to talk indignantly of "persecution" of Hoffa by "the Kennedys." Then I learned that in late 1963, following a year in which two dozen Federal indictments had been returned against Teamsters officials, Dodd had accepted a secret gift of $1,500 from the Teamsters. Later, in the spring of 1964, Sidney Zagri and Edward Corneaby, Hoffa's agents in the Capitol, called on Dodd. This time they were not thrown out. After a cordial meeting, they presented Dodd with a $2,500 check from the national Teamsters, along with a pledge of massive financial help from Connecticut locals. Dodd kept the check in his desk for two weeks, pondering what to do with it. To accept it was politically hazardous, since he was now in the campaign accounting period and when he, or the Teamsters, reported the check, its origin would become publicly known. But he rebelled at the thought of returning it. In the end, he found a way to cover it up. The $2,500 was turned over to the Democratic Senate Campaign Committee, headed by Senator Warren Magnuson. The committee then returned the $2,500 to Dodd—as coming from the committee itself. Dodd thus got Hoffa's money without his stigma. That transaction made a deep impression on me. The fact that a committee of distinguished Senators was permitting itself to serve as a front for unsavory contributions seemed to me to place a stamp of approval on deceit in financial reporting. Perhaps it seemed that way to Dodd, too.

Dodd's belated courtship of the Teamsters continued to ripen. When hundreds of that union's Connecticut members, fanatically loyal to Hoffa, came to Washington for a convention, Dodd invited their wives to the Capitol and warmly saluted them and their spouses. But a more substantial test of Dodd's new friendship was at hand.

In April 1964, two leaders of the Connecticut Teamsters, "Freddy" Roberto and "Sonny" Bets, notified Dodd, through Ed Sullivan, that they were expecting him to share the head table with Hoffa at a union banquet in Bridgeport. Dodd was in a tight corner; while he could defend his improved relationship with Connecticut Teamsters, he wanted no public display of rapprochement with Hoffa. He writhed and wriggled and held back from a commitment. "If I go," he told me, "there will be pictures of me and Hoffa shaking hands and grinning at each other, all over the newspapers. That's what they're planning. These fellows always want their pound of flesh." He noted that Governor Dempsey and other top political figures had flatly declined. But he did not decline, for the indelicate Teamsters bluntly let it be known that if he didn't show up he wouldn't get another cent from them.

The Brotherhood, however, was no match for wily Tom Dodd. Though he sent word that he would attend, he reserved to himself the final decision, to be made only at the point of no return. Hoffa, after all, was then undergoing one of his periodic trials, this time on a federal charge of misusing $20 million of union pension funds in a fraudulent loan scheme. He had to get the court's permission to leave Chicago for the banquet, and Dodd had received private intelligence that he would not get it. Still, one couldn't be sure; Hoffa was a resourceful fellow.

On the appointed night, Dodd went to Bridgeport and holed up secretively at a place near the site of the dinner. The assembled Teamsters were informed that delays on the campaign trail had slowed Dodd, but that he would be there soon. Dodd's staff had carefully studied the airline schedules from Chicago. His scouts were staked out, ready to flash the word instantly if Hoffa arrived. At ten P.M. there was still no sign of "Detroit Jimmy." Finally, it became clear that Hoffa had been unable to get away, and Dodd headed for the banquet hall. He entered to tumultuous cheers. His hosts were jubilant, and they avowed that they would know how to reward their friends. With Hoffa absent, there were no pictures, no bad publicity—

only happy Teamsters who made Dodd the hero of the evening. (A few months later, Roberto and Bets helped to organize a "labor-management dinner" that netted at least $31,853 for Dodd.)

Dodd actually enjoyed this sort of thing. In his mentality there was a strong penchant for the cloak and dagger. He periodically fretted over the security of his own operation; every volunteer was a potential spy. And, certain that his opponent was testing him, he methodically probed for weak spots in the security of his opponent. Within the confidential councils of ex-Governor Lodge, Dodd had succeeded in placing an agent, a prominent Republican. Before we had left Washington for Connecticut, the informant had turned over to him the results of a secret and expensive poll, taken by the Lodge forces, which showed Dodd leading Lodge substantially. Accompanying the poll was an analysis of the areas of potential gain for Lodge, in effect a blueprint of the Lodge battle plan. Dodd noted the areas carefully and had moved to bolster them. One night in October, Dodd invited me into the sitting room, where he was again conferring with his hidden agent, a dapper, agreeable gentleman who had with him the results of the latest Lodge poll, which showed Dodd widening his lead. But he had come on a matter of greater import. Lodge agents, he said, had begun to check rumors that Dodd had stayed at the Essex House and the Waldorf in New York City at the expense of a lobbyist. Apparently, in the last weeks of the campaign, Lodge had caught a glimmer of the Dodd-Klein relationship that was later to explode into front-page headlines. But Dodd, forewarned, had a chance to cover his tracks. The Lodge investigators never came up with anything.

These were satisfying days for Dodd. Observing him convinced me that electioneering satisfied many of his inner needs—the need for combat, for intrigue, for vindication, for excitement, for conquest, for being the center of attention, for being audibly on the stage of history, if only transitorily. The trumpet notes of battle sounded once more in his ears, and the radical iconoclasm of his youth would flicker and briefly take flame. He noted contemptuously that the aristocrats who controlled the insurance industry, austere Republicans who in the past had coolly ignored him, were now fluttering about, making contributions and even inviting him to make handshaking tours of their vast home-office buildings. "They don't fool me one minute," he said to me one night. "I know them. I can remember when the presidents of insurance companies used to sit around a table and draw up the list of young people to be invited to the Christmas Dance at the Hartford

Club, just to make sure no Catholic or Jewish boy or girl slipped in by accident"—and a trace of ancient enmity flared in his eyes. "I haven't forgotten. Oh, I've been feathering them along lately for my own reasons, but next year I'll put their feet to the fire. We'll get that insurance investigating committee of ours in high gear, Jim, and before we're through there'll be wigs on the green. They've been shortchanging and swindling the country long enough, and I aim to put an end to it. Next year—"

Politically, Dodd was certain of a "next year." This was the campaign in which he could feel anew each day the exhilaration of combat without the apprehension of defeat, or even of being hurt. Each day some newspaper declared for him editorially, with suitable encomiums. Local candidates jostled one another to be photographed with him. Men of power and wealth courted the sure winner, who was so close to the President. Politicians who had long scorned him now joined in the lionizing chorus. And the pace was relatively easy— three or four public appearances a day which created the illusion of a vigorous campaign without the exhausting reality.

Some nights when Dodd returned home he would be virtually floating in euphorious clouds. He seemed not to hear what we said; the day's ovations were still ringing in his ears. His pockets would be stuffed with checks and cash, sometimes amounting to thousands of dollars. He would nod with approval as the laudatory advertisements which had appeared in the day's press were shown to him. He enjoyed viewing his idealized biography, now being televised on all channels. Every imaginable device of prepaid glorification daily projected the image of Tom Dodd as he saw himself. And the day of Great Victory, sure and luminous, was inevitably approaching.

About three weeks before Election Day, I learned of the preliminary report on contributions and expenditures Senator Dodd was about to file with the Secretary of the United States Senate, as required by Federal law. Dodd was claiming to have received only about $12,-000, of which $7,350 had been donated by the Democratic Senate Campaign Committee in Washington, so that only about $4,500 represented funds not already reported to the Secretary of the Senate— $4,500 out of more than $300,000 I knew to have been collected. The Federal reporting law, I knew, had been enacted by Congressmen for their own convenience and it was filled with loopholes. So I did not know whether Dodd's skeletonized report violated that law. But I had no doubt, nevertheless, that the report deliberately concealed from the authorities and the public hundreds of thousands in contributions. Unanswered still was the crucial question: was the concealment of so large a sum a temporary tactic designed to forestall complacency among supporters and to deny useful campaign ammunition to opponents? Or was it another step in a calculated policy of fraud, to be consummated in a false report to the State of Connecticut on December 3rd?

Needless to say, news of the report revived the old suspicions that had lain dormant during weeks of total absorption in the election drive. Marjorie, Michael, and I resumed our investigatory conversations and, for the first time, we reached outside our intimate circle. James O'Connor, a young Hartford attorney, had a desk in our headquarters. He had formerly served, on Dodd's appointment, as Assistant United States Attorney for Connecticut. Now he functioned as one of Dodd's three nominal campaign managers, none of whom really managed anything. O'Connor, however, was also the house lawyer, having succeeded Judge Blumenfeld as legal advisor on campaign technicalities. One morning he volunteered concern over what appeared to be irregularities in Dodd's handling and reporting of campaign funds. So Marjorie and I, in separate conversations, spoke frankly to him. We discussed the absurdity of the recent report to the Senate and told him of our tally of contributions. We pointed out that contributions received by check were acknowledged in writing but that cash donations were not. We said that monies contributed to the Dodd-for-Senate Committee, the legal entity set up for this campaign, were actually being disbursed by the "Dodd Testimonial Dinner Committee," a relic of previous years that should long since have turned over its proceeds. O'Connor was highly disturbed. He said he shared our fears that Dodd would get into trouble and, a few days later, invited Marjorie to a private breakfast discussion at the Maple Hill Restaurant. There he told her he had looked at Ed Sullivan's financial records. They were kept in Ed's shaky handwriting, he said, and beside the name of some contributors Ed had written down two amounts. O'Connor seemed determined to get to the bottom of it. After all, he said to me, his own name might be on the final report.

We never learned the nature or results of his inquiries. He ceased abruptly to discuss the matter. Shortly afterward, he also ceased serv-

ing as house lawyer and became, curiously, a kind of personal attendant to Mrs. Dodd, keeping her company and driving her about to
ladies' teas. Just as abruptly, Marjorie's file of acknowledgment letters,
on which the amount of each contribution was carefully noted, was
ordered transferred to Ed Sullivan's office. Henceforth, Sullivan
would keep *all* the financial records. That left us with no means of
substantiating our estimate of contributions.

But we continued to receive information in bits and pieces, which
we fitted together as best we could. Big contributors, feeling perhaps
that it is advisable to have a Senator's staff fully aware of their services
to him, frequently advertised their generosity. Elliot Janeway, the
financial columnist, called me once to tell me he had raised "another
$1,500 for Tom." Tom O'Neil, of General Tire, who had already con-
tributed his plane and pilot, informed Marjorie that he was coming
to Hartford to give a large contribution to Tom, "personally." Marjorie
and Doreen, while working with the Senator on correspondence, would
see incoming checks and overhear conversations about large donations. A check for $6,000 arrived from Lazarus Heyman. A letter from
Gene Tunney, the former champ, now a vice-president of Schick's
Eversharp Division (controlled by Patrick Frawley), announced that
the proceeds from a cocktail party, of which he and Sam Pryor of
Pan American were hosts, amounted to $2,500. And the closing weeks
of the campaign featured a series of fund-raising affairs so large that
the results could not be concealed—if there was any intention to do so
—from people as intimately concerned with the campaign as we.
Arthur Barbieri, the Democratic Town Chairman of New Haven,
let it be known that a dinner he sponsored had raised $10,000
for Dodd. Quenton Hinton, a guileless business agent for one of the
building and trades unions, gave us day-to-day reports on a "labor-
management dinner for Dodd," he was helping to organize. "We've
got $32,000 in the till already, and the Teamsters' money hasn't all
come in yet," he volunteered a few days before the dinner.

As October drew to a close, our estimate approached the $400,000
mark, with no sign of a letup in contributions. Encouraged by the
burgeoning affluence of our campaign treasury, I suggested to the
Senator that we increase our newspaper and television outlay for the
final days before election. "Oh, no," replied Dodd. "Contributions are
lagging. I don't know what's wrong. Ed tells me we've got only $125,-
000 in, not enough even to cover present commitments. I don't see
how we can avoid a big deficit." Even the modest budget of several

hundred dollars submitted by Dave Martin for radio spots on foreign language stations was cut in half.

By November, several weeks of enforced togetherness in the house on Brace Road had yielded up its harvest of frayed nerves and dissension. In declining humor, the staff awaited the forthcoming liberation. As for the Dodd family, it had become apparent that, aside from the Senator, all felt toward their guests a hostility which ran deeper than the petty irritation which was inherent in our situation. Its origin probably lay in the Senator's unfortunate practice of making unfavorable comparisons between his children and his staff. These caused wounds he aggravated by assigning his sons only menial tasks—driving the sound truck, delivering packages of political "literature," handing out pamphlets at rallies. At our late evening conferences, Dodd, in front of us, would sometimes upbraid his sons fiercely. I particularly remember the merciless and illogical ridicule he heaped upon them on hearing that their sound truck had been stolen. Dodd's abuse of the "children" would understandably infuriate his wife, who would gather in her aging brood protectively. The end result was that our house was divided into two unfriendly camps, one composed of unwilling captives and the other of equally unwilling captors.

More than once I saw Dodd's morning optimism suddenly deflated by family complaints about our newspaper ads or the content of our television programs. At first, I thought it signified a natural penchant for being critical, but later I began, rightly or wrongly, to see in it a method of striking back at the Senator and at us. And I saw in it, too, a possible explanation for the early-morning tirades loosed for years in Washington. As we all knew, susceptibility to petty criticism was Dodd's Achilles heel. Any criticism of his public role, however insignificant, deeply disturbed him. If the chance remark of a cab driver could plunge him into gloom, the doubts implanted by his family gnawed into him with particular sharpness.

At night, with the day's campaigning over, Mrs. Dodd would carp about the Senator's drinking. To the staff that seemed unjustified and unreal, since during the campaign the Senator rarely took more than two or three drinks before retiring. Mrs. Dodd frequently saddled Michael with part of the blame, for he was the Senator's agile bartender. "Michael and that staff are turning my husband into a drunkard!" she shrieked hysterically one night and ran from the house. We sat in an embarrassed silence while she revved up the car motor in the driveway and roared off into the dark. Embarrassed himself, the Senator tried manfully to enliven the deadness in the room with small talk but despite our best efforts his attempt was a failure, and he went wearily off to bed. However cool we were then feeling toward Dodd, that sort of thing evoked our sympathy. In some ways, the wounded old lion seemed so superior to his environment; yet, it was an environment that he himself had created.

We had been at Brace Road only a few days when Mrs. Dodd protested to her husband that he should not permit Jim Boyd to live in the Dodd household, under the same roof with Marjorie Carpenter. "It gives scandal," she said. "He's a married man with children, and he's supposed to be a Catholic." I never concealed my affection for Marjorie, but we both took pains to see that our relations were circumspect. The Senator, apparently fearing that Mrs. Dodd was on the verge of provoking a scene, went to Michael. "Naturally," he said, "I've known about Jim's family situation for a long time. Years ago, I advised him against letting his marriage break up. And I know all about his relationship with Marjorie. I disagree with it on philosophical grounds, but I can live with it, because I don't interfere in other people's personal lives. But Grace has a bee in her bonnet. I'm afraid that one of these days she'll speak to Jim about it and he'll blow up." On conveying the conversation to me, Michael said he was sure the Senator wanted to reassure me that in this matter he was nothing but a helpless husband. In any case, it was a friendly gesture.

Mrs. Dodd never did approach me, directly. But one night, late in the campaign, she showed me an anonymous poison pen letter, warning Senator Dodd of a scandal in his official household. It rambled on, citing, in one contradictory sentence, Walter Jenkins and the Mann Act. It appeared to be the work of a crank. But I immediately recognized it as part of a calculated pattern, long familiar to me.

For almost four years I had been the subject of anonymous letters and phone calls to my family, the Senator, and even the police. Their message, if one could be found beneath the hyperbole, was that I was an office dictator, steeped in immorality and drunk with power, a corrupter of secretaries and a persecutor of those who were truly loyal to the Senator. After a groping period of experimentation, the immorality theme was upgraded, and romantic exploits were attributed to me that would have been flattering had they not been so disappointingly unspecific. My debaucheries were always enshrouded in a murky vagueness and my alleged companions were never identified.

Since most of the letters and calls betrayed inside information about the office, I knew the anonymous author had to be a staff member. I had often been warned by concerned friends of bitter verbal attacks made on me by a staff aide who was one of the Senator's political retainers, and who apparently blamed me for his failure to rise to a significant status and salary in the Dodd organization. For a long time I did nothing but, at length, I went to Dodd who, I reasoned, must have received many of these missives. Dodd confirmed that he had and said he shared my suspicions as to the secret author. "His wife has been at Grace about you for years," he said. "It's a common thing. He blames you for his own troubles. He's ambitious but without ability, and that's a terrible combination. All limited people have to blame someone for their own belly-flops, otherwise they would have to face the truth about themselves. I've been the victim of this, too." He reminded me of his lengthy efforts to place the fellow elsewhere and said he would intensify them, but he advised me to ignore the matter, closing our discussion with one of his aphorisms: "The higher you climb the tree, the harder they chop at the bottom."

I had the feeling that he was actually enjoying the rhubarb. He liked divisions among the staff and sometimes actually stirred them up. He encouraged gossiping and informing throughout his offices. He would privately side with someone whom I had disciplined for an infraction, while at the same time complimenting me for running a tight shop and urging me to bear down harder. I dropped the matter, assuming that my detractor would eventually tire of the game through lack of success in his major objective. That, I assumed, was to get me fired.

Then, one day, a police officer from Washington's fourth precinct paid me a friendly call and asked if I was being harassed by anyone. He showed me a letter, addressed to the police department, alleging that unknown to Senator Dodd his chief assistant, James P. Boyd, was living in sin with a girl in whom the Senator also placed great trust. The proof was a light-colored Chevrolet, bearing Maryland license plates, that was frequently parked all night outside Boyd's Washington apartment. Investigation had shown, the lieutenant explained, that the name signed to the letter was fictitious. And the Chevrolet was actually my own. The policeman told me that harassing letters of this kind were not uncommon on the Hill and sought my help in tracking down the sender. Did I have any idea who it was? I did not tell him of my suspicions, for I could not be absolutely sure. Instead, I warned my suspect that I knew what he was up to and pledged that if I ever heard of another such letter or call I would either have his resignation on the spot or resign myself. He maintained his innocence and studiously avoided me thereafter. But the poison pen attacks, so far as I knew, stopped at once.

Then, in the last days of the campaign, Mrs. Dodd triumphantly produced her anonymous letter and invited comment. I spurned the bait. Though I assumed the letter to be a revival of the old attacks, I saw no point in discussing the matter with Mrs. Dodd. By now, I had ceased to be concerned. I reasoned that any damage these twisted missives could do to me or those I cared for had been done long ago. Besides, I told myself, I would soon be leaving Dodd and the unhealthy atmosphere that seemed to surround him.

I was pleased, however, that this long, sustained assault had had no effect on Dodd. He had never questioned me about the accusations and, in recent months, he had shown more trust and public confidence in me than ever before. He had sent me as his representative to debate Governor Lodge on a number of occasions. I stood in for him at the important election year grilling by the AFL-CIO and substituted for him at other public functions that would not have been assigned to one he considered vulnerable to charges of scandal. His apparent confidence provoked in me twinges of guilt, because of my growing suspicion of him.

One Sunday night in late October, about a week before the election, something happened to deepen that suspicion. Several of the staff were enjoying a drink and hashing over the campaign in one of the sitting rooms when the door bell rang. I went to the door, and admitted David Martin. He was obviously excited about something; I remember the bright gleam in his dark eyes. I helped him off with his coat.

"Jim," he said portentously, "I have just made a major deal, a deal that will prove very important." Dave's sense of self-importance could be exasperating, but I always got a kick out of his unfailing enthusiasm.

"That's fine, Dave," I said. "What is it?"

"Well, I've been with Irving Ferman. I've had a wild day, full of confusion, but I finally managed to bring Irv and the Senator together down in Fairfield County. Irv, you know, is the Washington representative of A. N. Spanel, the head of International Latex."

I knew who Ferman was. He had called our headquarters from Washington, about a week before, saying he wanted to see the Senator on a highly important matter. I waited patiently for David, who always took a long wind-up, to make his point.

"Irv offered the Senator a $10,000 campaign contribution in behalf of Spanel. All Dodd has to do in return is to promise to do all he can with the President to get an ambassadorship for Spanel. Dodd agreed to do this."

I looked at David, disapprovingly.

"All Dodd has to do is *try*," David emphasized, as though that caveat somehow purified the arrangement. "Irv is much too knowledgeable about Washington to expect anything more."

"That's a lot of money, Dave," I said. "How will it be handled?"

"The exact method hasn't been firmed up yet," David said. "It will be disguised somehow. Irv is talking about making the contribution himself, and getting reimbursed by International Latex, as a bonus or something." David then walked into the room where Marjorie, Doreen, and Michael were talking, and with the same mysterious exhilaration, repeated the news of his success. I remained in the foyer for a time, half listening to David, half musing over this latest straw.

"But, David, don't you think this is wrong?" I heard Marjorie say.

David chuckled, in the manner of one absolved from apparent wrongdoing through the possession of a higher knowledge. "This is the way things are done," he said.

A. N. Spanel contributed $2,100 to Dodd's campaign. We later learned that in December, Irving Ferman delivered $8,000 in cash to Dodd. The $8,000 was from company funds of the International Latex Corporation.

Election night in Connecticut is like sudden death. The voting machines are closed at seven P.M., and the tabulation process is so swift that, unless the outcome is a cliff-hanger, it can be accurately determined by seven-twenty.* All over the country, politicians and commentators watch the state for a definitive indication of a nationwide trend, and within seconds of receiving the returns from Waterbury and Hartford and Greenwich, the television networks flash their national projections. Thus science, which has produced a completely tasteless tomato, has also managed to drain much of the drama out of what was

---

* Under a recent change in the Connecticut election law, the polls are now left open until eight P.M.

once the most exciting night of the year. Yet, for Connecticut politicians, the twenty-minute resolution of years of patient plodding can be an excruciating ordeal. Tom Dodd made elaborate preparations to endure it with a measure of privacy and dignity.

Remembering that in 1956 newsmen wrote of his children crying over the returns, Dodd rejected press requests that special lines be run into his home and that a news headquarters be established there. For the public and press his campaign storefront on Main Street would be open. He would meet them there when he was ready. As for his own election night plans, he resisted a dozen inquiries while secretly arranging, through Ed Sullivan, for a suite at the Statler-Hilton. Swearing them to silence, on election eve he invited a select group of relatives, staff members, and friends. But by seven o'clock, despite all precautions, his suite was inundated with an uninvited mob. Faces not seen for years pressed through the door and took possession. I was reminded of the Senator's words of a few days before— "There is a depressing thing about political campaigns. You always meet again all the people you'd like to forget." But the Senator remained a step ahead of his pursuers. He had prepared a hideaway, a small room equipped with television, a modest bar, and a reliable doorkeeper, where he listened to the earliest returns in near-seclusion.

At exactly seven, Marjorie and I were approached by the Senator's doorkeeper and led to his private room. He was sitting alone in the far corner, tense and motionless. We hesitated. His brooding, powerful, starkly chiseled profile bespoke a solitude that we cared not to penetrate. He looked up. "Come in, come in," he said, a flicker of warmth passing over his face. "Sit down over here, by me." Then, haltingly, he said, "I—am grateful—for all that you two have done for me. I thought the three of us might hear the results together."

For ten minutes we watched and listened in silence, while a scattering of small-town returns was reported. Normally Republican towns were giving lopsided pluralities to Johnson and Dodd. I put down my pencil and ceased trying to chart a trend; there was no need. A great relief settled over the Senator. The polls were right, his calculations had been accurate. "If I've carried Farmington," he said, commenting on the latest report, "then I've been elected by a landslide." He sent for Mrs. Dodd and the one newsman he had not barred, Bill Ryan of the *Hartford Times*. For another ten minutes the five of us sat, mute. In the Presidential race, President Johnson was toppling Democratic records set by Franklin D. Roosevelt in 1936. As the larger cities came in, they revealed Dodd pluralities so large as to be almost eerie.

I began scribbling out a short victory statement, with the accent on humility. Gallant in defeat, Dodd had shown that he could be a poor winner. Six years before, when he felt his first Senate victory marred because he ran behind his running mate, Governor Ribicoff, he had poured into the microphones a bitter denunciation of "the left wingers" whom he charged with splitting tickets against him. He actually threatened to drive them out of the Democratic party. There must be no repeat performance, for he would be the first important victor on the national scene and his words would be widely carried, creating the night's first impression.

By now the Senator's whereabouts had been discovered and he was enveloped in the chattering crowd he had sought to escape. But, no matter; it was all over anyway. News of Lodge's courteous concession quickly wrapped things up. I thought for a moment of the probable scene at Lodge's Westport home. Perhaps it was like the one at the Dodd home eight years before, when we had gone down in the Eisenhower sweep. In the last few weeks, I had seen the gray look of defeat on the faces of the handsome former Governor and his lovely wife Francesca, as they went about stoically trying to stave off the inevitable. They knew they were trapped in the Goldwater debacle, but they had hoped to salvage enough to remain in the running for the gubernatorial contest in 1966. That hope, too, was obliterated during the first twenty minutes of returns. Dodd was running close to Johnson everywhere, and ahead of him in some places, carrying towns that had never before voted for a Democratic Senatorial candidate. Already he had amassed the greatest plurality in the Connecticut annals of Senate elections.

I handed my draft to the Senator, who studied it briefly, nodded, and motioned for me to follow him. He inched his way through a sea of backslapping well-wishers and began the final round of formalities of the '64 campaign—a tour of television studios, a visit to his own headquarters and to the State Democratic Headquarters, and a private victory celebration at the house on Brace Road. At each stop we were informed that his margin of victory had risen by another great leap. By eight-thirty, it was over three hundred thousand. With more than twelve hundred thousand votes cast, he led two-to-one and had received only about forty thousand fewer votes than the President. At the first television stop I watched him on the monitor, after a newsman told him "this is going national." He and Grace looked very earnest and suitably awed. "To share in a victory of this size and scope has to be a very humbling experience," he began. "I do not regard it as a personal victory for me. It is a trust for which I shall be held accountable. We of the Democratic party are on trial. We have been given the mandate and the power, and the people will rightly expect us to live up to our promises." He was coming through beautifully, I thought.

Home at last, he trudged wearily upstairs, donned pajamas and bathrobe, and returned to share in our victory drinks and watch the election picture unfold across the country. For an hour the Senator, part of his family, Marjorie, Michael, and I sat in a quiet, cheerful glow, still a bit numbed at the degree of our success and that of the Democratic party, the realization that it was all over beginning at last to sink in. Before long, a loud, increasingly assertive voice told us that the Scotch, physical weariness, and nervous release were taking their toll on the victor. Uninvited guests now poured in, filling the house with the inane sounds of celebration. Dodd, still in his pajamas, finally went upstairs to sleep. At about midnight, the Johnson City White House called to say that the President wished to speak with the Senator. It was not easy to rouse the sleeping Dodd, and he was only half-awake when, still lying in bed, he took the phone. All over the house excited eavesdroppers picked up extensions to listen in on a footnote to history:

Hello, Tom. Congratulations on a great victory.

Well, Mr. President [Dodd mumbled rather thickly, with exaggerated courtliness], how generous of you to call. It's you who deserves the congratulations, not I.

You made a great run, Tom, just like I knew you would.

It was you who made it all possible, Mr. President. You have won the greatest personal victory ever in our state—for any office. Everyone here is talking about it.

They are? Well, get it out on the wire, Tom. You know how these commentators are. They've already started knocking me— saying that it's just Goldwater's unpopularity. You know that line.

Mr. President, you made the greatest run in—

That's wonderful, Tom, just get that out on the wire. Issue a statement right away, so they'll start quoting it. Just what you told me. It's still early in most places, you know. Congratulations again, Tom. God bless you, and give Grace our best.

Thank you, Mr. President.

The Senator surrendered the phone. I stood by for orders on the press release, but his eyes were already closed, a half-smile wreathing his face. There were to be no more statements from Connecticut's senior Senator for a while. Tonight he would sleep the sleep of those who have fulfilled their fondest hopes.

Immediately after the election the Senator and Mrs. Dodd embarked upon a Caribbean vacation, and the staff returned to Washington. For some, it was an interval of release and relaxation. But for those of us who reconvened nightly at the Carroll Arms it was a time of trouble. The Connecticut experience had in one sense strengthened the old allegiance; I felt closer to Tom Dodd than I had in years. And the staggering size of his victory seemed almost to place his stewardship in office beyond the questioning of ordinary mortals. Tom Dodd had made it, as a public figure and as a potential power in the nation. As the gay congratulations of our colleagues from other victorious staffs reminded us, we had shared in and were a part of an enormous general triumph. The contagion of victory among Washington Democrats in that heady November inflated us with glowing expectations. The L.B.J. era had dawned and would last a long time. Before it was over, we believed, decisive things would be accomplished for the nation. Few among the staffers who sat in the Carroll Arms did not reflect that among the chosen who had fought in the ranks, there would be thousands of promotions, hundreds of appointments, and the launching of dozens of promising new careers. But among the Dodd staff, there was a touch of foreboding. What Marjorie, Michael, and I had learned in Connecticut had made our old misgivings more ominous than ever. Large sums of money had disappeared. What had happened to them? We now bitterly regretted the dark curiosity that had drawn us thus far, but we had to know. We hoped that Dodd's forthcoming report would explain it all plausibly. But if it did not, we faced a decision.

Time was now a critical element. If there was massive fraud, the moment to uncover it was now, while the Senator was out of the country. Besides, Marjorie, a key link in our information chain, insisted that she was resigning, effective January 1st, regardless of what the forthcoming financial report revealed to us about the Senator's operations. She would, she said, inform Dodd personally as soon as he returned, and in the meantime was shopping around for another position. My own departure would be a far more complicated affair. As the Senator's administrative assistant, making $23,000 a year, I could look forward to a good position somewhere in the Executive Branch, but only with the Senator's full cooperation. Any future I might have in Washington was in his hands, and to leave him on amicable terms would be highly advantageous to me. We were always half-conscious at least that our efforts to pry into the Senator's secrets could have disastrous consequences for us. But we could not now turn back.

Our best strategy, we decided, was to try to recover Marjorie's acknowledgment file from Ed Sullivan. If we succeeded, we could check the actual contributions of hundreds of individuals against those listed in the official campaign report. In view of the circumstances under which the file had been taken from Marjorie originally, we knew the effort was full of danger, but we had to make it. During the second and third weeks of November, Marjorie, under the guise of wanting to bring the Washington records up-to-date, made several requests of Mary Hamil and Ed Sullivan to return her file of acknowledgment letters. And she requested that a copy of the official report be sent to the Washington office as soon as it was ready, to be put in the Senator's private file cabinet against the inevitable day when he would ask for it. Each of these requests was agreed to repeatedly, but neither the file nor the report arrived. Further inquiries to Hartford drew disingenuous replies. When we reflected that no previous request from the Washington office had ever been so consistently ignored, we concluded that Sullivan must be acting on the Senator's instructions. Was it merely a general security directive that Ed was following, or was it a specific order aimed at us?

At the beginning of December, Marjorie made her final request to Hartford for the financial information. The Senator was there now, going over the final version of the report, which was to be filed on the 3rd. When her request met with failure, we suspected that there was trouble ahead.

Lacking the documentary proof we sought, we completed our estimates as best we could. Our figure on total contributions would certainly be below the true figure, since we could not begin to know all that had been collected. But it would be close enough. Combining known facts with conservative estimates, I arrived at the following amounts:

Net receipts from testimonial dinner, November 1961			$55,000
" " " Washington reception, September 1963			13,000
" " " Dodd Day in Conn., October 1963			47,000
Known funds raised in 1964 prior to loss of our file			185,000
Estimate of funds raised after loss of file			101,000
	Total raised in 1964 campaign		$401,000

Estimating the approximate figure for expenditures was relatively easy. The main item, $102,000 for all forms of mass media and promotional work, we knew for certain, for I had supervised that expenditure and the final bill from the Randall Company had arrived in our Washington office in November. The lesser items we knew almost exactly—transportation, office space, the small payroll, billboards, telephones, the rent on the house on Brace Road, and miscellaneous matters—for Michael or Marjorie or I had firsthand knowledge of most of them. To be completely fair, I added $30,000 to cover the residue of the 1958 deficit, plus legitimate pre-1964 campaign expenses. Adding it all up, the top figure I could justify for legitimate expenditures of all kinds was $180,000.

On December 5th, two days after the report was filed with the Secretary of State in Hartford, the week's Connecticut newspapers arrived in Washington. I looked at the bundle for an hour before finally opening one. I leafed nervously through the pages of the Hartford *Courant* until I found what I had hoped not to find. In a few short paragraphs, Dodd's report was summarized. The Senator's major committee claimed to have received $167,497.67 in contributions and to have expended $174,159.44 on his campaign. Lesser committees reported a total income of $27,404.06 with an identical outgo. All told, Dodd claimed to have incurred a *deficit* of $6,661.77. It was unbelievable. I checked the other papers, anticipating a possible misprint, but they all told the same story.

Suspicion at last was replaced by certainty. More than $200,000 contributed for campaign use had been secretly siphoned off. An official report, required by law, had been grossly falsified. For six months I had questioned the Senator's honesty but had not acted. Now I had my answer. I would have to confront Dodd with the facts as soon as he returned to Washington.

On the morning of December 7th, Dodd appeared in the office, grim and remote. The routine pleasantries that attend a return from vacation were absent. His icy mien tended to confirm our speculation that he had intercepted our efforts to obtain the records. "I want to talk to you before you leave for lunch. Don't forget," was his only comment to Marjorie. And as the morning wore on he did not ask for me, though we had not seen each other for a month and his desk was piled high with matters that we normally would have had to discuss. I realized then how completely the office took its mood from the Senator. A tomb-like silence pervaded the suite, casting a pall over even the typists, who spoke to each other in whispers.

At noon, Marjorie buzzed the Senator. "I'm almost ready to leave for lunch," she said. "Oh, yes," he replied, "please come in."

She entered and sat down, prepared for dictation or instructions.

"I am reorganizing my office," he said, "and there won't be a place for you in the new organization. I will keep you on the payroll for three more weeks, but I want you to take your papers and leave right away."

"Well, frankly, Senator, I was planning to leave anyway and have already been to several job interviews."

"Did I say three weeks? No, I can only keep you on the payroll for two weeks."

He studied his desk calendar with mock intensity, as though the payroll, which had been flexible enough for the past six years to absorb several hundred thousand dollars worth of padding, had suddenly become an object of exact mathematical science.

"Let's see—I can keep you only until December 21st."

Marjorie, unconcerned with how long she stayed on the payroll but nonplussed at the Senator's valedictory, stared at him, unaware that he considered the interview over.

"Well!" he shouted, suddenly flushing, "What is this, a sit-in? Get out! Get out!"

About an hour later, the Senator's door to my office opened. But it was not the Senator. Though he was sitting only a few feet away in the perpetual twilight of his prized retreat, he had sent a minor aide, Jim Gartland. Pallid, eyes averted, Gartland approached my desk, left a message, and awkwardly withdrew. It consisted of one line, with a postscript. It read:

MEMORANDUM
TO: JAMES P. BOYD
This is to notify you that as of today your services in my office are terminated.

/s/ THOMAS J. DODD

P.S. If you have any personal property in my office you can call

Doreen Moloney and she will arrange to have it delivered to
you.

I do not recall having felt any particular emotion, except a strange
absence of feeling. It was like the vacant sensation I had experienced
several years before when, on our trip home from Norwich on that
winter night, our car had hurtled down the great hill, spinning round-
and-round. I had seemed then to be watching myself as though from a
distance, involved in an unreal event whose impact had not yet struck
me, and I again felt that weird detachment.

I put on my overcoat and left the office, without a word to anyone.

CHAPTER FOUR

ON the day after the firings, Dodd rescinded the order for my dismissal, restored me to full salary, and requested a meeting at his Georgetown home. I arrived at the appointed hour and was admitted by Michael, who winked encouragingly and ushered me into the sitting room. The Senator was upstairs, supervising some household task. From time to time snatches of his conversation, his voice mellow and amiable, floated down the bannister. I was left alone for some time, by design I was sure, to impress upon me my dependency. At length Dodd made his entrance, sportily clad in a plaid jacket and flourishing a pipe, which he used as a prop to bridge over the first awkward moments. He filled it, lighted it, puffed it, and mumbled incantations over it, as though performing an esoteric and meaningful rite. All the while, he remained standing.

"I didn't bring you here to lecture to you, Jim," he began at last, establishing at the outset the posture of the wronged but magnanimous party. "I must say, though, that I am deeply hurt by all this. It spoiled the whole campaign for me when I heard about it. If I've acted rashly at all, it's because I was hurt."

"What is it I'm supposed to have done, Mr. Dodd?"

"I'm getting to that," he replied brusquely, in a tone that indicated he had a definite plan for this conversation and intended that it would stay on course. "I have it from an unimpeachable source, a source I must rely on, that you and that Carpenter woman were disloyal to

95

me, flagrantly and cruelly disloyal, during the campaign. I learned that she attacked me in a public restaurant, in a loud voice that attracted attention, said unbelievable things about me, and you just sat there—didn't stop her, didn't defend me—just sat there. I think you owed me more than that. I've been pretty good to you over the years, and when I heard about this, a day or two after the election, I'm frank to tell you I was dreadfully disappointed." His voice swelled with emotion and there was color in his face. Even the set of his shoulders and the meter of his pacing about the room assumed an indignant character.

"I understand you didn't join in pillorying me," he continued, "and that's some small comfort. But you should have stopped her. You were disloyal and that's one thing I cannot tolerate."

"There was no such incident, Mr. Dodd," I said. "Marjorie and I never had dinner alone together all the time we were in Connecticut. Tell me what was supposed to have been said, and where. I think I deserve a chance to deny it or to confirm it, if there's even a grain of truth to the story."

"It doesn't need confirming. My source is irreproachable. People at a nearby table heard it and asked who you were. They just happened to be friends of mine. I can't say more without breaching confidences."

"Then you leave me in an impossible situation," I replied.

Dodd sat down, again feigning preoccupation with his pipe. I thought of a dinner conversation with Bill Curry, a close political ally of Dodd's, and his wife Beverly, who had been on Dodd's Senate payroll for six years. The most extreme interpretation of that conversation bore no resemblance to Dodd's description, but we had discussed irregularities in the handling of campaign money in the same manner in which we had broached the subject earlier with Jim O'Connor. Though Dodd had shown no intention thus far of openly discussing the real differences between us, I decided to explore the possibility. If he rejected it, I would let him lead the conversation to its planned destination and find out what his proposal was.

"Come to think of it," I said, "Marjorie and I did have dinner one night with Bill Curry and his wife, and we talked about you and the campaign. But they are staff people and old friends of yours. There was no shouting or abuse. I'd be happy to discuss that conversation with you."

"No, no—it wasn't the Currys," he interjected. "They have nothing to do with this. All I will say is that what Carpenter said about me was so bad, so vicious, that had it been overheard by enemies instead of friends it could have been disastrous to my campaign, disastrous! Anyway, that's over and done with. I don't care to discuss it further. It's too painful. But I do want a reasonable and fair settlement of our affairs. That's my only motive in asking you here. I don't think I'm a vindictive man. I don't believe in vengeance or retaliation. I guess I'm just not built that way. But I'm afraid all that has happened has made it impossible to continue our association as it was before."

"I agree, Senator."

"You've done good things for me. And I have no wish to hurt your family—those nice little girls. I didn't mean what I said about taking you off the payroll. I was angry, understandably, I think. You've got a lot of time off coming to you. I know you never took much vacation time. So I suggest that you go on a leave of absence at full pay until we find a suitable position for you elsewhere. I'll help you. In the meantime there are a lot of speeches coming up that you can do, if you want; in fact, I'd like to send out a Christmas newsletter next week."

I remained silent.

"We'll just say that you're on detached duty. You can work at home. I'll send you any equipment and information you need. You can still have quite a career ahead of you if you apply yourself. There are a lot of places in the Executive Branch that can use a fellow like you. Maybe even the White House. John Macy, the Civil Service Commissioner, was talking to me about these openings just the other day. He's from Connecticut, you know, and he's in charge of finding talent for the President. I'll talk to him about you." Then, as if it were an afterthought, he said, "You'd better let me handle these things, by the way. It will come out better."

The conversation had long since become a monologue, and now he was on his feet again, signifying that our meeting was over. He had a plane to catch.

"I'm sorry that things turned out this way, Jim. I had far different plans for you. But there's no reason why we can't continue to be friends."

"Well, I'd certainly prefer it that way, Senator."

"So would I," he answered, as he walked me to the door. "Good luck," he said, extending his hand. "Do you have a ride?"

"Good luck to you, sir. Yes, my car is here."

We shook hands limply, and I went down the stairs.

Twenty minutes later, Dodd, enroute with Michael to National Airport, emerged from a brooding silence to say, "Of course, I couldn't stand silently by and allow Jim Boyd to get a job in another Senate office, or in the House, or any place where he'd have anything to do with the White House. I have to exercise my prerogatives. After all, I have a duty to my colleagues and to my President. I'd just have to tell them the truth about Boyd's lack of character and his disloyalty. He was disloyal to me and would probably be the same with them. It would be better for him if he didn't even apply to those places. Too messy."

I had expected Dodd to put on a performance tinged with theatrics, but I had hoped that from time to time the veil would drop and enable me to glimpse his true motivations—how much he really knew about our inquiry, who or what had exposed us, and what his rationalization was for the defection of his closest aides. On all points, however, he had been resourcefully uncommunicative.

His tale about Marjorie's indiscretions in a Hartford restaurant was deprived of credence by its calculated obscurity and by his gruff refusal to specify the substance of the alleged lies. It probably had its roots in our conversations with O'Connor, or the Currys, or Dodd's Hartford secretary, Mary Hamil. But whatever the source, it made clear that Dodd had learned about our prying into his diversion of campaign funds. Our protracted effort to get the financial records from Hartford must have been the last straw, for it revealed, in addition to a troublesome curiosity on our part, a mulish persistence in meddling in his affairs. His manner of dismissing us by surprise, the immediate physical banishment from the office—these seemed the actions of a scared man, wary of exposure, and determined to cut off his pursuers from access to incriminating information. This view seemed confirmed in the days that followed by reports from Michael that Dodd had ordered all the locks changed and had forbidden his staff to have any contact with Marjorie or me, at risk of their own dismissal. If either of us phoned into the office, he ordered, the call was to be transferred without further notice to Gartland.

Why then did Dodd appear to relent and extend the hand of friendship to me? Like a mental juggler, Dodd often had several motives simultaneously in the air, and I could not be sure which one counted most. I believed that he had some regard for me and a considerable nostalgia for former days. I knew that I had some utility to him. I figured, too, that he might have had second thoughts about a compulsive anger which had driven him further than he had intended. It was in these terms that I at first examined Dodd's offers to return to his employ. But when I learned that, while paying me, he was systematically destroying my prospects of finding employment elsewhere, one explanation came to outweigh the others. He was obviously trying to reduce me to dependency upon him, because he was afraid of what Marjorie or I might reveal. By cutting us off from access to his office and staff he had appreciably lessened this danger, since he could be reasonably sure we had no incriminating evidence. But he had to face the possibility that we might already know enough to be troublesome. Hence, he decided to include me among his already sizable stable of retainers. To himself, however, I was sure he rationalized that he was simply being generous. Many times before, after he had indulged his vanity or wounded pride or insecurity or anger over thwarted efforts, I had seen him reverse his field. Such shifts could come swiftly when his welfare was at stake, and they were invariably accompanied by the satisfactions of a purge at the confessional.

There was the time he vented his wrath on the self-effacing Senator Mansfield, the Majority Leader, who to hasten action on an important bill had at the last minute canceled a Senate junket to Paris for which Dodd and his wife had planned. After smoldering all day, Dodd rose on the Senate floor and loosed an attack on Mansfield's leadership so lacerating as to astonish his colleagues, awaken the press gallery, and make front-page headlines the next morning. After thus relieving himself, and after Senator Everett Dirksen angrily threatened to make public Dodd's absentee record, Dodd realized he had committed a grievous error that could make him a Senate outcast. On the evening following his attack he publicly begged forgiveness. "I feel like a skunk at a lawn party . . . compared to Mike Mansfield, I feel small as a pin," he declared. His contrition won Mansfield's praise and a standing ovation from his fellow Senators.

Invariably, Dodd would go through a process of conditioning himself for these reversals of position, justifying them in terms of his personal magnanimity. To delude himself and others as to his real motives, he would indulge his capacity for sentimentalism. Two hours before his Mansfield recantation on the Senate floor, I could feel it coming when he said to me in his office, "I feel so sorry for Mike Mansfield. He's such a nice, mild, fellow; weak, surely, but there's no meanness in him.

His faults as a leader grow from his gentleness and decency as a man. He's a great human being. When I think how I must have hurt him yesterday, I feel like a sick frog."

Now it was the alienation of his ex-aides that posed a threat to him, I reasoned, and they, too, must be neutralized. But first he must paint at least one of the offenders in a sympathetic hue, since he could not admit his true motive. Though under normal considerations the defection of an impressionable young girl was a lesser offense than that of a twelve-year companion-in-arms, he could not bring himself to forgive Marjorie's "treachery." Her act of rejection had nurtured in Dodd an extraordinary bitterness. For years she had been his office favorite. Two years before he had asked her to move into his house and be as a daughter to him; now he could not bear to utter her first name—she was "that Carpenter woman." Eighteen months hence, her appearances at the Senate hearings would incite him to public tantrums. Under the rules of Dodd's morality play, Marjorie could not be approached. Nor could he hope to intimidate her, since for a girl with her qualifications and previous references, jobs were going begging; and on the secretarial level Senatorial vetoes were not always honored. I was a likelier prospect for neutralization. Dodd well knew that my financial burdens were heavy and that my career hopes were at the mercy of his good will. Once I had fallen into line, Marjorie could be expected to do the same, out of concern for my welfare.

Whatever Dodd's motives, I was now cast before his intimates as a sympathetic character. My only sin had been to *listen*, Dodd insisted to friends, and thus I was eligible for redemption. In discussions with Michael and Carl Perian, Dodd's references to me were increasingly friendly, expressing hopes that a way could soon be found to bring me back to his official family. "I've always liked Jim," he said to Carl. "I feel bad about that boy; such a waste. I don't know what happened between us, maybe I failed him somewhere. But I think it was his personal life—he was all mixed up, you know. A bad woman can do that. Maybe it's not too late to rehabilitate him. But he's got to *want* to be rehabilitated."

Less than a month after the fiery dismissals, he made me a concrete offer to return and help him reorganize his office, which I courteously evaded; and each month thereafter I was to receive for consideration a new proposal, sometimes through emissaries, sometimes from Dodd himself. In the meantime, I remained in splendid exile, writing speeches for him and receiving my handsome salary, which I began to hoard against an uncertain future.

Dodd had thus put me on a long and comfortable leash, but I was not to be allowed to slip off of it. I was subtly warned, through reports from Michael and Carl Perian on their conversations with Dodd, against seeking employment on the Hill or through White House contacts, a warning I knew Dodd could make good. While pretending to be helping me with the Civil Service Commission, Dodd caused a file filled with derogatory material to be opened on me by the commission, even though I had never applied there for a job. He concealed from almost everyone the fact that I was still working for him and was still carried on the official rolls as his administrative assistant, while in all quarters where I might logically look for work he sowed the most damaging and imaginative canards. Encountering a Senate official on an airplane, Dodd invented an explanation of the dismissals that he was later to repeat with varying pornographic embellishments. "I caught them in bed together and had to get rid of them," he said. For newspapermen and other people on the Hill he had an improved version: "I caught them in the very act on the divan in my office. I told them to get dressed and get out—and stay out." To John M. Bailey, who, as chairman both of the Democratic National Committee and the Connecticut Democratic Central Committee, was a key figure in my employment hopes, he said, "I found Boyd and Carpenter playing house together. It got to be such a scandal I had to fire the both of them." He made it clear to Bailey that I was on the proscribed list. Bailey, who had always been friendly toward me, thought Dodd's explanation ridiculous but, as he said to Marjorie, "I could use Jim and would like to help him, but until he gets straightened out with Dodd I just can't touch him. Tell him to patch things up."

And so Dodd was right in considering me vulnerable to his carrot and stick game. For me, all roads led back to him. After twelve years he was my only real employment reference. "He'll soon find out that good jobs are mighty hard to come by around here," Dodd told Michael.

But Dodd, as it turned out, overplayed his hand. Back in that first week of December when I at last faced the truth about the campaign funds, I had felt betrayed and disillusioned. But I had no intention of proceeding against Dodd. It seemed response enough to get away from him and to cease being involved in his affairs. Conditioned by the popular ethic that condemns the informer more than the culprit, I had no wish to be a stool pigeon. Nor could I contemplate risking the total dislocation of my life that would inevitably result from challenging a powerful Senator.

It was prolonged exposure to the visible workings of Dodd's design to prevent me from doing what I had no intention of doing that caused me to see and, more importantly, to feel the full significance of the corruption of a high public office. His engaging in one misuse of power to hide a previous misuse gave flesh and color and scent to what had once been distant abstractions: profiteering, misappropriation, conflict of interest. By his menacing maneuvers, Dodd had made it impossible for me to further deceive myself and to accept the easy deliverance he offered. Where an unspoken appeal to genuine sentiment and affection might have carried the day for him effortlessly, he had heavy-handedly thrust me into a moral dilemma. Where fear of the future might have dissipated the strictures of conscience, he had by his vulgar display of strength turned fear into shame, and shame into an anger that was heedless of the future.

There was resentment in that anger, to be sure, a long-repressed urge to strike out at the lordly hands that manipulated the strings. But that was the smaller part. I had too well learned self-discipline from years of coexisting with Dodd's tempestuous excesses to act rashly out of personal pique. "Why should I ruin my life," I had maintained hotly to a skeptical Marjorie, "just because Dodd turned out to be a bastard?" And, on the purely practical level, there was no need. Dodd was willing and anxious to restore to me the temporal things he had taken away.

But it was no good any longer, for he had laid bare my delusions. He had stripped away the layer of rationalization by which men shield themselves from the recognition that their noisy labors are without honor or meaning. I was compelled to acknowledge that the man I had so long excused as ambitious, temperamental, and artful was in reality narcissistic, irresponsible, and unprincipled—and that my excuses were really for myself, not him, for they were designed to help me live with the fact that my interests advanced along with his. But in the end, I could not work for a fraud, and I would not be bullied into remaining silent. Had Dodd allowed me to walk away quietly with my illusions I would probably have done so, and thereafter looked back fondly and recalled the era as it existed in its early years. But he had become too overbearing, too fond of the tools of power and intrigue, to rely on my good will and uncoerced choice. "People are either with me or against me," Dodd had often said. And so he had forced a confrontation. I accepted it, not exultantly, nor mournfully either, but in angry resignation that Dodd and circumstance had put me to a test I would willingly have foregone.

It was at this crucial juncture that I learned of two new abuses, one small, one large, that revealed a continuing and expanding pattern of behavior. A young man named Gene Cullen was placed on the Senate payroll, but was to serve as chauffeur, valet, and handyman to the Dodd family. And Dodd was again dunning political supporters and government contractors for $1,000-a-table contributions to yet a new dinner, for the ostensible purpose of meeting an alleged campaign deficit. It was being planned as the biggest fund-raiser of them all, big enough to add seventy or eighty thousand dollars to Dodd's private coffers. Vice-President Humphrey, who had been lied to about the purpose of the dinner, was sucked in as the featured speaker and prime attraction.

I resolved on Dodd's public exposure; it remained only to devise the means.

I remember, in those first February days of rebellion, being awed and in a way stimulated by the sheer size of my undertaking and the measurable odds against its success. The Senate protected its own. Never in history had the Senate taken formal disciplinary action against a member for financial misconduct. And Dodd, at the height of his prestige and influence, lately chosen by the State Department as a representative of the United States at the funeral of Winston Churchill, with a great election victory just behind him and a full six-year term stretching ahead, seemed secure and unassailable.

He had phoned me from London, my answering service reported, but I was out taking a walk at the time, trying to determine what posture I should assume toward this former chief whose downfall I now was plotting. To succeed I had to be duplicitous; but what degree of duplicity was permissible? Certainly I had to do everything possible to conceal my designs and to encourage in Dodd a feeling of complacency. Should I resign from the twilight position I held with him? Since he knew I had no job, such a course would likely reawaken the fear that I was working against him, probably in the pay of his enemies, and put him irrevocably on guard. On the other hand, if I agreed to go back to his office, a tactic that would be ideal for espionage purposes, it would badly compromise my credibility later on. To pretend to be fully reconciled with him, to resume my old position of trust only to uncover scandal against him, seemed to exceed the limits of what is fair even in war.

I thought it prudent and reasonably honorable, in such a murky situation, to remain in the status to which he had consigned me after our break. I would write speeches when asked and treat his proposals of accommodation cordially, while resisting as diplomatically as possible any formal return to his office and to his full confidence. When it was all over I would have to leave Washington and start again, perhaps as a newspaperman or a schoolteacher, but I had to stay on until I had collected enough information to enable me to turn the project over to others.

The first step was to develop a network of informants within Dodd's office; the next was to gain access to the documentary evidence in his files. The natural recruiting ground was among those who had in the past taken some part in our nightly sessions at the Carroll Arms. They had done so, of course, in a spirit of gossiping within the family; none had then contemplated public disclosure. Since that had now become my objective, I felt obliged to so inform all those whose help I sought.

There were several on the staff who knew as much as I about Dodd's covert activities, perhaps more, but most of them I considered to be unlikely prospects. It was my opinion that they found Dodd's conduct tolerable or that their livelihood came first to them or that they were themselves implicated. I narrowed my list to a trusted handful. One mistaken confidence, one leak that reached the Senator or his palace guard and the project would be finished.

I was fully confident of Marjorie alone, though I knew well what I was asking of her. Within a day or two after Dodd's dismissal she had accepted a secretarial position with the prestigious Lawyers' Committee for Civil Rights Under Law, a group of nationally prominent attorneys originally called into being by President Kennedy to enlist the organized bar in the fight for civil rights. Working in this field, with people she highly respected, she had found the sense of positive involvement she had been looking for when she first applied for a position in Dodd's office. Already she was being considered for promotion to the post of assistant to the executive director, which carried important responsibilities and a substantial salary.

For Marjorie, the chronic tension and anxiety of the previous years magically vanished once she left the Dodd office. Embryonic ulcer attacks that had plagued her with increasing frequency suddenly ceased. To engage in a clandestine inquiry into Dodd's conduct in office was to reenter a bad dream, now almost forgotten. It would not only endanger her new position but might also involve the Lawyers' Committee in embarrassing and even damaging publicity. But Marjorie had been the first to see "something evil and frightening" about Dodd and to perceive a responsibility to oppose it. She immediately agreed to help and would start by trying to enlist the aid of girl friends who still worked for Dodd. If her participation should ever take on a character that figured to affect the Lawyers' Committee, she said, she would resign.

Michael's help would be indispensable. He and Marjorie and I were the closest of friends, in and out of the office, and the widening division between Michael's friends and his employer, to whom he also felt obligated, now cast a shadow over his habitual good humor. Conscientious to a fault, he was torn by conflicting loyalties and responsibilities—as a friend, as a trusted employee, as a citizen. He was now Dodd's closest aide, and Dodd talked of his some day becoming administrative assistant. Violating Dodd's ban, he continued to see us regularly and to advise us of day-to-day happenings in the office. But he was reluctant to impart the information we needed most—the facts in Dodd's financial records. He drew a line between those things he considered it ethical to divulge, such as Dodd's moves against me, and revelations he deemed a violation of professional responsibility to his employer, principally the data he acquired as the Senator's bookkeeper.

"I know that Dodd is a hypocrite and that he's done things that are dead wrong," he said to me. "Whether those things are illegal, or whether they go beyond what other Senators do, I don't know. I'm not sure it's right to single him out for exposure."

Having so long wrestled with the problem ourselves, we well understood Michael's dilemma. Our trust in him was such that we kept him fully informed of our daily progress, hoping to heighten his sense of involvement. At any time, he could have won Dodd's total favor by telling him of our objective, but we knew instinctively that he would never betray us. Concerning Dodd, there was one chord of memory that would always bind us together. If nothing else, our experience with Dodd the day President Kennedy died was the guarantee of our mutual fidelity.

On the afternoon of the assassination, Mrs. Ruth Weldon of the United Aircraft Corporation called our Washington office to inform us that the company's official plane had just left Hartford for Washington, carrying Senator Dodd, and that he wanted his key staff people to meet the plane. She had been told that the new President wanted to confer with Dodd at the airport as soon as he arrived from Dallas and, given the national emergency, Dodd had asked UAC to make its plane available as a public service. We had spoken with Dodd several times on that memorable afternoon and we knew that the story was a preposterous fabrication, more of his theatrics, this time in petty exploitation of a great tragedy. But when the UAC Convair, of commercial airliner size, touched down at National Airport with its momentous passenger, Marjorie, Michael, and I were there. The normally bustling waiting room was muted. Dodd seemed somehow out of place as he entered, looking rumpled and argumentative. He directed that we proceed to his house. It was obvious that there was no valid reason for us to have met him. He had no business to discuss. He just wanted to be met and to have an audience.

"Just before you landed," Marjorie said, "a plane arrived carrying Senator Smathers. He was wearing a black armband."

"Well," said Dodd, "Smathers was a friend of the *old* Administration. I am a friend of the *new* Administration." We sat in appalled silence as it dawned on us that Dodd considered this a day of victory. Unable to contain himself, Dodd launched into a harangue against the man whose flag-draped casket was expected in Washington momentarily. Reaching a bitter climax, Dodd crowed:

"I'll say of John Kennedy what I said of Pope John the day he died. It will take us fifty years to undo the damage he did to us in three years."

When we reached Dodd's house, he turned on the television. As statesmen paraded one after another across the screen, paying tribute to the fallen President, Dodd would deride and even mimic them. He was particularly abusive toward the remarks of Prime Minister Lester Pearson of Canada, so much so that we got up and walked out on him, coldly declining his command invitation to dinner. Never before had we been offered so unguarded an insight into the self-centered world of Thomas Dodd. Michael, who had all but worshipped President Kennedy, was affected even more than Marjorie or I. With Celtic amiability, he had cheerfully forgiven a hundred personal indignities at

Dodd's hands, but he never forgave him for that night. He brought it up often, his eyes still narrowed in bitterness and disbelief.

"The son of a bitch," he would mutter. "The son of a bitch."

I was confident that in time Michael would find it impossible to observe the fine line he had drawn, and then he would come fully to our side.

I next approached Carl Perian. A thirty-five-year-old bachelor whose handsome, sensitive features were framed by a five o'clock shadow that was impervious to the keenest edge, Carl had served on the Senator's Juvenile Delinquency Subcommittee for eleven years, working under five successive chairmen. It was on my recommendation that he had been promoted to staff director, but for years I considered him something of an enigma. He was a talented saxophone player, a student of psychology whose sympathetic counsel was sought by so many that Dodd called him our staff psychiatrist, a sports car fancier who dressed colorfully and fastidiously, and let his dark hair grow long between public hearings. When off-microphone, Carl talked in the lingo of the beat set and cultivated people who were way out. He was a professional criminologist, a part-time professor at George Washington University, and a consultant to the Kennedy and Johnson Administrations on juvenile problems, on which his expertise was widely recognized. His was the moving spirit and organizing mind behind our subcommittee investigations into the criminal traffic in narcotics and firearms and the antisocial dangers of television portrayals of crime, violence, and depravity. No armchair expert, Carl relished his role as an investigator. Once he had masqueraded as a dope-addicted ski bum, with recording equipment hidden under his parka, to get evidence on the drug-pushing racket at Aspen, Colorado. On several occasions, posing as a narcotics buyer, he had entered the opium-growing regions of northern Mexico and had smuggled heroin and marijuana back into the United States to demonstrate both the culpability of Mexican officialdom, which allowed the open cultivation of opium, and the inadequacy of our own border patrols, which contributed to making Mexico the principal source of narcotics in this country.

Carl's devotion to his work was beyond question. In the past he had complained to me repeatedly about Dodd's handling of investigations, but in the unending press and clamor that was part of my job I had paid little attention. Now I remembered.

"Every time we are on the verge of a major breakthrough," Carl had once said, "when we have these crooked slobs in a corner and could blow things wide open, Dodd always splits and cuts out on us. He's castrated everything we've tried to do, and it's happened too often to be a coincidence. Man, it's tearing me up." So I went to see him.

"Do you know what you're getting into?" he asked. "Are you going to stick it out to the end?"

"This will go all the way," I replied.

"Well," Carl said, "what you're doing is bound to get screwed up, but—what do you want *me* to do?"

"Just tell the truth. Once the story of these squashed investigations comes out, I'll need back-up, and you'll be put on the spot. You'll be asked lots of questions."

There was a pause. Then Carl said, "You can count on me to tell the truth—to a committee, to anyone who has a right to ask. If I did less, I'd be a whore."

Marjorie was successful in winning the cooperation of two young secretaries in Dodd's office—Judith Berling, my former secretary, and Terry Golden, who divided her duties between Gerry Zeiller and Dave Martin. In the past, both had expressed disillusionment with Dodd and now, with the spunk of their twenty years, they were ready to help. From Judy, Marjorie obtained a key to the new locks in Dodd's office. From Terry, we began to receive bits and pieces of information about Dodd's unusual efforts in behalf of particular business firms. Terry, who for several months had been "going steady" with Michael, was a conscientious girl with rigorous personal standards. She felt a strong obligation to become involved, and she gradually became a full partner in our enterprise.

By mid-February, then, we had gained the help of several strategically placed collaborators. Now began in earnest the task of digging out the facts. Initially, we limited our quest to personal testimony; the more crucial search for documentary evidence could wait until we had become a more cohesive group and better knew what we were looking for. From week to week throughout February and March, 1965, steady progress was made at night meetings. Our method was informal discussion—the matching of recollections of almost forgotten events that now seemed suspect. The results were encouraging but progress was slow. Our sessions had to be infrequent and carefully planned, for we knew that in times past Dodd had used his cronies to spy on employees. By the end of April, I had compiled lengthy notes on more than a score of cases. Some clearly pointed to misconduct, others to acts that were, at the least, highly irregular.

The question of what to do with this information now loomed perplexingly. Our accusations against Dodd rested on personal statements. As yet, we had no supporting proof. And there were wide gaps, the closing of which would require thorough investigative work. But to whom do you go to get a United States Senator investigated? The express refusal of the chairman of the Senate Rules Committee, Senator Everett Jordan, to investigate the misconduct of Senators implicated in the Bobby Baker case, and the perennial rejection by the whole Congress of proposed rules of ethical conduct for members left no doubt of the Senate's hostility to probing or punishing misconduct within the Club. After the charges of "whitewash" and "cover up" made against the Rules Committee by the press and by a small band of reform-minded Senators, we felt we could not expect to achieve anything by taking our accusations there. If we did, it seemed a certainty that, under the tradition of Senatorial courtesy, Dodd would be immediately informed of our charges against him. Thus, before an investigation could ever get off the ground, Dodd would be given a chance to destroy the evidence in his files and to coordinate the alibis of his accomplices. Besides, going to a Senate committee was a moot question anyway in May of 1965. The jurisdiction of the Rules Committee had been superseded by that of a newly created Committee on Standards and Conduct. But such was the Senate's zeal for policing its members that eight months after the committee had been established it still had no chairman, no members, no staff, and was not destined to have its first meeting until almost a year after its creation. We were left in a procedural no-man's-land.

I doubted that we could go to the F.B.I. or to its parent, the Justice Department, with any more assurance than we could go to the Senate. The F.B.I. will not order a field investigation of charges against a Senator without written instructions from the Attorney General himself. The protocol involved could easily turn our effort into a political football to be kicked around the higher echelons of the Justice Department and the White House. It would only magnify the danger that Dodd, a former Justice Department prosecutor and a friend of the President, would be forewarned instead of investigated.

And, politics aside, Dodd was too close to the F.B.I. He was the nation's highest-ranking ex-F.B.I. agent, a prize exhibit. As chairman of the Senate Juvenile Delinquency Subcommittee and vice-chairman of the Senate Internal Security Subcommittee, Dodd enjoyed a particularly close working relationship with the bureau and had a key voice in legislation in which it was vitally interested. For years, Dodd had used his position to harass in secret committee proceedings and to attack in privileged floor speeches those who had dared to criticize some aspect of F.B.I. performance. For years, Dodd had specialized in speeches of praise for the F.B.I. and its chief, J. Edgar Hoover, which I had ghosted with undercover assistance from the bureau. In return, Hoover's men rendered unusual services to Senator Dodd. On at least one occasion, F.B.I. agents in New York City were detailed as chauffeurs to drive Dodd around town on social calls. I knew, too, that the F.B.I. at times made its agents available to Dodd as private detectives, to tail members of his staff who had incurred his suspicion. In April of 1962, during a barrage of those anonymous poison pen letters, Dodd had me followed night and day for two weeks by Federal agents, who submitted written reports to him on my hour-to-hour movements. One of Dodd's secretaries saw one of the reports and, years later, told me about it.

A discouraging precedent further deepened my reluctance to entrust our case to the F.B.I. In 1962, a man named Arnold Foster had walked into F.B.I. headquarters in New York City and charged that Senator Dodd's office had tried to shake him down for money in return for help on a routine constituent matter. Before investigating the charge, which involved the possibility that the Senator himself might be implicated, the F.B.I. in Washington called Dodd and told him all about Foster's allegations. Only after Dodd and I had first questioned our staff was the F.B.I. interrogation of the persons named by Foster begun, with Dodd's knowledge and assent. The matter was soon dropped for lack of evidence. I had always assumed that the charges were unfounded, but I could not now forget the opportunity given Dodd to cover his tracks or the manner in which sound police procedure was abandoned out of deference to Dodd's position and influence. If the F.B.I. dealt with our charges in the same manner, by telegraphing every move to Dodd and reporting to him on the results of their interrogations, our informants within Dodd's office would be exposed and our chance of getting solid documentary proof lost forever. I felt that the F.B.I. was not for us.

It was not that we presumed to sit in judgment on the Senate and the Justice Department and found them indifferent to corruption in high places. It was indisputable, though, that they looked on a Senator as *a priori* above suspicion and his conduct as beyond their normal jurisdiction. A United States Senator was regarded as an ambassador from a state, an independent sovereign among his peers, a feared tyrant over the executive bureaucracy, a worthy foe or needed ally of the Presidency itself. He was a maker of laws and a selector of judges. The Constitution itself protected him from certain kinds of interference and arrest. About him had been spawned an undergrowth of official attitudes and immunities which rendered him all but above the law. Only public opinion, we judged, had the power to cut through this web. Our sole chance of success lay in arousing that opinion.

There is but one institution in the American system with both the facilities to expose Senatorial misconduct and the independence necessary to pursue it. That is the press. I was confident it would help us to complete our work of discovery, while keeping it secret from Dodd until it *was* completed. And when our information was fully assembled, verified and ready to print, we could then go to the authorities in a position of strength. With the press and public in possession of the facts, Authority could not long ignore them. There would have to be official probes, backed by the power to subpoena documents and put balky witnesses under oath. That, in any case, was my hope. It was a long shot, but it seemed the only course available to us.

To whom among the press should I go? Drew Pearson and Jack Anderson came immediately to mind. They wrote the nation's most widely syndicated column, carried by over six hundred newspapers. They specialized in government scandals and had already shown an interest in Dodd, having both praised and attacked him during his first term. They had proved in many a lonely battle that they had courage and that neither editors nor libel suits nor official intimidation could scare them off. With an insight that was almost eerie, Anderson had phoned me twice within the preceding weeks. He had been eyeing Dodd skeptically for some time, he said, since receiving a tip from a former Connecticut Congressman that Dodd could stand some investigating. When he heard, through his long grapevine, of my departure from Dodd, he thought he saw an opening. He told me that he had heard some bad reports on Dodd and that if I had any information of wrongdoing it would be in the public interest for me to help him. I had remained noncommittal; it was too early then. But his interest had encouraged me. I discussed it with my cohorts and, with their approval, decided to follow up my phone conversations with Anderson by going to see him.

At that juncture, however, early in May, Dodd sent me what he called a final offer to return to his official family and restore our old relationship. He required a quick answer, contending he could no longer delay the reorganization of his office. If I declined, he said, he would be compelled to end our existing arrangement.

His proposal had come at a bad time. I could not accept the offer for reasons long-determined, but to reject it would risk fracturing the era of complacent relaxation that had gradually set in since the December binge of firings and lock changings. I tried to play for time. I replied, as I had to previous offers, that though I would like to resume our old association, I felt that for various reasons this particular proposal was impracticable. This time it did not work. Dodd refused to be put off further. He called a meeting at Washington's University Club at which we were to come to a definite conclusion, once and for all.

When Michael and I joined Dodd in the dining room, I was surprised to find Mrs. Dodd present, along with an elderly, white-haired sugar lobbyist named Jim Markham. The Senator, tanned and rested, quickly established a mood of warm cordiality. He fairly exuded that assuredness one associates with impeccable respectability. To see him again, serenely puffing his pipe, nodding approvingly at Grace as she described churches and convents they had visited on their last trip abroad, to hear him discuss the progress of his children, his legislative goals for the coming year, his latest "Meet the Press" appearance on television, was a dismaying experience. It made the Tom Dodd I was pursuing seem an unreal phantom. After a while, he left the table. When he returned he wore a solemn air and made a shattering announcement.

"I just called Hartford," he said. "The latest word from the hospital is that Ed Sullivan has slipped into a coma and won't last the night. Poor Ed." For a time, as gloom spread around the table, Dodd reminisced in sepulchral tones about "my friend and political mentor." Then he rose and said that he had business to discuss with Jim and Mike. We adjourned to one of the sitting rooms and he came to the point immediately.

"My proposal is very simple, Jim. I want to end this mix-up. It's not doing either of us any good. I suggest that you come back to your old desk right away, Monday in fact, as legislative assistant. You'll be in charge of legislation, policy, speeches, and such, as you always were. And you have my solemn assurance, with Mike here as a witness, that within sixty days you'll be in full charge of the office again, as administrative assistant, and we'll go on just as in the past. I need that sixty days to move people around and to clear things with my associates in

Connecticut. They're pretty steamed up against you, but I'm sure I can cool them down. Now, for the first few weeks I'll have to cut your salary a bit, only temporarily until I can move someone off the payroll —we're strapped, aren't we, Mike? But you have my word that within sixty to ninety days you'll be back up to your old salary, and that's a commitment. Now I think this is a good offer."

When I did not accept immediately, but instead raised tentative reservations, his attitude stiffened as though he sensed a personal rebuff. A steeliness came into his eyes; the timbre of his voice hardened. "This is my last offer," he said. "Under the circumstances I don't see how it could be more generous. I'm not going to bargain with you. Think it over and make up your mind, but I'll have to have an answer within forty-eight hours. I've promised Grace that I would have the matter resolved one way or the other by the end of the week."

I was dejected as I rode home with Michael. Dodd had been so inflexible that an open collision loomed. I found that the old days, represented by Ed Sullivan, still had a grip on me; the desire to please Dodd and to agree with his schemes was still almost automatic and had to be consciously resisted. And the hard consequences of an open break now loomed with bleak immediacy.

But I decided to keep up the game as long as I could and in the morning I began the touchy business of drafting a formal, if deceitful, letter of refusal. I made it a question of professional pride, saying that though I esteemed the Senator and was grateful for his offer, I could not agree, even temporarily, to return to a post lesser than the one I left. Dodd obviously knew that the sixty days of penance was the weak point in his proposal, since its only conceivable purpose was to proclaim that he had emerged the victor. He would assume, I hoped, that a matter of such importance to him could also be important to me and would attribute my rejection to vanity rather than enmity or conspiracy.

I was relieved when Michael brought word that there was no outburst from the Senator when he read my letter and that he seemed rather defensive and subdued. And I learned something that showed Dodd's essential vulnerability. Michael, troubled over Dodd's announcement about Ed Sullivan, had sorrowfully informed the office staff of his momentary decrease. Then he called Mary Hamil in Hartford to learn if Ed had survived the night.

"Mr. Sullivan is fine," she said. "Why do you ask, Mike?" It turned out that Ed was not in a coma, had never been in one, had already been discharged from the hospital, and was expected in the office soon. His premature demise had been just another bit of stage management. The incident reminded me of Dodd's reckless addiction to falsehood as a working tool. He must have realized, in the back of his mind, that I would eventually find out about Ed, but it was characteristic of him to think only of the advantage of the moment—in this instance the creation of a sympathetic atmosphere for his negotiations. The minor complications and embarrassments of tomorrow, after today's objective had been achieved, he could attend to if and when they arose. Surely, I thought, in the long contest that lay ahead such a weakness was bound to prove crucial.

I watched and waited for a week. The reaction I had feared did not materialize. There was no purge of my friends and collaborators, the locks were not changed again, no new security measures were introduced. The office remained empty and unwatched on weekends. As Dodd had stipulated, he took me off the payroll but soon sent hints of a new offer, in response to which I made the old conciliatory sounds. It was now May 19th. I made an appointment to see Jack Anderson on the following day.

In the flesh, Anderson belied his shadowy image on Capitol Hill, where his victims call him "Dirty Jack." I found him rather handsome, in a clean-cut way, and decidedly agreeable. As though to confound his detractors, his unlined face glowed affably with an altar-boy radiance, an outward guilelessness that seemed to deny both his profession and the edge of gray at his temples. He was soft spoken, voluble, open. In an attempt to put me at ease, he rambled with disarming frankness about personal matters—a close relative who had disappointed him, a great scoop that had eluded him, the nature of his relationship with Drew Pearson. He spoke, perhaps purposefully, about his eight children, the Sunday School class he taught, and of his mission as an investigative reporter: "Every time we expose one chiseler in Congress, a dozen others that we can't get the goods on straighten up for a while." Would I like a drink? "Yes, I would," I said. But he was thinking of diet cola. Only later did I learn that he was a practicing Mormon, a former missionary who neither drank nor smoked and who shunned even coffee and tea. But there was in Anderson's exterior nothing of the grimness that one often links with sectarian austerity. With shoes off and feet up, he was relaxed and jovial. On his desk I noticed a little statuette of what appeared to be the traditional three monkeys—hear no evil, see no evil, speak no evil. But on closer look the monkeys bore perverse expressions, the first cupping his hands to his ears, the second peering through long binoculars, the third shouting into a megaphone. When I began haltingly to tell my story, grasping for ways to make the tangled skein intelligible, he listened intently, expressions of sympathy, concern, and indignation passing across his mobile features at reassuring intervals.

I sped through an abbreviated recital of our evidence of misconduct, skimming over my notes and citing only the highlights. Even so, two hours passed. When I finished I was overcome by a feeling that I had presented the matter poorly, that the events I cited must have seemed trivial and insignificant.

"Do you think there is anything here?" I asked.

"If we can substantiate half of this," he replied, "it will be the most significant disclosure of corruption in Washington in forty years, certainly in all my time as a reporter."

A working relationship thus began. I went to Anderson's office almost daily, locked myself in by prearrangement so as not to be observed there, and dictated my notes in full to his secretary and associate, Opal Ginn, a tall, talkative, nonteetotaler with an infectious warmth and a remarkably proficient shorthand. The notes soon amounted to more than one hundred typed pages.

During the early days of our association, the guidelines were drawn. Anderson would treat the Dodd story as a top-priority matter and would be available at any time of the night or day to work on it. I would assist him until my dwindling finances ran out. We agreed that I would receive no remuneration of any kind, either for the information I provided or for the work I did in developing it. That was to apply to all our group, for nothing must be done that would later taint our revelations or discredit our motives. Nothing would be published until every scrap of available information was in, and then we would inform the Senate and the F.B.I. of all that we knew. Anderson, for his part, committed himself to make a crusade out of the case, to do all within his power to lay it before the public and the authorities, and to persevere in it no matter what pressures were brought to bear on him. I agreed to provide sworn affidavits whenever needed and to testify in any legal forum, and I expressed confidence that everyone in our group would do the same.

The further I proceeded in relating the individual episodes the more apparent became the need for documentation. "I believe what you tell me," Anderson would say, "but we can't go to press on that basis. Some of this we can print, based on your testimony and the others; but for most of it I need proof of some kind that I can show to Drew and our lawyers."

For months the key to Dodd's office, which lay beside my telephone, had been a daily reminder of what was ahead. Now that moment had come. To invade Dodd's office and remove his files was an ugly business. Anderson always stopped short of recommending it; but there was no other way to get the proof. I was aware of the ethical questions involved, if not the legal. What about Dodd's right to privacy, the inviolability of a Senator's official papers, the precept that the end does not justify the means? But I concluded that traditional concepts of civil liberties, developed with reference to the rights of private citizens versus the state, had little relevance when applied to elected officials versus the public. I reasoned that an elected official, by his very calling, renounces much of his right to privacy. Certainly he has no right to conceal his conduct in office from his constituents, in whose name he acts. The office he holds belongs to the people and his actions in it are to a large extent public property. If the functions of a public office are misused, the public has a paramount right to know about it. When an erring Senator will not open his records voluntarily —and Senate committees and the Justice Department refuse to subpoena them—then the public has no way to acquire the information that rightfully belongs to it unless an individual with inside knowledge takes the burden upon himself. Such a burden may or may not involve a technical violation of the law, depending on the conflicting interpretations of lawyers. Should one shrink from this debatable violation when to do so means that massive wrongdoing will continue and go undetected? I concluded that this was a unique situation for which I knew of no precedents. Rightly or wrongly, I judged that the larger ends of justice would be served by my trespassing in Dodd's office and removing all files containing evidence of misconduct. Marjorie agreed, and when we told Michael and Terry of our plans, they offered to join with us.

Our plan was simple. Michael and Terry, who were still members in good standing of Dodd's staff, were to remove files in all suspect areas and at periodic intervals bring valises full of documents to Marjorie and me, who would be waiting in a car outside the Senate Office Building. We were to take the files to Marjorie's apartment, two blocks from the Capitol, where we would sort them out, rush the pertinent documents to Opal Ginn for photocopying and return the originals to our rendezvous point, where we would pick up another load and repeat the process. Should someone come into Dodd's office unexpectedly—and with a staff of fifteen that was always a danger—there would be no cause for suspicion, for Michael and Terry frequently worked with the files. Marjorie and I were not to enter the office. Should we be observed there or in the adjoining halls by a staff member or by a Capitol Hill policeman who might have been warned against us in the days of suspicion, the operation would be immediately undermined.

On the night of Friday, June 10th, Michael, Terry, and I gathered at Marjorie's apartment for a final rehearsal of our document raid on Dodd's office, planned for the following day. Circumstances had delayed us. Marjorie, who had by now received her promotion, had been away for a week in Jackson, Mississippi, helping to set up a field office for volunteer civil rights lawyers. Then Jack Anderson was stricken with appendicitis, followed by complications, and was hospitalized for two weeks. Now, at last, all was ready. Dodd had left for Connecticut for the weekend. According to Michael's best information, no one would be in the office on Saturday or Sunday.

As we began our final review, the spontaneity that normally marked our meetings was absent. Michael quickly explained why.

"Terry and I have thought this thing through," he began. "We've tried hard to figure out the right thing to do, and we just can't go along with you. We sympathize with what you're trying to do, but we're in a different situation. We are still Senate employees, and we don't think it's right to copy your employer's files and turn them over to a reporter. We've been willing to help you, and still are, but not this way."

I felt suddenly flat, as though the air had been let out of me. They were our closest friends. Every day they risked their jobs just by associating with us. If they disagreed with what we were doing, who on earth would agree?

"I understand how you feel," I said finally. "This is a rough thing to figure." And after a friendly drink they left.

For a moment Marjorie and I sat in defeated silence. Finally, I said, "I think we should go in there by ourselves tomorrow and get those files. I have a feeling that if we don't do it tomorrow we never will."

"That's how I feel, too," she replied. "We can use the key Judy gave us. You'll have to call Opal Ginn and tell her about the change in schedule."

Our enthusiasm quickly revived, and we began formulating a new plan.

On Saturday, while waiting for the late afternoon, when our entry into Dodd's office would be the least subject to detection, we went to see Jack Anderson for a final huddle. Jack was now recuperating at his Bethesda home. Clad in sky-blue pajamas, he was painfully hobbled but his demeanor was that of a patriotic archbishop blessing the troops as they left for the battlefield.

"What you are doing is morally right and I don't think it can, therefore, be legally wrong," he began softly. "In good conscience, I can't urge you young people to take this risk—that's entirely up to you. But I must warn you of the consequences. If you're caught at it today, you may be ruined. And even if you don't get caught and we get all the documents and are completely successful in exposing Dodd, it will all come out when you testify, as you well know, and it will follow you all through life. People won't want to hire you. You may be all through in Washington because so many here will identify with Dodd. He'll pressure the Senate and the Justice Department to go after you, make no mistake about that, and it will be touch and go.

"But if you do take this chance"—now the old missionary ardor sounded in his voice—"Drew and I will never abandon you, and we have fifty million readers. We'll protect the documents, and we'll print all the stories, down to the last sordid detail. If they want to prosecute you, they'll have to prosecute Drew and me, too, because we'll demand to be tried as accomplices. And every day in our column we'll ask the country 'Why are they not prosecuting all the Senators and high officials who leak official papers and classified documents to the press to serve their own ends?' And we'll name them, day by day. We'll make this a test case to prove whether or not the free press in this country has a right to get the facts about that gentlemen's Cosa Nostra they call the Congress!"

As Jack escorted us to the door, his air of militant evangelism gave way to a reflective look that seemed to embrace recollections of fire escapes, stake-outs, and hairbreadth getaways.

"Those doors in the Senate Office Building," he said expertly, "don't they have inside locks that can't be opened from the outside?"

"Yes, I think they do." I said.

"Well, the minute you get in Dodd's office lock all the doors from the inside. If anyone tries to get in, tiptoe up to the door and listen carefully. They'll have to go back to the police office to get help. Wait until you hear the footsteps die away in the hall, then run for it with the documents the quickest way out. If you think you've been detected, come right here with the documents. They'll be safe here. This house is never empty. If all goes well, call me, but keep your comments guarded. Always assume that the phones are tapped, especially mine."

There are five entrances to the Old Senate Office Building that lead, on three different levels, to Senator Dodd's offices in the south wing of the first floor. At each entrance there is a police desk and an officer on duty. Among the tasks of these gentlemen, especially at night and on weekends, is that of carefully observing all who enter and leave the building for signs of questionable intentions. We had scheduled our raids for periods when Dodd's offices were most likely to be empty, but these were also the periods of minimum traffic in the building, when our comings and goings would be the most conspicuous. By alternating our use of the various entrances and exits we hoped to hide the extent of our movements.

At five forty-five P.M., Marjorie and I passed through the Delaware and "C" Street entrance, and nodded with pretended familiarity to the officer on duty, who returned our nod routinely. The policeman was new and gave no indication of interest in us. Then we started down the long, echoing hallway. Except for the magnified sound of our footsteps in the void, there was complete silence. We each carried an empty valise, mine of almost suitcase size.

As we passed the offices of Dodd's next-door neighbor, Senator Paul Douglas of Illinois, a comparison between the two was unavoidable. For sixteen years Senator Douglas had imposed upon himself a code of ethics that was well-known throughout the Senate. He accepted a modest scale of life and each year made public his total income and net worth. He refused to accept from contributors a single dollar, under any guise, for his personal expenses. He returned all gifts, however innocent, that were worth more than five dollars. And he refused campaign contributions from any person or group who had a financial interest in any matter before him as a Senator, be it a business tycoon or a labor union with an axe to grind. Was it quixotic to hope that one day his code would be universal in the Congress?

Dodd's suite was a long string of interconnected offices, each with a door opening to the hall. When we reached our destination, we saw light shining through the transoms of two of the offices. Was someone in there? Probably not. Five minutes earlier we had phoned Dodd's office, dialing both the regular number and the private line, and there had been no answer. Probably someone had been there earlier in the day and had failed to turn off the lights. In any event, we would have to risk finding out. We continued down the hall to the entrance furthest from the lighted rooms. I turned the key silently and inched open the door. The suite was dark at that end. We tiptoed in and closed the door quietly behind us.

We listened for sounds coming from the other end of the suite and moved silently towards it, through Zeiller's office, through mine, to the edge of Dodd's sanctuary, where two small lamps burned dimly. The room seemed to exude Dodd's presence. We stepped across the threshold and looked anxiously toward his desk; we fully expected to see him sitting there, staring at us. We *did* see him, almost, but it was only a trick of the imagination. The remaining rooms, where we had seen the light, were also vacant. I moved quickly from door to door turning all the inside locks. The one on the door to Dodd's personal office was broken, but the door stop, when pressed all the way to the floor, caught in the edge of the carpeting and seemed to hold fast, though I could not tell how much force this makeshift arrangement would withstand.

Marjorie was thoroughly familiar with the filing system and soon began deluging me with stacks of letters bearing names we had been discussing for months—Klein, Spanel, Kluge, O'Neil, Blinken, Dunbar, Janeway. I leafed through them, hurriedly deciding what was important, and stacked the folders to be removed on the now celebrated red leather divan in Dodd's office. Our immediate success somewhat dazzled us. We whispered our finds to each other excitedly, until we realized it was slowing us down. The Klein folders, hundreds of pages in extent, threw light on many a transaction between the Senator and the registered foreign agent; the highlight, at least to my speeding eye, was a packet of instructions from Klein to Dodd, detailing whom Dodd should see and what he should say in Klein's behalf on a trip to West Germany.

Though the full significance of all that I was stacking up on the divan must, I knew, await further study, particular documents jolted me with the excitement of discovery. "As instructed by Mr. Thomas F. O'Neil, I am enclosing herewith check for $1,000 which we have made payable to the Testimonial Dinner for the Honorable Thomas F. Dodd," began one letter. This was important, for I knew that all the proceeds from that dinner had gone straight into Dodd's personal pocket. If O'Neil had intended it for political purposes, then Dodd had deceived both him and the Internal Revenue Service, and had misappropriated the money. If O'Neil had intended it for Dodd, then Dodd must answer how he could justify accepting this large sum of money from the man who headed General Tire and Aerojet, two prime government contractors, and RKO, which operated in a field Dodd was supposed to be investigating.

There was a paper listing the names of two dozen corporations that had been assisted by Dodd in obtaining government contracts and whose officers had in turn made large contributions to him; in the margins were occasional handwritten notes appraising the extent of their generosity.

There was a memorandum dictated by Dodd himself recounting how Julian G. Sourwine, chief counsel of the Senate Internal Security Subcommittee and renowned Red hunter, had gotten Dodd to endorse a bum check for $2,500 and how, when Sourwine's check bounced in Las Vegas, he had pressured Dodd into making it good, though Dodd had to take out a loan to do it. Dodd had told me about this eighteen months before, but here it was in writing. We later learned that Dodd had written off the $2,500 on his income tax returns as a business expense for "professional assistance in the preparation of lectures." Sourwine had never helped Dodd with his "lectures." What hold did Sourwine have over Dodd that would explain this shakedown of a Senator by a Senate employee?

There were voluminous copies of thank-you notes acknowledging gifts received from television executives, lobbyists, and businessmen dealing with the government. Invariably, the gift-givers had a direct stake in Dodd's official acts. We had known about the gifts before. Now we had proof.

There were vouchers claiming travel expenses we knew to be bogus, a strange intervention for the pardon of a convicted criminal, a document proving that Dodd was receiving personal income from a publishing venture whose expenses he had charged to his campaign. The evidence was mounting.

"I have the folders containing Ed Sullivan's weekly reports to the Senator," Marjorie whispered, handing me three thick files. "They should tell a lot about the fund-raising." The sound of heavy footsteps outside cut short our mood of celebration. But they passed by. "Let's stay another half hour," I said. "We've got almost as much as we can carry."

In that half hour we located Dodd's official diary for 1964, complete travel itineraries and speaking-engagement lists for the previous three years, and appointments schedules and telephone logs for the previous two years, including Dodd's notes on the purposes and results of his meetings and phone conversations. All these were vital to us, for they would enable us to fix precisely where Dodd was on any given day, who visited him, whom he visited, whom he talked to on the phone, where he made speeches, who paid the fees.

At eight o'clock we packed up. Soon the approaching dusk would reveal to passersby on Constitution Avenue, and perhaps to the Capitol Hill police, that something strange was going on in Senator Dodd's lighted office. The files that we could not squeeze into the valises we carried under our free arm. We were comically overloaded and, on coming out of Dodd's office, we would be visible the entire length of the hall. I opened the door a crack and listened for the sound of footsteps. Hearing nothing, we slipped out into the hall and in three minutes were past the desk and safely in our car.

Later that night I returned alone, through a different entrance, and replaced some of the files which, on examining, we found we had no need to photocopy. This time I was back in my car within fifteen minutes. I returned to Marjorie's apartment, where documents were piled on chairs and tables in disorganized profusion. For several hours we studied and classified in terms of what would be photocopied the next day. At about two A.M. we reached the folders filled with Ed Sullivan's handwritten letters, more than two hundred in all. By four o'clock we had waded through all but five or six of them and had discovered nothing of real significance. Dutifully we read on, only for the sake of completeness, and in these last letters we found three financial reports on the 1961 Dodd dinner in Hartford which showed, in ledger form, that $64,000 had been raised, and that the entire net proceeds, $55,000, had been sent to Dodd in Washington and deposited in his personal bank account. For the first time we had documentary proof of what heretofore we knew only from deduction. Of the quarter-million dollars in political funds which we estimated Dodd had expropriated, more than one-fifth was now accounted for.

Four hours later, at eight o'clock Sunday morning, we drove into the underground garage of the new Senate Office Building and parked near the door leading to one of those subterranean corridors in which the Capitol complex abounds. This particular corridor led from the new Senate Office Building to the old, and was one of the shortest routes to Dodd's offices. In everything we saw, we imagined danger. As we got out of our car and started for the door, Marjorie spotted the duty officer at the garage police desk reaching for the phone. A moment later, we passed another police desk which commanded a view of the entire corridor we were to traverse. We simulated carefree conversation, and felt questioning eyes burning into our backs. But in three minutes we had climbed the marble staircase and were again inside Dodd's suite.

This time we were a little cooler, more methodical. Like archaeologists grubbing for fragments of old bones, we knew that the smallest relic, the one which appeared most trivial, might be the piece which completed a skeleton. Scrap by scrap, we uncovered items that were full of meaning: copies of letters from Dodd to the President recommending high appointments for a group hardly distinguishable from his major contributors; a missive to Dodd from his single-minded retainer, George Gildea, recounting how firms that had received constituent services from Dodd's office were being solicited for contributions to the 1961 testimonial, the proceeds of which we knew had gone into Dodd's pocket; a file which traced Dodd's requests to Hartford insurance companies to grant large business loans to a real estate speculator with the musical name of Manlio Liccione, for which Dodd received thousands of dollars in finder's fees; a curt letter to Dodd from Presidential Assistant McGeorge Bundy deploring the attempt to enlist White House muscle in behalf of a contract for Avco's Lycoming Division. Bundy would have deplored it more, I thought, if he had known that Avco often placed a company plane at Dodd's disposal for personal use and that Avco's president, Earl "Red" Blaik, had been a speaker at Dodd's $80,000 bonanza in Hartford in March, 1965.

"Listen!" Marjorie warned. Again the approach of footsteps in the hall. This time they stopped right in front of us and the door was tried, followed by vigorous knocking. Marjorie bolted and tried to hide behind the file cabinets. I pursued her and dragged her out. "You must sit behind your old desk," I whispered urgently. "If he starts to force the doors, and Dodd's starts to give, I'll let him in and ask what he wants. You start typing and look natural." Our visitor was now knocking on Dodd's door. I went to it and listened. He moved on. Each doorknob was tried, each door knocked on. Then he went away.

Frantically, we gathered up our contraband and started to evacuate. But the more we reconstructed the event, the more it seemed to be just a routine door check. "Cops are always trying doors," I said hopefully. "He didn't use a key so he couldn't know they are locked from the inside and that someone is in here."

We decided to stay and in the next hour, which we vowed would be our last, we unearthed records of Dodd's activities involving five corporations that had for months figured prominently in our speculations. I took the files into Dave Martin's littered office and, with one ear on the door, raced through them. Page by page, adding what I already knew to fill in the blank spaces, I grasped the bare outlines of five significant cases:

Allegheny Airlines: As a Senator, Dodd had helped Allegheny to obtain millions in subsidies. Later he had secretly purchased Allegheny stock under the name of a friend.

Kaman Aircraft: Dodd had lobbied effectively for Kaman with defense agencies and even with a private corporation having subcontracts to let. In gratitude, President Charles Kaman, a Republican who had never contributed to Dodd in four previous campaigns, came to Washington personally in the late summer of 1964 to give Dodd a $4,000 check.

The Mite Corporation: Dodd had asked the White House to exempt Mite from competitive bidding on one valuable contract and pressed the Navy for prompt approval of another. In September 1964, President Robert Blinken of Mite made a pilgrimage to Washington to bring a brown envelope containing $2,100 in cash, which Dodd pocketed and never reported, either as personal income or as a political contribution.

The Frouge Corporation, builder of Marincello, a vast housing development near San Francisco's Golden Gate: President Tom Frouge spoke of Dodd as "my attorney," and paid his travel expenses in California when Dodd went to see Governor Pat Brown to urge a change in policies of the state of California which were impeding the project. Dodd treated this reimbursement as payment for business expenses, and the Frouge file contained documented records of Dodd's activities as a private agent for Frouge. The shocker was that the file also contained lengthy letters from Frouge to Dodd directing Dodd's step-by-step intervention with Federal agencies, in his capacity as a Senator, to clear the way for Marincello, along with detailed reports from Dodd on his progress in these efforts. Dodd thus was acting both in a private and public capacity in Frouge's behalf. "This will be good for me and for you," Frouge wrote, as Dodd descended deeper and deeper into the quagmire of conflict of interest.

The Conetta Company, manufacturer of rifle components: Albert Morano, from whom Dodd borrowed $15,000, was an official of Conetta when he joined Dodd's Senate staff, and he continued to work for Conetta while a Dodd aide. Working with Dodd, Morano used his Senate post and Dodd's office facilities to lobby for contracts for the Conetta Company. Swiftly turning over the letters in the Conetta file, I came upon one from Morano to Dodd, mailed under the free government frank, which seemed to symbolize the multiple conflicts of interest: "Dear Senator, the trigger purchase from Conetta is critical. Nothing has been heard. Please contact [Secretary of Defense] McNamara again." Conetta got the contract.

There was much more in the file cabinets, we were sure, but we had stayed as long as we could without risking discovery by some conscientious Dodd employee who might drop by the office unexpectedly.

At nine-fifty we left Dodd's suite and began what we had come to call the last mile. If I had been wrong about the "routine door check," someone could be lying in wait for us. The desk at the end of the corridor was strangely unoccupied, but in the garage stood a captain and a lieutenant talking with the officer on duty. We went to the car without looking left or right, our bulging valises now feeling like huge albatrosses. As I backed out of the parking space, a vehicle suddenly pulled up short in back of me, but it was only a laundry truck. When we drove past the captain and his men, they smiled and waved at us. And in a moment we had gone up the ramp and out into the bright Sunday morning stillness of the Capitol streets.

Ahead lay a day of photocopying and then the return of all originals to Dodd's files. When the Senator's office opened for business Monday morning, all had to be back in perfect order. At this point, Marjorie was required to leave to catch a plane to New York. Later in the day she was to give a brief talk to a group of philanthropists in behalf of her Lawyers' Committee. I insisted that I could handle things easily, but before the day was over her absence and that of Jack Anderson were to have serious consequences.

Opal Ginn was waiting, cool with conspiratorial aplomb, when I arrived at the K Street address Jack had given me. Our meeting place was a half-finished office suite. The air conditioning was off. The incomplete furnishings and decor gave no hint of what business normally was transacted there, except that phonograph albums, featuring nudes on their jackets, were strewn about the floor. But the essential item of equipment was there, dominating the office—a large Xerox copying machine. For half a day, as we crouched mechanically in front of the humming, heat-throwing monster, all went smoothly. We copied thousands of papers. Then, without warning, a paper got stuck somewhere in the interstices of the machine, causing it to jam. Had Marjorie been on hand she could have fixed it, for she was familiar with Xeroxing. But Opal was not, nor was I. Opal phoned for help. I assumed it was to someone in the Pearson-Anderson organization.

When our helper arrived she was carrying a large container filled with daiquiris and was in a holiday mood, having in tow a tall, blond, beach-boy type. Her name was Marilyn Homer, a not unattractive young lady, although too plump for her lavender stretch pants. When it became apparent that she was not a part of the Pearson-Anderson band I realized that a major security goof had been committed. As casually as possible I turned the topmost documents on each pile face down. Without ado, Miss Homer removed two wrinkled letters and had the machine humming again. But had she noticed that the letters were from Senator Dodd to Julius Klein? Full of bouncy conviviality, she invited us to the daiquiri party at her place when we had finished whatever we were doing and, followed by her boyfriend and her perfume, she undulated out the door.

An hour later a man named Irving Davidson entered. He turned out to be Marilyn Homer's boss and an acquaintance of Jack's. This, it turned out, was his office. He looked around cheerfully for a few moments and then left. He had come, on a hot Sunday afternoon, to see what was going on, perhaps after a call from Miss Homer. Irving Davidson—his name struck a note in my memory—a lobbyist of sorts, a friend of Jim Markham's, the white-haired man who was at the University Club with us on the night of my last meeting with Dodd! But there was nothing to do but go on and finish the job.

Nine hours after we began we were still at it. We had copied at least three thousand documents. Opal's rugged veneer was at last pierced. She was woozy from the heat and thoroughly whipped. But she hung on and in ten minutes the last page of the last folder came down the chute. It was after seven, but it would still be light out for almost two hours. If I hurried, I had time to return to Dodd's office.

Inside the cool depths of the old Senate Office Building again, I stopped at a public phone and dialed the two numbers to Dodd's offices. No answer again. I lifted up my burdens, glanced over my shoulder to where the guard, bored with his uneventful Sabbath, lolled at the entrance, and plodded forward. Cumulative tension now began to bore in forcefully. An hour before, I had returned a load and had found lights on again, though I had carefully turned them off that morning. Someone was just barely missing me. Concern over the unknown visitor, over Marilyn Homer, Irving Davidson, the law of averages itself, dogged my weary steps. How ironic, I thought, if I were nabbed in the act of *returning* the stuff. As I passed the office of Senator Quentin Burdick, a door opened and there emerged a girl in slacks, with a kerchief tied over haircurlers. I knew the people in Burdick's office; fortunately, this girl was new. But the omens seemed to be multiplying.

In twenty disciplined minutes I had returned each file to its appointed drawer, in its alphabetical place, recalling with perverse satisfaction that in all the years I was in charge of Dodd's office I had never been able to fathom the filing system and that now I had mastered it.

Once more down the hall, a smile at the desk to one who could not distinguish me from the thousands who passed by him each week, and out through the revolving door into the street. As I hit the evening air an excruciating sense of conquest came over me, strangely reminiscent of my feelings on the moment of Dodd's victory over Chester Bowles so long before. The originals had all been returned, the copies were all secure in Jack Anderson's safe. Whatever else might happen, inexorable consequences would flow from this. I was suddenly very, very tired, as never before, and could feel nervous sweat trickling down my arms and sides. For a long while I sat motionless in the car, enjoying the stillness and the sight of couples strolling in the park across the street. I thought of Marjorie in New York and wondered how her maiden speech was going.

"Irv Davidson is all right," Jack assured me. "He and I used to share an office together and he has never violated a confidence. But that Homer gal is the last person in town I'd trust with a secret. Opal will try to divert her with a cover story, but you'd better not go into Dodd's office again. It's too risky."

We waited two weeks. Our informants reported no change in Dodd's attitude, no sign he had heard anything disturbing. And Terry Golden had pinpointed for us the location of a number of hot files. So we decided to go back. On Saturday evening, June 25th, and Sunday morning, June 26th, Marjorie and I made three more trips and spent several fruitful hours among the file cabinets. This time, we did the Xeroxing at Marjorie's office.

There were now upwards of five thousand pages of documentation in Jack's safe and, in the weeks that followed, the store was augmented repeatedly. We obtained a large cache of confidential records that traced the collapse of Dodd investigations to persons and interests that had later turned up on various contributions lists. Terry Golden procured copies of valuable documents and mailed them to Marjorie from Dodd's office. Michael now became the key figure. The financial records to which he alone had access were essential if we were to tie down some of our most important leads.

Michael had continued to help us in various ways and seemed more and more to share our view about the documents. One September night he agreed to come with us to Jack Anderson's house. Jack made a persuasive appeal, saying that we had put together a case against Dodd that would shock the nation and force reforms, and that Michael's help was essential to put it over the top. "I know you are trying to do the right thing, Mike, or you would not be here tonight. I know you are hesitating to take the last step only out of a sense of duty to your employer. I have lived with this problem for twenty years and, believe me, your ultimate duty is to the public, your real employer, and to the democratic system, not to a crook like Dodd who has betrayed his office and every honest person associated with him."

Michael was visibly moved. Soon after, he learned accidentally from Mary Hamil that Dodd had opened a new checking account in Hartford, from which his personal expenses were paid. Neither the deposits nor withdrawals appeared in the books Michael kept for income-tax purposes. He agreed in principle to furnish to us the financial records after he had brought them up to date. It was now just a matter of timing. But time was to prove short. In October, Terry Golden was fired, without explanation. Shortly before that, Judy Berling had been forced to resign. They were a part of what Dodd's cronies called "the Boyd clique" and their meetings with Marjorie had been discovered. Apparently, word of our activities had reached Dodd in some form, and a purge was on. Terry's firing came without warning on a Friday afternoon as Dodd was leaving town. Like us, she was forbidden to return to the office. We judged that Michael might be next, on Monday, and our last chance to get the financial records would vanish. He saw the urgency and made his decision. Spending all day Saturday in the office, on guard for signs that he was under surveillance, he brought the books up to date and late that afternoon took them to Marjorie's office where it took seven hours to Xerox them.

The books covered five years and included day-by-day records of Dodd's income and expenditures, including all checks by number; all of his recorded loans and their present status; his lecture and legal fees; the complete records of his travel expenses, down to the last airline ticket stub; records that showed payment of personal and family expenses out of political contributions; the financial report of the D.C. Testimonial Reception for Dodd; complete income-tax returns; records of large sums invested in his property; and on and on. We took the duplicate records to Marjorie's apartment. Around midnight, Jack came by with a big black bag to pick them up. We urged him to stay for a while but he demurred. "I have to get up early tomorrow," he said. "I'm teaching Sunday school."

All told, we had acquired from all sources about seven thousand pages of documents, more than enough to start several official probes. Except for a stray find by Michael, whose role remained unsuspected, the document phase of our effort was now ended. And none too soon. For in the meantime Marilyn Homer, of the daiquiris, had gotten word to Dodd of what she had seen.

The Senator did not at all grasp the extent of what had befallen him; but he immediately reactivated his security apparatus. The old retainers, who had been asleep at the switch, were appropriately rebuked. The locks were again changed. The building superintendent and the police were summoned to emergency conferences and instructed to put Dodd's office under strict watch. Dodd's peculiar underground was alerted and assigned missions of state. And he told Michael that private detectives were at work and would expose the "plot" in a number of days. After years of anticipating a conspiracy against him, Dodd finally had one.

Shortly thereafter, Dodd's legislative assistant, Milton Wernstrom, who had been with Dodd for six years, was surprised at his desk on a Saturday afternoon by the Capitol Hill police. He was just doing his job, he insisted, trying to catch up on the legislative mail backlog. His elaborate efforts to identify himself got nowhere. He was unceremoniously hustled out of the office on "the Senator's orders" and reported.

But it was all too late. The deed was done. Now we had to see where it would lead.

CHAPTER FIVE

To counter the uncertain danger disclosed by Marilyn Homer, Dodd decided on personal diplomacy. In late August he sent his friend Jim Markham to Jack Anderson with a message. A discharged and embittered employee named Jim Boyd was going around spreading malicious stories about Senator Dodd, cautioned the elderly Markham, and, though Dodd felt sorry for Boyd, he thought Anderson and other newsmen should know, for their own protection, that Boyd was "demented."

Anderson, adept at candidly revealing what his interrogator already knows while masking the more important unknowns, admitted interviewing Boyd some time before but said the talk had been of no value. Anderson explained that for years he had been pursuing a registered foreign agent named Julius Klein. In June, a cache of papers that linked Klein with several Senators had come into his hands. During the process of checking out these papers, Anderson said, he had called Boyd, whom he had once met, and together they went through the file, but Boyd maintained there was nothing irregular about Dodd's relations with Klein so he decided to move on to the other Senators. Markham returned to Dodd with that assurance.

A day or two later, Dodd asked to see me and suggested we meet at eleven P.M. at France's Restaurant in Georgetown. I agreed to go. There was a chance, I thought, that he could be set at ease, and that would take the heat off our informants in Dodd's office. When I arrived, Dodd was waiting. He led me to the cocktail lounge, which was quite dark. The small red lamp on the table illumined only our faces. As we parried our way through the preliminary chitchat, I was conscious of Dodd's eyes fixed on me, and I recalled that he had once told me: "When I'm talking with someone, I always concentrate on his eyes and facial expressions. Long after I've forgotten what he had to say, I remember what his face revealed."

I thought Dodd's face revealed something, too. Whatever he had heard from the Homer girl had shaken him, and it showed through his disguise. The equilibrium that had so long existed in our relationship had shifted perceptibly. No longer did I discern in him the old assuredness. And I awaited his words not in deference and anticipation but in hard calculation. A debased equality existed between us now, founded on mutual suspicion. Each of us was aware that the other knew more than he was conceding. He would lie to me, I would lie back to him, and I sensed momentarily how life becomes dehumanized and degraded by intrigue.

"Jim," he said, in a hesitant tone that meant we were now to talk of serious things, "I don't know quite how to say this but—do you know Jack Anderson?"

"Yes, sir. Not very well, but I know him. As a matter of fact, the last time I saw him we talked about you."

"What on earth about?"

I repeated an account similar to the one Jack Anderson had given Markham. Dodd listened and watched until I was through.

"I understand," he said casually, "that Anderson has got hold of some nonsensical story—something about General Klein giving Grace a Persian rug and buying champagne for Martha's wedding. Nothing to it, of course. Did he ask you about that?"

"No, he didn't," I answered. This time I was being truthful. For at that point Anderson and I had never discussed a rug and the champagne story was altogether new to me.

Dodd remained silent for a moment. Then, bending forward into the reddish light, he asked huskily, "Jim, do you think I'm a crook?"

"Why no, Mr. Dodd, of course not," I replied.

"Then that's all I have to hear. I accept your explanation fully, and I'll not raise the matter again. If you say it, it's enough for me," he declared, though a little too sweepingly for me to believe him.

"Now that that's cleared up," he continued, "I can get to what I really have in mind tonight. I'd like you to come back to work with

me. I'm getting rid of Gartland and all the deadwood. No room for
that any more. I know I've said this many times before, but I had to
accept certain things in my first term. I'm over that hump now. It will
be your staff, and I want it to be to your liking. This whole row between us has been a mess, and I take the blame for it because I'm
older and should know better. We were a good team. We had a good
operation. And at this stage of my career it's damned foolishness to
pull it all down and try to start from scratch again. I need you and I
want you to come back. What do you say?"

"Well, I'd like to be back with you, Mr. Dodd. I'm not after anyone's scalp there, but as you say there are things that would have to be
worked out, and I suppose that would take time."

"Yes, but not much," he said, with a wave of his hand. "A few weeks
at the most. Can we agree in principle then? You'll come back as
soon as proper arrangements can be made regarding staff, salaries,
and that sort of thing?"

"Yes, sir, I'll agree to that."

"Good!" he said, expansively. "That sets my heart at ease. I want
this for you as much as for me, you know. There are great days ahead
for us. We're just at the beginning really."

By September, I had been without income for four months, except
for unemployment compensation, which amounted to only about ten
percent of my former salary. By carefully measuring out the money I
had saved during my last months on Dodd's payroll, by selling my car
and borrowing from friends, I had managed to meet my family obligations. But I was now at the end of my resources. I had received a
court summons, preliminary to eviction for nonpayment of rent. I
was threatened with liens for late payment of taxes. I had received a
cutoff order from the phone company and a drawer full of legal
notices from collection agencies.

The candid advice I had gotten months before from the United
States Employment Agency had, not unexpectedly, proved prophetic.

"There are three potential groups of employers in Washington for a
person with your background, Mr. Boyd," said Mr. Wartholowitz, a
counselor at the professional employees office. "There is the Hill, the
executive agencies, and the lobbyists. Without Senator Dodd's approval, none of these groups will touch you. Why should they borrow
trouble? Now, I might be able to find someone who's hunting for a

bargain in damaged goods, if you don't mind the expression, someone who would pay about one-third of what you used to earn. But even that's doubtful and it's the only hope I can hold out to you. I'll keep trying, but if nothing turns up for you within two months, my advice is to leave town and give it a try somewhere else. I've run into cases like yours before."

The two months had long since come and gone, but I hung on in hope. Late in August, Jack Anderson learned of an opening in research and speech-writing on a House Public Works Subcommittee, headed by Congressman John Blatnik of Minnesota. Jack recommended me. I was interviewed for an hour by Mr. Blatnik, a straight-talking but cordial veteran of twenty years in Congress. I told him that I had had a personal falling out with Dodd and that he might give me a poor reference, but I left a thick folder of speeches and articles I had written. In the middle of September, Blatnik phoned and offered me the job. I accepted it, gratefully.

The thought of a new beginning, under such an appealing and respected figure as John Blatnik, seemed a magical deliverance. And during the same week I also got part-time work ghostwriting speeches for the newly created Equal Employment Opportunity Commission. My first effort evoked a favorable reaction, and thereafter I was assigned to the chairman, Franklin D. Roosevelt, Jr. Though I received only $150 per speech, I looked on this as another opportunity to return from oblivion. It would take a long time, I knew, to work back up to a level comparable to my old one with Dodd, but I had escaped, for the moment at least, the personal disaster that had for so long shadowed me. When Dodd sent word that he was ready to act on the agreement we had made at France's Restaurant, I could reply—quite honestly—that since I saw him I had made other commitments which I would have to honor.

Throughout the late summer and the autumn months of 1965, Marjorie, Terry, Michael, and I held regular evening and weekend "document sessions" at Jack Anderson's twelve-room house in a prosperous section of Bethesda, where he lived comfortably with his family of ten. We worked at the dining room table, the longest I have ever seen. Attired in old slippers and faded sportshirt, Jack presided. He had set up a filing system and, week-by-week, we relentlessly broke down the thousands of papers into his twenty-eight categories. Each night, Jack began methodically by distributing colored pencils and stacks of documents, and for hours we would plod away, classifying each paper and appending notes about its significance. Later in the evening, using my original memos as a base, Jack would lead us step-by-step over a particular incident, gathering together the relevant documents, while he furiously took notes in his self-taught shorthand. The smallest details were important. If a phone call was to be cited, we would locate it in the phone log and in the telephone bills that listed all long-distance calls. If a meeting played a part in any prospective revelation, we would find its date and time in the appointment schedules. Any trip, we would confirm through travel vouchers and airline tickets. In the case of a check or a bank deposit, Michael would get out his ledgers and give us the check number or the date and place of deposit.

At regular intervals, Jack would surfeit us with diet cola, candy bars, peanut brittle, and ice cream, the vices of a teetotaler, and we would work on into the night, often until one or two in the morning. If, around midnight, one of us suggested it was time to break up, Jack would pretend not to hear and would straightaway introduce a new subject for our scrutiny. It was a slow, tedious grind, but there was an undeniable fascination to it and, as the project came to dominate our lives more and more, we came to look forward to these meetings. They became our principal social activity.

Michael, with his detailed knowledge of Dodd's financial affairs, made signal contributions to our effort. Many a muddy transaction was clarified through his painstaking mastery of our voluminous store of ledgers, invoices, and vouchers. His explanation of Dodd's manipulation of travel expenses was particularly revealing, not because huge amounts were involved, but because of the pattern of deliberate fraud it demonstrated.

Whenever Dodd delivered a paid lecture, he would receive, in addition to his fee, the cost of his travel expenses. He developed a scheme for profiting from these travel reimbursements by having two different groups pay for the same expenses. For example, in February 1964, the American Medical Association's Political Action Committee paid him $2,000 for a speech and $739.80 for air fare to San Francisco and hotel accommodations. By billing his campaign committee in Hartford for the travel expenses, Dodd was able to pocket almost the entire $739.80 paid him by the AMA affiliate. Similar double billings were made for trips to Los Angeles; Bal Harbour, Florida; Claremont, California; Tyler, Texas; and Westerly, Rhode Island. Another variation of this pattern was to bill the United States Senate for the identical travel expenses already paid for by the group sponsoring Dodd's appearance. To do this, Dodd would carefully arrange for some subcommittee activity at the approximate time and place of his paid lecture. Then he would double bill his expenses. In this way, both the Senate and private sponsors paid Dodd the same air travel costs for trips to Philadelphia, West Palm Beach, San Francisco, Miami, Seattle, Tucson, and Los Angeles.

On these thirteen trips, Dodd made a personal profit of more than $4,000 on expense reimbursements.

In November 1965, we finally obtained a copy of Dodd's official campaign contributions and expenditures report for the 1964 election. Ironically, this was the last important document to come into our hands though it was the first we had sought a year before, when we were all in Dodd's employ. To get it, Jack Anderson had sent an associate, Robert Byrd, formerly of the *Baltimore Sun*, to Hartford, accompanied by his wife. Byrd posed as the representative of a publishing house making a national survey on campaign spending. He was told at the Secretary of State's office that there were no copies, nor was he allowed to have Dodd's report photocopied, though it was supposed to be a public document. But Byrd and his wife were not easily discouraged. For two days, they camped, morning and afternoon, in the Secretary of State's outer office, copying the original report by hand. It contained the names and alleged amounts of hundreds of contributors, as well as itemized expenditures ranging from $3.50 for the rental of a TV set up to $110,000 for advertising. But they got it all, and it was worth the effort.

We quickly established that not a penny of the $55,000 raised in November 1961, or the $13,000 raised in September 1963, or the $47,000 raised in October 1963, was listed in the report. Nor was there any supplementary report to cover the $80,000 raised in March 1965. We turned next to the listing of individual contributions. We did not have accurate records against which to measure Dodd's official entries, having failed in our effort to obtain them from Ed Sullivan a year before. But circumstance had fixed in our memory several large donations and we checked Dodd's report for these as a preliminary index of its honesty. We recalled, for instance, the $2,100 in cash which Robert Blinken had brought to Washington and, in Dodd's absence, had left with Marjorie; the $8,000 in cash from industrialist A. N. Spanel and associates, delivered after the election to Dodd by Irving Ferman, Spanel's Washington representative; and a $1,000 check from the Seafarer's International Union, which had been ceremoniously presented to Dodd and which three of us had seen. Not a single one of these test contributions was listed in Dodd's report. We knew, too, that at least $32,000 had been raised at the Labor-Management Dinner for Dodd in Bridgeport in October 1964, but the report listed only $16,000. If our partial recollection revealed these falsifications, what would an exhaustive official probe uncover? It did not escape our attention that the names of many of Dodd's biggest supporters as well as key members of the lobbyist corps which courted him were conspicuously absent from the lists.

Dodd's companion report on campaign expenditures we found equally distorted. We were unable at that time to undertake a complete item-by-item check, since it would have involved calling people who would run straight to Dodd, but a spot check, based on our own knowledge of the campaign and reenforced by our documents, identified numerous false entries. There was, for instance, an entry of $697.50 listed as payment to a Vincent Shields for "campaign photography." In fact, the payment was for photographs taken at the Dodd's thirtieth wedding anniversary party, which were presented to Mrs. Dodd, bound in white leather, as a memento. $5,560 was charged to the campaign for air travel. But we had ticket stubs and financial statements to show that most of this was paid to American Airlines for personal travel for Dodd and his family and that much of the amount was not even an expense at all, since Dodd had been reimbursed for it by either the government or private groups. The entire dining bill for Dodd and his family at the Senate Restaurant in Washington for the year 1964, a total of $1,458, was listed as a campaign expense under the heading "political meetings."

A claimed campaign expenditure of $8,500 to Edward Lockett for "preparation of campaign literature" masked a double duplicity. Lockett, an honest and legitimate writer, had contracted to ghost a book entitled *Subversives in America,* to be published in Dodd's name sometime in 1965. It was intended purely as a profit-making venture. Dodd had already signed a contract with MacFadden, the publishing house, and had received an initial advance of $2,000, which went into his personal bank account, minus ten percent for his agent, Donald MacCampbell. Instead of paying Lockett out of his personal funds, however, Dodd directed Ed Sullivan to pay him out of political funds. The book was not even completed when Dodd filed his campaign report. Yet, Dodd not only claimed the $8,500 paid to Lockett as a campaign expense, but he had, in making payment, used political contributions to bankroll a personal financial venture. As it happened, the book was later abandoned.

The falsifications were not limited to large items. An American Express dining card bill for $59 was paid by the campaign and charged off to "shipping material." A $57 heater Dodd had bought for his North Stonington home was listed as a campaign expense. So were the entertainment tabs run up by Dodd's children at the Congressional Country Club in Washington, the liquor he drank in his office, described euphemistically as "buffet luncheons," and the gasoline his family used throughout 1964, including purchases made by Mrs. Dodd in Nova Scotia and by his sons on trips from Rhode Island to California. $136 was listed as a payment to Jersey Airways for a campaign trip, but we had a document showing that Metromedia, Inc., had reimbursed Dodd for that expense.

Our study of the reports confirmed our previous estimate that Dodd had raised a quarter of a million dollars more than he had spent on campaigning. And on this enormous sum he had paid no income tax.

By December 1965, the story that lay behind the thousands of papers and the hundreds of pages of notes in Jack Anderson's safe had been almost assimilated. There was some investigating to do and some people to question, but that was to be the job of Anderson, who planned to act at the last possible moment before the publication of each story. The element of surprise, he said, was crucial in flushing admissions out of people. "If I catch them unawares and flash enough facts to convince them I know the whole story anyway, there's a fifty-fifty chance they'll blurt the whole thing. But if they've been forewarned, or given time to prepare an alibi, I usually can't get a word out of them."

It was decided that publication of the Dodd columns would not commence until the distractions of the year-end holidays were over, when Congress had returned from adjournment and settled down for the long session ahead. January 24th was designated as D-Day. As that date slowly approached, an almost unendurable feeling of expectation, tinged painfully with anxiety, began to build up. That the secret labors of so many months were soon to burst upon the public scene both thrilled and disturbed us. After the revelations, reprisals would surely follow, and each of us wondered what shape they would take and what their impact would be.

Michael O'Hare's position was particularly vulnerable, for he was between jobs. His original intent had been to make his break with Dodd's office immediately after turning over the financial records. But his inside post was so valuable to us that he agreed to stay on for as long as possible. For months he lived in daily expectation of exposure by Dodd. In November and December he tried to extricate himself, writing formal letters of resignation. Dodd disregarded the letters and forcefully pressed Michael to remain "for a few more weeks." To avoid arousing Dodd's suspicions, Michael stayed on tentatively. By January, he could wait no longer. He stopped going into the office and began looking for another job. But he had allowed insufficient time to locate and entrench himself elsewhere and, as D-Day approached, he faced the unlikely prospect of seeking work at the very moment that his role in the Dodd case was being revealed to every employer in town. He did not ask for a postponement in our publication timetable, however. It had been delayed long enough, he felt, and he would take his chances.

Several days before the scheduled appearance of the first column, Carl Perian observed a restiveness in Dodd, as though he sensed that something was amiss. He was preparing to leave for a long weekend in Connecticut, but he seemed reluctant to go. He appeared to be plagued by an uneasiness that he had to assuage before beginning his holiday.

"What's Jim Boyd doing these days?" Dodd asked Carl. "He must be bored stiff with highways and sewers by now." He then authorized Carl to offer me a position with the Juvenile Delinquency Subcommittee, with the understanding that I would work for Dodd part of the time and after a few months would transfer back to my old job in his office. Had his antenna picked up danger signals again, or was it a genuine attempt at a reconciliation? I would never know.

On Friday night, January 21st, the Senator called Carl from his Connecticut home. Carl told him of a long and pleasant chat he had had with me. He said I was thinking over the job offer and seemed quite favorably disposed. The information relaxed the Senator, who waxed unusually complimentary.

"You're a good man, Carl," he said. Then turning to a little squabble of personalities on the Juvenile Delinquency staff that Carl had managed to smooth over, "It's good to have our own staff psychiatrist. I don't have any trouble sleeping nights, but if I ever do, I'll know who to call on."

On January 24th, the first column on Dodd appeared in most of the 635 newspapers that carry Drew Pearson's "Washington Merry-Go-Round." Dodd began the day casually at Laurel Glen, unaware that it was to mark a watershed in his life. When edgy, Dodd often called his office at exactly nine, to catch those who were late for work; today he called at nine-thirty in an affable mood. Fascinated as always by weather phenomena, he graphically described a snowstorm that had enveloped much of New England the previous night. He canceled a noon luncheon appointment with Assistant Attorney General Ramsey Clark and announced that he and Grace would "wend our way leisurely" to Washington by car and that he would check in with the office en route. A half hour later, the Washington office received an alarmed call from Waterbury, Connecticut.

"Have you read the Drew Pearson blast on Dodd in this morning's paper?" asked Mayor Joe McNellis, a staunch Dodd ally.

"The *Washington Post* doesn't have anything about the Senator," replied Milton Wernstrom.

"Well, the *Waterbury Republican* does," said McNellis, "and it's not good." The entire Pearson column then was dictated over the phone to a Dodd secretary.

Early in the afternoon Dodd called in again from a phone booth along the New Jersey Turnpike. David Martin was waiting and commenced to read, in his stentorian tones, the full Pearson piece. "This column has uncovered correspondence between Senator Tom Dodd, the Nuremberg prosecutor, and Julius Klein, the West German agent, showing how Dodd has worked behind the scenes to promote West German interests," Martin began. Dodd, normally impatient with David's sometimes protracted declamations, listened without interruption until the final disturbing sentence: "Startling facts, that were successfully hidden from the Senate investigators, will be revealed soon in another installment of the curious Dodd-Klein story."

Dodd now hurried toward Washington along the sixty-mile-an-hour turnpike. When he reached the Baltimore area, he called the office to say that he would go straight home and that he wanted to talk to Jim Markham as soon as he got there. "Tell Markham it's an emergency," he said.

For the moment most of Washington was ignorant of the newest scandal, for the *Washington Post* had suppressed the Pearson column that morning. It was a surprise omen that we read with some foreboding. In the afternoon, Drew Pearson conferred with the editors of the *Post*. Why had they pulled his column that morning? They said frankly that they had reservations about its accuracy and were concerned over Pearson's plan to publish a whole series on Dodd. They had frequently received complaints of misstatements of fact in the Pearson column, they said, and to publish charges against Dodd day after day might expose the *Post* to costly libel action, since sustained attack might be taken as evidence of malicious intent. Pearson patiently explained the scope of the Dodd project, said that he regarded it as one of the major scandals of his entire experience, and vowed that he could personally vouch for the massive documentation on which it was based. He reminded the *Post* editors that they had hammered away at Bobby Baker day after day for many weeks and argued that the Dodd story was far more significant to the nation. In the end, the *Post* agreed to print the columns, but reserved its prerogative to edit out portions to which it objected. In the days to come occasional surgery was performed, but in the main the Dodd revelations were printed by the *Post* and thus reached official Washington, our most important single audience.

With publication under way, we promptly undertook Phase Two of our plan—the briefing of key officials. Marjorie and I felt that the President himself should be informed, for Dodd would be sure to importune the White House to intervene in his behalf. Unless the President knew something of the extent and validity of the charges, we reasoned, he might, out of loyalty to an old friend, try to help Dodd and thus implicate himself and the Democratic party. To approach the President, however, entailed the risk of having our own roles prematurely revealed. It might set off a chain reaction that could harm us and set back our cause. But it was a risk that had to be taken, we decided, and we asked Marjorie's boss, Berl Bernhard, who had performed several missions for the President and was an intimate of the White House staff, to be the bearer of the bad news. Marjorie told Bernhard the major aspects of the Dodd story and the source of the information in the hands of Pearson and Anderson. She did not tell him the exact nature of her involvement, and he studiously avoided asking her.

At eight-thirty the following morning, January 26th, Bernhard called at the White House. Thirty minutes later, the President was briefed by an aide. It was an unusually busy day, even for the President. Earlier, he had personally briefed twenty Congressional leaders about the war in Southeast Asia. In an hour he was to unveil to the public his six-billion-dollar program to renovate the nation's slums. And he was in the final hours of his decision on whether to end the month-old moratorium on the bombing of North Vietnam. But he took the time to investigate thoroughly our advance intelligence on Dodd. In contrast to those who would scoff, even after two dozen Pearson columns had appeared, Johnson immediately perceived it as an explosive matter. He asked for more information, firing incisive questions, some of which had to be referred back to Marjorie and me for details: Will this cause us to lose any Administration legislation? Does the exposé involve government contracts, bribery, tax violations? Are there inside informants, confidential records, extensive material? Who uncovered the story—Pearson or Anderson? He asked, too, if his appearances at Dodd's fund-raising affairs could be used as a pretext for dragging his name into the scandal—and we passed back the word that Ivan Sinclair, a former Johnson aide, had made the proper inquiries in Johnson's behalf about the purposes of the fund-raising and was assured that the money was to be used for campaign purposes.* The President's questions were all that we ever learned of his reaction, except that he sent thanks to Bernhard for our information. (Later, we learned from White House reporters that from the time of our warning, the Presidential door was closed to Tom Dodd.) Bernhard, now fully aware of the dimensions of our effort, urged caution.

At about the same time, Jack Anderson went to see the Senate Majority Leader, Mike Mansfield, and told him he was just at the beginning of extensive revelations about Dodd that would pose for Congress a major ethical challenge. Anderson outlined the shape of the story to come, said he would soon begin pressing publicly for a Senate investigation and cautioned that it would be a calamity if there was a repetition of the failure that had marked the Rules Committee's probe of Bobby Baker. Mansfield replied that if the facts were as An-

---

* It was I to whom Sinclair had telephoned and who informed him, on Dodd's instruction, that the dinner was for campaign purposes. During the Ethics Committee investigation of Dodd, he signed an affidavit in which he confirmed this story. But curiously, in testimony he personally gave to the committee six weeks later, he insisted that he did not recall such an inquiry at all and had signed the affidavit without understanding its true significance.

derson stated them to be, he would use what influence he had to see to it that the Senate met its responsibilities. He expressed complete confidence in the newly formed Ethics Committee, but added, "It's up to you to make out the case and create the climate for action. If you do, I can tell you the Senate will respond."

John M. Bailey was briefed too. He was interested, but neither surprised nor alarmed. With eyeglasses resting back on his forehead, his face immobile except when he shifted his cigar from one side to the other, he listened with the passive skepticism of one who has seen many attempted coups misfire. He had figured that Dodd would get into trouble sooner or later, he said, because he knew the crowd that hung around him, but he was not convinced that the story would ever really get off the ground. Bailey possessed an instinct for assessing political trouble; it was said he could measure at once the meaning of every obituary column in the Connecticut papers on the clashing ambitions of the host of office-seekers within his domain. But if he was already calculating the impact of an unexpected Senate vacancy, he did not show it. "If it gets off the ground at all," he said cheerfully, "it will be a minor embarrassment, but it won't do us any real damage. Tommy has always been an off-horse, always at odds with the organization. The Republicans won't be able to hang him around our necks. But don't write him off. He's a master at exploiting tough situations, and he's got the greatest luck of anyone I ever saw."

After four or five columns had appeared, Jack Anderson called J. Edgar Hoover's deputy, Cartha "Deke" DeLoach, and told him that he had information of criminal misconduct by Dodd, that he was requesting an F.B.I. investigation, and that he had thousands of documents and several witnesses to make available to the bureau. DeLoach said that Mr. Hoover would have a letter incorporating Anderson's charges drafted and sent to the Attorney General. The F.B.I., he explained, could not investigate a United States Senator without explicit direction from the Attorney General.

In the meantime, Drew Pearson demanded an investigation by the Senate Ethics Committee over his weekly radio broadcast, carried by more than one hundred stations. A day or two later, Committee Chairman John Stennis of Mississippi was quoted in the press as saying that there were no charges properly before the committee on which it could act, whereupon Anderson sent him a formal request for an investigation, specifying charges and offering to furnish full documentation as well as a list of witnesses who would willingly testify. But Stennis did not respond.

In seven weeks, from January 24th to the middle of March, seventeen Pearson-Anderson articles on Dodd were published in newspapers having a combined daily circulation of fifty million. In addition, several Pearson radio broadcasts carried an account of Dodd's activities into millions more homes.

The first articles spotlighted Senator Dodd's global errand-running for Julius Klein, the free-spending lobbyist for West German interests. Subsequent columns and broadcasts, laced with incriminating data from Dodd's files including extracts from his financial ledgers and income-tax returns, told in rapid sequence how Dodd profited financially from his anti-Communism. They described the fleet of airplanes and automobiles provided him by firms which either sought his help in obtaining government contracts or which came under the investigative jurisdiction of one of his committees. They itemized the cash and valuable gifts he regularly accepted from people who sought and obtained his help in obtaining appointments to government posts. Finally, they sketched the story of Dodd's massive personal enrichment from the diversion of political contributions.

The first seventeen columns were the opening phase of the Pearson-Anderson campaign. They quickly became a major conversation piece on the Capitol cocktail circuit. Riding the bus to work down Connecticut Avenue each morning, Marjorie noted with satisfaction that most newspapers were turned to the Pearson page. But January passed into February and February into March, and there was still no measurable official reaction.

How was Dodd reacting, we wondered as the exposé began. With Michael no longer in Dodd's office, we had no sure way of keeping up with the Senator's daily moves. From Carl Perian, who saw the Senator frequently and was sometimes employed by him as an emissary to me, I got periodic glimpses of Dodd. And we still had friends on another fringe of the Dodd operation. Glenn Cooper, a researcher in the office, and a part-time secretary there, kept Michael informed of all they saw and heard. They knew little about our enterprise, but they seemed sympathetic to its objective and wanted to play a part. Our information was more fragmentary and less reliable than it had been, but it enabled us, nevertheless, to maintain the measure of the adversary.

I had begun to keep a diary, into which I painstakingly copied every event and every snatch of conversation from Dodd's office. Its pages revealed Dodd in crisis—besieged, canny, preposterous, angry, and at times, pathetic, but always formidable. I had long known Tom Dodd as a man who found release and joy in combat. Restraint had never been among his virtues. When attacked on policy matters or slighted in personal affairs, he would compulsively mount a ferocious riposte, and he seemed to relish it. His office staff had once had an inside joke to the effect that the Senator could not be disturbed at the moment because he was busy preparing replies to attacks that had not yet been made.

Now Dodd was in the gravest dilemma of his life. In the beginning, he was necessarily ignorant of how much Anderson knew—was it a few embarrassing scraps that he could ride out, or was it the mother lode? A check of his files showed that everything was in place and, at first, Dodd could hope that the barrage involved only the Klein relationship, a relatively minor facet of the story, and would soon end. He sent word to Anderson that he would be glad to give him an interview when the "series" was over, and he inquired when that would be. Though eager to interview Dodd, Anderson was noncommittal about the termination date and to avoid any commitment he referred vaguely to "new information coming in." Anderson was determined to be at least as canny as Dodd.

From all over, Dodd was getting letters from critics who denounced him and from supporters who asked why he didn't defend himself. But what could he do? A public defense on the floor of the Senate? A press conference? These were luxuries reserved for those who dared to submit to questioning. He could not disprove the charges against him. At best, he could dwell on an occasional minor error, but that would be small satisfaction. To respond to Pearson at all would only draw attention to the scandal and put it on the front page. Dodd's silence was rightly calculated, for Pearson and Anderson were counting on his well-known temper to escalate the affair. But to take it lying down, day after day, was an ordeal for which Dodd was poorly constructed. To act was for him an imperative. For a time he found a substitute for active public defense in small intrigues and marathon war councils.

His counselors included Thomas G. Corcoran, "Tommy The Cork" of the Roosevelt brain trust, now one of Washington's most successful lobbyists; Carmen Belino, a political troubleshooter for the Kennedy family; U.S. Court of Appeals Judge Irving Kaufman of New York, who in happier days had introduced Klein to Dodd; Judge Paul McNamara, a Connecticut political ally; and Senator Russell Long, the Assistant Majority Leader, who frightened as much as reassured Dodd when he said, only half in humor, "I'll support you all the way on this, Tom, even if you're guilty." And there was the evening cabinet, too, now enlarged by the arrival of one Bill McCue, an old friend and land developer from New Britain.

David Martin, though he recognized Dodd's vulnerability on some points, was convinced that the attack was, in the main, part of a worldwide Communist conspiracy against what he called "liberal anti-Communists." He urged that Dodd take the Senate floor immediately to offer a point-by-point rebuttal. But from all other quarters, Dodd was advised to continue to say nothing, make no defense, force Pearson to carry the whole load. He received encouragement from his fellow Senators, who reminded him that in the past more than thirty Senators had publicly denounced Pearson and that no less than three Presidents had called him a liar. "We're all with you," wrote Senator Birch Bayh, "on this yellow attack by Pearson."

Since the preponderance of advice jibed with his own instincts, Dodd decided to follow it for the time being. But he was by nature distrustful of the opinions of other men, even though some inner insecurity habitually drove him to consult about his problems with almost everyone with whom he came in contact. When too many agreed with him, he generally began to worry, a reaction which must have been strengthened when he received counsel from Jim Gartland. "I've told Tom there's nothing he can do about it," Gartland told Glenn Cooper. "I told him he's got to let it roll off, just like water off a duck's back. Tom is just like me, an honest man, and an honest man has nothing to fear because he can't be hurt."

While waiting for Pearson's offense to subside, Dodd launched an intensive grilling of his staff, which went on day after day and brought the normal operations of the office to a standstill. I was the leading suspect, but now no one was free of suspicion and from day to day the onus shifted—to O'Hare, to Zeiller, to Marjorie, even to a former legislative aide named John McEvoy who long before had come and gone. While trying to nail down who did what, Dodd made emergency efforts to mollify his tormentors. His approach to me was multiple and perhaps significant, for it revealed his conception of how men can be moved, even in the midst of hostilities.

On January 26th, two days after the first Pearson column, Dodd conducted a series of interviews in his office with people he knew were my friends. He talked to Chuck Hamel, a former aide, Carl Perian, and Michael O'Hare, each of whom called me after leaving the office. Dodd had not specifically asked them to, but they are recognized from his tone that he expected them to relate the conversations to me.

The word from Chuck Hamel was direct and simple: All Dodd's sources of information had assured him that I was behind the Pearson columns. I had no reason to be against him, Dodd said, because he felt kindly toward me and had always tried to help me. I still had time to "get off the hook" by calling off the attacks. If I didn't, I would be in serious trouble with the law; and if Dodd became angered, he could take my job away "by picking up the telephone."

Carl's message was less a threat, more a bribe. The Senator was still anxious to have me return to his staff on the terms he had offered the week before, but of course this would not be possible if I was conspiring against him.

An altogether different approach was conveyed by Michael. "I am in trouble, Mike, terrible trouble, and I know you'll help me," Dodd began. "I don't care for myself about these Pearson articles, but they're killing Grace. She has a form of heart trouble, you know, very serious. I've borne this in silence up to now. Not even the children know, although they must have noticed something. Only extraordinary care can save her, but these Pearson articles have so upset her that she no longer responds to treatment. She looks terrible. Her complexion is gone. There's no life left in her, and you know how lively Grace used to be. You wouldn't recognize her. Regardless of how this Pearson thing got started, I know that Jim Boyd is not aware of the damage it is doing to my family. I don't think he's that down on me. I know you'll help me, Mike."

While the Senator was making this appeal to Michael, Mrs. Dodd was attending a social affair sponsored by the Congressional Wives Club, as we learned the following morning when she appeared, looking chic and quite fit, in a photograph on the society page of the *Washington Post*.

Dodd thought the story about Grace was particularly effective, and he spread it around town. Senator Symington of Missouri was moved by it and told a group of Senators who were discussing what to do about Dodd that the Pearson articles had already put Mrs. Dodd in the hospital.

Terry Golden, who had obtained a position as secretary to Judge David Bazelon of the United States Court of Appeals, obtained a variation of the story firsthand. Judge Bazelon phoned Dodd one morning to congratulate him on a crime study released by the Juvenile Delinquency Subcommittee. Dodd seemed in low spirits and when Bazelon asked him what was wrong, he replied that Grace was in the hospital, her health broken by Pearson's scurrilous attacks. The Judge was moved and instructed Terry to send flowers to Mrs. Dodd. When Terry called Doreen Moloney in Dodd's office to find out which hospital was treating Mrs. Dodd, there was a long pause. Then Doreen returned to the telephone with the explanation that it wasn't Mrs. Dodd who was in the hospital but the Senator's son Christopher, and that Mrs. Dodd was there looking after him. "I'm sure Judge Bazelon will want to send flowers to Christopher then," Terry said, sensing a ruse. "Which hospital is *he* in?" There was another long pause, while Doreen went for further instructions. "There's been some confusion," she said at length. "It seems that neither Mrs. Dodd nor Christopher is in the hospital. Christopher is at the farm in North Stonington. He's not feeling well and Mrs. Dodd has gone up there to look after him."

To Anderson, Dodd sent a roundabout message that *he* was dying. Jim Markham passed this word to his friend, Irving Davidson, to deliver to Jack. "Dodd's got only a little while left," Anderson was told, "maybe a few weeks, maybe a couple of months. His weight has dropped off to nothing and he's developed a nervous twitch. Markham feels that if you realize that he's on the way out anyway, you're not the kind of a fellow to hound him to a premature death."

"If we thought he was dying, we would stop the columns," Anderson replied. "But I don't believe him. I can't believe him. He's cried 'wolf' too many times. First it was his wife, then she turned up in the pink. Now *he's* at death's door. I just don't trust him."

In the past Dodd had usually been successful in playing upon people's sympathies. It had begun working when he was a boy, the baby of a family which included four indulgent older sisters. For years pretended illnesses had explained away his broken appointments, his frequent absences from duty, his drinking. He had learned to make the role of the underdog serve him well. "In politics," he often said, "there's nothing better than being the victim of an outrage." But the old tricks were not working now.

As the columns continued to appear, breaking fresh ground each week, Dodd became overwhelmed with a morose and despairing self-pity. Carl, the sympathetic listener, was called frequently to Dodd's office to sit with him.

"You have no idea how unfounded all this is, Carl. A fellow calls me up and says, 'Tom, I know you've devoted your life to public service and haven't got any money. The demands of public life must be hard on you. Let me loan you a car to make things easier.' So I let him. What's the matter with that? And look what they do to me. Before long they'll be investigating who gives you a stick of chewing gum—if you happen to be an anti-Communist that is." The proposition that he was being persecuted for trivialities because he was a danger-ous enemy of Communism soon became a cardinal tenet of Dodd's defense.

At other times he would be preoccupied with the theme of betrayal. He would stalk around his office, a man at bay. "Boyd is a mad dog, a savage, a literal savage. After all I did for him, this is my reward. It's unnatural, his hatred is unnatural. I couldn't be like that. And look at Mike O'Hare. O'Hare is an Irish rat, and there's nothing lower than that. Irishmen, you know, can be very good or very bad. All these years I thought O'Hare was a good one. I took him in off the street, just a threadbare lad, a starveling. I felt sorry for him. I bought clothes for him, brought him along, gave him a good salary, a career. I had him in my home. Think of it! At the very table with Grace and me! And after all this he turned on me, like the Irish rat he is."

When two or three days would pass without a Pearson attack, he would revive and brighten with the righteous glow of vindication. But when a new blast sounded, he would as suddenly redescend into the blackest depths.

"I know beyond a doubt who it is now," he said to Carl one afternoon. "Boyd, that Carpenter bitch, the Rat, and Golden. They've turned me over to my enemies. Sure I took the plane rides, what of it? But they twist everything. They're disfiguring my image. They're going to destroy me. And there's no hope. We've seen only the first wave of a massive attack. The entire history of the Senate shows no precedent for this.

"Now I know what it must have felt like to be in a concentration camp. The rats have been nibbling away at my feet, and now it's my ankles. Before long, it will be my whole leg. And there's nothing I can do except wait for slow destruction. Nothing like this has ever happened before, Carl. Mad, mad dogs."

He rejected all attempts at consolation and commenced to sob quietly, his shoulders shaking. "Death is a precious gift," he began again, when he had recovered. "Some men are lucky. At the moment of stress a heart attack takes them away. But I won't be so fortunate. I'm too strong. I'll have to swallow the whole bitter dose, down to the dregs. I've done nothing that all the others don't do, but the worst defense in the world is 'you did it, too.' No, I am helpless before their insatiable appetite for my blood. Everyone else is getting off, but I have to go through this hell alone. It will be unending, and nothing can be done."

So pitiable and bereft of hope was the picture Dodd conveyed that Carl, though steeled for these performances, found that he, too, was reduced to uncontrollable tears. Later, when Carl, with his gift of near total recall, told me of that conversation, it was obvious that he was still filled with sympathy for Dodd.

It was Dodd's nature to suffer reverses more acutely and demonstrably than other men, but he was too tough and too resilient to remain in abject despondency for very long. Even as he proclaimed ruin he was formulating a new offensive. The policy of "no comment" had become untenable. It might have worked had the Pearson onslaught petered out after a couple of weeks. But the attacks persisted and were spreading into new areas. Over the protests of most of his advisors, Dodd decided that he must put a better face on things before he found his protracted silence judged irrevocably an admission of guilt.

A Pearson story about Dodd's acceptance of the Dunbar automobile had been picked up in Connecticut and, for the first time, Dodd was approached by the local press for comment. Asked by the *Hartford Times* if he had arranged appointments with government agencies for David Dunbar, Dodd said, "I never did it. Someone in my office may have. I don't know."

It was an inept remark. We had memoranda showing that Dunbar had discussed his problems with Dodd personally, that Dodd had instructed Gerry Zeiller to make the necessary appointments, and that Zeiller had reported to Dodd faithfully on the progress of Dunbar's bids for transportation contracts, receiving Dodd's approval every step of the way. But Dodd's comment was nevertheless significant, for it was the first public indication of what was to become a consistent element of his defense. *He* had not done the things charged to him; if they had been done at all, *his staff* had done them without his knowledge.*

The new policy unfolded further when Dodd quietly requested J. Edgar Hoover to investigate the theft of documents from his office. That was the first step in a studied campaign to divert attention from the scandal itself and fix it on the lawlessness and treachery of the accusers. Dodd also offered to turn over to the F.B.I. his files on the Julius Klein matter for evaluation of the Pearson-Anderson allegations. And in a letter to Senator Stennis, he privately offered his Klein files to the Ethics Committee, asserted that his relationship with Klein was blameless, and requested an investigation of it. If investigations into his affairs were ever undertaken, Dodd could claim that *he* had initiated them as a means of clearing himself of false charges, and that he was actively cooperating with the F.B.I. and the committee as they proceeded to expose the frauds perpetrated against him.

Thus far these moves had been unpublicized, as Dodd held on to his options. But on February 24th, an unforeseen event forced an acceleration of the timetable. Freshman Congressman Joseph Resnick of New York rose on the floor of the House of Representatives to make a prepared speech. Resnick intended to condemn ethical laxity in the Congress and to cite the Pearson-Anderson articles on Dodd as proof of the need for a new code of Congressional conduct. At the first mention of Dodd's name, however, he was gaveled down by House Speaker John McCormack, Dodd's good friend, on the grounds that he had broken the rules of the Club by speaking ill of a member. But Resnick, whose eye for an issue and whose disdain for restrictive tradition were, ironically, reminiscent of the early Dodd, had taken the precaution of distributing advance copies of his talk to the press. The

---

* Later, when Dodd came under attack for having received double reimbursement for travel, he blamed it on the faulty bookkeeping of a "deceitful employee," Michael O'Hare. When he was charged with not having reported the $2,100 cash contribution which Robert Blinken had delivered to Marjorie, he maintained for a time that Marjorie had kept the money and had never turned it over to him. Confronted with widespread irregularities in connection with his payroll, Dodd blamed me, to whom he said he had delegated complete authority over such things. When his income-tax treatment of $6,000 he had borrowed from political-dinner funds was questioned, he charged the C.P.A. who prepared his tax returns with making a clumsy mistake. And the myriad discrepancies found in his official campaign reports he attributed to the incompetence and inexperience of his campaign associates. He had had nothing to do with any of it himself, he contended.

story broke immediately, its news value enhanced because Resnick had been silenced. Pursued by newsmen for comment, Dodd issued a statement:

> Because I have absolutely nothing to conceal in the matter, I wrote to Mr. J. Edgar Hoover . . . asking that the F.B.I. investigate the charges made against me by Pearson and Anderson and offering to turn over my files to them. I have also written to Senator John Stennis, Chairman of the Senate Committee on Ethics, offering to turn my complete files over to the Committee.

"Dodd Calls for Probe" read the headlines the next morning, upstaging Resnick's charges. Dodd's advisors complained that he had made a major mistake. He had put the Pearson vendetta on the front page and had added to the mounting pressures for an official inquiry. "Never ask for an investigation, you might get one," remonstrated evening advisor John O'Keefe. Jack Anderson was delighted. "Dodd fell for it," he said. It was the response he had hoped for when he had shown the Dodd-Klein files to a Resnick aide.

Yet, my own reaction was to see an element of sagacity in Dodd's move. He had reached the point where he must come out of hiding or lose by default all appearance of honor—and then he would really be fair game for snipers. He knew that the clamor from Pearson for an official investigation, now spreading to Congress itself, could not much longer be resisted by a committee called into being for that very purpose. It would look far better for him to request an investigation than to have one imposed upon him as though he were a defendant.

What had he lost? In offering his files he had given away nothing and had laid the basis for a profitable hoax. His offer, without his saying so explicitly, was limited to the Klein files, which Anderson had already given to the F.B.I. and had proffered to the committee. The most damaging portions had appeared in print a month before. From the time of his offer, Dodd, while stoutly refusing to surrender his papers on a dozen other topics, could repeat at every provocation, "I have turned over my files in toto," and present a reassuring image of forthrightness.

Requesting an F.B.I. investigation was also a hazardless gesture, one designed to inspire confidence while covering silence. As an old F.B.I. man, Dodd knew that the bureau never makes findings of guilt or innocence and does not make public the results of its investigations.

Only in the unthinkable event that he, a United States Senator, was tried in court, would F.B.I. evidence emerge from secrecy. And if things ever reached that unlikely stage, the jig would be up anyway, and it wouldn't matter what his strategy was.

The Ethics Committee was a less predictable quantity. If it operated like the Rules Committee, which had investigated Bobby Baker, he had no worries. After all, many other Senators were involved with Klein. It was reasonable to believe that after the committee had seen Dodd's file on Klein, which named these Senators, it would probably shy away from a formal investigation. Even if it decided on a probe, Dodd could count on several months of elbowroom while the committee inquired in private. And he would far rather have the matter localized in the hands of his friends and colleagues who would be mindful of his privileges as a peer, than to have it spread wildly like napalm as it was fought out in the press.

For the foreseeable future, Dodd had forestalled a major inquisition and stilled public discussion. The press would wait to see what the committee decided. Dodd had struck on a formula which would permit him to refuse righteously all questions from newsmen, while posing as the outraged victim of yellow journalism. "I have asked the F.B.I. to investigate the false charges made against me," he would now say at every challenge. "I have asked the Ethics Committee to investigate. I have offered my files. What more can I do? Having asked for these investigations, I think it would be unfair to the committee and to the F.B.I. if I impeded their work by making public comments on the matter. That's all I have to say."

But what was Connecticut thinking? That, Dodd told his staff, was his main concern. The Connecticut press had been all but silent on the case. Pearson's outlets in Connecticut were few. The public there knew few of the details that were available to the rest of the country —a circumstance which had given Dodd considerable freedom to maneuver. But among the state's politicians, whose business it is to be fully informed on such things, Dodd was the chief topic of conversation. The scandal buzzed through the halls of the State House.

Resnick's blast and Dodd's counterstroke had been made on the eve of the annual Jefferson-Jackson Dinner in Hartford, a $100-a-plate conclave of party functionaries that constituted, in effect, the Democratic party of Connecticut. The dinner posed an important decision for Dodd. If he ducked it, he would show weakness under fire. But by attending it, he exposed himself to foe as well as friend and risked a hostile reaction. Some of his counselors cautioned him against going. They argued that much of the party organization had always been against him and might jump at the chance to embarrass him. One of the gimmicks associated with the dinner, they reminded him, was the so-called applause meter, by which newsmen judged the relative standing of the state's top Democrats. In his past battles with Bowles, Benton, and Bailey, Dodd had used this to advantage, but a bad reaction now might be seized upon by the heretofore quiescent press as a reason for airing the whole Pearson business.

Beyond the political considerations were the personal. Dodd was a proud man. To submit himself, at this vulnerable moment, to the rump judgment of a mob of hack politicians would be intrinsically humiliating. Characteristically, he withheld his decision until the last moment; then decided to go. He knew the Democrats of Connecticut, he said; they wouldn't let him down.

On the night of February 26, 1966, Hartford's Statler Hilton Hotel was jammed with a jubilant throng of more than two thousand prospering politicos. There was good reason for the expansive smile that wreathed the features of John M. Bailey, the perennial toastmaster, as he looked out on the festive host that had overflowed the main ballroom and spilled over into adjoining banquet halls. This was Bailey's annual command performance, through which he financed the operations of the Democratic State Committee. The attendance was an index of his organization's strength.

Bailey was fond of reminding the party faithful that when he had first taken up the reins two decades ago, a sparse hundred or two would turn out for these dinners, half-filling the small banquet room of the old Bond Hotel. And he liked to speak of the dismal head table of those days, graced by an assortment of machine politicians of the lower cut whose presence did more to advertise than to hide the dearth of major Democratic office holders in Connecticut. But the dinners had grown so successful that now even the Statler Hilton could not accommodate them; and the glittering eighty-foot head table was crowded elbow to elbow with the foremost personages of the state— the Governor, all the state's Senators and Congressmen, the leaders of both houses of the legislature, the mayors of the major cities. Here was gaudy testimony to his stewardship as party leader.

As the affair began, the place reserved for Dodd, to the left of the principal speaker, Senator Edward Kennedy, was empty. Dodd had not appeared for the traditional picture-taking ceremonies before the dinner when the galaxy of Democratic stars posed together for the next day's newspapers. Some were beginning to doubt that he would show at all. Then he was spotted, a bit pale and apprehensive, moving quietly toward his seat. A round of applause greeted his appearance, and he brightened perceptibly. An hour later, when his turn came to speak, he stood solemn and motionless at the lectern as the din, normally irrepressible, subsided into a hushed, expectant silence.

"You all know me pretty well," Dodd began. "I've done the best I know how for you and the people of Connecticut. Unfortunately for me, some people on my staff robbed my files and turned them over to a newspaperman who has distorted them with half-truths. There has been a relentless and vigorous assault on me. This is not an easy thing to go through—it's not easy to take the darts and swords of the enemy."

His voice, a bit thin at the start, was gaining in resonance and authority. His gaze, downward when he commenced, measured his rapt audience from end to end. Gradually his countenance lifted.

"It was Harry Truman who said that if you can't stand the heat, then don't stay in the kitchen. I have no intention of leaving the kitchen because of these lies and distortions. I am not about to turn in my chips.

"There was another man in public life who said 'Don't ever explain.' But I *believe in* explaining. You needn't worry about me letting you down. I'll be around when the truth is known, and you'll have no reason to be ashamed of me. All I ask of you is that you give me a chance to demonstrate to you that I'm the same person I've always been."

As he turned away from the microphone, applause began, punctuated by shouts of "We're with you, Tom!" It continued to mount as Dodd took his seat. People began standing here and there and in a moment the entire gathering was on its feet in a mighty ovation that rolled on and on. When it finally died away, toastmaster Bailey approached the microphone and, turning to Dodd, said, "Tom, I think you got your answer from this crowd tonight."

For Dodd, that night in Hartford was a turning point. From then on he fought us with all the tenacious resourcefulness I had long known he possessed. He returned to Washington in a bullish mood. His difficult decisions of the past fortnight had all turned out right, as was demonstrated by editorial reaction, which widely credited him with having acted forthrightly and honorably to clear his name. "The only time I ever get into trouble," he was fond of saying, "is when I stop following my own instincts and start listening to other people."

Dodd now began his counterattack in earnest, as I learned when my phone rang one afternoon in early March.

"Hello, this is Sarah McClendon," said a pleasant voice. I immediately recognized the Texas twang of the lady reporter whose provocative questions had enlivened so many of President Kennedy's press conferences. But I was hardly prepared for what was to come.

"Are you the James Boyd who was discovered by Senator Dodd on his office divan with a young secretary, in a highly compromising position? And did you . . ."

"Whoa!" I interrupted. "Give me a chance to catch my breath. The answer so far is 'no.' But would you mind telling me, if it would not appear boastful of me to ask, what particular secretary you're talking about, just in case I've overlooked someone?"

Miss McClendon began laughing. "Well, Mr. Boyd, I'm just checking a story. Senator Dodd has told people on the Ethics Committee and a lot of other folks around here that one stormy afternoon last winter a plane he was supposed to take from National Airport was canceled, and when he returned unexpectedly to his office, he found you and a Miss Carpenter cavorting in his office in the altogether. He says he fired you both on the spot and ordered you out, and that while you were getting yourselves rearranged, the airport called saying that Dodd's plane was leaving right away. So he rushed back, and after he left, you and Miss Carpenter pilfered his files and went to Jack Anderson with them. Do you have any comment on that?"

"Well, I hesitate to explode such a good story," I said, "but the day Miss Carpenter and I were fired is a matter of public record—December 7, 1964. It was a beautiful, sunny, cloudless afternoon, and Senator Dodd was here in Washington all that day and for the next two days. He hired me back the next day. And really, Miss McClendon, in a big office like that with people coming in and out all the time, you can't . . ."

"All right, I believe you," she said. "I never fell for it anyway, but you should know that Dodd and his people are spreading it all over town."

During the months ahead, I was to be contacted by a dozen newsmen with whom that story had been planted. No one ever printed it, but word-of-mouth carried it to most places Dodd wished to reach. Drew Pearson first heard it in New Haven, Connecticut, where he happened to be making a speech.

Dodd soon added a supplementary story, relayed to me both by Carl Perian and Jim Canan, a correspondent for the Gannett news chain, which owns the *Hartford Times*. I had been paid $5,000, the story went, for turning over Dodd's files to Anderson. "I wish some one would print it," I told Canan. "I'd slap a lawsuit on them within twenty-four hours." No one ever did print it, to my knowledge, but a Washington magazine called *Capitol Hill* sneaked up to it in its March issue, with a florid editorial broadside:

> The alleged theft of Senator Dodd's papers by a former em-ployee has cast a black shadow of suspicion upon every em-ployee on the hill. No member of Congress could feel secure again if this reincarnation of Judas Iscariot is allowed to go un-punished.
>
> We are curious as to what law Jack Anderson and Drew Pearson feel they are operating under. Was there any inducement offered to the individuals in the way of compensation? Was it offered be-fore or after the theft? Did it take the form of silver, or the prom-ise to help the thief obtain a position with another member of Congress?

That editorial, in a magazine aimed exclusively at Hill people, re-flected a major theme of Dodd's underground offensive: If Dodd could be damaged by staff informers, every other Senator and Repre-sentative was in danger. Such an argument was hardly complimentary to the Congress, but there were indications that it was having a pow-erful effect. "Washington Buzzes Over Theft of Senator Dodd's Files" ran one five-column headline over a story that said concern over how Pearson obtained the files overshadowed interest in what they con-tained. In another article, Robert Walters of the *Washington Star* quoted an unidentified Senator as saying, "The first two questions I asked myself were 'What do I have in my files that might be damag-ing?' and 'Can I trust my staff?'" Even the august Foreign Relations Committee, the Senate's Holy of Holies, began looking over its shoul-der. Committee members were embarrassed that Dodd had been se-cretly involved with Julius Klein at the same time that the committee, in 1963, was conducting a major investigation into the affairs of Klein

and other international lobbyists. The possibility of summoning Dodd
for testimony was raised. But, as one committee member revealed to
the *New York Herald Tribune,* the discussion shifted to the contention
that Dodd was "a victim of his staff" and died out right there. Later,
the committee members voted down a motion to make public the record of that discussion.

There was a corollary to the thesis that Dodd's misfortune set a
precedent that placed all Congressmen in peril: Dodd's faithless employees were unfit for employment anywhere. Dodd himself did not
hesitate to strike directly to cut off the livelihood of those he had identified as the conspirators against him.

Terry Golden was the first casualty. Her call to Dodd's office about
the flowers for Mrs. Dodd had revealed her place of employment. A
week later, following a visit to Judge Bazelon by Jack Fleischer, an
occasional member of Dodd's evening cabinet, she was dismissed, al-
beit with kindness, severance pay, and good recommendations. Bazelon's explanation was that he had forgotten, when he hired her, that
he had promised the job to someone else, who was now available.

We were, of course, puzzled by the explanation. Our most unfavorable interpretation of the episode appeared confirmed, however, when
Marjorie learned from Berl Bernhard that Dodd had lately denounced
her to Bernard Segal, one of the founders and driving forces behind
the Lawyers' Committee for Civil Rights Under Law. Dodd had insisted "violently" that she be fired* and had repeated to Segal the
usual fabrications, including the one about my receiving $5,000 from
Anderson. Dodd was on a first-name basis with Segal and may have
thought he had a hold over him, for Segal had represented NBC's top
brass during Dodd's probe of television programming and had won a
number of concessions beneficial to his clients. But Segal stoutly refused to be pressured. He told Dodd that the Lawyers' Committee
was highly pleased with Marjorie's work and would not respond to
outside interference. Tactfully, he suggested to Dodd that retribution
of this kind by a powerful Senator against a working girl might be
viewed by some as an admission of guilt.

Before Dodd's calls to Segal began, Marjorie had informed her superiors of her role in the case and, in order to forestall embarrassment
to the committee, had offered her resignation. But the new cochair-
men, the eminent Whitney North Seymour of New York and Burke

* When Marjorie later testified concerning Dodd's attempts to have her fired,
Dodd nodded vigorously in agreement.

Marshall, the Assistant Attorney General for Civil Rights during the Kennedy Administration, declined to accept it, as did Bernhard, the Executive Director. They expressed confidence in Marjorie's integrity and respect for her motives in the Dodd matter. They said they would leave it to her to decide, as the case developed, whether the Lawyers' Committee would be damaged by the attendant publicity she might receive. But as the days passed, Marjorie saw signs of their growing apprehension and submitted an irrevocable resignation, to take effect as soon as a replacement was found and trained.

Dodd's success in my case was more immediate. Early in March, I learned from inside sources that the Senator had walked over to the House side of the Capitol to see his old friend, Speaker McCormack, who was himself a frequent target of Drew Pearson. In the third week of March, Congressman Blatnik called me to his office. I approached his door with an intuitive feeling that it was to be the last time.

"Jim," he said, "I'm sorry but I'm going to have to drop you from the subcommittee staff. I think this is wrong, I fought against it, I delayed it for weeks, but I haven't got the power to stop it. George Fallon, the chairman of the Public Works Committee, has cut my budget by an amount that's roughly the same as your salary, and I've just got to let you go. All I can do is promise you my help and my best references in getting a new job."

I knew that the earnest Blatnik was the unhappy man in the middle and that there was no use prolonging his discomfort, so I left with a half-smile; but to lose my job at that moment was a crushing blow, for I could not hope to get another in Washington until the Dodd scandal was finally resolved and my role in it vindicated. At the rate things were going, that would be months and maybe even years; perhaps never.

The story of my firing was leaked to the press by Dodd, and first appeared in the Connecticut papers. Newspapermen told me the dismissal was arranged by Speaker McCormack, through a simple phone call to Fallon. Pearson and Anderson came up with the same finding and printed several stories to that effect, which were never challenged.

The circle of unemployment among our group was now complete. Michael had been out of work since leaving Dodd three months before. He had gone to one job interview after another and had never received the slightest encouragement. This unbroken reaction had discouraged him from further efforts.

"Everyone wants to talk to me for hours about the Dodd case," he said, "but no one ever calls me back about the job." His meager resources were exhausted. The Senate Employees Credit Union, acting with unusual speed, repossessed his car, even though he had in his Credit Union savings account an amount of money almost equal to what he owed. Michael had all but decided to go back home to Jersey City and seek a job as a construction laborer when the rest of us scraped up a hundred dollars and presented it to him as a St. Patrick's Day gift. But now we were all just about broke. Jack Anderson and Drew Pearson were willing to help us, but they knew, as we did, that we could not accept their aid. Even a loan from them would be suspect.

Simultaneously, Dodd's legal counterattack was being launched under the aegis of one of the world's largest law firms. Dodd had retained Cahill, Gordon, Sonnett, Rheindel, and Ohl, of New York. Even before the announcement was made, his Senate staff, now headed by Robert X. Perry, lately of the United States Attorney's office in New York, had begun working with a covey of the firm's lawyers. They were led by senior partner John Sonnett, formerly a high Justice Department official. This legal task force, which ultimately numbered eight attorneys, busily prepared arguments to buttress Dodd's demand for criminal prosecution of those who had "purloined" his files. And word reached Jack Anderson, through his underground network, of a multimillion dollar libel suit soon to be filed against him.

Dodd also hired a New York private detective firm. Its principal activity, judging from the alarmed reports I received each day, was digging into the personal lives of the suspected informants against Dodd. The firm's chief investigator was a gruff, red-haired man of enormous girth named James Lynch, an ex-F.B.I. agent. Working out of Dodd's Senate office, Lynch rang doorbells all the way from New York to North Carolina in search of spicy material. He called on my former wife, Gloria, but she refused to let him in. As the door closed on him, he fired questions about why and where we had been divorced. He visited a girl who had worked as a secretary in Dodd's office three years before and pressed her for derogatory information about my reputation in general and the possibility of extramarital relationships in particular. He visited Marjorie's former husband, Eric Carpenter, now remarried and living in New York, and probed vainly for discrediting information about her. Similar inquiries were made about the others. Lynch must have been either disconsolate or footsore when he reached the door of Walter "Joe" Stewart, a staff member of the Senate Appropriations Committee. "Sure, I know all of them," said Stewart, as Lynch read off our names. "Do you know anything bad about any of them?" blurted out Lynch, fresh out of subtle approaches. Gently, Stewart turned the intrepid giant away.

On other occasions, Lynch was more persistent. He gave Judith Berling the impression that he was a Federal agent, working with a grand jury that was about to hand down an indictment against the document thieves. He could keep Judy out of it, he said, if she told him all she knew.

"I don't know a thing about it," said Judy. Lynch told her that she had been identified going through Dodd's office files. "I've been in those files many times," said Judy. "It was part of my daily work." Lynch told her that since she wouldn't cooperate with the investigation, he was on his way back to Senator Dodd's office and would have to make a bad report on her. "Do F.B.I. agents generally report to Senators on their investigations?" Judy asked. Sensing trouble, Lynch modified his story. "Oh, I'm not an F.B.I. agent," he said. "I'm an ex-F.B.I. agent."

The following night, Lynch called Judy's father, Thomas Loftus, an official reporter of Senate debate.

"If you want your daughter to stay out of trouble, come to my room at the Fairfax Hotel right away," he said. Loftus replied that his daughter wasn't in any trouble and wasn't going to be and that he had no intention of meeting Lynch anywhere. Lynch then hinted that Loftus' own job with the Senate might be endangered by such an uncooperative attitude. "I've held a responsible position with the Senate for fifteen years," Loftus replied. "But if I thought for one minute that I could lose it for refusing to play ball with bums like you, then I wouldn't want it. And I warn you right now to leave me and my family alone!"

We heard, of course, only from our friends. When a week or two would pass without word of Lynch's movements, we wondered where he was and what he had uncovered. Had he discovered, for instance, that in 1947 when I was a private in the Marine Corps, I had received a deck court martial for disorderly conduct, following a payday celebration in the regimental tavern, and was sentenced to ten days in the brig on bread and water? Upon all of us fell a spooky foreboding that we were being followed, that our phones were tapped, that our friends and relatives and critics were being grilled about our personal lives. Scarcely a night would pass without one or all of us receiving repeated phone calls, with nothing on the other end except the sound of heavy breathing.

On March 28th and 29th, 1966, came the first solid official reaction to the Dodd revelations. Separate teams of F.B.I. agents called on Marjorie, Michael, Terry, and me. At long last, I thought, we could give them the information we had been preparing for a year, which Jack Anderson had offered in our behalf. But the agents had been instructed not to take any information concerning Dodd.

"We are interested only in what you can tell us about the removal of documents from Senator Dodd's office," said a man who identified himself as "Agent Chisolm."

The Department of Justice had thus adopted a curious order of priorities. Our action in removing proof of misconduct from a public office not only lacked a criminal motive, but on its face was designed to expose illegal acts. Even Dodd's lawyers were later to admit that no case could be made for a violation of Federal law and that even a misdemeanor charge under local trespass ordinances would be of shaky validity. In the weeks to come, Dodd's attorney-in-chief, John Sonnett, called repeatedly for a "new law" to protect Senators' files, thus admitting our action had not violated existing law. And Sonnett filed with the Ethics Committee an analysis prepared by the legal department of the Library of Congress, which concluded that our actions lacked various elements, including criminal intent, necessary to bring us afoul of Federal law. A number of distinguished lawyers and law professors went further and defended our actions on the positive ground that it was a praiseworthy and necessary "citizen's response" to uphold the law and expose unlawful acts which otherwise would have gone undetected.

In contrast, Dodd stood publicly charged with a variety of major Federal offenses, ranging from larceny, conflict of interest and the receipt of bribes, to large-scale income-tax violations. To back up these charges, Jack Anderson had made available to the F.B.I. several thousand of our documents. Yet, it was our improbable transgressions, not the conspicuous felonies, that were now being studied with all the resources of this, the world's most celebrated law enforcement agency.

I told Mr. Chisolm, a thoughtful, soft-spoken man who seemed a bit embarrassed at the anomaly of the situation, that after looking forward for a long time to working with the F.B.I., it was a real disappointment to have to be uncooperative when the chance finally came.

In my judgment, I said, Senator Dodd was trying to create a diversion, to which the Justice Department was lending itself. If Dodd succeeded in discrediting the witnesses and tainting the evidence against him, he could block an inquiry into his affairs before it ever got started. Under these circumstances, I was unwilling to abet a scheme that would work against the larger ends of justice. I said I was anxious to testify, with no holds barred, before any grand jury, court proceeding, or Congressional committee convened for the purpose of investigating Senator Dodd, and that I would gladly answer any question put to me on any subject, including my own conduct. But as long as the authorities refused to investigate Dodd, I would not give them information that could be misused to create a side show.

"That's all you have to say on the subject, Mr. Boyd?" asked Chisolm, politely.

"Yes, sir," I replied, "but I hope you'll be back some day to question me about some real offenses."

"Perhaps we will," he said.

The F.B.I. questioning of me had been conducted on a high level, but Marjorie's interrogation, by Agent Philip King, was at times carried on in the Lynch tradition. "A serious crime has been committed here," said King of the document removal, and he asked Marjorie her weight, height, age, and the color of her eyes, as though taking a description for a prospective WANTED poster. Marjorie, as well as Michael and Terry, took the same position I had on discussing the removal of the documents. They were willing to give information about how the evidence against Dodd was removed, but only as part of a general inquiry into Dodd's conduct in office.

For the next few days, the corridors of the old Senate Office Building swarmed with F.B.I. agents. They used Dodd's personal office for questioning his employees, except when the Senator was on the premises, in which case they moved to another room in the suite. This made it look as though the F.B.I. was working hand-in-glove with Dodd. Doris O'Donnell, a secretary who was known to have been friendly with us, was questioned about us for three hours behind a partition that did not reach the ceiling. Whatever she said could be overheard by any Dodd employee who happened to be planted on the other side.

Whatever the motives behind the F.B.I.'s performance, whether mere bureaucratic bungling or a conscious effort to bail Dodd out, nothing could have been more effective for intimidating potential witnesses into silence. Our supply of daily intelligence dwindled to a

trickle. Some of those we had hoped would be our allies, with important information we had counted on getting when things began going
badly for Dodd, in fact went over to his side. There now seemed to be
visible proof to back Dodd's repeated claims that the authorities were
behind him and that his accusers would wind up in jail.

For instance, Margaret Bray, Gartland's secretary, had once told
Terry Golden that she knew things that would put at least one of
Dodd's retainers behind bars; but when Terry now tried to set up a
luncheon meeting to discuss this, Mrs. Bray was suddenly distant and
unavailable.

Another case in point was Gerry Zeiller, who had resigned from
Dodd's employ ten months before. Zeiller had handled Dodd's dealings
in behalf of business firms and had frequently expressed his contempt
for his boss's ethics. The week he left, he invited Marjorie, Michael,
and me out for a farewell drink. He told us of a number of suspicious
episodes. Among others, he told of an alarmed vice-president of the
Colt Firearms Company, a Mr. Bolles, who had come to Zeiller with
the story that his company had been approached by a man named
Victor Hess who purported to be associated with Senator Dodd's "top
aide," James Gartland. He suggested that, in return for appropriate
commissions, Dodd's office could be of great assistance in obtaining
government contracts. Bolles was upset, for Colt was unwilling either
to offend Senator Dodd, who was then writing legislation to regulate
the gun industry, or to be involved in any illegal shakedown. In his
last week on the job, Zeiller declined to handle such a hot potato and
arranged an appointment for Bolles with Dodd, the outcome of which
was unknown to him. Much later Zeiller told Michael that he had
recounted this whole story to the F.B.I. but that nothing had come of
it.

A few months after Zeiller left Washington, Michael and Terry visited him at his New Hampshire home, and when Michael commented
that he had been fortunate in separating from Dodd on amicable
terms, Zeiller responded, "I have nothing to fear from Dodd, I have
too much on him." He then said that he would like to see Jim Boyd,
that he had a lot to tell me. But I was never able to get together the
money to make the trip to New Hampshire. Now, in the midst of the
F.B.I. barrage, Zeiller was back in Washington, visiting Dodd's office
each day. Michael called on him at the Skyline Inn, and found that his
former attitude had shifted 180 degrees. We were fools, he told Michael, to have tried to cause trouble for Dodd. The whole establish-

ment was against us, he said, and had rallied around Dodd. He himself was going to help Dodd in every way he could.

Those working in Dodd's office watched for news of the arrest of "the Boyd clique," and, one-by-one, the informants we had hoped to recruit slipped through our fingers.

As the middle of April approached, twelve weeks and twenty-three columns after publication of the Dodd story had begun, our enterprise could only have been characterized as a failure. The help we had counted on—from the press, the authorities, the public—had not materialized.

We had thought it the function of the press to move in quickly on any story that gave off the smoke of public corruption, before the fragile flame was snuffed out and the informants scared away. We did not ask the press to accept at face value the Pearson-Anderson charges. But we did expect the news services and the great papers to make their own investigations of the facts, and we stood ready to help them with our testimony, as Pearson and Anderson did with the documents. But, except for Jim Canan of the Gannett News Service, no one came looking.

As far as we could determine, the vaunted news departments of the great broadcasting networks, NBC, CBS, and ABC, had not uttered a single word about the Dodd disclosures. The Associated Press and the United Press International had carried nothing but a few ambiguous statements by spokesmen for the Justice Department and the Ethics Committee, who said only that they had nothing definite to say.

The *New York Times* and the *New York Herald Tribune* had carried nothing of the allegations against Dodd. The *Washington Post,* though it was printing the Pearson columns in their regular place on the back pages, had carried only two articles on its news pages—one pointing out that since a majority of the Ethics Committee had actually opposed its creation, there would probably be no investigation of Senator Dodd at all; the other a general debunking of the Pearson-Anderson charges, under a six-column headline that proclaimed "Dodd's Image in Connecticut Unstained by Charges Against Him." The *Chicago Tribune* had printed only attacks on Dodd's accusers. There had been nothing in the *Wall Street Journal,* the *Philadelphia Inquirer,* the *Christian Science Monitor.* Of the great papers, only the far away *Los Angeles Times* had published a strong editorial demand for a Senate investigation.

Even among those papers that regularly carried Pearson's "Wash-

ington Merry-Go-Round," our sampling indicated that the practice of
pulling columns and editing out key paragraphs was widespread. In
Connecticut, three of Pearson's five clients had refused to print the
columns on Dodd, cutting Pearson's circulation in Dodd's home state
to about thirty thousand, out of a total population of three million.
And on the news pages there had been a virtual blackout in the
Connecticut press as to the specific charges against Dodd. There were
a couple of Sarah McClendon columns in a small weekly tabloid
called the *Sunday Herald*. Of several stories filed by Jim Canan, only
the emasculated remnants survived heavy censorship by the editors of
the Gannett chain and the *Hartford Times*. All told, the two dozen
charges made by Pearson and the massive documentation behind
them had failed to reach Dodd's constituents.

Every one of the national news magazines had thus far ignored the
story completely, except for *Newsweek*, which had done a piece that
in the main questioned the Pearson charges, defended Dodd, and
closed on a prediction that nothing would be done. As for the journals
of opinion, they had no opinion.

Of the nationally syndicated columnists, for whom reform of Congress is in the abstract a favorite topic, only two, both extreme conservatives, had even taken notice of this latest Congressional scandal—
and both had defended Dodd. Holmes Alexander, of the McNaught
Syndicate, depicted Dodd accusers as "vultures . . . birds of prey
. . . who do not like his militant anti-Communist stand in the affairs
of Latin America, Africa, and Asia." Alexander urged Dodd's Senate
colleagues to rally around him.

The inside story of how copies of Dodd's letters and papers became available to enterprising reporters is spicy with the sauce
of gossip and intrigue. None of it reflects adversely on Dodd, and
all of it throws a red glare of warning on other occupants of the
Senate office buildings. Every senator on Capitol Hill knows that
what had happened to Dodd's files could happen to others.

On Dodd, Alexander made this judgment:

I have found Tom Dodd to be a sensitive, kindly, trustful, industrious and often exhausted man—a diligent and important public figure . . . I am sure that any erosion of his status as a person of integrity would be injurious to the American cause.

And from columnist John Chamberlain came the solemn assertion that Dodd, because of his firm positions in foreign policy, was being pilloried for "practices that have been accepted for years by scores of Congressmen."

"I am sufficiently ornery to doubt," wrote Chamberlain, "that anything much would have been done about the Dodd finances if Dodd had been a supporter of Senator Fulbright."

But it was the official reaction that was most important and, therefore, the most disappointing to us. Outside of the Justice Department's investigation of us and my dismissal by the House Public Works Committee, there had really been no reaction. The Ethics Committee had held some closed meetings on the Dodd matter, and staff members of the committee had questioned some of us informally about the allegations against Dodd. But apart from an occasional mention that it was "considering the matter" and that "Senator Dodd is giving full cooperation," the committee was silent, and twelve weeks after the Pearson charges began, had reached no decision on whether they were worthy even of a formal inquiry.

Connecticut authorities had reacted—or failed to react—in the same manner, though the state's Corrupt Practices Statute was patently involved. Despite demands for an investigation from the Republican State Chairman, A. Searle Pinney, neither Governor Dempsey nor State's Attorney John Labelle would even comment on the matter, let alone order a probe. When Pinney tried in March to get Dodd's campaign reports from the Secretary of State so that the Republicans could start their own investigation, he was informed that they had been burned in February. The state authorities pointed to a convenient statute which said that such records could be destroyed fifteen months after the election. The law didn't say they had to be destroyed, but they were, despite the fact that charges involving campaign contributions had been made public as far back as January 24th.

Pearson and Anderson had poured out seventeen thousand words of copy on Dodd; it was widely known that they had thousands of documents and several inside witnesses to back up their charges, and for months they had vociferously sought an official inquiry before which proof could be presented. Yet, with the exception of the chastened Resnick, not a single member of the Congress had seen fit to demand an investigation or even to emit a word of comment on a matter that directly involved the integrity of the Congress. Not one Senator, not one law enforcement officer, not one Connecticut official, not one civic or religious leader had ventured a public statement of any kind.

The Pearson attack itself had stalled and ground to a halt. For three weeks, Pearson had held up all columns on Dodd. A few had been written in protest of the Justice Department action against us, but no new material was published about Dodd, though the ammunition was still plentiful. Editors were protesting, Pearson explained to Anderson. They were getting tired of the Dodd series and worried about libel action. Pearson himself seemed worried. Another major libel suit, on top of the six he was currently battling in the Federal Court of the District of Columbia, would practically immobilize him.

A cold chill set in among our ranks. With cheerful resignation, we had accepted the unemployment, the turning away of old friends, the assault upon our motives, the public denunciation as thieves and liars, the dirty stories, the threats of criminal prosecution, the pursuit by private detectives, the investigation by the F.B.I. All that was a price to be patiently endured, if it served an end. But by the middle of April, all the portents indicated that no end might be served at all, except it be the further entrenchment of Dodd and those like him, and the intimidation of those who would some day be in our shoes and would cite our sorry example as good reason for keeping silent about what they saw. I remained stubbornly hopeful, but I felt more and more that I had failed the group, by leading it into a labyrinth of meaningless sacrifices.

Carl Perian described Dodd as triumphant with the air of vindication. He had outmaneuvered and outlasted his foes. Eighty days of almost continuous fire had failed to tarnish his image, and his accusers were now on the defensive.

Dodd had already drawn up the battle plan for final consolidation of his victory. His battery of attorneys was putting the finishing touches on the libel suit against Pearson and Anderson, which was to be built around an ingenious charge of conspiracy that sought to discredit all of us. John Sonnett was confident of winning the suit, and even the filing of it by such a prestigious law firm seemed designed to satisfy any remaining doubters in the Senate and among the press. Finally, Dodd laid out a program of public speeches and televised committee hearings that would once more bring him before the public in a positive light, as the crusading investigator of old.

But first, he and Grace were off to Florida for a holiday. After ten days in the sun, he would fly to Connecticut, he said, where he would be honored in a religious ceremony on April 24th by the Knights of Columbus, the strong lay arm of the Catholic Church. The highest order of Knights, the Fourth Degree of the Northern District of Connecticut, had announced an "exemplification" ceremony in Middletown in honor of Dodd, to be followed by the pageantry of a religious parade to Holy Cross Church for Benediction of the Blessed Sacrament. A dinner would follow, at which Dodd would be the principal speaker. On Dodd's desk was a resolution passed by the Fourth Degree that declared Dodd was "unstained from the malicious and slanderous articles being published by certain newspaper columnists."

As Dodd gave Carl final instructions before leaving for Miami, his eyes gleamed in anticipation.

"The F.B.I. has broken the document theft," he said. "Naturally, I'll demand prosecution. When I come back, I'm going to finish them off for good. I'll come out of this stronger than ever, and my enemies will go to jail. That's the way it all had to end, from the start."

CHAPTER SIX

SINCE there was no reason for the four of us to act in secret any longer, we began to meet occasionally at A. V.'s, a spaghetti house on New York Avenue, where the food was copious and inexpensive and the thunder of recorded operatic arias assured that our conversation would not be overheard. We did not have to analyze events to recognize they were going badly. Apparently, we had underestimated public indifference to corruption in Congress. From the start we had foreseen the reluctance of officialdom to move against a Senator, and we had sought to circumvent it by taking our information to the press. But now we saw that this reluctance was, in fact, massive resistance—by the Senate, the Justice Department, the Internal Revenue Service, and the Connecticut authorities. That we, rather than Dodd, might be prosecuted was a definite possibility. If so, we resolved to admit freely that we had copied the documents and turned them over to the press. We decided we would make our defense the necessity to do so in the public interest. We determined that if all other means failed, we would use our own trial as a forum for bringing out the Dodd story. But that would be a last resort. The immediate need was to get off the defensive and start our attack rolling again.

First, we decided to try to revive the stalled Pearson-Anderson series. We accepted as a matter of faith and reason that what had come out thus far must have had some effect, even if only underground. If twenty-three newspaper columns had not done the job, then, we reasoned, perhaps forty-six would. We wanted to know why Pearson had stopped running the columns and what we could do to persuade him to resume.

On a Saturday afternoon in early April 1966, Marjorie, Terry, Michael, and I called on Jack Anderson at his Bethesda home. Jack needed no urging. He promptly agreed that things did not look good and that the delay in new exposures had caused a loss of momentum.

"I don't understand why Drew is holding this up," he said. "I know some editors are kicking, but I've never known him to back away from a fight. He'll take on battles that even I would duck."

When I suggested that we all go to Pearson, tell him what we thought and ask him directly what his reservations were, Jack agreed and went to the phone.

"He'll see us in an hour," Jack announced, on returning. "Let's be on time. Drew can't stand to have people late. After twenty years together, if I'm not on time for something he'll start calling me 'the late Mr. Anderson.'"

It was dusk when we drove, in Jack's silent Lincoln Continental, through the newly green countryside toward Pearson's weekend retreat in rural Maryland. We had never met Pearson before, though we had long been curious about this celebrated and reviled personality. Until the slowdown began a month before, things had gone so smoothly that there had never been sufficient occasion to approach him. Now that we were on the way, I found myself trying to form a picture of him, and wondering what to say.

He must be about seventy now, I thought. I could not remember a time in my life when his name had not been a household word. I had first become aware of his "Washington Merry-Go-Round" more than twenty-five years before, when I was a newspaper delivery boy for the *Portland Evening Express.* My father was always quoting from it. "Pearson really gave it to the Republicans tonight," he would say with partisan glee. "It's the only part of the Maine press a Democrat can look forward to." And I could remember how our family would gather in the living room on Sunday nights to listen to Drew Pearson and Walter Winchell, when their provocative shows were the top attractions in news broadcasting. To me, Pearson was something of an institution.

We arrived at our destination just at nightfall. It was a secluded, rambling old house that overlooked a stunningly picturesque stretch of the Potomac River. We were admitted by a maid and shown into a large, rustic sitting room, tastefully done in brightly hued chintz and comfortably crowded with chairs and divans. In a few minutes, the object of our troubled pilgrimage appeared. He had on a pair of old bedroom slippers, but was otherwise impeccably attired in a brown tweed jacket, gray slacks, and a soft, gold-tinted sport shirt. Erect and dignified, he conveyed an undeniable presence, almost a forbidding one. He had a fascinating, bristling white moustache, pointed at both ends. Behind it, his face was surprisingly youthful, his complexion clear, eyes sharp. During the introductions he was solemn, almost distant. He sat down without a word.

Jack opened things up by saying that we all felt the Dodd story was flagging, and then he turned the floor over to me. Pearson peered at me expectantly, perhaps impatiently, making me almost forget what I wanted to say. Somehow things weren't going as expected. I began in disorganized fashion, expressing grateful recognition of Pearson's great investment in effort, column space, and risk in undertaking the Dodd story. I spoke of how we had made considerable headway until the last few weeks, how Dodd had then taken over the initiative, and how we needed to regain it.

All the while, our host gazed at me enigmatically over his elegant, sometimes twitching moustache. Neither by nod, gesture, smile, nor question did he do anything to ease my feeling of awkwardness. On the contrary, he distracted me, almost intimidated me, with a variety of disconcerting mannerisms. He would pull at his moustache, clear his throat with a nervous *harrumph,* hitch up his trousers for no apparent reason, scrutinize his socks and pull them up, scratch his shoulder, and then recommence his deadpan gaze. I struggled on haltingly, all hope of persuasiveness gone, just trying to finish. Pearson finally spoke.

"So you think I've got cold feet, eh?" Before I could disclaim such a thought, he continued. "Well, I can't say I blame you." His voice was surprisingly mild and pleasant, but so soft you had to listen attentively. He *harrumphed* again.

"I agree with everything you've said. I've been out around the country on a speaking tour. Everywhere I go, people ask me if anything will be done about Dodd. If we don't get action, I'm afraid the little people of this country will become terribly disillusioned with their government, and that would be a very bad thing. No question about it. Having started this, we have a duty to push it to the right conclusion. What do you have in mind?"

I suggested a resumption of the columns, pointing out that we had never completed the series about the diversion of campaign funds.

"All right," he said. "I was looking at Jack's draft on that just before you came. I'll clear it tonight and it will be carried next Wednesday. But I think we are being repetitious and dull in some of these columns. They're hard to understand. *We* know that these columns about campaign funds refer to different years and different amounts, but to housewives and working people who skim over the column, it all seems to run together, as if we're repeating ourselves. I don't want to overwhelm my readers with masses of confusing facts and figures. I'm looking for fresh stories, new subjects that have a moral to them, things that affect *people*. What do you have?"

Marjorie, Michael, and Terry joined in now, suggesting unexploited topics. There was a ferment, reminiscent of our early meetings with Jack. Pearson entered into the discussion with warmth and spirit. He left the room, returned quickly with three or four folders, and sat down in the middle of our circle. "I have some material here on Dodd and the insurance companies, and the gun industry, and I'm checking into his involvement with a pipeline that's being constructed up there," he said. I received the impression that it was important to him to make personal contributions, beyond editing and rewriting. Then it would be *his* story and not just the product of his organization.

Suddenly, it seemed as though we had known Pearson for years. His early reserve—or perhaps it was my misconception of it—had vanished. He was surprisingly easy to talk with, unopinionated and approachable, making us forget the gulf that separated us in station, age, and experience. There was in this feared and notorious muckraker, a kindliness, a gentleness, a sensitivity that we had not expected. The battles, feuds, intrigues, and libel trials of forty turbulent years seemed not to have marked his personality. He seemed a shy man, actually. A wry, self-effacing humor played always on the edges of his conversation. Surprisingly, he was not a cynic; there was an unblighted idealism and enthusiasm in his words and demeanor. When he spoke of "the people" there was an obvious but unaffected emphasis, a feeling of personal bond, of championship. His confidence in the public, in eventual progress, in the democratic system, seemed undiminished after a lifetime of chasing official corruption and fighting public apathy.

Far into the night, we planned together the next phase of our campaign. The columns would resume regularly, we agreed, and other newsmen would be invited to share our material. And there was more.

"I have friends in the Senate, strange as that may seem to you," Pearson said. "I'm going to talk to them. I think it's time we had some speeches urging a public investigation." Jack looked on affably and stayed in the background. Most of the discussion was old stuff to him, but he was obviously pleased at Pearson's reaction to us, and a couple of times I thought he winked at me.

We drove homeward in a state of high excitement. "We should have done this before," Jack said. "When Drew Pearson gets personally involved in something, there's no holding him. We'll finish up the campaign stuff and then get into the insurance companies and the arms industry. He's really hot on that."

Once more we had marching orders, and we could feel the battle resuming.

"I don't see how they can avoid public hearings," cried Oregon's Senator Wayne Morse a few days later, standing at his front row desk on the Senate floor. Lean, glowering, with piercing eyes and the fierce countenance of a ruffled eagle, Morse pointed his finger as if at absent villains. The long Senate silence on the Dodd case was broken. It was April 14, 1966.

He was incredulous, Morse declared, over an Associated Press story which said that the Senate Committee on Standards and Conduct was to shut down the Dodd investigation quickly, without public hearings, and quietly draw up a report behind closed doors. "The record ought to be made public," exploded Morse. "The American people are entitled to it, because it has become public business."

Morse turned to press reports that the Ethics Committee and the Justice Department were devoting primary attention to uncovering how the Dodd documents came to be furnished to the press, instead of evaluating what was in them. As usual, his voice was raspy with hoarseness on its lower register but clear and powerful when raised.

"I do not know what the facts are, but I know the press and the people are going to continue to ask the controlling question: What about the *contents* of the documents? Are they true or false? I do not think I need to tell anybody in this body my feelings about stool pigeons or betrayers of trust, but those questions are irrelevant to the question of determining innocence or guilt!"

Ominously, Morse introduced into the Record a speech he had delivered twelve years before, at the time of the censure of Senator Joseph McCarthy, which outlined the proper procedure to be followed in the impeachment of a Senator. Then he yielded the floor to Senator Stephen Young of Ohio, a small but fiery septuagenarian who lifted weights each morning and made public each year a complete record of his income and assets. Accustomed to speaking his mind whenever he became indignant, Young was one of the mavericks of the Senate.

"It has seemed . . . that the committee's proceedings have been shrouded in a cloak of a secrecy," Young began. "I feel it would be in the best interests of the Senate and of the nation if the committee were to conduct open hearings on the subject without delay. Certainly, were a Senate committee to be investigating similar charges against any high official in the Executive Branch of the government, open hearings would be held, and the matter would be fully aired before the American public. Have we the moral right to create a double standard of conduct, one for the Executive Branch and another for the Legislative Branch of our government?"

And the Ohio Senator had a few words for the F.B.I. "There are reports that the Federal Bureau of Investigation is harassing the newspapermen who originally made the allegations that resulted in the investigation, and that knowledgeable individuals who are in a position to testify to the facts have been intimidated by F.B.I. agents . . . If these reports are accurate, they constitute conduct on the part of F.B.I. agents that is reprehensible."

Freshman Senator Paul Fannin, a conservative Republican from Arizona, rose to congratulate his liberal Democratic colleagues and to join in their recommendations for a full inquiry and public hearings.

In the past, the Ethics Committee had given the silent treatment to all speculation about its activities, but it could not continue mute when Senators began voicing misgivings. Prompt assurances were given by Chairman John Stennis of Mississippi that the Committee would be thorough and unhurried. Vice-Chairman Wallace Bennett, a Utah Republican, a past president of the National Association of Manufacturers, and an elder of the Mormon Church, went further.

"The Senate itself is on trial," said Bennett, echoing Morse and Young. Though noncommittal about public hearings, he promised that the complete record of committee actions would eventually be made public.

On the day of the speeches by Morse and Young, the Pearson articles resumed, as promised. The opening column related how $47,000 raised by Dodd in a series of political events on October 26, 1963, had been diverted to Dodd's personal use, without the payment of income taxes. Added to the $55,000 revealed in an earlier column, the total topped $100,000, apparently a magic figure to the press. This time we could feel the impact immediately. Pearson's disclosures caught the attention of Richard Harwood, a feature writer for the *Washington Post*. After checking Connecticut sources, he asked for an interview with Dodd. A few weeks before, Harwood had done an article on the Connecticut reaction to earlier Pearson charges. It had been friendly to Dodd, so Harwood was now rewarded with an interview. It was not with Dodd to be sure, but with David Martin, who had become his most practiced defender. Dodd's plan, we later learned, was to use the session with Harwood for the launching of a trial balloon in answer to Pearson's charges. If the respected *Washington Post* once more responded sympathetically and prominently featured Dodd's reasonable explanation, it would go far to discredit the Pearson assault.

This gamble ended up an unqualified disaster. A front-page, three-column spread on April 20th pictured Dodd as admitting to having pocketed the $100,000, and as denying any impropriety. The money came to him, he said, not in the form of political contributions, but as "tax-free gifts." With his penchant for overstatement, Martin, the unidentified source, went on blithely rubbing it into the taxpayers of the land, for whom the April 15 deadline was still a fresh wound. "There is no question about the legality of such gifts and no question of tax liability," he said. "That is why no taxes were paid on this money . . . Testimonial dinners enable a poor man to remain in office. They are part of the American way of life."

Martin regarded the published interviews as quite a coup, according to our inside sources, and phoned Dodd in Florida with the good news. He began excitedly to read aloud the Harwood story. Halfway through, the look of satisfaction suddenly faded from his face and loud objurgations could be heard from the other end of the phone. Dodd instantly recognized the debacle. He was on the next plane back to Washington.

Predictably, the "American way of life" was seized upon by cartoonists and pundits far and wide. No matter that Dodd's trial balloon revealed only the tip of his financial iceberg. For the first time his affairs began to receive widespread press attention.

Prompt and alarmed challenges to Dodd's version rolled in, from the White House all the way down to the Connecticut precincts. President Johnson, asked about his attendance at two of Dodd's "tax-free testimonials," said that he had never attended a dinner which he knew was being held "for anyone to obtain funds for personal use." Vice-President Humphrey, headliner at a third affair, also denied knowledge that the money raised was to be used as a gift to Dodd. Senator Clifford Case said that even if Dodd could establish that the money was really intended for him, his conduct was improper. The receiving or giving of contributions, apart from campaign purposes, Case said, was "thoroughly bad public policy." Senator John Williams, who two years before had waged a near single-handed struggle to keep alive the Bobby Baker probe, described Dodd's contention as a "farce" and said Dodd owed taxes on all the political money he had diverted to personal use. Williams contemptuously dismissed the claim that the solicitations had nothing to do with campaign funds, backing up his stand by inserting in the Congressional Record one of the invitations, which began:

In 1964, our friend, Sen. Thomas J. Dodd will campaign for re-election to the United States Senate. It does not seem necessary for me to stress the heavy financial burden this campaign will involve. For this reason, it is necessary for those of us who respect and admire Senator Dodd to lend whatever aid we can to assist him in presenting a vigorous campaign.

Four members of the Ethics Committee told the *Washington Star* that Dodd's contention was new to them and that they had never siphoned off dinner contributions for their own use. Senator Bennett said, "I have never been a party to that good old American tradition. I have never heard of other dinners for Senators and Congressmen for that purpose. So far as I know, all of these dinner exercises are for paying off past campaign debts or for re-election."

In Connecticut, head table guests at Dodd's many affairs expressed surprise at his explanation. "I thought I was just going to a dinner," said John M. Bailey. State Senator Gloria Schaeffer, who had opened her fashionable home for one of Dodd's receptions, said, "I understood the funds were being raised for political purposes. I've never known them to be raised for any other purpose. The local newspaper reported the party as a fund-raising affair." Checking out the Dodd claim that "testimonials" for personal benefit were commonplace in Connecticut, the *Washington Post* polled political observers and newsmen there and reported that none had any recollection of any dinner "where an announcement was made that the proceeds would go to the personal use of the person for whom the dinner was given."

After the long drought, we were overwhelmed at the sight of the press in action. We knew, of course, that Dodd's explanation was a fabrication. His dinners had always been represented to the donors, the press, the guest speakers, even to his own staff, as strictly campaign affairs. On the rare occasions when newsmen would inquire as to the specific purpose, Dodd would instruct me to inform them that it was to retire old election deficits or lay a foundation for upcoming campaigns. "Tell them I may be presented with a gold watch by my friends," he said, and I believed him. The campaign motive dominated his many solicitation and thank-you letters. We had several of which Senator Williams was not even aware.

The solicitation letter to the March 1966, dinner, drafted by me on Dodd's instructions, approved by Dodd, and sent out to 2,000 people over the signature of Arthur Barbieri, a New Haven politico, read:

> Tom Dodd was re-elected to the Senate of the United States by an overwhelming majority last November. His vigorous campaign made a significant contribution to the unparalleled landslide in Connecticut. He spared himself no personal effort and sacrifice, and undertook every financial expense necessary to bring to the people his record and platform. The result justified the efforts and expense but a considerable deficit was incurred and must now be met. A testimonial dinner will be held at the Statler Hilton Hotel in Hartford, Conn., on Saturday, March 6. This affair will celebrate his record-breaking majority and assist in meeting the campaign deficit.

To all who contributed to Dodd's Washington reception on September 15, 1963, he wrote:

> It gives me confidence and encouragement as I enter a campaign for re-election to a second term, to know of your approval of the record made during my first term.

In connection with the 1963 affairs, Dodd wrote to Vice-President Johnson:

> First of all, allow me to thank you again for your generous offer to come to Connecticut to assist me in my forthcoming cam-

paign. I wish I could convey to you how enthusiastic everyone is about your visit and how much it will assist me in getting my campaign drive under way.

All the dinners, luncheons, breakfasts, receptions, and other assorted happenings that Dodd staged over a four-year period were advertised and reported in the press as campaign functions. Never had a correction been issued. Never was the word "gift" ever breathed in public, before or after the funds were salted away. For if the press, the public, or the Democratic party had ever grasped the fact that Dodd was planning to expropriate the proceeds, it would have been regarded as a public scandal; none but the most brazen of lobbyists would have attended, there would have been no head table of luminaries, no famous guest speaker. Dodd would have been roundly condemned, and it is doubtful if he could ever have been re-elected. Only Dodd and the silent Sullivan were privy to how much had been raised, where it had come from, where it went. All others who had played any part in the events—the staff, the nominal treasurers, chairmen, toastmasters, committee members, solicitors—were mere names on letterheads, dupes who were told nothing about the origin, size, or destination of the huge amounts collected in their names.

But now it was out. For a year I wondered what Senator Dodd's explanation of the missing treasure would be when we finally confronted him. The ploy of the tax-free gift must have been conceived in fear of the Internal Revenue Service. But it seemed to me that in the long run this explanation would raise as many legal problems as it solved. A large percentage of the testimonial donations came from people who had official business with Dodd as a Senator. Taking money from these people he had officially aided was questionable enough even when the contributions were political. But at least it had the sanction of common usage. To accept these contributions as personal gifts, however, was bound to raise black questions—vote buying, influence peddling, conflicts of interest, violation of state and Federal corrupt-practices laws. Every donation was now suspect, whether the standard one- or two-hundred-dollar offering from Washington lobbyists, the $1,000 from the board chairman of General Tire, the $1,500 from the Teamsters, the $5,000 gift from the buildings trades unions, the $8,000 from the International Latex Corporation, or any one of hundreds of other donations.

The universally adverse reaction jolted the Senator. Back from Florida, tanned but drawn, he quickly disowned Dave Martin's carefully rehearsed interview. Though within three months Dodd would offer exactly the same explanation, and would progressively enlarge on David's rhetorical embellishments as to the prevalence of $100,000 appreciation tributes ("common as nutmegs in Connecticut, common as raindrops"), the Senator now branded Martin's statement as completely unauthorized, and returned to his former policy of silently hiding behind the Ethics Committee. But the press had caught a sniff. It was now acknowledged that, at the very least, there was smoke.

Up to now the only contact that Marjorie, Michael, Terry, and I had with the Ethics Committee had been through its counsel, Benjamin Fern, a forty-four-year-old retired Navy captain who had only recently taken up the law. We instinctively liked and respected Fern. In a capital bustling with bogus "colonels," "judges," and "commissioners," Fern was a real captain who preferred to be called simply "Mr. Fern." Soft-spoken, spare, with thinning red hair and an honest, reflective face, he had questioned all of us at length and seemed to believe we were telling the truth. To a doubting committee, which thought of us primarily as informers and file thieves, Fern had vouched for us as witnesses upon whom a Dodd hearing should be built.

But Chairman Stennis, cautious and skeptical, decided first to call us in secret session before a special subcommittee, composed only of himself and Vice-Chairman Bennett.

"Don't be alarmed when you get a subpoena," Fern reassured us. "It may appear unfriendly and unnecessary to you, since you've all volunteered to appear willingly, but the chairman likes to have things official and proper."

With a sense of heightening anxiety, we waited for our first meeting with Chairman Stennis. More and more we had come to see that the fate of the Dodd case would be largely shaped by this austere man whose attitude was so difficult to divine. The power of the Pearson column, though vital as a catalyst, was limited in the Senate. On the whole, the press remained dormant and, except for a sporadic foray now and again, content to take its cue from the committee. Word had leaked out of both the Internal Revenue Service and the Justice Department that their own reluctant probes would be held in abeyance until the Ethics Committee had made a pronouncement on the case.

And it was clear that John Stennis of Mississippi dominated the committee and was the key man in the proceedings.

Dodd privately called Stennis "the Swampfox." When I first heard it, I thought it was a crude lampoon, such as Dodd delighted in fashioning for his peers. But as the months had passed, I came to see there was more of chagrined admiration in the epithet than of ridicule—a tribute to Stennis' shrewdness and elusiveness, his mastery of the brambly Senate environment and the arts of camouflage, his talent for swallowing up an adversary in a hundred hidden ways.

Though not well-known to the public, Stennis was a pillar of the Senate Establishment and enjoyed a considerable reputation for astuteness among his colleagues. During two decades in the Senate, he had not noticeably risen above the narrow prejudices of his constituency, but neither had he sought to exploit them unduly through demagoguery. He took his turn in the filibusters against civil rights, but concentrated his attention on matters of national defense and military preparedness, on which he was a recognized authority.

I had watched Stennis for years on the Senate floor and at committee hearings—grave, authoritative, impatient with delay, oblivious of the cloakroom camaraderie of his colleagues. In his sixties, beginning to gray, he was a rather big man with a deep chest and solid build, always immaculately tailored in dark, conservative suits. His face was rugged, deeply lined, plain, but touched with dignity and the hint of sagacity. His voice was exceptionally deep, with a thick accent. His idiom was a mixture of folksiness, gallantry, and officialese, which meant that sometimes his speech would get tangled. The impression he left, however, was not one of confused thinking but of veiled objectives, of a mind that often raced ahead of the immediate discussion to concentrate on the next move. Stennis seemed disciplined, industrious, and shrewd, rather than brilliant, imaginative, or profound. His manner was suffused with the ingrained courtliness of the Southern gentleman, but after the fleeting smile and the bow there was about him a certain severity, an attitude of habitual command, a no-nonsense approach to the business at hand and to life. He could not abide the slightest sign of disorder or disrespect. Whispering among busy aides on the Senate floor, inattention by bored Senators to debate, laughter by the public at a hearing, would provoke his instant rebuke. He had once been a judge, and he carried about him an air of the courtroom.

So dominant was his sphinx-like quality that some reporters called Stennis the "great stone face." Under questioning he would often

respond with oracular ambiguity and could never be lured into un-
wanted channels of discussion. Newsmen who were granted rare private interviews on the Dodd probe would emerge in a state of bafflement. "I would artfully set up a loaded question for him," one reporter
told me, "and Stennis would all the while smile encouragingly at me,
nodding his head vigorously in seeming agreement. Then he would
state his answer with great authority. 'My mind is not closed on that,'
he would say, or 'the door is still open,' or 'that certainly is a serious
problem you have raised and you can be sure it will be given consideration.' When I got out in the hall and thumbed through my notes, I
found that after a half-hour interview I didn't have a single usable
quote."

Like other Senators, especially Southerners, who held great power
and secure seats, Stennis wanted to govern, to decide, not to debate or
posture. He was unsympathetic to the role of the press and public in
the day-to-day operations of the Senate. He liked to function behind
closed doors where "orderly progress" could be made and unanimous
recommendations hammered together without the distractions and
theatrical atmosphere of a public hearing room. Stennis was of the
view that the Senate had powers in and of itself, quite apart from an
electorate far from Capitol Hill. He seemed to regard the people as
something of an irritant, standing between him and the job he wanted
to do.

But it was not alone for integrity, or judiciousness, or effectiveness
that Stennis was chosen, above ninety-nine colleagues, to be chairman of the committee to investigate other Senators. It was also because Stennis was an insider, a defender of the prerogatives of Senators, a natural oligarch instinctively hostile to outside intrusions into
the privacy of the Club. Impervious alike to public clamor or the lure
of headlines and dedicated to perpetuating the exalted image he held
of the Senate, Stennis could be trusted to wield carefully the unique
power of his Ethics Committee chairmanship—the power to destroy.
There would be no televised circuses at a colleague's expense. The
dirtiest linen would be washed in private, if at all. Any Senator under
attack would be treated as an ambassador from a sovereign state, entitled to privileges and protections not available to ordinary subjects of
Senate scrutiny. This is what the Senate wanted, and Stennis was prepared to furnish it.

I recalled Jack Anderson's assessment of Stennis, which I found disturbing. "Remember this," he said. "Stennis may not have any use for

Dodd, but he loves the Senate. The Senate is his whole life, the summit of his aspirations. And if he can help it, he's not going to let the Senate be dragged through the mud. He may decide to sacrifice Dodd for the good of the Club, or he may decide to cover up for Dodd for the same reason." Jack gave me some pointed admonitions: "When you appear before Stennis," he said "he'll probably try to limit the questioning to a few cozy areas. Don't let him do it. Get in everything you can. Take a list with you and insist on getting it into the official record. It's possible that this will be your only chance." I was skeptical of what Jack said, but I decided to follow his advice.

On the afternoon of April 22, 1966, Marjorie, Terry, Michael, and I were led through a maze of narrow hallways and winding staircases in the upper regions of the Capitol to an unmarked, sparsely furnished room. There we waited, until, one-by-one, we were conducted through another series of passages to a second unmarked room, where two Senators and a court stenographer were seated. I was the first to be brought before Stennis and Bennett and after being put under oath was questioned for more than two hours. Fern conducted the examination, though the Senators intervened whenever they wished. Stennis was cordial and formal. He tried to set me at ease, while at the same time stressing the gravity of the proceedings. He maintained a judicious, reserved neutrality, but I had the feeling that the circumstance of a mere Senate employee testifying against a Senator was a painful spectacle to him. Bennett was more affable but tended to take his cue from the chairman.

The questioning focused on but three subjects: Dodd's fund-raising ventures, his trip to West Germany in 1964 and its possible connection with Julius Klein, and airline travel for which Dodd might have improperly billed the Senate. It was not until I was about to be dismissed that I recalled Jack Anderson's warning. I said there were many other subjects on which I wished to be heard, and pressed for permission to read into the record more than a dozen areas of misconduct on which I requested to be recalled later. Stennis told me to proceed. After I began reading from my list, Stennis interrupted me. "Since you have it all written down there, let's just give it to the reporter and he can put it in the record as is." I handed it over to the chairman and withdrew from the room. Marjorie followed me into the chamber, then Michael, then Terry. Their interviews followed the same pattern as had mine. Each was politely thanked by Stennis at the conclusion and cautioned not to reveal our appearance to anyone.

"The proceedin's of executive sessions must be kept secret," he drawled. "That is why they are held behind closed doors. It will be better for all concerned if our friends in the press are not informed of anything that transpired heah."

In all, the session lasted four hours. Fern seemed highly pleased. "I'm sure the committee was impressed," he said. "I'm sure they believe you." In the days that followed, he and his assistant, Mike Spence, questioned us at length on the matters not entered into at the formal hearing.

Jack Anderson urged me repeatedly to prepare careful notes on all the testimony given to the committee and its staff. "I may be wrong, but my instinct is not to put any trust in them," he said. "I've seen too many of these inquiries fizzle in the past. I know you like Fern, but Fern is just an employee of the Senate. They can turn him on or off as they wish. Our strongest suit is that they now have your testimony and the documents and are stuck with the responsibility of following through. If they don't, we'll call them to account—but you must keep accurate records."

Again I thought Jack was exaggerating but, out of deference to his suspicions, I prepared careful notes on all information presented to the committee and later to the F.B.I., whose teams of agents now reappeared and took more than thirty signed statements concerning Dodd's activities from the four of us.

I often studied my notes, hoping to gain new insights and uncover hidden aspects that might stimulate those who somehow had failed to take an interest in the Dodd case. Throughout the more than fifty episodes we had related there ran the common denominator of misuse of office for personal gain. But to show merely that Dodd was profiteering from his office had proved insufficient to really arouse people. There seemed to be a sort of jaded acceptance of such conduct. It was not news.

"So what if Dodd is 'knocking down' a little," confided one reporter. "A lot of them are. Isn't this small change? Who is he really hurting?" But we had seen enough to know that every time a Senator puts personal gain ahead of duty, someone gets hurt. And, out of the many matters on which we were giving testimony or interviews, we began to emphasize several that served particularly to illustrate this.

*   *   *

In January 1964, Senator Dodd had announced an investigation of the motion-picture industry by the Juvenile Delinquency Subcommittee. It was to concern a particular kind of salacious film which glorified violence and crime and was produced primarily for teenage "drive-in" audiences. Dodd formally requested and received committee funds for this investigation and the staff began preliminary work. Covertly, the F.B.I. helped by furnishing note books filled with pornographic advertisements, reviews of films, and notes on a series of crimes that had apparently been motivated by scenes from particular movies.

The response from the movie industry was immediate. Edward Cooper, Washington representative of the Motion Picture Association, at once became active. He began a courtship of Dodd. At considerable expense, the movie people printed up in a fancy brochure some remarks ghostwritten for Dodd on the evils of censorship. Pleased with the publicity, Dodd allowed the Motion Picture Association to circulate the brochure widely. Next, movie people showed up for a fund-raising reception for Dodd held in, of all places, Hollywood. The Motion Picture Association then joined forces with the Metromedia television company in staging a soiree for Dodd *at* the MPA's showplace headquarters in Washington. Meanwhile, Cooper paid regular visits to Dodd's office to discuss the pending investigation with the Senator and the subcommittee staff. In June of 1964, Cooper approached Carl Perian with a $500 check for Dodd's campaign. "This will help you with the Senator, Carl," he said.

"I can't have anything to do with any money from you, Ed," Carl said. "In view of our investigation, it would be improper." Cooper, unabashed, then went directly to Dodd, who accepted the check personally.

In the aftermath of all these attentions and favors to Dodd, Perian noticed a change in the attitude of the normally affable Cooper toward the subcommittee staff. "He became arrogant and demanding," said Carl, "as if he had a hold over us." Cooper had good reason. Nothing more was ever heard of the investigation.

*   *   *

In 1961, Senator Dodd requested and received the vacant chairmanship of a special unit within the Antitrust and Monopoly Subcommittee. This unit had a number of tasks: to investigate abuses within the insurance industry by which the public could be defrauded; to determine the adequacy of state regulation, whereby fifty different state commissions tried to supervise the insurance colossus; and to probe monopolistic activities. For several years, Dodd held this responsibility, during a period of increasing attack upon insurance practices—from ordinary policyholders, from students of the industry, and finally from members of Congress.

Letters poured in from irate people all over the country who complained that their insurance costs were unconscionably high, that they had been hoodwinked by fast-talking insurance men, that their automobile and hospitalization policies, maintained for years at great sacrifice, had been peremptorily cancelled without just cause, that their benefits had been diluted by the fine print.

More sophisticated critics of the industry pointed to the annual statistics compiled by insurance companies as proof of the need for investigation and reform. Advances in medical science, which steadily increased the life span, were being studiously ignored by life insurance companies in the calculation of premium rates, they said. It was charged that insurance company practices were dominated by the quest for new sales, and figures were cited to show that year after year companies were spending more funds on sales commissions and advertising hoopla than on death claims. Even surplus reserves, supposed to be a safeguard against unexpectedly high claims, were being gambled on promotional activities. The hunger for ever-rising sales, the critics said, was encouraging high pressure tactics and phony presentations that resulted in disillusioned policyholders, who, burdened with insurance they did not really want or could not afford, soon dropped their policies. Statistics showed that of every hundred life policies sold, seventy were later abandoned by the purchaser; of every $2.00 in coverage sold, the buyer surrendered $1.00 at a loss. To be sure, much of this could be attributed to the imprudence or gullibility of the purchasers, but critics insisted that such an unstable condition, in an industry supposed to be the financial bedrock of the American family, should be exposed and remedied. And the purchaser frequently was not at fault. Early in 1962 the *National Underwriter*, a trade journal, reported that Missouri Superintendent of Insurance Jack L. Clay was planning action against ten percent of the insurance companies doing business in his state because of distortion and misrepresentation in selling policies. But, though these companies operated in other states too, Missouri's action was not characteristic. There were serious signs that state control was failing dismally, that many state insurance commissions were a patronage haven for political hacks, and that others were loaded with retired insurance executives who were drawing pensions from the very companies they were supposed to regulate. In most states the commissions were understaffed, underequipped, and underfinanced for the task of controlling the insurance giant—and the giant liked it that way.

Beyond the question of fraud and abuse was the antitrust issue—central to the work of Dodd's subcommittee. Students of monopoly charged that the insurance companies, with their tens of billions in premium dollars to invest and bank each year, threatened more and more to dominate the money markets of the world. It seemed to be standard for directors and officials of insurance companies to serve also as directors and officers of banks—ostensibly a competing business. Dodd did not have to look farther than his own Hartford, Connecticut, for examples of monopolistic practice. While Dodd presided over his insurance investigating unit, effective competition among Hartford's commercial banks was being undermined through dominance of those banks by insurance companies. Nine insurance firms controlled one-fifth of the voting shares of Hartford's two largest banks. More than sixty "corporate interlocks" placed officers of insurance companies on the boards of Hartford banks.

The insurance lobby had answers to all these charges, of course, and they deserved to be heard. But the need for a full-fledged Senate investigation into the little known insurance world could not in good faith be disputed. The very existence of Dodd's subcommittee presupposed such a probe; the volume and gravity of the complaints demanded it. There was, however, to be no investigation—no public look at the rigged mortality tables, or the misrepresentation, or the inadequacy of reserves. There would be no inquiry into the sixteen million lapsed policies each year, or the monopolistic practices, or the laxity and conflicts of interest that rendered impotent many state commissions.

Instead, to the great relief of the insurance industry, Dodd conducted two trivial inquiries, one into the practices of *foreign* insurers which competed with American firms, the other into fly-by-night com-

panies that were irritants to the great established corporations in
Hartford and elsewhere. That was all. In 1964, Dodd actually diverted
his staff to the task of finding ways in which he could be of assistance
to the insurance industry's Washington lobby. "Cooperation meetings"
were held in his office with groups of insurance officials, and plans
were made for such projects as turning over to private insurers the
government insurance on grain in Commodity Credit storehouses.

There were complaints about Dodd's inactivity, some of them coming from a Connecticut man named Norman Dacey, who had written
a book called *What's Wrong with Your Life Insurance?*.* After Dodd
made a series of speeches to chummy audiences of insurance officials
and state commissioners asserting that he could find nothing much to
investigate, Dacey turned up in the office with his book. He tried to see
Dodd, but Dodd refused. And Dodd declined to read Dacey's book.
Instead, he made more speeches in which he said that the only fault
he could find with the insurance industry was that it was too bashful
and didn't lobby vigorously enough in support of its interests.

It was not until we seized the documents that I found out how
profitable the goodwill of the industry was for Dodd. Our records,
which probably told only a part of the story, showed that Dodd received more than $24,000 in testimonial gifts, honorariums, fees, and
favors from insurance industry sources after he became responsible
for the insurance investigation. Some $4,000 of it came in outright
testimonial gifts from insurance executives and sales people. Another
$4,500 came in fees for pro-insurance speeches. In a $1,000 speech to
a group of auto insurance executives in Chicago in 1965, Dodd demonstrated the ethical compromises involved in this practice of taking
honorariums from those whom one is supposed to be investigating.
His prepared text, submitted to his hosts in advance, included a proposal for an automobile insurance guarantee fund, to protect policyholders when insolvent insurance companies default. The fund was to
be operated by the states and involved the levying of an extra tax on
auto insurers. Dodd's well-heeled benefactors objected to that proposal, and Dodd obligingly deleted it, apparently on the theory that
those who paid his fee were entitled to call the shots.

In one chunk, $5,000 went to the Senator in the form of a legal fee
for helping the Bankers Life Insurance Company of Chicago obtain a
charter to do business in Connecticut. Dodd's only effort was a couple

* Mr. Dacey later wrote the best seller *How to Avoid Probate.*

of phone calls to Connecticut Insurance Commissioner Al Premo, long a Democratic party functionary, and two brief letters to the insurance company's lawyers, one of them enclosing a bill for $5,000 which was promptly paid.

Another $6,000 came in as "finder fees" for helping a business associate, Manlio Liccione, obtain two loans totalling a million dollars from Aetna Life and Connecticut General. When Pearson broke a story on this incident, indignant spokesmen for Aetna and Connecticut General rushed forward to deny that Dodd had had anything to do with the granting of the loans. But Liccione gave the game away. Contacted by the *Hartford Times* at poolside at a Florida resort, Liccione confirmed that Dodd had been his go-between with the loan czars of the insurance world.

"Tom did nothing wrong, and I was very happy to let him earn some extra money," said Manlio.

And from the time Dodd began "investigating" insurance abuses, he stopped paying his own insurance bills. Years passed and by 1965 these unpaid premiums amounted to $3,500. But the Charles McDonough Agency of Hartford didn't bother to collect. There were no nasty ultimatums or canceled policies. Dodd had solved the "lapsed policy" problem for himself, if for no one else.

In the end, others would step into the six-year void created by Dodd's refusal to investigate the insurance industry. In 1967, for instance, investigators of the House Banking and Currency Committee would lay bare the monopolistic tie-up between insurance and banking in Hartford and elsewhere. In the same year, a dozen protesting Congressmen, headed by William Cahill and Peter Rodino, both of New Jersey, would demand the creation of a special committee to probe excessive rates and unethical practices in the field of automobile insurance. And in late 1967, Senator Philip Hart, Kefauver's successor as chairman of the Senate Antitrust and Monopoly Subcommittee, at last took over Dodd's function and announced a major investigation of the auto-insurance industry for the following year. But for the time being, in the spring of 1966, Dodd held the field alone and kept the lid tightly on.

No single activity gained more publicity for Senator Dodd during his first term than his probe into the rampant portrayal of crime, violence, and depravity on television. And for a time none of his ventures seemed to hold out such promise of public benefit. Psychologists told the Juvenile Delinquency Subcommittee that prolonged exposure to television "action" shows tended to implant in the viewer an acceptance of violence and brutality. The more impressionable and less stable the viewer, the greater the impact. A new generation had grown up in front of the television set—a generation which seemed to find violence more acceptable than its predecessors. In the steaming ghettos where the television screen is too often the slum mother's babysitter, absorbing television violence hour after hour is the principal household activity.

From 1961 on, Dodd's Juvenile Delinquency Subcommittee staff gathered impressive information pointing to the social dangers of this kind of programming, which had come to dominate totally the prime viewing hours on the three major networks. Further, the staff was prepared to show that the steady diet of crime, sex, and violence had been deliberately designed for the American public by a small group of top television executives in order to jack up ratings and advertising income.

The hearings began, the television moguls and their records were subpoenaed, and for a time Dodd pressed doggedly ahead, reaping headlines and a flood of approving mail from concerned parents. Apprehension mounted among the network top brass. Resignations were accepted from programming executives, plans for new "action" shows were hastily abandoned, and promises of improved fare were piously made. Then in July 1961, information came into the subcommittee's hands that clearly identified President Robert Kintner of the National Broadcasting System as the personal architect of the violence craze on NBC television and of systematic violation of the industry's broadcasting code. A major breakthrough that might accomplish the fondest hopes of the Subcommittee investigators was thus at hand, and aides industriously prepared for hearings that would expose to public view both the decision-making process which governed a great television network and the shabby considerations that dictate the type of programs saturating the television screen and the minds of its millions of young viewers.

The NBC empire drew protectively around President Kintner. A subcommittee subpoena for NBC documents was evaded. Company officials changed their stories and suffered incredible lapses of memory under oath. According to the documented legal opinion of the Juvenile Delinquency Subcommittee counsel, Paul Laskin, perjury was committed repeatedly in an attempt to shield Kintner from personal responsibility for company programming practices. Only a former vice president, David Levy, told the whole truth—and his most important testimony, which singled out Kintner as the driving force behind crime, sex, and violence on NBC programs, was given in secret session.

A crucial point in the subcommittee investigation was thus at hand. The staff pressed for a showdown with its mighty adversary, for a resolution of the conflicting sworn testimony, for a confrontation between Levy on the one hand, and Kintner and his apologists on the other. But Dodd began to back off. He rejected all pleas to carry forward the NBC probe. He refused to act on the evasion of the subcommittee subpoena. He would not permit the cross-examination of Kintner or Levy on the conflicts in their testimony. He intimidated his subcommittee staff and abused chief counsel Laskin savagely in the presence of NBC officials for "persecuting" NBC. He eventually fired Laskin for "disloyalty." When a second subcommittee counsel, Don Scarlett (now Dean of the South Dakota University Law School), presented a legal argument for pursuing the NBC investigation that was almost identical with Laskin's, the brief was locked in a safe by Dodd and never acted upon.

Dodd shut down the investigation. He forbade publication of the crucial executive-session testimony. He rejected one staff report after another on the investigation, and finally specifically forbade any mention of the Kintner-Levy conflict. On his orders, the watered-down report he finally approved was shown to NBC officials for their clearance before it was distributed to the other Senators on the subcommittee. NBC Vice-President Peter Kenney reported back that, while his company conceded the report was "fair" to NBC, it would, of course, prefer no report at all. Dodd obligingly never made the report official. He waved the thick "committee print" aloft in rebuttal to the charge of his campaign opponent, John Lodge, that he had wasted a million dollars on a television investigation that had not even resulted in a report or in official recommendations. But, unknown to Lodge, the "committee print" had no official standing, and after the election Dodd quietly dropped it. To this day, no bona fide committee report on the four-year television probe has ever been issued.

Staff members who knew the inside story of this investigation bitterly deplored it as a sell-out. But the motive we did not know. We accepted the fact that, for his own reasons, Dodd was determined to protect Kintner, but we held out the hope that the general investigation into television practices was not entirely dead and from time to time we tried to revive it.

There were indications that it would be revived. In both 1963 and 1964, Dodd requested and received subcommittee budgets of about $200,000—with completion of the television probe as his number one stated objective. Perian mapped out a set of hearings. His proposals called for a new look at the three major networks, plus a probe into smaller groups of independent broadcasters that specialized in unsavory programs.

One afternoon Carl invited me to a private showing of a special film the subcommittee staff had spliced together from segments of a dozen top-rated programs. It was an unrelieved portrayal of violence. To see all at once the savagery that was being ladled out to the TV public in nightly portions was a shock to the nervous system. The opening scene concerned a Western gunslinger who liked to shoot people "right between the eyes." Another featured a prolonged and sadistic beating of a young man with heavy chains by a mob of hoodlums. There was a torture sequence in which the victim's lips were seared off with a blowtorch. Then came the inevitable fist fights of almost unbelievable brutality, followed by the stabbings, maimings, sniper killings, and mass murders that make up the nightly entertainment of the American public, with its twenty-five million young viewers. When it was over I was almost sick to my stomach and overcome with a numb sense of depression that I found difficult to shake.

"How did you like it," Carl said.

"God. It's awful."

"What do you think a steady diet of this, night after night, year after year, will do to people—especially all those millions who are unbalanced to start with?" Carl asked. "The scenes we just saw were from shows produced by the three major networks. They were all condemned by the committee at the last hearings, and the networks apologized for them and said they'd do better. Instead, they've put all this garbage in syndication, for reruns. A new network, Metromedia, bought the worst of it. They're showing these programs earlier in the evening, to an audience made up largely of children. One of them even has a homosexual theme. Metromedia stations are now showing almost as much crime and violence as the three major networks put

together. It's as if they used our 1961 hearings as a shopping list."
We agreed to work together on this.

The subcommittee staff made a thorough survey. Tables were prepared for Dodd, showing the comparisons between Metromedia channels and the other broadcasters. Subpoenas were drawn up for Metromedia officials and their files. But Dodd refused to issue them. "It
wouldn't be fair to single out this one independent," he said. "Check
the others again."

We figured it might be a stall, but the staff ran another survey, on
Storer Broadcasting, Westinghouse, and other independents. Carl reported back to Dodd.

"We have no real basis for investigating the other independents," he
said. "They devote less than thirty percent of prime time to shows that
feature violence. For the big networks the figure is fifty percent. For
Metromedia, it's eighty percent!"

But the answer from Dodd was still "no." I interceded to no avail.
Carl followed Dodd over to the Senate floor to make a last appeal. "If
we let Metromedia get away with this, after all our brave pronounce-
ments, it will make a mockery of our whole investigation," he told
Dodd.

"I told you before, Carl, I'm not investigating Metromedia," Dodd
said, reddening. "That's final."

"Even if they're the worst?"

"Everything is relative, Carl. I don't want to hear another word
about it." Dodd turned away.

He remained adamant. We began to add up the reasons. During
Dodd's first probe into television in 1961 Carl had asked Metromedia
to send him several of their films for monitoring. That was the signal
that touched off an intensive wooing of Dodd by Metromedia executives. It began with a series of invitations to social events from Mrs.
Florence Lowe, an attractive, aggressive widow, appropriately titled
"Coordinator of Special Projects." As the months passed, the Dodds
were wined and dined ever more frequently by the tireless Mrs. Lowe.
Then Metromedia President John Kluge took a hand.

Kluge began to entertain Dodd regularly, even had the Dodd family to his Beverly Hills home, recently purchased from Frank Sinatra.
Highly impressed, Dodd made this entry in his official diary:

It was very beautiful and unusual, built high up on the moun-
tains. The girls visited all over the house. It has its own movie

theatre. Mr. Sinatra had his own barber chair, in which the girls all sat.

Kluge's attentions gave the Dodds social prominence they had not before enjoyed. In the summer of 1965, the Dodds were honored at a lavish party at Kluge's Virginia estate, in the heart of the fox and hound country, to which Cabinet members, Senators, a Supreme Court Justice, and Washington columnists and celebrities were transported on a special bus equipped with a bartender. And the gifts poured in: a television set from Mrs. Lowe, imported champagnes from Kluge, testimonial and political contributions from Metromedia officials. And there were other financial contributions from friends of the Kluges and Florence Lowe. For instance, in October 1964, Mrs. Lowe steered millionaire Mortimer Gordon to Dodd. "I think that the two of you will become good friends, and I know Morty will be your ardent and meaningful supporter," she wrote. At their first meeting, "Morty" had a $1,000 contribution for his newly found friend.

To make sure that the subcommittee staff was not quietly investigating Metromedia behind his back, Dodd placed Mrs. Lowe's son, Roger, a three-time school dropout, on the subcommittee payroll as a professional employee. There he could spy on the staff, examine the confidential files, and report back to his mother at night on all its investigative activities. And while Mrs. Lowe was entertaining Dodd at dinner or at the Ice Capades, she could keep him posted on his staff's movements.

There was never a formal probe of Metromedia, nor were the surveys and tables already compiled by the staff ever released to the public.

During the last years of a Senate career noted for its honest and courageous investigations into powerful interests, Senator Estes Kefauver doggedly tracked a final opponent—the drug industry. Kefauver maintained that illegal rigging of prices and strangling of competition by the drug barons enabled them to charge as much as forty times the cost of producing a given drug. The chief victims, he said, were the aged and the sick who desperately needed these wonder drugs and frequently suffered pain and death when they were unable to pay prices that were artificially inflated by the companies. For two stormy years, Kefauver kept one controversial case before his Anti-Trust and Monopoly Subcommittee, a case involving the drug giants of America and one which he thought would prove the need for prosecution and reform.

It was based upon a dispute within the industry itself. McKesson & Robbins had begun producing non-brand-name drugs and selling them at low cost in an experimental program involving the South American nation of Colombia. The rest of the drug industry was aghast and, according to Kefauver, had ganged up on McKesson to break up this experiment and freeze the company out of the South American market. To prove his case, Kefauver needed subpoena power over company records, but the drug trust, through its friends in the Senate, led by Senator Everett Dirksen of Illinois and Senator Roman Hruska of Nebraska, managed month-after-month to withhold that power from Kefauver. The Tennessee Senator would not give up, however, and continued to press for action.

Dodd, the number three man in subcommittee seniority, was a key figure, for every vote counted in the recurring confrontations between Kefauver and the Dirksen-Hruska group. Moreover, the international nature of the case brought it before the Foreign Relations Committee, making Dodd the only Senator to judge it in two separate capacities.

In a manner that was now familiar to his staff, Dodd began receiving favors, this time from *both sides* to the dispute. From McKesson & Robbins, he accepted the regular use of a plush company plane and crew. At a moment's notice, the Cessna Queen Air would wing toward Washington from its home base in New Jersey, take the Senator wherever he wanted to go, and remain at his disposal for as long as he wished. The cash value of such a service, used on a weekly basis, had to be at least $10,000 annually. Dodd also received a $1,000 campaign contribution from McKesson Vice-President Laurence C. Ehrhardt. We knew that, meanwhile, Dodd raked in $1,000— it may have been more—from representatives of the firms lined up against McKesson, beginning with a gift from Thomas G. Corcoran, who represented the Pharmaceutical Manufacturers Association. Corcoran met Dodd frequently in Washington and New York on "business matters" and helped organize the D.C. reception for Dodd in 1964, which netted $13,000 for him.

Such was Corcoran's influence with Dodd that when the Senate Committee on Health, Labor, and Public Welfare was meeting behind closed doors to complete action on a drug-control bill, of which Dodd was the original author, Corcoran appeared in Dodd's office with a letter requesting amendments to the bill that were favorable to one of his clients—McNeil Laboratories, makers of the drug Butisol. He asked Dodd to have his letter retyped verbatim on Senate stationery for Dodd's signature and forwarded to the committee. Dodd signed Corcoran's letter without change and had it hand-delivered to the committee, which adopted the suggested amendments unaware that they had been drafted, not by the bill's author, but by a paid lobbyist.

Dodd walked a tightrope between both sets of benefactors. On the rare showdown votes in committee, he would support Kefauver and McKesson. In the equally important maneuvering to prevent show-down votes and thus delay the investigation interminably, Dodd would side with Corcoran's clients. He would stay in his office, some-times in Corcoran's company, while Kefauver was desperately trying to round up a quorum. He would have Marjorie call Kefauver's staff throughout the afternoon on showdown days. So long as there was no quorum present, he would remain in his office, thus, by his absence, preventing a quorum. If a quorum was at last assembled without him, he would go to the meeting. But periodically he would slip out of the closed hearing room to phone messages to Corcoran, informing him of the latest confidential developments inside, in direct violation of a sacrosanct Senate rule.

The delaying tactics dragged on successfully for years, frustrating Kefauver's efforts to get at the truth. The death of the great Tennes-see Senator in 1963 brought final victory to the Corcoran group, and after a time the drug inquiry petered out inconclusively. The price of many vital drugs at the corner pharmacy would continue to be twenty to forty times the production cost.

In his capacity as chairman of the Juvenile Delinquency Subcom-mittee, Dodd was also "probing" other facets of the drug industry. His special target was the criminal traffic through which half of the one billion "pep pills" and "goofballs" produced in this country each year were being sold illegally, mostly to thrill-seeking juveniles and drug addicts. Most of the time, this investigation was on the level, since Dodd needed a legislative achievement to take home to the voters during his forthcoming campaign. Legislation placing minimal con-trols on the amphetamine and barbiturate traffic seemed the surest bet for passage of a bill bearing his name. But even here the usual pattern set in.

Investigative staff work had isolated Endo Laboratories as the major producer of an addictive synthetic narcotic called "Percodan" which

Attorney General Stanley Mosk of California said had spread to twenty thousand youths in that state alone. The staff had subpoenaed the records of Endo, Dodd had announced public hearings at which Mosk would be a key witness, and Mayor Sam Yorty of Los Angeles revealed that Dodd's hearings would be held in that city. But then the versatile Corcoran turned up in Dodd's office as the lawyer for Endo. He haughtily announced to the staff that he would deal only with Dodd on the matter. The records turned over to Dodd by Corcoran were incomplete. Perian found ample evidence that key documents had been withheld in violation of the subpoena, and he sent a memorandum to Dodd apprising him that Endo was thus in contempt of the Senate, as well as deeply involved in the Percodan mess. But from the moment Corcoran entered the picture, the Endo inquiry was dead. The highly publicized hearings were called off. The fight to place controls on Percodan was abandoned. Fortunately, others took up the effort many months later, and Percodan was eventually placed in the class of drugs requiring a triplicate prescription. But that wasn't Dodd's fault. His relationship with Endo Laboratories and Tom Corcoran was unimpaired.

In the summer of 1963, a young boy named Steve Pederson was swimming in a Wisconsin lake. A prankster lobbed a souped-up firecracker, called a cherry bomb, in his direction. It went off underwater, and the boy quickly sank from view. Hours later his body was pulled out. Examination showed that the underwater explosion had blown open his stomach and ruptured the aorta in his heart. Blood had rushed to his lungs and he had drowned internally in his own blood, before the water got him.

Shortly after this incident, a similar mishap had blown out the eye of twelve-year-old Randy Berkley. His father, an army colonel, came to the Senate Juvenile Delinquency Subcommittee to plead for an investigation and the *Washington Post* took up the cause.

The staff began checking into the fireworks industry and found that in place of the relatively innocuous roman candles and Chinese firecrackers of former days, several firms were now producing dangerous explosives and selling them to children. They were variously called "ash cans," "M-80's," and "plastic cherry bombs," the latter having the added hazard of spewing plastic pellets at high velocity, like a hand grenade. Testing showed that one of these toys, set off underwater, could actually blow a coconut in half—to say nothing of a human. The probe further revealed a tragic toll of deaths, blindings, and cripplings, some caused by accident, others by malicious intent.

Much of the traffic in the new fireworks was illegal. It was, for example, a violation of the Federal Fireworks Law to transport any kind of fireworks into a state where their sale was prohibited by state law. But this Federal law had never been enforced. Despite the widespread prevalence of obvious violations, there had never been a successful Federal prosecution.

Dodd jumped into the matter with a loud bang. He would make war on those who merchandised in death and tragedy. Crates of business records were subpoenaed by the subcommittee staff. The first producer called to testify, Bernard Semel, took the Fifth Amendment. His files and testimony were turned over to the F.B.I. He was promptly convicted and sentenced to jail. But Semel was only a small producer. Perian and the committee staff went on examining records and built what Perian considered to be far more serious cases against several of the larger operators, including one Tony Fabrizio of Elkton, Maryland. The staff was on the verge of a brilliant success. Plans were readied for a sensational set of hearings, and a bill to tighten up the Federal law was drafted and given to Dodd for introduction.

Then, one day, Fabrizio and two other fireworks producers, Milton Dropo of Moosup, Connecticut, and H. W. Lloyd of Pittsburg, Tennessee called on Senator Dodd at his office. They protested to Dodd that the pending investigation would put them out of business. They must have said other things that were very persuasive, too, for Senator Dodd telephoned Carl, in their presence.

"Carl," he said, "I want you to stop harassing honest businessmen for stretching the law a little. I want you to drop this investigation and get off their backs. And stay away from the F.B.I. You're not to turn over to them another shred of the information you've gathered, understand?"

Carl understood. He had learned that while Semel was awaiting trial, Lloyd and other cherry bomb manufacturers called on him to boast of how they had "gotten to" Dodd to stop the probe, and how Dodd had humiliated Perian. Semel didn't think they were very funny, however, and tape-recorded their boasts. One day, Fabrizio and the other fireworks people visited Carl and told him they had just called on Senator Dodd to give him their contribution. They had enjoyed a very friendly chat with the Senator, they said; there would be no further fireworks investigation, they were sure.

They were right. The probe was never revived. The new fireworks bill was never introduced. The killings and the blindings of children remained immune from Senate interference.

CHAPTER SEVEN

ON April 28th, six days after our appearance in executive session, Chairman Stennis made his first public move in the Dodd case. He announced that the Ethics Committee would conduct public hearings "on matters relating to the alleged relationship of Senator Thomas J. Dodd and Julius Klein, owner of a Chicago public relations firm." A date would be announced later, he said, and on completion of the Klein hearings a decision would be made as to whether additional sessions would be held on other allegations against Dodd.

The announcement, emblazoned in black headlines, seemed to us a thrilling vindication of a year and a half of effort. But not to Jack Anderson. He was more wordly-wise.

"Why did they pick the Klein case?" he asked. "We used it first in the column because we wanted to start off with the small stuff and work up. The Klein thing all boils down to a matter of intent, and it's Dodd's word against yours. They may be setting the stage for a white-wash."

Dodd appeared to think so, too. The *Hartford Times* reported an "air of confidence" in Dodd's office after the Stennis announcement. "This will be a pushover," said a key aide. And in a public statement, Dodd pointed out that it was he who requested the investigation of the Klein matter in the first place. "I am therefore pleased that the Senate Ethics Committee has today announced that it plans to hold hearings," he said. "These hearings will demonstrate to my own constituents and to the American public not only the malicious untruth of the charges made against me, but also the systematic theft of documents from my office and the motivations of those who conspired in that theft."

Weeks passed, without word of when the hearings would be held or of how wide would be their eventual scope. Talk of the Dodd case died out, as reporters waited for a lead from the committee. Newsmen told us that there was a tacit understanding among the major newspapers with bureaus in Washington to leave the Dodd matter alone until the hearings started.

Into the vacuum moved Dodd and his attorneys. On May 6th, Dodd, with great fanfare, filed the five-million-dollar, fourteen-count libel suit against Pearson and Anderson that he had long planned. It charged an illegal conspiracy between the columnists and the ex-employees who had burglarized his files. The full text of Dodd's twenty-nine-page complaint was mailed to the one thousand press names on Dodd's mailing list. Late that night, attorney Sonnett obtained the issuance of subpoenas for pre-trial hearings for Michael, Terry, Marjorie, Drew Pearson, Jack Anderson, and me. They were served on us by United States Marshals. In another blaze of publicity, Sonnett announced that it was necessary to move against us quickly and by night, because he believed Dodd's ex-employees were the kind of people who might suddenly skip town.

I assumed that the libel suit was a multipurpose ploy, intended to stop the Pearson columns, frighten the "ex-employees," give Dodd a public relations boost, and elicit, through the secret pre-trial hearings, just how much of Dodd's affairs was known to us and hence to the Ethics Committee. We learned that private eye Lynch was again making his rounds. And one of Dodd's lawyers, Walter Kinney, called Michael in an attempt to lure him back to the Dodd camp.

"Terry Golden is a nice girl, from a good family," Kinney said. "It would be a shame to endanger her reputation. When you see the kind of questions we are going to throw at Boyd you'll know what I mean."

"When our turn comes, we'll be there," Michael replied coldly.

By court order, I was the first to be called for pre-trial interrogation by Dodd's attorneys. I was required to be available for four days and to bring with me all documents in my possession.

The deposition, as it was called, was scheduled to take place in the offices of Dodd's lawyers in the presence of the attorneys for Pearson and Anderson and the witnesses. In theory, its purpose was to establish the basic facts before the trial began, thus speeding and making more meaningful the court proceedings. No judge would be present, but the action was under court surveillance and any dispute that arose between the opposing lawyers would be referred back to the judge for a ruling. An official court reporter would administer the oath and make a transcript that would be used later in the trial. The perjury laws applied.

I was represented by Jack Anderson's lawyer, Warren Woods, a genial and able veteran of many libel suits. Our strategy provided that I would answer all questions that were even remotely relevant—about taking the documents, about my personal life, my finances—and thus to set a precedent that could be cited to the judge if Dodd proved evasive and uncooperative when his turn for questioning came.

I arrived at the appointed hour at Sonnett's Washington offices. To Sonnett's vast annoyance, I was accompanied not only by Woods but by Anderson, who, as a party to the case, was entitled to be present. John Donovan, another skilled libel lawyer representing Drew Pearson, also joined us. Sonnett was waiting, flanked by a large staff of young lawyers. I looked him over carefully.

He was about sixty. Combative looking, puffy, perspiring, his collar open, he reminded me of H. L. Mencken's description of William Jennings Bryan at the Scopes trial. "There was a vague, unpleasant manginess about his appearance; he somehow seemed dirty, though a close glance showed him as carefully shaven as an actor and clad in immaculate linen."

Sonnett was a courtroom performer of the old school, well-practiced in all the tried-and-true forensic devices. He was by turns calm, sympathetic, angry, scornful, indignant. He gestured and eye-rolled. He resorted, with painful obviousness, to the insulting remark to goad a witness into an unguarded reply, the pointed finger to unnerve, the suddenly raised voice to frighten, the theatrical ogle to mystify, the exaggerated use of massive, irrelevant documentation to intimidate. The questions came in rapid sequence. Why had I "stolen" Dodd's files? Why did I sell out my benefactor to Anderson, whom I knew to be a liar? Why didn't I trust the F.B.I.? How much money had I taken from Anderson and Pearson? Where did my associates now work?

Something of a legal prestidigitator, Sonnett made exhibits appear and disappear. He would wave under my nose a check cashed by me four years before in a cabaret, as if it contained the revelation of a corrupt past. He would note that he had before him a copy of my divorce decree and then lay it aside with the implication that he would later return to it with devastating effect. He asked me to identify the signature of a girl who was once a close friend, but whom I hadn't seen for many years, and then claimed possession of an affidavit she had signed which he would one day read into the record in all its sordidness. He asked me to identify my own signature, as if a drawerful of bad checks were coming up any minute. He would direct me to read my oath of office as a Senate employee, as though to underline the depth of my betrayal. As he went on and on, junior attorneys would come and go with stacks of documents. What was the source of my income? Where did my children live? Was I meeting my financial obligations? How much money did I have in the bank? Had anyone loaned me funds in the past year? Laboriously, he would set the stage for some presumably damning admission that would expose the kind of fellow I was, and then not ask the critical question, as though saving it for a grander occasion. He was trying, I knew, to muddle me, to pressure me into lying on some small point, to elicit a different answer from me today than he got yesterday, and thus to show the Senate later on that I was a duplicitous and untrustworthy witness. So far as I could tell, he did not succeed. By the fourth day, the fire had gone out of his performance. He asked a series of routine, factual questions in a tired monotone and dismissed me with half the day still left.

If Dodd and Sonnett were engaging in psychological warfare, they must have been disappointed with the results. There was no break in the ranks of the prospective witnesses against Dodd. Pearson and Anderson continued to pour it on in their column and showed their determination to fight the libel suit to a successful verdict. In a key decision, they won a court order permitting the interrogation of Dodd. He was ordered to follow me to the stand. Suddenly Dodd backed away from the suit he had launched with such fanfare. He dropped ten of his original fourteen counts and began to ask for postponements in the schedule of depositions. Nothing more was to be heard of the libel suit.

Early in June the Ethics Committee announced that the Dodd-Klein hearings would begin on the 22nd of the month. As that day approached, the design of Chairman Stennis slowly emerged, through a combination of cryptic committee statements, news leaks, and information we acquired while working with the committee staff. I had taken part in many Senate investigations, but the Dodd hearings were shaping up to be unlike anything I had ever seen or studied.

A brand new set of rules that turned upside down the precedents for past Senate probes was being created for Senator Dodd. The institution of the Congressional inquiry, with its reputation for toughness and its capacity to instill fear, never took a more curious or more impotent form.

By rule and tradition, Senate investigative hearings are not circumscribed by the restrictions that apply to criminal trials. The ordinary object of such an inquiry does not have the rights of a defendant in court. His files may be subpoenaed by Senate investigators. His business partners and employees can be placed under oath and required, on penalty of contempt of Congress, to divulge what they know about his transgressions. He is required to take the stand himself, often under the TV lights, and is asked questions which, if answered truthfully, might put him in the penitentiary. If he refuses to answer on grounds of self-incrimination, he tacitly admits guilt in the public eye, signaling the end of his reputation and perhaps of his livelihood. He faces a highly organized prosecution, composed of skilled committee counsel and prestigious Senators. He is protected by no strict evidentiary standards. Masked witnesses, unverified affidavits, transcripts of secretly monitored phone conversations, testimony from staff investigators about the alleged admissions of absent persons—all are admissable if so ordered by the Chair. Against this formidable assault, he has no means of defense except his wits. He has no advance information about the case against him, no power to protest unfair questions, no right to challenge hostile exhibits or to cross-examine adverse witnesses or to call witnesses in his own behalf or to introduce evidence that gives his side of the story. While he may bring a lawyer with him, the lawyer is not allowed to play any part in the proceeding and can do nothing but give advice on whether or not to take the Fifth Amendment.

The Senate has long justified these procedures on the grounds that Senate hearings are fact-finding inquiries aimed at illuminating matters of national interest and legislative need. No jail term is meted out by the Senate, no criminal punishment imposed. Hence, it is argued, the safeguards that surround a court trial are not justified. They would, it is said, inhibit the operations of the Senate and prevent it not only from obtaining the facts it needs to legislate intelligently but from informing the public of the grave abuses which victimize the country. True, the object of investigation may be condemned in a committee report and damned in the press, but this, it is argued, is the natural hazard faced by anyone who involves himself in the public arena. True, evidence obtained may be turned over to the Justice Department for criminal action—but *then* he shall have all the Constitutional rights to which he is entitled.

The argument in favor of the free-wheeling Senate inquiry is most cogently made when the object is a public official accused of misdeeds. Here, the usual justifications are enhanced by the public's right to know about the official conduct of public servants. Hence, Senate aide Bobby Baker could be asked scores of incriminating questions in front of watching millions; his papers were commandeered and used as evidence; his secretary, Carole Tyler, his staff, and his legal associates were required to testify against him and to help the staff build its case. So strong is the right of Congress to probe official misconduct that Mrs. Adam Clayton Powell was required to testify about her husband's alleged sins, although in court a wife cannot give testimony against her husband.

But for reasons unexplained, Senator Stennis and the Ethics Committee had no thought of investigating Dodd as though he were a mere Cabinet officer, or a Congressman, or a Senate employee, or an ordinary citizen. The Senate's finely honed investigatory procedures were not to be used on a Senator. For the Dodd inquiry, a marvelous and lopsided hybrid had been created. It consisted of an oversized defense apparatus mated with a dwarfed prosecution. No one had ever seen anything like it before on Capitol Hill.

Contrary to normal Senate practice, Dodd was to be informed of the list of witnesses against him and of their expected testimony. A dress rehearsal of the public hearing was to be held in private, at which the committee would unveil all the evidence and go through its case under the eye of Dodd and his lawyers. There would be no direct television or radio coverage. Dodd and Sonnett were to be accorded the right to challenge any action of Counsel Fern, protest questions he might ask of witnesses, object to the introduction of evidence, cross-examine all committee witnesses, and present their own evidence and witnesses. They could even interrupt Fern's presentation and bring on their own witnesses to refute current testimony. In cross-examining, they were to be permitted to attack the witness's character and reputation as well as his testimony. And Dodd—in a decision totally without precedent—was not to be required to testify. To grant

Dodd and his counsel some of these privileges, the Ethics Committee had to reverse its own rules adopted only a few months before.

I could not help but regard the special privileges given to the defense as evidence of favoritism and hypocrisy. But believing as I did that Dodd deserved a fair chance to present his side of the matter, I did not particularly oppose the defense part of the arrangement. It was the other half of the hybrid, the emasculated prosecution, that caused me to worry.

There was to be no prosecution, per se, despite the full-blown defense. This was not an adversary proceeding, Stennis said. Counsel Fern was supposed to impartially present both sides of the case. But in presenting the side against Dodd, he was to be severely limited. First, the scope of the inquiry was to be rigidly restricted. How rigidly, I did not yet know, but Fern had hinted to me that the committee would not challenge Dodd's profiteering on his payroll, his squashing of investigations, his accepting favors from people interested in legislation. These, he said, were considered to be matters "involving a Senator's judgment," though I was hard pressed to understand what that meant. Even the inquiry into the Klein relationship was to be limited to one main question—whether or not Dodd went to West Germany in 1964 to speak to government officials there in Klein's behalf. But Fern was forbidden to submit questions, even in writing, to those officials.

Fern was not allowed to subpoena either Dodd's or Klein's files. Nor could he use the files we had provided. They were "tainted," said Stennis, although the Justice Department had ruled they were quite valid, F.B.I. agents used them in questioning us, and court precedents held that they would be admissible, even in a criminal trial, to say nothing of a Senate hearing.

Fern could not call as witnesses any of the forty-odd members of Dodd's various staffs, even though some of them had direct knowledge of wrongdoing. That, Stennis maintained, would be in violation of the privileged relationship which should exist between a Senator and his underlings. Only if Dodd gave his permission could committee investigators talk to a member of the staff.

In cross-examining witnesses produced in Dodd's behalf, Fern was put under wraps. He was forbidden to attack their character and reputation, however dubious their testimony, as Sonnett would be allowed to do to us.

If Dodd chose to appear in his own behalf or if he produced Mrs.

Dodd as a witness, Fern would not be allowed to cross-examine at all. Stennis, the gallant Southerner, ruled that only a Senator could question another Senator or his consort. Thus the prospect of a skillful dissection of Dodd's defense, which could come only from a prosecutor totally immersed for weeks in the subject, went glimmering. It was highly unlikely that a Senator, his time occupied by twenty other matters, could, on the basis of a briefing, do an adequate job, even if he had the stomach to pursue the evasions and maneuverings of a fellow-member of the Club.

I was troubled but not surprised at these procedures. This was what the four of us had apprehended when we decided in the first place to go to Pearson and Anderson, rather than to a Senate committee. But the confirmation filled us with misgivings. We were to be the only witnesses against Dodd, and we could not tell whether we were striking a blow for reform, or walking into a trap specially constructed to shield Dodd while exposing us to public condemnation and the hazard of Federal prosecution.

Who was Julius Klein, anyway? Despite forty years devoted largely to publicizing himself, Klein remained a shadowy figure in the public mind. Because he was little known, the significance of his relationship with Dodd was unclear to the average observer. But as the hearings approached, Klein could not resist undertaking a campaign to draw attention to himself. He held press conferences and issued pronunciamentoes. This stimulated newsmen to check on his past, to look up the last time he had been investigated by the Senate, and to write long and revealing stories. By the time the hearings began, the image of Julius Klein hung palpably over the hearing room to form a backdrop against which, for the first time, the public could get a clear view of the world of Senator Tom Dodd.

Once or twice in Dodd's office I had seen Klein, short, thickset, with a German accent. I had read his letters, florid, self-serving, demanding, sometimes abusive, frequently inscribed with such marks of secrecy as "confidential" and "Please destroy this. I made *NO* copy." And I had met his harried retinue, the apologetic instrument of his massive ego and of his blatant persistence in pushing himself into prominence. But it was not until the week before the Dodd-Klein hearings were to begin that I made a concerted effort to find out, from investigative reporters and former employees, just who Klein was.

Both at home and abroad, he traveled in the highest circles. He claimed to be a confidant of Senators and generals, of Adenauer, Foreign Minister Brentano, and the major German industrialists. According to his prefabricated Walter Mitty image, he was Major General Julius Klein (United States Army Reserve, ret.), and was surrounded by all the aura of the Joint Chiefs and the German high command. On the masthead of his stationery was a general's flag with two stars. Pictures of himself with Eisenhower and MacArthur dominated a wall of his Essex House suite. He was a comrade-in-arms, he was always saying, of Douglas MacArthur. His chief assistant, General Kenneth Buchanan, was once, he said, "the right arm of General Marshall." His chief American client, the eccentric, seventy-five-year-old Schenley whiskey baron, Lou Rosenstiel, who sported a Swiss Alpine hat but had never worn a uniform, was always referred to by Klein as "the Supreme Commander." Served by a staff of military men, Klein, with flair and Teutonic efficiency, directed a far-flung public-relations empire which had offices in Frankfurt, Chicago, Los Angeles, New York, and Washington. When he traveled by train, it was in a special deluxe compartment. Each time he crossed the Atlantic, it was aboard the liner *United States,* and he occupied the stateroom reserved for the Duke and Duchess of Windsor.

Before his current splendor, Klein had led many lives, all of them glamorously gilded and assiduously publicized by his firm. At age thirteen, during World War I, he had been a boy war correspondent in Germany. At seventeen, after America joined the fighting, he was a "doughboy." At eighteen, he became a member of the United States Military Commission in Berlin. During the Capone era in Chicago, he was a Hearst "editor," then a Washington correspondent. During the golden age of the screen, he became a "$75,000-a-year" Hollywood movie executive. Still later, he was a decorated war hero and commander of troops in the Pacific in World War II, the originator of the Defense Department's first antisubversion program, an officer of the General Staff, an "advisor" to Congress on the Cold War, an author of important books, and Republican candidate for the Senate in Illinois in 1950. Then he donned yet another uniform as National Commander of the Jewish War Veterans, a 100,000-man organization with considerable political leverage. Now, he fashioned himself Julius Klein, the international statesman, counselor to chancellors and presidents.

But painstaking press inquiry deflated the heroic image he had created for himself. The war correspondent was, in fact, the contributor

to a high school paper in Germany, where he was raised, of a single
puerile story which praised one of the Kaiser's war messages for its
"glorious words to his people in this dreadful hour of need." His successive careers as doughboy and member of the United States Military
Commission turned out to be his embroidery on the fact that, a week
after the war ended, he obtained a job as office boy with a United
States Army detachment in Berlin and later moved over to the Military
Commission as a lowly clerk. His editorial career was totally unknown
to Hearst veterans, said the *Washington Post*, although he is remembered as a reporter and the backer of a Republican German-language
paper that came out only at election time.

Layer after layer of the image continued to peel off. No records
could be found of his contributions as a movie executive—no credits,
no listing in the Motion Picture Encyclopedia, although some vaguely
remember him as an occasional public relations man for the late Louis
B. Mayer of MGM. The "noted American soldier" and commander of
troops in the Pacific was a rear echelon quartermaster officer engaged
in the necessary but unheroic task of storing and moving supplies in
the forgotten backwater of New Caledonia. His service with "the general staff" turned out to consist of several months as a public relations
man in the office of the War Secretary. His general's stars came by
political appointment in the Illinois National Guard, after loyal service as a contributor and leg man for the Republican party. The 1950
Republican candidate for the Senate in Illinois was in fact a self-
declared candidate in the Republican primary that year, who ran
ninth in a field of eleven. The Cold War consultant to Congress? One
of the Senators who used his Essex House suite had appointed him for
a time to the staff of a Senate Committee, so he could travel in Europe
with official credentials. The author of books? In reality he had turned
out a couple of private puffs about himself.

Even Klein's true age and place of birth were enshrouded in doubt.
He had spent a small fortune in legal and other fees to have Chicago
officially declared his birthplace—perhaps in anticipation of running
for President. But some of his confidants believe he was really born in
Austria or Germany, where he grew up. And, after pressuring Dodd
and other Senators for years, he finally managed to have a reprimand
removed from his military record that was placed there in the first
place because he had lied about his age on his official papers.

A few nights before the hearings opened, Marjorie and I spent a
hilarious evening with Klein's former secretary, Helen Batherson.

Fortyish, an attractive and voluble blonde, she recalled eleven years under Klein with both humor and bitterness.

"I was his girl Friday," she said rolling her eyes, "and that covered a broad territory. One of my jobs was to keep visiting Senators comfortable, even the ones who couldn't keep their hands off my fanny." Miss Batherson said that Klein usually carried thousands of dollars in cash on his person, and that he would often have her cash large checks at the bank before he went calling on Capitol Hill. "He used to fix up double-sealed envelopes, one inside of the other, which I would carry to the offices of friendly Congressmen, including Dodd," she told us.

"General Klein was a genius at conning people," she said. "He took the Germans for more than half a million dollars and never did anything for them that I could find out. Instead of building up the new Germany to American officials, Klein had American officials like Dodd build *him* up to the Germans. All he ever did for Germany was to travel there five or six times a year on the *United States*. The pleasure of his company, that's all they ever got out of it. Before every sailing he would throw a big going away party for himself in his stateroom to which a list of big shots would be invited—and the Germans had to pay for it all.

"Nothing was too gauche for Klein to attempt if it would promote his image," Miss Batherson recalled. "When the body of General MacArthur was lying in state in the Capitol Rotunda, Julius rushed to Washington, borrowed a uniform of the Jewish War Veterans, hired some photographers, and obtained special permission from House Speaker McCormack to have his picture taken in front of the bier. There he was, while legitimate mourners stood waiting in line, leaning over the casket with his ridiculous cap on, mugging in grief-stricken poses while the flash bulbs popped. It was awful. He sent those pictures all over the world."

The Jewish War Veterans had eased him out when they learned he was in the employ of German industrialists and, for $40,000 a year, was lobbying for the return of impounded war assets to their former owners, many of them ex-Nazis. The military front was exploded by Major General Harry Bolen, Klein's superior in the National Guard. Bolen told the *Washington Post* that the unit Klein commanded "couldn't shoot at a kid's box kite . . . we needed that unit like I need a damned buggy whip on my jeep . . . that kind of man [Klein] is dangerous, and we can't have him in the Illinois National Guard, and I threw him out."

Even the public relations empire was tottering. The Germans had canceled one contract after another since Senator Fulbright, chairman of the Senate Foreign Relations Committee, had investigated Klein and found him an example of a man who "by exaggeration or misuse of his relationships with members of Congress can, for his own purposes, create for government officials and business interests a mistaken and sometimes unflattering picture of how our government institutions function." Klein's former Senate boosters—Humphrey, Javits, and Dirksen—had turned their backs on him. But Klein's hold over Dodd remained intact. At Klein's insistent behest, Dodd wrote to Fulbright:

> . . . I hope the record can also show that I have known General Klein for many years, and I consider him to be a man of sterling character and of great competence. In addition, he is one of the most patriotic Americans I have met and he is dedicated and devoted to the best interests of our country. Over the years I have had a full and complete opportunity to know him and I can state without qualification that he is a man of unblemished honor and integrity.

And to Dr. Ludger Westrick, minister of the West German Cabinet, Dodd sent a letter, dictated in the first instance by Klein himself, which said:

> I noted that you had a visit with General Klein and all of us, of course, shall appreciate it if his problem, in the interest of both countries, is solved to a mutual satisfaction . . . I don't have to repeat the high regard we have for the General and the great help he has been to us in the past, but most important we value his advice and counseling. I assure you that my and my colleagues' friendship and my desire to underline General Klein's value as advisor and counsel is a purely unselfish one and it is based on our feelings that he is an understanding bridge between our countries. These statements are not only shared with my Democratic and Republican colleagues, but also with our newly elected Vice-President Hubert Humphrey, who recently stated how he will need the advice and counsel of his friend Julius Klein.

But now Dodd, the last of Klein's mouthpieces, was himself under investigation—for his association with Klein, among other things. The future must have looked bleak indeed to the general, but with his gambler's instinct and his flair for stuntmanship, he saw the hearings as another chance for fame. Since the Ethics Committee had not scheduled him as a witness, he began to issue broadsides demanding that he be called.

With de Gaulle-like pomp, the Old Soldier held a televised press conference in Paris.

"I have given money to many Senators," Klein said, "but in the present witch-hunting climate, I will not reveal their names. I will go to jail first." He would journey to America by ocean liner for the hearings, he said. "Since the war, I always travel by boat to avoid hemorrhaging."

He made the most of the moment. On his arrival in New York the press carried photos of General Klein waving from the gangplank in the manner of a returning hero. He released a "shipboard statement" in which he said: "I am anxious to testify because I am aroused by the character assassination of my good friend, Senator Dodd. He and I are under attack because we are strong Americans, anti-Communists, and I don't hesitate to say that Drew Pearson is left-wing."

But Stennis had decided not to permit the unpredictable Klein to play a decisive role in the hearings. Klein would be allowed to testify, since he demanded it, but only as an anticlimax, three weeks after the rest of the hearings were scheduled to end. This was to be Dodd's show, not Klein's.

On the night before the public hearings were to open, the four of us met at Marjorie's place. A year-and-a-half had passed since we first began to plot our improbable scheme. In many ways it had been a barren period. Our lives had been in a sort of suspension, in a temporary existence that had stretched on and on. But we were still together. Our relationship had survived a hundred tense moments when the mistake of any of us would have hurt us all. And, as the hour of testing approached, we all felt good about that.

Michael had finally found employment. It was a tough job that took him out on the road every week, doing personnel work for the Southern Railway Company. But he stuck with it. Terry, after losing her position with Judge Bazelon, had landed an administrative post with a research firm.

Marjorie and I were not so fortunate. On leaving the Lawyers'

Committee, Marjorie was hired as a legal secretary by Arnold and Porter, a distinguished Washington law firm with a reputation that had been fully earned for defending unpopular causes. Marjorie had explained her role in the Dodd case before she was hired and was told that she would not be penalized for it. But during the deposition I had revealed to Sonnett her place of employment. The next day, she was peremptorily—though apologetically—dismissed. Now she was living on unemployment compensation and some past savings. As for myself, except for an occasional ghostwriting chore, I was far along in my second prolonged period of unemployment.

We talked about the next day's events. From the hesitant beginnings of the early days of our plot, we had all grown very militant about the Dodd case. We had become hardened to the derisive terms much of Washington used to describe us: informers, document thieves, betrayers of trust. We became the more obstinate, even as the hole we dug for ourselves grew deeper and deeper. What had started as a personal protest against the power-bred venality of one man, what had continued as a contest, a battle joined, had inevitably grown into a mission, with all the trappings of a cause. We had come to identify ourselves, perhaps presumptuously, with the general struggle for political reform and we looked on the Dodd hearings as a means of showing the country some of the reasons why the democratic process was being daily undermined by influence peddlers, fixers, and bribers, whose activities were encouraged and protected by the ethical laxity and the collusive secretiveness of the Congress.

We broke up early that night. I was to take the stand in the morning. My turn was expected to last for about two days. Then would come Marjorie, then Terry, then Michael. Tomorrow, Wednesday, though the first day of the public hearing, would be my third consecutive day of testifying, for on Monday and Tuesday the major part of the case against Dodd had been presented in closed session through testimony by me and Marjorie. Sonnett, therefore, could prepare for renewed cross-examination with exact foreknowledge of the adverse evidence.

I was hoarse and tired. I hadn't been able to get any real sleep in several nights. Though outwardly I felt calm and confident, I found that I had an inner life which seemed to go on quite independently of my conscious, willed existence. It followed its own pattern, one that infuriated me. A tenseness I could not reason away kept me awake until three or four each morning and awakened me as soon as the light came at six. Whatever I might be doing, my mind was constantly engaged in imaginary colloquy with Sonnett or the committee.

As I lay awake again that night, imaginary fears loomed large. Would my memory fail me? Would I look haggard and unconvincing? Would my cracked voice last? If it rained tomorrow, how would I get to the hearing without cab fare? Finally, I drifted off. When I awakened I felt taut, clear, and ready, as though somehow sharpened to a fine edge. As I mulled over the expected questions for the thousandth time, the answers automatically came forth. I tried my voice, and it was still there. And it wasn't raining after all. The phone began to ring—words of encouragement from Marjorie, Michael, Terry, Jack, Drew Pearson. A telegram was delivered. It was from an old service friend whom I had not heard from for fifteen years and who had read about the hearings in the paper. "Fine business you're in," it read, "pulling rugs out from under Senators. Good luck old buddy."

At nine-fifteen I started walking toward the Hill. "Tonight," I thought, "when I walk back home, my life will have greatly changed, for better or worse." When I arrived at the Senate Office Building, I found the hallway crowded with national newsmen, onlookers, Connecticut reporters I had once known well, friends of Dodd, and TV and radio teams of all descriptions. Two cameramen panned me all the way down the hall, backing up in front of me as I walked along trying to act as if nothing was happening. When I reached the great door to the Hearing Room, from which the TV and radio men were barred, two policemen came forward and led me in.

I was astonished at its size. Large as a football field, one reporter wrote. It was jammed with hundreds of spectators. People were milling around and a buzzing din rose higher and higher. Way up front I saw a long, lonely-looking table with one chair and a microphone placed in front of it. I started toward it, down the center aisle, through the crowd. A pleasant-looking woman ran up to me, her round arms outstretched. "God bless you," she said. "Don't let them frighten you, now. I'm Sarah McClendon." Then she leaned forward and whispered: "You should get a load of this crowd. Every crook in town is here."

I saw Senator Stennis approach the rostrum, a look of vexation crossing his face as he peered at the confused scene before him. I waited in the aisle, wondering if I should go forward.

"All right. All right," boomed the Mississippi voice. "The committee will come to ordah. We *must* have ordah heah. Standees will find a seat or retire. Our photographer friends may take pictures for two or three minutes only. We feel we are goin' to have the cooperation of everyone in heah. If there should be someone who doesn't cooperate, why we are goin' to have to resort to othah means . . .

"All right, we will now begin the proceedin's. You gentlemen with the cameras can be active now. Mr. Fern, call the first witness, please."

Hesitantly, I looked past the microphone, across the polished witness table, toward Dodd. He was seated at a table to my left front, surrounded by his lawyers. For a second our eyes met. Then he turned to Sonnett and I could hear the low rumble of his voice. He looked well, I thought, a bit trimmer, clearer of eye, less florid of face than I remembered him in bygone days. His silver hair was carefully brushed and his old props were in place—the pipe, the gold watchchain suspended from his lapel. He affected a pose of nonchalance, as though a disinterested party to a scene somewhat beneath him.

On the other side, Chief Counsel Fern shuffled papers. There were a few opening preliminaries: Did I understand I was still under oath? Yes. Was I accompanied by counsel? No. Did I realize I had the right to counsel? Yes. And then it was under way.

Stennis had defined the crucial question to be determined. Had Senator Dodd traveled to Germany—at taxpayer's expense and during important business on the Senate floor—primarily to contribute to the business interests of a lobbyist and registered agent of a foreign government? Within the limitations imposed on him by the committee, Fern made an earnest effort to prove that he had. In three days of testimony from me, Marjorie, Terry, Michael, and Helen Batherson, and through the introduction of dozens of supporting documents first brought to light by Pearson and Anderson, the story of Dodd's complicated involvement with Klein was presented.

For years, Dodd had accepted favors from Klein while supporting the lobbyist's interests. From eight to a dozen times each year he moved into Klein's $700-a-month Essex House suite, off Central Park in New York, and holidayed free of charge. Meanwhile, he had supported Klein's interests by making speeches at his request, placing in the Congressional Record tributes which the general reprinted and distributed, acting as host at Senate luncheons and parties for visiting German clients, and boosting Klein for prestige government appointments. Then, it was shown, following the 1963 Fulbright probe into the effect of lobbyists on American foreign policy, Klein had strenuously pressed Dodd, through letters and telegrams (which were placed in the record), phone calls and visits (which we described), to fly to Germany to help save his vanishing contracts. Dodd had promised Klein repeatedly to go and even planned the trip with Klein and his aides. General Buchanan, Klein's top assistant, delivered a thick bundle of instructions to Dodd, which contained not only dossiers on the people Klein wanted Dodd to see, but also prepared blurbs outlining exactly what he wanted Dodd to say to them. Dodd made arrangements to call on everyone on Klein's list and, after carefully packing the dossiers in his valise, left Washington suddenly, in the midst of the most important filibuster-breaking effort in fifty years (on the 1964 Civil Rights Act), because, as he said to me, "Julius has been pressing and pressing me to go."

When Dodd arrived in Frankfurt, it was shown, his plane was met by two members of Klein's staff, Herr Kimpel and Frau Reich. Dodd visited four of the six people on Klein's original list, the other two not being available. After Dodd returned to Washington, David Martin, who had accompanied him to Germany, stated in four separate conversations that Dodd had boosted Klein to everyone he saw, "even Adenauer," and that he (Martin) was afraid Klein would get Dodd in trouble. As a follow-up to the trip, Dodd sent two letters drafted by Klein to German Chancellor Erhardt's chief of staff, Dr. Ludger Westrick. The letters were placed in the record, alongside Klein's original drafts.

Perhaps more revealing than the details of the machinations between a confidence man and a United States Senator was the peremptory and sometimes abusive tone of Klein's letters, which caused Chairman Stennis to inquire what kind of a hold Klein had over Dodd.

Of a speech he had drafted for Dodd, Klein wrote:

As soon as you have edited the copy, please deliver it and have Jack Fleischer release it, not only to the American press, but also to the German correspondents accredited to the National Press Corps, and send a copy over to the press attache of the German Embassy, including Minister Krapf, so that this will get the widest circulation in Europe.

When Dodd failed to deliver on an appointment Klein wanted to the United States Advisory Commission on Information, Klein reproved him:

"You know, Tom, friendship is a two-way street."

And when Dodd, fearing for his own reputation, did not come forward strongly enough to satisfy Klein at the time of the Fulbright hearings, Klein wrote him:

> I asked you to be present at the executive session. You promised me the night before that you would attend—but you were not there. I wired you to be present at the public hearings—you were not there either. What are you afraid of? Do you consider friendship a one-way street? All I can say is I am ashamed of you . . . With this. Tom, I close the chapter for good."

It was to keep the chapter from closing that Tom Dodd went to Germany.

This was as far as Counsel Fern was permitted to go by the Committee. He had not been allowed to seek the clinching testimony from the German officials to whom Dodd had spoken in Germany, nor to examine Klein's business records and correspondence in search of corroboration or payments to Dodd, nor to examine Dodd's records, except such as Dodd volunteered, nor to interrogate, prior to the hearings, either Klein or Dodd or their staffs.

"We are not prosecutors," said Stennis, all too correctly. But the partial evidence Fern was allowed to introduce—most of it previously published by Pearson—was proving quite effective.

John Sonnett obviously judged that the best way to handle Dodd's defense was to discredit personally the opposition witnesses. For most of the day-and-a-half that I was on the stand, he concentrated, not on disputing my testimony, but on attempting to picture me as a traitor to a man who had been like a father to me, a man who had been forced to fire me because I was disloyal and immoral and because my work was "deteriorating," whereupon I, out of vengeance, had distorted Dodd's blameless record by feeding misleading documents to unscrupulous columnists who twisted them and used them out of context.

With Marjorie, too, Sonnett had little interest in the facts of the testimony but a great fascination with her divorce of three years before and her subsequent "social relationship" with me. The Senators were visibly unsympathetic to these tactics, and when Sonnett asked

Marjorie if she was planning to marry me, Stennis at last intervened, saying he had gone too far.

With Michael, the thrust of Sonnett's attack was again to show that all of us had acted out of vengeance because the righteous Dodd had interfered with office romances that were springing up all around him. At one point, he actually asked Michael to recount to the committee all the discussions he had ever heard or in which he had taken part concerning "the relationship between Mr. Boyd and Mrs. Carpenter." Surprisingly, this attempt to solicit wholesale gossip and hearsay was not stricken by Stennis. But when Michael started off his answer by saying he had conversed with Senator Dodd about the relationship a number of times, Sonnett abruptly dropped the whole thing and changed the subject. For Michael's answer would have shown that Dodd knew all about the "relationship" a year before he now claimed to have discovered it. This would have nullified his contention that the plot against him arose because he had uncovered his chief aides in a liaison, had fired them, and that this moral act was the cause of their treachery and his present ordeal.

It became increasingly evident, if only by the conduct within the Dodd camp, that Sonnett's gambit was not succeeding. Dodd's people did not act as if they thought they were winning. Dodd himself lost the air of aplomb he possessed at the outset.

On the first day, he suffered through my testimony with audible grunts and growls and an occasional focusing of the evil eye. On the second day, he angrily denounced Counsel Fern for bias and irresponsibility, and he disrupted Fern's questioning of Marjorie by jumping out from behind his table, accusing her of perjury, and threatening to have her prosecuted by the Attorney General. On the third day, Dodd's son, Jeremy, now on his father's senate payroll, accosted and shoved Michael just before he was to testify. "When this is over, I'll follow you to your f———g grave," young Dodd threatened, touching off an uproar that several hours later evoked an apology to the committee from Senator Dodd. Later that day, it was revealed by the *Washington Star* that one of Dodd's lawyers had threatened a smear of Terry Golden unless she cooperated with the Dodd defense. On the fourth day, Dodd stunned the Senate by charging the vice-chairman of the Ethics Committee, Senator Wallace Bennett, with bias and prejudice. Dodd demanded that Bennett be disqualified from participating further in the deliberations.

These outbursts caused a progressively stiffening attitude on the part of the committee, the members of which were certainly aware that they had heavily weighted the procedures in Dodd's favor. Sonnett was overruled with growing frequency for dilatory and tasteless tactics. Dodd was rebuked and silenced for his attack on Fern. "If he is impugned, why *we* are impugned, because he is our voice," declared Stennis, as though from Mount Sinai. To the threats against Marjorie and Michael, Stennis reacted with knitted brows and icy severity. "The committee just cannot stand by now and see any of these witnesses threatened, coerced, or intimidated," he said. He called such tactics "an assault on organized society" and solemnly read aloud a law providing for a $5,000 fine and five years in prison for anyone who attempts to intimidate a witness at a Senate hearing. To Dodd's attack on Bennett, Stennis responded in a voice quivering with anger:

> Gentlemen, we are going through with this hearing. There is no question about that, in spite of the fact that charges have been publicly made here . . . in request of the Attorney General to start a prosecution of one of these witnesses, in spite of allegations . . . that one of the witnesses was threatened directly and one indirectly . . . and in spite of the fact that now one member of this panel, who has the right to sit and deliberate here, has been challenged. Those things do not deter us, not one bit, not one iota!

Dodd had crossed Stennis at his most sensitive spot—orderly procedures, the maintenance of control, the decorum that must prevail among Senators. In the past, Dodd's bullying, his emotional outbursts, his special pleadings had generally worked—but now he looked up at the immovable Stennis and heard a tone even more ominous than the carefully chosen words. Dodd's motion to disqualify Bennett was curtly dismissed, without discussion.

Dodd himself took the witness chair on the fourth day. Stennis was careful to point out that he did so at his own request, not because he was called. Dodd wore the expression of one who was above the battle. He spoke sorrowfully of those he had befriended and who had betrayed him. "I had liked Boyd," he said. "I had taken him out of, I almost say, the basement of the Aetna Insurance Company . . . I thought he was a mighty decent young man . . . Mrs. Dodd and I treated him almost like a fifth son." And of O'Hare: "When I hired O'Hare, as a student attending Catholic University, he was an emaciated, poor lad, and a likeable one, I thought." He had trusted Mrs.

Carpenter and had let her handle his confidential affairs. He had been misled. All three were in league to destroy him. "They were robbing me blind," he said sadly. As he looked back, his only mistakes in life were a preoccupation with the great issues of his time and poor judgment about the character of his underlings.

Yes, he had been glad to stay in General Klein's "apartment" about "seven or eight times a year." He used the accommodations of other friends in New York almost as often. He was a poor man. He was not ashamed of it, he said, not ashamed to take favors from friends.

Yes, he had entertained Klein's associates and recommended him for government appointments. Why not? He had known Klein for many years. Klein was "a decent human being" with "a distinguished war record." He was "a close friend of the late Senator Robert Taft. I believe he was with him when he died," Dodd said, resurrecting the old blurbs. "He was a close friend of General MacArthur and Herbert Hoover and men of such standing." Klein was exceptionally well-informed about foreign affairs, Dodd continued, and understood the Communist menace as did few men.

On the question of the trip to Germany, Dodd's defense was simple. He had gone there only to interview an imprisoned murderer named Bogdan Stashynski, who had been a member of a "Soviet assassin ring." He had interviewed Stashynski for two hours, maybe longer, and "looked him in the eye," had talked to the German judge, and had then gotten out a 157-page Senate report alerting the American people to the threat of "the Soviet terror apparatus."

Klein had had nothing to do with the trip, Dodd insisted. Dodd had never seen the Klein briefing papers. He did not know why in the world Klein's staff had met him in Germany and followed him around. He had not even mentioned Klein's name to anyone, except to Adenauer, and then it was Adenauer who brought the matter up.

As Sonnett's questioning of Dodd ended, the Senator exuded a confident air as though everything had been explained to the satisfaction of any reasonable man. But there were inherent contradictions between Dodd's explanation and the content of the Dodd-Klein documents. It was the reluctant and embarrassed task of the Senators on the committee to question Dodd, they explained, and they began to do so—not with the incisiveness of a prosecution, but with the gentleness of mildly disbelieving old family friends.

How could Dodd reconcile his testimony with his three months' correspondence with Klein about the trip, in which Klein's contracts were mentioned constantly and the Stashynski matter not once? Or with the letter to Klein, who was waiting in Germany, in which Dodd said:

> As you know, I have been trying and trying to get away to join you . . . I have been thinking about this, and I believe that I might be more successful with the people in Germany if I talk to them alone. I don't think it is at all necessary for you to accompany me and there is a chance that it might be misunderstood. You know how anxious I am to help you and it is for this reason that I want to present your case in the best possible light.

Well, Dodd explained, he *was* interested in correcting the false impression of Klein that the Fulbright investigation had caused. "I do that on any trip anywhere in the world. If I thought a man had received an unfair deal and I had a chance to straighten it out, I would do it, whether it was Klein or anyone else."

Had he, then, corrected that injustice?

No—he corrected it only if *someone else* brought the matter up. And only Adenauer did.

Why then, if Dodd was so interested in justice for his wronged friend, was he so passive?

Well, said Dodd, he was "not on any mission for Klein."

Was it possible that Dodd, who had at Klein's behest taken the trouble to send those glowing letters of praise to Dr. Westrick, would not even have mentioned Klein's name when he visited Westrick in Bonn—after the dossier and the briefings and all that?

Yes, the question of Klein just didn't come up.

Why, it was asked repeatedly, would a United States Senator take the guff Klein had dished out to Dodd? What permitted Klein to talk that way?

Dodd did not regard Klein as obnoxious, he said. He forgave his unfortunate mannerisms. He (Dodd) was by nature courteous and forgiving, recognizing that we all have our faults.

As the questioning continued, Dodd's story of the Stashynski mission rapidly dissolved. It was shown that for a year before Dodd's emergency trip to Germany, he had known that Stashynski was in a German jail and would be there for several years to come. The C.I.A. and other intelligence agencies had long since questioned him and their findings were available to Dodd. Why then, did Dodd pick this particular time for his trip—when his presence was so important in the

Senate? Was it not precisely because Klein's problem was at that time so critical?

No, Dodd had wanted to make the trip for a long time, he just couldn't get away earlier.

Why, after Dodd returned from Stashynski, did he do nothing about the matter for a whole year—not even mention it to a single Senator? And why, if the Stashynski report was so urgent that it pulled Dodd away from a filibuster, did he wait for a year and a half before issuing that report?

Well, Dodd said, he wouldn't know how to explain it really. One would have to know how his particular committee operated. These delays were common. The members never spoke to each other about committee business.

And the Stashynski report, which Sonnett had waved aloft, turned out to be something of a hoax. Of its famed 157 pages, all but 2½ turned out to be reprints of old public documents that had been moldering in Dodd's files for fourteen months before he went to Germany, plus the transcript of an interview held right in Washington. The remaining 2½ pages consisted simply of an introduction written by David Martin, of which not a word reflected information obtained during the German trip. And it was shown that *Life* Magazine, with its circulation of seven million, had revealed the Stashynski story to the American people two years before Dodd had rushed headlong to Germany. So there was nothing new to reveal after all. Finally, under questioning, Dodd admitted as much. The diary of the trip was introduced in evidence and revealed that Dodd had spent twice as much time visiting the people on Klein's list as he did on the Stashynski matter.

The details of the hearings were incredible and confusing, and would soon fade away. But the insight that emerged into Dodd's character, as he became increasingly harried by accusatory headlines and skeptical Senators, would not be so easily forgotten. As he talked of the treacheries committed against him, he forgot his stage manners. He leaned forward. His eyes seemed to glitter. His hands clenched and unclenched.

He spoke repeatedly of "the Soviet terror apparatus," intimating that if he hadn't been fighting it, he wouldn't be under investigation. Anyone who fights it, he said, "usually gets lambasted in one form or another." But it wasn't just the Communists who were out to get him.

While he had been campaigning in Connecticut in October 1964, he said, everyone in Connecticut knew that his closest associates were traitors. "I was surrounded by people who were betraying me, and nobody ever told me about it until the campaign was over," he said. His description of Marjorie's dismissal, though distorted, reflected a fear completely at variance with the divan stories he told when not under oath.

"I called Mrs. Carpenter into my office and I said to her 'I have new plans . . . and they don't include you.' She said, well, she would like to remain until the end of the year. I said, 'You can't remain one minute. And pick up your personal effects and leave the premises.' She sat in her chair and glared at me. I said 'What is this, a threat?' And I walked to the door and opened it, and I said, 'Now leave,' and she left."

Before the hearings were over, Dodd was convinced that the committee, too, was betraying him. During the testimony of a witness friendly to Dodd, a faint pounding could be heard in the Hearing Room, caused by some workmen down the hall. The disturbance was so minor that Stennis, a stickler for silence in any hearing room, did not interrupt the testimony. But Dodd stormed to his feet and precipitated this bizarre exchange:

DODD: Can't we have that hammering stopped?
STENNIS: We are trying to have it stopped. If it disturbs you too much—
DODD: I can't hear the witness with the hammering. I hope it is not prearranged.
BENNETT: I object to the statement that it is prearranged.
DODD: I don't say it was prearranged. I said I hoped it was not prearranged.
STENNIS: Let's not make an issue out of that, Senator Dodd.
DODD: I just don't think we ought to have hammering going on while this important witness is testifying.
SONNETT: [trying to get Dodd to sit down] Let me take a fresh start at it.
STENNIS: Wait just a minute. Senator Dodd says he cannot hear.
DODD: [up again]. I can't hear with that hammering and I don't think anyone else can.
STENNIS: [slightly aghast] All right. Suppose we suspend until we can get—
[short recess]

None could tell exactly when the blow had landed that had so decisively damaged Dodd, or at what particular point his self-revealing antics and the weakness of his defense had combined to transform what should have been an easy exhibition match into a mortal struggle. But it had happened. Dodd had, all about him, the telltale look of guilt, the symptoms of a brittle vulnerability, the scent of humiliating defeat. A discernible cloud hung over him. And the concluding, anti-climactical testimony of Julius Klein—preposterous, evasive, contrivedly unintelligible—described by pro-Dodd columnist John J. Kilpatrick as "The Death of a General Salesman"—darkened and thickened that cloud.

When the last gavel came down, the press stridently demanded to know when further hearings into the more serious charges against Dodd would begin. Senators agreed that the Dodd investigation could not end at this point without touching off a nationwide cry of "whitewash" and "cover-up" that would be far more damaging to the collective image of the Senate than the revelation of one Senator's misdeeds could ever be. For months, Chairman Stennis said nothing definitive. No verdict was issued on the Klein case. Then, in November 1966, five months after the Klein case had been considered, Stennis announced that new public hearings would be held sometime in 1967 on Senator Dodd's "political and official finances." This, everyone knew, would be a more serious matter.

CHAPTER EIGHT

I needed the money. This has been a cumulative thing over many years. I would pay off one and in order to do so I had to borrow from another. I can't remember beyond that . . . I got in the hole in 1956, and I was never able to get out, and some of these things had to be paid off. I used what money I had to do some of it, and then I would be behind and I would have to get help from somewhere else . . . and that is the best I can tell you. That is really all I know about it.

THE words came haltingly, as Senator Dodd testified in his own defense at the fifth and final session of the Ethics Committee's public hearings into his "political and official finances." It was, ironically enough, St. Patrick's Day, 1967.

Dodd's appearance had changed markedly since the Klein hearings. His once celebrated white mane was now lusterless and, beneath the meticulous combing, one could detect the approach of baldness. There was a gauntness in his lined face that emphasized its high cheekbones and Roman nose. His eyes seemed dulled, his speech lethargic, his voice flat and toneless. He had the look of a noble but ghostly old Indian, unable to comprehend the meaning of captivity.

On the witness stand, Dodd was under oath. However unlikely the prospect, he was liable to a perjury charge if he lied. Within the valises of his inquisitors, he knew, there were piles of ledgers and bank statements and affidavits that traced his every financial transaction, documents that would disprove any explanation he might contrive. So Dodd spoke only in generalities. His testimony wandered fitfully. Patiently and sorrowfully, Senators waited, now and then prodding him gently for some word of explanation that would help his case. But Dodd insisted he could remember nothing of the hundreds of thousands that had passed through his hands. Avoiding any confrontation with fact, he insisted only that his conscience was clear.

The best I can say would be that I always thought these things [testimonial dinners] were on the level. That is why I said repeatedly if there was anybody who was under any misimpression, all you have got to do is tell me and I will give him his money back, if I have to sell my shirt. That is the way I have lived and that is the way I intend to live.

I don't want to get money from people under false pretenses or have them donate it under false pretenses. I guess if I had I wouldn't be in such tough shape, but I try to do things on the level and do them right.

I could not forget Dodd's old mastery of artifice, and I suspected that his forlorn appearance was, at least in part, staged. For months he had been stimulating alarums that the ordeal was breaking his health and clouding his mental powers. Today he looked the part. He was obviously under heavy tranquilization, administered perhaps to avert the emotional outbursts that had marred his comportment at the Klein hearings. I knew that for several years he had been taking powerful drugs for high blood pressure. His listlessness and slowness of speech in the hearing room reminded me of the occasions when he had exceeded the prescribed dosage. Yet, despite his outward memory lapses, his thinking processes seemed to me intact. I felt that he was, beneath the crestfallen exterior, alert and prepared for the challenge.

His defense was, first, that after thirty years in public life, he was the model of honest poverty, and second, that he did not know what had been done in his name with large amounts of money that had passed through his various accounts.

It was not an easy feat for a man who pictured himself as struggling relentlessly to keep a roof over his family's head to claim, at the same time, total ignorance of the details of what he had done with $120,000 in loans and $200,000 in diverted campaign contributions. If he recalled the specifics of some point in his favor, he could not convincingly pretend to have forgotten the details of transactions he wished to hide. And he must keep constant guard against the danger of some glaring admission, involuntarily wrested from him under pressure in the heat of exchange. For a man walking through a mine field, Dodd's footwork was deceptively nimble. His silence on the specific charges irritated the Senators, but failure to give proof of innocence was better for him than providing evidence of guilt. An ordinary witness, of course, would have been grilled mercilessly, until he was forced either to testify responsively or take the Fifth Amendment. But Dodd knew that as a Senator he was exempt, and he took full advantage of the gentleness of examination to work his wiles of obfuscation.

Chairman Stennis conducted the questioning almost apologetically. He never pressed Dodd and would prefix his interrogations with such phrases as "If I may ask," or "If you don't mind," or "Excuse me." And, in response to Dodd's evasions, he would say, "All right, Senator," or "I am certain you are doing the best you can on this."

In contrast to Dodd, the sixty-five-year-old Mississippian was nowhere marked, neither in his granite face nor his regal bearing, by the passage of a year since the beginning of the inquiry. With brisk, athletic stride he continued to move purposefully from office to hearing room to the Senate floor in the methodical procession of dutiful twelve-hour days that had filled his twenty years on Capitol Hill.

From Stennis's viewpoint, the hearings must have seemed a triumph of precision and control. Whereas the McCarthy hearings in 1954 and the Baker hearings in 1964 had dragged on rancorously for weeks, the Dodd hearings were winding up on their fifth day, exactly on schedule, after a pace so fast that the press had been able to digest only a fraction of all that had been revealed. With scarcely an audible dissent, Stennis's committee had followed his lead through the tangled maze of his precedent-making decisions. With barely a murmur, the press had accepted his drastic limitation of the scope of the hearings. Even Dodd and Sonnett had been reduced to a spiritless non-defense.

But a great price had been paid for this precision, at least by the public. The larger part of the case against Dodd had been abandoned by the committee. The open examination into corruption within the legislative process and into the Congressional system of influence peddling, an examination that might have generated a demand for fundamental reform, had been successfully averted. For Stennis, the golden mean had been achieved. Enough misconduct had been laid out to discredit Dodd and set the stage for some discipline that would pacify the press and public. But enough had been concealed to spare the Senate's honor and avoid a head-on collision with the deep-seated abuses that command tenacious, if covert, support on Capitol Hill.

The exclusion of explosive issues was only one element in the Stennis approach, however. The surrender of Dodd himself was also essential to the plan. If Dodd had persisted in the belligerent tactics he used at the Klein hearings, if he had pursued his threat to implicate others in order to show that his behavior was typical, if he had charged that he was being hypocritically singled out as a scapegoat for the common abuses of the Senate—then the Dodd case would surely have degenerated into an indiscriminate Senate bloodletting. Stennis wanted none of that.

Fully a year before, Chairman Stennis had devised his preventive formula. Out of the multitude of possible charges against Dodd, he had singled out three that were peculiar to Dodd alone and as remote as possible from the Senate as a whole. They consisted of what Dodd had done for Klein *in Germany,* how Dodd raised and spent campaign money *in Connecticut,* and the instances that Dodd had double-billed the government and private groups for the same travel expenses. The delineation of this last charge was the tip-off on Stennis's plan to isolate Dodd's conduct from that of the Senate generally. Dodd was not to be charged, as he could have been, with taking personal or vacation trips at the taxpayers' expense, under the false front of Senate business, an offense of which many a junketing Senator was guilty. It was only the double-billing aspect that was to be examined, which was Dodd's peculiar twist to an old racket, an extreme that more prudent colleagues forswore.

That, I concluded, had been the Stennis plan as far back as April 1966. At that time, when he and Senator Bennett had examined us in secret session, it was those three charges that were the basis of the inquiry. All our efforts over the ensuing year to interest the committee in what we considered more fundamental abuses had failed to evoke any real response.

I saw now that the Klein hearings had been an experiment—a dry run in which Stennis and the committee tested the witnesses, the Dodd defense, the public temper, the rules and procedures he had fashioned, for the more critical phase that would follow. The Klein hearings had taught Stennis, among other things, that Dodd's belligerency had to be subdued if order was to prevail. By forcing an admission on the basic facts of the charges, Stennis knew he could head off a demagogic defense such as Dodd was already making to the public, based on emotional tirades against the treachery of the witnesses, the perfidy of the press, the unfairness of the committee, and the Communist direction of the plot against him. No, Stennis had concluded, Dodd must be indicted out of his own mouth and tried by the Senate on the basis of facts conceded by his own lawyers.

The moment Stennis divined his solution to the riddle, he cast a net over Thomas Dodd, though he took his time in hauling it in. He would let the fight slowly go out of the prey. And so for months the wild and undisciplined Dodd thrashed, fumed, struggled, resisted, and evaded the tightening web of witnesses, bank statements, affidavits, and hard facts that progressively encircled him. Dodd and his legal staff fought Stennis at every turn. Despite Dodd's frequent assertion that "my books are open" and "I am cooperating fully in the investigation I requested," his books and files were closed tight to the committee and everyone else. Though he said again and again to the committee that he had nothing to hide, he steadfastly refused permission for the committee to question involved members of his staff, such as David Martin. Stennis, who was determined to treat Dodd like a lord no matter how knavishly he responded, continued to bar such questioning without Dodd's permission, and to prohibit the use of our "stolen documents" as evidence. But though Dodd and Sonnett counted heavily on this restriction to prevent damaging facts from coming out, it made little difference. The documents, the newspaper stories, and our verbal testimony provided all the *leads* to conscientious investigators that were necessary. Fern and his staff subpoenaed the records of a dozen banks and a score of business firms. They obtained sworn affidavits from more than one hundred people. In the end, Fern had a set of documents that, in the limited areas under consideration, surpassed our own in the indictment they made.

Dodd stalled and fought for time, hurling one legal challenge after another at the committee. The committee lacked jurisdiction, he said. It was violating his Constitutional rights. It had no right to look into his role as a campaigner for office, but only into his role as a Senator. It was using witnesses against him who should be "impeached" because of bad character. Its investigation was prejudicing his defense against possible charges by the Internal Revenue Service.

Stennis and the committee heard each challenge, one by one, and rejected them all.

"Senator Dodd is receiving the benefit of every right known to American jurisprudence, and some that are not known," he said. Slowly he tightened the net. Time was not crucial to him. The committee staff was ready for hearings in September 1966, but Dodd was not yet prepared to submit. So Stennis delayed, until November, until January, until March, always tightening his lines.

While Dodd dragged out his capitulation, the case of Adam Clayton Powell, a powerful chairman with twenty years seniority, erupted in the House of Representatives. The swift, insensitive treatment Powell received was a direct challenge to the Stennis concept of the

Dodd investigation. On December 19th, a House subcommittee began three days of hearings into Powell's alleged misuse of salary and travel allowances, which we regarded as among Dodd's lesser misdeeds. Powell's staff was called to testify against him. Two weeks later, the subcommittee, having found that Powell had engaged in "deceptive practices," ordered his wife removed from the payroll. On January 9th, Powell was stripped of his committee chairmanship by the House Democratic Caucus. A day later, the House voted to deny Powell his seat temporarily and created a select committee to investigate his case and report back in five weeks. Under the chairmanship of Emanuel Celler, the dean of the House of Representatives, the select committee investigated Powell without granting him any of the special privileges which Stennis had accorded Dodd. Powell was formally requested to appear, and would bear the onus of guilt if he did not. His staff again was called to give damning evidence. Even his wife was subpoenaed and compelled to testify. On February 23rd, the Celler committee recommended a $41,000 fine, censure, and complete forfeiture of seniority. The recommendation was backed by Speaker McCormack and by the leadership of both parties in the House. But the aroused House membership judged it too lenient, bolted the traces and, on March 1st, voted by an overwhelming margin to exclude Powell from House membership.

It had taken ten weeks, from beginning to end, for the House to dispose of Powell, whereas the Dodd case was now in its fourteenth month of Senate consideration, with no end in sight. The press made many a pointed comparison, and some speculated that it was the difference in race that determined the difference in treatment. But the taciturn Stennis remained unhurried. The House action seemed low-class to him. The repudiation of the Celler committee by a stampeding membership spurred on by press and public appalled him.

Stennis quietly continued private negotiations with Dodd over the signing of "stipulations" by which Dodd would admit the basic facts of the charges against him, while leaving open the question of intent and motive. At length, Stennis had increased the pressure by announcing that public hearings would begin on March 13th. Dodd was told that if he would not agree to the stipulations, the committee was prepared to prove its claims, point by point, over the course of several weeks. An hour-by-hour public revelation of his complicated machinations would, Dodd knew, destroy his reputation once and for all.

Finally, on March 11th, the eve of the hearings, Dodd surrendered.

John Sonnett signed his name to 116 statements of fact. The long wait had achieved its objective. Dodd, no longer struggling, had been gathered in.

On the morning of March 13th, while I waited alone in a nearby room, the stipulations were read aloud in the hearing chamber.

In those 116 statements of admitted fact, and in the tables and bank statements and reports that accompanied them, Dodd conceded the accuracy of the committee's case. He admitted having raised, at seven fund-raising affairs, at least $203,000 that had never been publicly acknowledged or reported. Most of the $203,000, the stipulations revealed, was spent for non-political purposes—home renovations, personal air travel for himself and his family, club dues, limousine service to a race track, household expenses, liquor tabs, football tickets, florist bills. Among the details were expenditures of $6,000 for Federal income taxes, $28,000 to retire tax loans and $27,000 to retire other personal loans, $4,900 as a gift to Dodd's son, Jeremy, and $9,000 for improvements to Dodd's property. Dodd's campaign committee was listed as having financed trips by Dodd and his wife to Jamaica, Curacao, Miami, and London. Dodd further conceded that he had received, on seven different occasions, identical travel expense reimbursements from both the government and private groups—amounting to a false billing to the government of $1,767. He also admitted accepting $2,100 from R. H. Blinkin of the Mite Corporation and $8,000 from the International Latex Corporation, as well as exclusive use of three successive new Oldsmobiles registered to the Dunbar Transfer Company, on which $2,700 in finance and insurance costs had been paid.

The facts were thus established. It remained only to show the intent. For four days Dodd had sat impassively behind his long table in the hearing room, listening to testimony from me, Marjorie, Terry, and Michael. We disclosed that he had organized and directed the dinners and had knowingly misrepresented them as campaign affairs, even to the Vice-President of the United States, Lyndon Johnson; that he had deliberately and specifically instructed Mike O'Hare to double bill and to pay personal expenses out of political funds; that the money from the International Latex Corporation came following agreement by Dodd to help obtain an ambassadorship for the company chairman, A. N. Spanel. And Dodd listened to Edward Lockett, who had received $8,500 in campaign funds for what had been listed as "preparation of campaign material," testify that the book he had written for Dodd was a personal venture that—by agreement—had nothing to do with any campaign.

By the time Dodd took the stand on the fifth day, public interest was at its peak. For months, Dodd had asked the Senate, the press, and the public to suspend judgment on the charges, in the American spirit, until he had presented his defense before the Ethics Committee. And so, when he took the oath, it was universally assumed that, under Sonnett's rehearsed questioning, he would attempt a careful rebuttal. To the surprise of all, however, Sonnett announced that there would be no organized refutation of the charges, no "direct testimony" by Dodd, not even a formal statement. Dodd, he said, would be happy to answer any questions the committee might have. Since the committee had repeatedly disclaimed the role of a prosecutor, since it had stated that it would not force admissions from Dodd, the tactic was transparent. Dodd had to be conceding that no point-by-point defense *could* be presented, and was throwing himself on the committee's mercy.

And so Dodd now sat caged in the witness chair, alone. After a lifetime in politics, the poverty and inconsequence of his associations stood pitifully revealed. Where were all the judges, the tycoons, the officeholders who had once fawned on him and upon whose fealty he had counted? Over and over again, Dodd and Sonnett had proclaimed that Judge M. J. Blumenfeld, his lifelong friend and law partner, whom he had personally caused to be elevated to the Federal bench, would appear and would testify that Dodd had acted on his advice, making his behavior obviously faultless. But the hearings were in their last hour and Blumenfeld had not come. To defend the claim that his personal use of testimonial funds was openly done and was the norm in Connecticut, Dodd could produce, under subpoena, only an unprepossessing band of figures from the lower levels of Connecticut politics. It would have been better for him had they not appeared for, under Fern's questioning, each revealed that he had been kept entirely in the dark about Dodd's handling of the testimonial money.

Dodd's major contention was that most of the funds he had received from the testimonials had been used to retire debts incurred for campaign purposes. To test this claim, Stennis had, time and again, identified sums Dodd had received—$10,000, $2,500, $10,000, $6,000, $5,000—and asked what had happened to the money. Dodd said he could not remember. When Stennis asked the purpose of $7,500 borrowed from a Chicago businessman, Howard Brundage, which was

repaid out of political funds, Dodd slipped characteristically into ir-
relevance. He told of how he had met Brundage at Nuremberg twenty
years before, of how they became friends, of how Brundage had
served as a colonel in World Wars I and II, of how Brundage was a
wealthy man, of how Brundage, from his deathbed, had called in his
son to say that he didn't want Tom Dodd to pay back the $7,500, of
how Dodd had nonetheless repaid it to Brundage's widow, which reminded him of how he had paid back a lot of widows, and he began
to name them. But what had he done with the $7,500? Dodd wasn't
sure. It went for personal-political bills, or political-personal—but he
wouldn't identify any of the bills.

Again Stennis reminded Dodd that it was in his own interest to tell
the committee where more than $200,000 had gone. But to no avail.

"I don't remember exactly what the need was, but it would again be
the same thing. They were all the same thing," Dodd said.

Turning hopefully to a comparatively recent transaction, Stennis
asked:

"Could you say that the $2,500 went to pay off another loan, or did
it go for personal matters, or what was it?"

"It could have been either or both," replied Dodd.

After a time, the fruitless questions ceased. Dodd's failure of memory on matters that another man would have had to recall, especially
if he had enjoyed the assistance of a platoon of lawyers and accountants and fourteen months to prepare his defense, went unchallenged
by the committee. The perfunctory examination ended without a
voice having been raised against Dodd or a sharp question asked. But
Dodd's inability to challenge so much of the case against him left
intact the adverse testimony. What implication the committee would
draw was not yet certain. For the moment, the Senators listened re-
spectfully, if impatiently, to Dodd's rambling peroration on his conduct and his life.

> If my life ended now, or my political life, I wouldn't want to
> go to my grave feeling that I had flimflammed anybody at a din-
> ner, and I haven't done that. . . . You know, the most consoling
> thing to me is that I have made no personal profits out of all this.
> I would be so ashamed if I had to come here and say I bought
> all these stocks and bonds, I speculated in this or that, or I got
> myself all these fancy personal things, but I did not at any
> time. . . .

I venture to say that I may be the only member of the United States Senate whose files have been systematically rifled, ransacked, and the contents taken to creatures who deal in this sort of traffic. And so who are those who stand against me? Four former employees, two of whom I had to fire, for good reasons, and two who joined them after their dismissal, but continued to work for me pretending to be honest, faithful assistants. . . . I do not think anybody else in the history of the Senate ever went through this kind of a situation, but I can look you in the eye this morning and say despite all of it, all their thievery, all of their dishonorable, deceptive conduct toward me, I do not believe that anybody can look me in the eye and say I did wrong.

An hour after the hearings ended, Marjorie, Michael, Terry, and I met to evaluate what had happened. The abrupt termination of the case, with so much left unexplored, mystified and dismayed us. We did not question the authority of the Ethics Committee to limit its hearings and were willing to assume from the reputation of its members that its motives in doing so were honorable. Yet it seemed to us that the privilege of secrecy which protected both a Senator and the Senate from exposure could not be in the public interest. It defeated every purpose for which we had so long waged the battle. We decided to make a formal appeal to the committee to reopen the investigation.

After two weeks of reviewing our documents, I drew up a two-thousand-word letter which cited twenty-four cases in six broad areas that the committee hearings had neglected. The letter did not attempt to enumerate *all* the unpursued charges, just those that could be stated concisely and sustained easily by our documents and testimony. It was signed by all four of us, and a copy was sent to each member of the Ethics Committee.

A week passed without answer or acknowledgment from any of the six Senators. I then made contact with the *Washington Post*, to determine whether the letter was newsworthy. It was, they replied, and they asked me to come to their offices immediately for a point-by-point examination of its contents by their editorial and legal staffs.

Two hours later, Managing Editor Ben Bradlee gave the order to remake the front page and to print both the complete text of the letter and a story on its contents. The following morning, April 13th, the 100 Senators, the 1,400 accredited newsmen in Washington, and anyone else who was interested could read, with their morning coffee, what we told chairman Stennis and the committee.*

Protesting the exclusion of more than a score of serious matters from the hearings, we wrote:

> Were it merely an individual episode here and there that the committee did not feel worthy of public inquiry, we would have assumed that the evidence had proved insufficient or that the committee, in its superior judgment, considered certain offenses negligible. But since several whole areas of misconduct, about which we had given exhaustive testimony, were not pursued, we are left with the conclusion that there was a policy decision to limit the scope of the hearings. Upon what considerations it was based we do not know. But we feel that the areas not covered in the hearings constitute the heart of the Dodd case.

In its lead story, under the banner headline "4 DODD EX-AIDES DEMAND SENATE REOPEN PROBE" the *Post* summarized our "principal allegations":

> • That Dodd accepted cash donations and valuable gifts from executives of six industries under investigation by committees on which he served.
> • That Dodd promoted government contracts or legislation for men who had given him thousands of dollars in campaign and testimonial donations. In one such case, according to the letter, Dodd's efforts to get a government contract were so strenuous as to draw a rebuke from Presidential Aide McGeorge Bundy.
> • That nine men who had given or loaned Dodd nearly $90,000 were recommended by the Senator for Federal appointments, including ambassadorships. Two men who loaned him $35,000—George Gildea and Albert Morano—were placed on the Senate staff.
> • That Dodd, while serving in the Senate, promoted government assistance for three of his private clients.
> • That at least seven members of Dodd's staff devoted the bulk of their time on the public payroll to raising money for Dodd's personal and political use, that thirteen members of the Juvenile Delinquency Subcommittee staff were diverted to work for Dodd on matters unrelated to the subcommittee's business, that some members of the Internal Security Subcommittee staff

---

* See Appendix I for the complete text.

were used as fund-raisers by Dodd, and that some Senate employees were exploited as personal servants.

In each instance listed, the letter named specific companies and individuals and cited dollar amounts.

The first response from the Ethics Committee to the *Post*'s publication of our letter came from Vice-Chairman Wallace Bennett. Our allegations, he said, were being considered by the committee and might have a bearing on its recommendations. Meanwhile, we learned that Senator John Sherman Cooper was pressing the committee to re-open the hearings and go into these very areas. But Stennis remained adamant and in the end his formula for a limited inquiry prevailed.

In the ensuing weeks, committee spokesmen offered a variety of reasons for the restrictive policy—some designed to defend against press attacks, others to reassure the Senate that the Dodd case was indeed under tight control.

Stennis assured Senators that no attempt would be made to prove or even to suggest that Dodd had violated any law. That was not the Senate's function, he said. Senator Eugene McCarthy, a committee member, elaborated:

> We did not raise any questions which we thought involved existing law, either the Internal Revenue law or the Corrupt Practices Act, or any other law that might be brought to bear on this case. There is no doubt that some of the issues raised are related to existing law, but when the committee reached the point where we thought we were impinging on existing law, we refrained from going into the question of illegality with reference to any actions attributed to the Senator from Connecticut.

Thus, the committee had adopted the curious position that when a violation of ethics turned out to be so serious as to constitute a violation of law, the Senate must cease to pursue it. Such an approach was in complete contradiction to long-standing Congressional policy, demonstrated so sensationally in the cases of Jimmy Hoffa, Bobby Baker, Billy Sol Estes, Adam Clayton Powell, the General Electric Company executives, and many others whose violations of law were first exposed in Congressional hearings.

McCarthy also explained why other large areas of Dodd's conduct were not to be considered—such matters as the "finder fees" Dodd received for obtaining commercial loans for business associates and the "legal referral fees" received from lawyers for cases steered to them. Since no specific rule on these matters had been established by the Senate, McCarthy said, the committee did not want to single out Dodd. The ethical morass in which the Senate as a body was submerged was starkly revealed here. Any Cabinet member or ordinary bureaucrat would be automatically dismissed in disgrace for engaging in such practices. The American Bar Association long before had branded the acceptance of referral fees as unethical. But what was outlawed in the Executive Branch and condemned by an eminent body of lawyers was not even to be investigated, said the Ethics Committee, when indulged in by a United States Senator.

"I don't think we're ready to tell a man what he can and can't do on the outside," one member of the committee told the *Wall Street Journal*.

By use of the same sophistry, the committee had declined to examine the $50,000 Dodd had received in speaking fees, thus shielding from view the honorarium practice, by which Senators regularly receive $1,000 or $2,000 as fees for addressing special interest groups and backing their positions—fees which, if obtained under less contrived circumstances, might be called bribes or conflicts of interest. It had always been the announced policy of Senator Paul Douglas to refuse an honorarium from any group that had a legislative goal to promote. But Douglas had few imitators in the Senate, so few that Dodd's honorariums were not examined. Even if McCarthy's premise were to be accepted, it missed the point. It was not the legal kickbacks, or finder fees, or lecture fees, per se, that we had asked to have examined. It was the fact that, in Dodd's case, the money was coming from the very sources which he had been directed by the Senate to investigate.

The committee simply overlooked the mutilated investigations over which Dodd had presided, the vacation travel at taxpayers' expense, the patent misuse of Senate payrolls. Chairman Stennis, Fern had told me, felt that these were matters involving the discretion that must be granted to Senators. Besides, Senators would be hostile to any committee which began looking into those practices which had become commonplace in the Capitol.

There were two other excuses frequently expressed to explain committee omissions.

"Some of these charges are based on stolen documents and we can't use them," said Senator Bennett, conveniently overlooking the facts that: (1) the Justice Department did not consider the documents tainted, and based its own investigation on them; and (2) all the charges we had made in our letter could be substantiated from public and business records readily available to the committee—if it wanted to obtain them.

Perhaps sensing this weakness, Stennis did not rely much on the "tainted" document theme in his rare public explanations of committee policy.

"We do not have the staff or the investigative resources to cover everything," he said, though he refrained from saying why he had deliberately kept his staff and resources so limited—three professional men and two secretaries—when the subcommittees that Dodd chaired had staffs of between twenty and thirty members, many of whom were now working daily with Dodd's seven lawyers and numerous accountants to prepare his defense.

All of the excuses for limiting the Dodd hearings had, in my judgment, a contrived and hollow ring to them. The ends they served were those of the Senate, not of the country. To be sure, it lightened the work of the Committee, which was not a small consideration. It also narrowed the scope of the decisions Stennis was called on to make. But, mainly, it spared the Senate the disgrace of a public cataloging of all the ways one Senator had found to profiteer from his position. It prevented the furnishing of fuel to those reformers who had long urged mandatory disclosure by all Senators of income and assets—a measure that Stennis, Dirksen, and other powerful Senators opposed. And an open hearing on all, or even many, of Dodd's offenses would probably have led to irresistible public pressure for his expulsion from the Senate, a step which Stennis opposed, not for Dodd's sake, but on grounds of public policy, Constitutional theory, and the stability of the Senate as an institution.

By the last week in April, the Ethics Committee had reached its verdict. How should the news be told to Senator Dodd? For days, according to aides, the sensitive Stennis had fretted over the manner in which Dodd should be informed of the findings. Manfully, he decided that Dodd should be the first to know and that he, as chairman, should do the job himself. On the morning of April 27, 1967, Stennis summoned Dodd's administrative assistant, Robert Perry, to his office, thence to escort him back to the waiting Senator. The committee report in his hand, Stennis arrived at Dodd's suite, funereal in dress and solemn in manner. He was led immediately into Dodd's private office, where the Senator waited with his wife, Grace. Stennis shook hands with Dodd and bowed to Mrs. Dodd.

"I have the report, Tom," he said softly. "It's not all good." Then, after a strained exchange of pleasantries, the chairman left.

Indeed the report was not all good. While newspapermen and television cameras collected in the hall, word of the result spread swiftly among Dodd's office staff. Rose Marie Allen, Dodd's darkhaired, $7,200 a year receptionist, burst into tears and tried to handle the phones through hysterical sobs. A tense Dodd aide snapped at an intruding newsman, "Don't you realize the Senator has been censured on two counts?"

A few minutes later, Stennis reported briefly to the full Senate. As expected, he had brought in a unanimous committee recommendation. The report condemned Dodd for converting to personal use "at least $116,083" that was raised ostensibly for political purposes, and for obtaining on seven different occasions identical reimbursements for travel expenses from both the Senate and private organizations. The committee further cited $45,233 in political funds that Dodd had used for purposes that were neither clearly political nor personal, most of it to pay personal debts of which the original purpose could not be determined.

The report found that Dodd had received $8,000 in cash from the International Latex Corporation "as the consummation of a promise made during the campaign," and had accepted the use of three automobiles from David P. Dunbar. These matters, it said, would be referred to the Attorney General of the United States for investigation of possible violations of law, just as other matters were to be turned over to the Commissioner of Internal Revenue for investigation into possible tax violations.

The report also announced that other allegations made "in the press or encountered by the staff in its investigation" would remain within the jurisdiction of the committee, and that some of these allegations "which, if proven, might possibly constitute violations of existing law," had also been referred to the Department of Justice for further study.

And then the dread word came. The committee recommended "censure" of Dodd for a course of conduct between 1961 and 1965 that "is contrary to accepted morals, derogates from the public trust expected of a Senator, and tends to bring the Senate into dishonor and disrepute."

As for the matter of Julius Klein, the report found that Dodd had traveled to Germany on Senate business "under circumstances that suggest he was influenced to go by Julius Klein," who "sought to improve his image because he was losing clients." The committee found that Dodd's relationship with Klein was "indiscreet and beyond the responsibilities of a Senator to any citizen;" but "because a sovereign foreign government was involved," the committee could not pursue its investigation to a conclusion and was "unable to obtain sufficient evidence to warrant recommendation of specific disciplinary action by the committee." *

And so Dodd had been recommended for censure—a condemnation visited upon only five senators in the nation's history.

Later, we learned from the newspapers that the committee report had dealt with us, too. It had asked the Attorney General for "action or recommendation" in the matter of our removal of papers from Dodd's office. And it went on to say:

> While the committee recognizes the duty of every . . . employee of the Senate to report wrongdoing to responsible authorities, the committee believes that the unauthorized removal of papers from a Senator's office by employees and former employees is reprehensible and constitutes a breach of the relationship of trust between a Senator and his staff . . .

The committee, of course, had *not* recognized "the duty of every employee of the Senate to report wrongdoing to responsible authorities." On the contrary, it had refused to interrogate or to call as witnesses several Dodd employees who, it knew, had direct knowledge of wrongdoing. Nor did the committee explain how a relationship of trust could or should continue to exist between a corrupt Senator and his staff, whose duty presumably was to the public. In its investigation, the committee had established the precedent that Senate employees could properly remain silent about the wrongdoing of a Senator, and would be protected in that silence, even if it hid their own collusion. That precedent, now joined to the committee's attack on us, constituted a double-edged notice to all Senate employees that silence in such cases was golden.

* See Appendix II for the complete text of the committee report.

I assumed that the referral of our "offense" to the Justice Department was meant to appease those many Senators who looked upon their staffs as private retainers rather than public servants. Even Dodd's lawyers had been unable to show an adequate basis for our prosecution. We had openly revealed our actions a year before and were fully prepared to defend, in any court or forum, the proposition that a Senator's office must not be a sanctuary for records of corrupt transactions. But we could not view lightly the fact that the committee action effectively blacklisted any of us from obtaining employment again with the Congress or anywhere else in the government. It was a price we had been willing to pay from the beginning, but we had hoped for a chance to present our side of the argument.

In a way, I took a perverse satisfaction from it, for it proved to me that all the committee talk about the rights of the accused and the fairness of its procedures was so much posturing to cover what I had always suspected was mere favoritism, intended for Senators only. We had been in continuous cooperation with the committee and its staff for more than a year, but had never once been told that there were any charges against us. We had appeared as the principal witnesses at both hearings, and had submitted freely to all interrogations on the removal and copying of the documents, but we had never been apprised that we should present a defense of our actions. We had been given no right to introduce evidence or call witnesses or reply to the attacks that were frequently made against us at the hearings. We had not even been given an opportunity to present a written statement of the reasons for our actions. A couple of ad lib justifications of our motives, in response to the attacks of Dodd's lawyer, was all that the record contained in our defense. When Dodd's attorneys had produced a paid handwriting expert who sought to undermine Michael's testimony that Dodd had signed certain checks, Michael urged the committee to have an unbiased examination performed by an independent expert. The committee refused. It was satisfied, said Counsel Fern, that the testimony of Dodd's expert was irrelevant and had not damaged its case.

"But it has damaged my reputation," said O'Hare, and he renewed his plea for an official examination of the signatures. The committee, however, was not concerned about O'Hare's reputation or the protections he was supposed to enjoy under its own rules.

But, no matter. Though the committee deplored our methods and ignored our rights, it had accepted our testimony and recommended censure of Dodd by the Senate.

"I'll get Tom Dodd out of this mess or I'm not half the lawyer I think I am."

With those words, Russell Billiu Long, the Senate's Number Two Democrat, volunteered himself as Senator Dodd's floor defender against the censure charges brought by the Ethics Committee. His opening brief was not so much that Dodd was innocent as that other Senators were equally guilty.

"Why, this man hasn't done anything that hasn't been done before by many other Senators," Long said. "Half the members of the Senate Ethics Committee couldn't have survived the investigation given to Tom Dodd's affairs." On reflection, Long broadened his indictment: "Half of the *Senate* couldn't have survived such an investigation!"

Newsmen buzzed with expectation at the prospect of Russell Long in the Senate china shop. Before his entry, the Dodd case seemed neatly tied up and destined for a quiet and dignified disposal. Dodd would be censured with a minimum of turmoil, sparing both him and the Senate a further spectacle. The date for burial had already been announced.

But Long had other ideas. His client was to have a Louisiana-style defense, with all the trimmings, and he demanded a six-week delay. The usually mild Mike Mansfield, the Majority Leader, was angered. He and Minority Leader Dirksen had worked out a mutually agreeable date with Dodd and Sonnett. All other Senate business had been canceled. All Senators had been notified to reschedule outside engagements so they could be present. But things were too well arranged to suit Dodd's new defender.

"If those who would like to hang that man have had sixteen months to smear him, why are you boys so concerned about giving us a few more weeks to defend him?" Long asked. Mansfield and Dirksen gave in reluctantly and granted a three-week extension.

It was said of Russell Long's father, Senator Huey P. Long, that he always rejoiced in tormenting the powers that ruled the Senate. Each time he made a particularly telling debating point at their expense, he would break into a special victory jig on the Senate floor—to the red-faced consternation of his targets and the immense delight of the galleries.

If Russell Long fell short of his legendary father in some respects, he was nonetheless cut from the same cloth. He, too, was an icon smasher. And at forty-eight he had come to exercise more power in the Senate than did the Kingfish, whose career was cut short by assassination at forty-three.

Bright, articulate Russell was a wizard at parliamentary maneuver. Eighteen years a Senator, chairman of the ultra-powerful Senate Finance Committee, already the Assistant Majority Leader of the Senate, he seemed destined, at the least, to succeed Mansfield in the top Senate post.

But a penchant for the preposterous and the irresponsible, which in recent years Long had suppressed, seemed to be emerging again, making him the Senate's most unpredictable character. During the years I had worked in the Senate, I never missed an opportunity to watch Russell Long perform. In debate, he would freewheel about the Senate floor in his rumpled suit, his arms windmilling, his voice rising mercurially from its natural resonance to a stuttering screech when excitement took hold of him. He could be scholarly and serious, as when he successfully defended President Johnson's 1964 tax bill against 150 amendments, without losing on one. But his native element was exaggeration, hyperbole, ironic humor, and earthy stories. He was a pitchman, a snake oil salesman, a rural demagogue—and that part of him was never far from the surface.

With impish grin, bulbous nose, round cheeks, and sensuous mouth, Long had the mark of Bacchus on him. A periodic celebrant, his office refrigerator was stocked with champagne and his public escapades were a part of Capitol Hill lore. In the old days, before he became the Democratic Whip, I once saw Russell Long appear on the floor of the Senate, shoeless and coatless, break away from the restraining grip of his worried aides, jump to the top of his desk, and unloose a wild harangue in a mighty voice that almost shook the great Chamber. No newsman ever reported it, and no Senator called the popular Long to order. But this sort of thing raised serious questions, to say the least, among responsible Senators and kept them guessing on what to expect next.

Why had Long decided to help Dodd? Once, when Dodd had tried to dissuade him from hijinks on the Senate floor, he had looked at Dodd with his hazel eyes and said, "You remind me of my Daddy." Some recalled that Huey Long, too, had once fought impeachment by the Louisiana Senate. Others said Russell was always for the underdog. Long himself explained it to a Washington reporter: "Tom Dodd is my friend. I owe him this. All his other friends have run out on him."

For sixteen months not a single Senator had said a public word in Dodd's behalf. Now he had a defender, one of the most influential and incendiary figures in the Senate.

"Members of the Senate . . ."

There was a melancholy note in the rich Southern voice. Ninety Senators, perched gravely behind their diminutive, antique desks, looked toward the place where Senator John Stennis stood, erect and stolid, a sheaf of papers before him. Two hundred reporters, filling every space in the press gallery, peered down on the rare sight of a nearly full Senate. The public galleries were packed and silent. From the front row of the section reserved for families of Senators, Grace Dodd and four of her grown children smiled down on Thomas Dodd, who nodded confidently in recognition. The debate on the censure of a Senator was under way.

"This matter is . . . resting in the bosom of the Senate," Stennis was saying. "It is the pending business, and it is Senate business only. . . .

"We are not prosecutors. We have not been. No man's case was ever heard with more unanimous personal sentiment for the man than this one. It is our duty, however, to present this matter to the Senate."

He reviewed in detail the seven testimonial affairs—how Dodd and his inner circle had organized them, how solicitation letters and public announcements had concealed their true purpose and misled the public, how a large part of the proceeds was then secretly diverted to Dodd's personal use.

Exasperation showed as Stennis recounted his efforts at the hearings to get an accounting from Dodd of what he had done with these funds.

He said they were all mixed up. That was a disappointing answer to the committee. I know it was to me. This testimony was disappointing. He said they were all mixed up . . . there emerges an inescapable conclusion that unfortunately the Senator from Connecticut deliberately engaged in this course of conduct to divert to his own use funds over which he held only a trustee or fiduciary control.

For two hours, Stennis, plainly and without embellishment, cited facts and figures, then he concluded:

> What are we going to do about it? . . . I could be as forgiving as any Senator. As I say, that is not the issue. If we pass up this matter, then sometime, somewhere, in some way, something big will slip out of this Chamber, and a lesser standard or lesser rule or lesser conduct will have to be accepted.
>
> Sad as it is—and I say it is sad for every one of us, for the Senator from Connecticut and for the rest of us—I do not believe we can afford to do it.

The following day, when Senator Dodd rose to present his long-awaited defense, the Senate Chamber and its galleries were again crowded and expectant. He looked well. The thinness, the listless pallor of his appearance before the Ethics Committee three months before seemed to have vanished. Perhaps he felt that, whatever happened, the worst was behind him. Under the unwritten rules, nothing new could be raised against him, and any change from the unanimous condemnation by the committee would have to be an improvement.

The Senate floor was inherently more to Dodd's liking as a battleground than the witness chair. Here, *he* was in command. Here, there was an honored place for dramatics, for acting, for performance. Oratory had always been his forte, and he well knew that in oratory, facts don't really count. Emotion and eloquence, stagecraft and generalities —these are the essence of a speech. On the Senate floor *he* would have the initiative. He could *make* them see how he was suffering and what an open, honest, decent man he was, without being pinned down by all those questions, questions which on the Senate floor could usually be averted. Not only was he no longer under oath, he was actually constitutionally immune from all libel and perjury laws. His fellow Senators would treat him with their customary deference. His targets could not reply to him. It would be his word against the word of those who were absent and without a voice.

Dodd found himself holding the spotlight, as he had always hoped to, under different circumstances. His posture before the Senate was properly humble. His bearing was appealing—a beleaguered man, seeking only to save his honor. His voice was finely tuned. He knew this was the most important performance of his life.

> Is there anyone [he asked], who has not felt in some—per-
> haps fleeting—moment of anguish that goodness has suddenly
> fled the world? That all of the canons of justice have been
> repealed? That the minimum requirements of human decency
> have been suspended? A moment, I mean, when without deserv-
> ing it, you come under general attack; when you know the at-
> tack is unjust, yet others deny or doubt what you know?

Any Senator sitting there on the floor could be betrayed by his staff
into such a predicament, Dodd conjectured, and, as the Senate listened in rapt attention, he painted the base origins of his own betrayal. He had been forced to dismiss James Boyd and Marjorie
Carpenter for "conduct which no Senator could have tolerated." What
that conduct was, he did not specify. Michael O'Hare had been lured
into the plot by the "mesmeric influence" of Boyd and Carpenter.
Terry Golden, the fourth conspirator, was O'Hare's girl friend. The
conspiracy thus originated in a pathological desire for revenge.

His apparent transgressions, Dodd insisted, were actually the work
of distortions, half-truths, and lies by his former aides. "In the entire
history of the Senate . . . no dismissed employees had sought to do
what Boyd and Carpenter had done."

He concentrated his fire on the double-billing charge, the lesser of
the counts against him. It was O'Hare, he shouted, "that witless
bookkeeper," not Dodd, who had done the double billing, and when
O'Hare joined the plot he had tried to frame Dodd by blaming him
for it.

Dodd knew that his ridicule of his former staff struck a sympathetic
chord with Senators, to whom the thought of staff rebellion was a
nightmare. The Senate roared with laughter as Dodd said. "O'Hare
might very well have been the alltime most inefficient bookkeeper in
the history of the Senate." Again and again, he drove home his point
that the double-billing charge rested on the word of a mere employee
against that of a United States Senator.

"It is very simple," Dodd declared. "Either you believe me or you
believe O'Hare." And he said that thirty years of honest dealing served
as evidence that he would not suddenly have turned to petty chiseling
from the government.

Dramatically, he raised his right hand. "I swear now and I will
swear forever. I am telling you the truth. If I had to face my Maker in

a minute, I'm telling you the truth, and may the vengeance of God strike me dead if I'm doing otherwise!"

Dodd looked around the Chamber, his gaze pausing on the face of first one Senator, then another. "I have walked among you. I have talked with you. I have lived with you for more than eight years. Does any one of you know that I have ever lied to you? That I have done any dishonorable thing, ever broken my word, ever cheated you, ever said I would do this and then done something else? Is there anyone here who says I lied? Get up! If I lied—get up and say so!" He looked across the Chamber. No one rose.

Between the peaks of emotion, his argument was skillful and plausible, though it artfully skirted the thrust of the committee's indictment. He devoted little time to the major charge—covert pocketing of campaign funds. He recited his poverty as further proof of his honesty. He read letters from friendly donors who said that they had wanted him to use their money for himself. He claimed there was no law against it. And he insisted that the money had gone for what in reality were political debts and the expenses of office. Should politics be only for the rich? Should the poor men be driven out?

Dodd was giving the performance of his career.

"It is my life that is at stake. I would rather be dead than dishonored." For three hours he held his judges spellbound. Then he concluded:

"I do not ask for mercy. I ask for justice."

As he made his way off the floor, Senators grasped his hand warmly.

"This was the greatest speech I've ever heard Tom Dodd make," declared Senator Abe Ribicoff of Connecticut. Said the Baltimore Sun: "Most Senators, whatever their views on the Dodd case itself, thought the Connecticut lawmaker had made a stirring, almost classic appeal." A jubilant Russell Long announced that the case of the Ethics Committee had been destroyed. "Now they'll be trying to put Humpty Dumpty together again and we'll just destroy it again," he beamed. In front of the cameras, Dodd received the congratulations of his chief defender. But there was about it a trace of the Last Hurrah.

On the third day, general debate began. One by one, the members of the committee—Senators Bennett, Pearson, Monroney, Cooper, and McCarthy—defended in detail particular aspects of the charge which Chairman Stennis had laid down in broad outline. Their contributions were at times useful and perceptive,* though at no time did the joint presentation approach anything resembling devastating precision. Stennis was throughout the commanding, if sometimes distant, figure. Well remembered as the lion of the McCarthy censure thirteen years before, Stennis did not have to use tooth and claw now to prove his prowess. Somehow, his total impact was far greater than the sum of his words and acts.

But there was surprising sentiment for Dodd. Great waves of emotion would surge from the Dodd camp and wash across the floor, only to dash imperviously against the clifflike Mississippian and recede. On rare occasions, the Chairman's argument might falter in the maze of detail and contention, but never his presence, his sense of certitude, which dominated the proceedings and held the ship on the course he had set.

As the week progressed, Dodd, now without a script and perhaps encouraged by the disposition of Senators not to question him closely, descended further and further into evasion, distortion, and then to demonstrable falsehood.

When the point was raised that Dodd had spent $9,000 in testimonial dinner funds on his home, he said: "I have to have a place to live. It is a place I check in when I go to Connecticut. . . . A small amount of these moneys was used to keep the place up." The truth, well known to the committee, was that Dodd had poured $50,000 from political funds into transforming an abandoned farm in North Stonington into a $100,000 property.

He told the Senate repeatedly that he could not possibly have enriched himself out of public office since his net worth was only $54,000. But, in fact, we knew his net worth at the time we left him to be at least a quarter of a million dollars, as contrasted with a net worth of minus $100,000 when he had first assumed office, six years before.

Now immune to perjury action, as are all Senators when speaking on the Senate floor, Dodd insisted categorically that the $120,000 he had stipulated as personal debt was in fact campaign debt. "The loans were not personal in purpose," he said, "but I assumed these debts and paid them off. One was to a printing company which did my printing in 1956. . . ." Hidden away in the printed volumes of the committee hearings that were stacked on each Senator's desk was Dodd's official campaign report for 1964. It showed that the $10,192

* Appendix III furnishes a digest of the principal arguments and counterarguments.

that was paid to the University Press of Cambridge, Massachusetts, to clear up that 1956 printing debt was paid, not by Dodd personally, but by Dodd's 1964 campaign committee and duly claimed as a campaign expense. But no Senator looked it up; or if one did, he kept courteous silence.

When asked by Chairman Stennis if personal bills were paid out of his campaign account, Dodd answered, "Yes," but explained that Ed Sullivan had done this inadvertently, because O'Hare had never indicated which bills were personal.

"For example, on the airline tickets," Dodd said, "all O'Hare would do was send up a general bill. He would not go to the trouble of delineating, and say 'This was a personal trip of Senator Dodd's' . . . They should have been separate. But certainly I did not know about it, and that's how it came about."

Stennis and the other Ethics Committee members knew otherwise, and had long ago rejected Dodd's claim unanimously. The Committee had documentary proof that O'Hare had painstakingly divided the bills into personal and political travel and would send the political bills to Sullivan for payment while referring the segregated personal bills to Dodd. For instance, the total airline bill for one ten-month period in 1962–63 was $3,018.43. O'Hare carefully audited the bill, sent the political expenses, $1,392.38, to Sullivan for payment, and took up the question of the personal expenses, $1,626.05, with Dodd. But Dodd ordered the personal bill to be paid out of campaign funds, too.

"This is one way the campaign fund can help me," he told O'Hare.

Dodd's own campaign accounts verified this. For the American Airlines bill in question (November 25, 1963), for $3,018.43, was paid by Ed Sullivan in two installments. The initial payment was made with a campaign check for $1,392.38 for the expenses O'Hare had designated as political travel and sent to Sullivan first. Two months later the remaining $1,626.05—the personal expense—was paid by Sullivan, after Dodd ordered that bill, too, to be paid out of campaign funds. If O'Hare had not carefully delineated the bills, if they had been all jumbled in together, as Dodd claimed, these separate payments could not have been made. Stennis, however, did not directly challenge Dodd's false statement, nor did he edify the Senate and the public as to the documented truth of the matter.

"All right," he said, cryptically, and turned to another subject.

The question hung over the Senate—if the testimonial dinners were intended solely to raise money for Dodd's personal use, as he stoutly maintained, why had Dodd sent out letters of solicitation that announced their purpose as campaign kickoffs or for the retiring of previous campaign deficits?

Because, Dodd kept insisting, he never knew about those letters. Specifically, he denied ever having seen the letter sent out to prospective donors by New Haven political leader Arthur Barbieri, which stated flatly that the purpose of the March 1965 dinner, which raised $79,000 for Dodd, was to pay off the 1964 campaign deficit. "I never saw it," Dodd said. "I was not writing letters for the [dinner] committee. They wrote them all. I would have written them differently if I was doing so." But, in fact, the letter in question was initiated by Dodd and approved by him before Barbieri ever saw it. Dodd had instructed me on what he wanted the letter to say. After further suggestions from Ed Sullivan, I had drafted the letter. It was delivered to Dodd, who had it sent to Barbieri. All that was in the testimony, in those green volumes on each Senator's desk.

Perhaps they knew Dodd was lying and refrained from humiliating him. But it is in the nature of debate, however circumscribed, that sooner or later some inquisitive Senator will force a confrontation with the truth. It all but happened when freshman Senator Edward Brooke of Massachusetts rose to make an inquiry. His reading of the record indicated, he said politely, that on February 1, 1965, when Dodd or his lieutenants were sending out their announcements of a forthcoming victory dinner to wipe out a campaign deficit, there was, instead of a deficit, a favorable balance on hand of $55,000. If that were true, Brooke asked, was not a fraud committed on the public?

Dodd was cornered. Again he resorted to falsehood. He said that after his official expenditures report was filed in December 1964—a month after the campaign ended—somehow another $55,000 in unexpected campaign bills came in and were paid. There was a false ring to this explanation. Brooke pursued the matter, establishing that no supplementary report had ever been filed with Connecticut authorities accounting for this alleged $55,000 in further expenditures and that no proof had ever been presented to the committee, or to anyone else, to substantiate the payment of a single dollar of that $55,000. Mercifully, other Senators joined the debate and changed the subject, giving Dodd a breather. But the near escape had shaken his aplomb. He was foundering.

Then another freshman Senator, Charles Percy of Illinois, rose to speak. Percy addressed himself to the key question of Dodd's insist-

ence that he personally had never misled anyone into believing that
any of the testimonial dinners were for campaign purposes, though his
friends may mistakenly have done so. Percy had a letter in his hand,
taken from the *New York Times* of May 28, 1967. It had purportedly
been written in 1963 by Dodd himself to Vice-President Lyndon Johnson just before the series of Dodd-Day testimonial affairs. Silence settled over the Senate as Percy began to read the text.

> Dear Lyndon,
> First of all allow me to thank you again for your generous offer
> to come to Connecticut to assist me in my *forthcoming cam-
> paign.* [Author's italics.] Since receiving definite word from your
> office that you will be available on October 26th for the entire
> day, I have scheduled a variety of activities that will cover the
> principal centers of the state.
> "I wish I could convey to you how enthusiastic everyone is
> about your visit and how much it will assist us in getting my
> *campaign drive* under way. . . .

Percy finished reading the letter and picked up another document.
Russell Long, seeing the abyss yawning in front of Dodd, moved
quickly to have Percy ruled out of order. Dodd had yielded to Percy
only for a question, not for a speech, Long argued, citing a seldom-
invoked rule of debate. Long was sustained by the Chair, and Dodd
regained the floor. But then the wily Dirksen intervened.

"If you are going to play that kind of pool," he said to Long, "two of
us can play." Dirksen had not declared a position on the censure, and
Dodd, hoping against hope that the Minority Leader—never a stickler
about Senate ethics—would come to his side, was alarmed at Dirksen's ire.

Percy again confronted Dodd. "Will the Senator yield for a question?" There was no place to hide. Dodd yielded. This time, Percy
posed his remarks in the form of a query. Asking Dodd if what he was
about to present was correct, Percy read an account published in the
Hartford *Courant* of October 27, 1963, the day after four fund-raising
affairs were held in Connecticut:

"Throughout the trip, Senator Dodd expressed his gratitude to Vice-
President and Mrs. Johnson for coming to the state to help him build
up a *campaign war chest* for 1964. 'It is difficult to adequately thank
you for doing so,' Senator Dodd said." Then Percy asked whether that
was a true account.

"No," Dodd replied lamely, "that is not true."

This was too much for John McClellan of Arkansas, an incorrigible cross-examiner, who suddenly, with his voice of doom, began plying Dodd with rapid-fire questions.

MR. MC CLELLAN: Did these articles come to your attention? You say you did not know it before, and that you did not see it. Did these come to your attention immediately?

MR. DODD: I am sure I saw it at the time.

MR. MC CLELLAN: Was it after that that you made this disbursement of funds in the way in which you have?

MR. DODD: Yes.

MR. MC CLELLAN: It was after these articles and the letters; you knew about the letters later, did you not?

MR. DODD: No. I did not.

MR. MC CLELLAN: With all of this political atmosphere about the letters going out for invitation, and the Vice-President being invited for political purposes, you knew nothing about it?

MR. DODD: I knew the Vice-President was going to be there.

MR. MC CLELLAN: You did not know it was going to be for political purposes?

MR. DODD: No. It was not for political purposes.

MR. MC CLELLAN: Okay.

McClellan wheeled angrily, turned his back on Dodd, disbelief etched unmistakably on his severe, battleworn face. He stomped off the floor, as though to say he had had enough.

For a time other Senators took over to argue procedural matters, while Percy waited patiently for another opening. He finally found it. Again he cited the letter in which Dodd stated that the purpose of the Vice-President's visit to Connecticut was "to assist me in my forthcoming campaign." He asked Senator Dodd if he had, in fact, written the letter.

"Sure, I wrote the letter," Dodd snapped back, blanching at the admission.

A crisis point had been reached in the debate, from which Dodd's fortunes would never recover.

It was ironic that this letter should play so vital a part. It was one of the documents that Marjorie and I removed from Dodd's office, copied, and returned. Our copy was in turn copied by the Justice Department, which later furnished a copy to the Ethics Committee.

Somewhere along the line we had lost our copy and repeated searches failed to uncover it. Though it contained proof of Dodd's personal involvement in a hoax, proof upon which the case might well turn, and though I had testified as to the existence of such a letter during the committee hearings, the Ethics Committee declined to bring forward their copy as evidence. It was "tainted," the committee said.

But three weeks before the censure debate opened, someone from the Ethics Committee showed the letter to E.W. Kenworthy of the *New York Times* and permitted him to photostat it. Kenworthy read me the letter over the phone, and I verified its authenticity. Then he took it to Marjorie who, from the markings in the upper right-hand corner, confirmed that it had indeed been sent out by Dodd to the Vice-President. A few days later, the *New York Times* printed it.

The Ethics Committee would continue to profess, virtuously, that it had never used the documents it had stigmatized as "tainted." But suspicion showed on Dodd's face as he surveyed the wreckage of his exchanges with Percy and McClellan.

Only something spectacular could turn the tide now, Russell Long told his confidants. Long had thrown himself wholeheartedly into Dodd's defense. He had harassed, without stint, the various presentations of Ethics Committee members. He had tied the Senate in procedural knots to delay the hour of reckoning. Each day he had come to battle equipped with colorful charts and graphs that claimed to prove that Dodd, far from profiting out of campaign funds, was actually deep in the red. Adroitly, Long juggled figures which, when challenged, he admitted he could not authenticate at the moment.

"I am the only man who understands Tom Dodd's finances," he said. Irrepressibly, he pointed again and again to a chart covered with figures which demonstrated, he said, that Dodd was blameless and had profited "not one red copper cent"—until Stennis forced Long to admit that, as Stennis said, the chart was "just imagination" and was "not in the realm of reality."

But there was one chance left, and Long boasted that he would yet save Dodd's neck. Each day the Louisiana Senator promised that before week's end he would make new revelations "not yet even hinted at" about the moral corruption and twisted motives of the witnesses against Dodd. His exposé, he promised, would "blow the lid off the Senate."

I knew the Dodd camp had primed Long with stories that Dodd himself had been leaking for a long time, but had been afraid to use openly. David Martin had planted the basic content of the "exposé" with a newsman who had conveyed it to me. Dodd claimed to have an affidavit from a former secretary in his office that could be used to support a charge that I had maintained her on the payroll without his knowledge and had exploited her sexually. They had, as well, a statement from George Gildea, one of Dodd's old retainers, that he had once surprised me "in passionate embrace" with another office secretary. They claimed to have a third statement charging Michael O'Hare with having brought a prostitute into the office for the purpose of entrapping Dodd. Long, presumably, was prepared to argue that these were the kind of people who had turned on Dodd when he found them out—yet the Ethics Committee had relied upon them as witnesses. In the talented hands of a Russell Long, such material might indeed cause a sensation and bring off the explosion he had predicted.

Long's "bombshell" had been well advertised, and when he took the floor at week's end, he faced a capacity audience, at a peak of curiosity. I had given a statement to reporters denying these anticipated attacks, to be distributed the moment they were made.

But Long appeared strangely subdued, and it soon became apparent that he was not to explode his bomb after all. The reasons had to be pieced together. Senator Stennis, to whom the thought of such a debasement of Senate debate was unthinkable, had had a talk with Long. What he said to dissuade him was not divulged, but some things were known.

The Ethics Committee had obtained a notarized affidavit from the first young lady, who swore that a private detective hired by Dodd had forced his way into her home, threatened her, and frightened her into signing a statement that he had written out. She had signed it, she stated, only to get the intruder to leave her home because she feared he would physically attack her. She stated further that she had worked for Senator Dodd personally, in his outer office, so that he could not have been unaware of her employment. As for the second charge, the committee knew that George Gildea had drawn a Senate salary for several years without working for it, and Senator Stennis had described him as a dubious witness on which to base anything. "He was an elderly gentleman and his memory was confused," Stennis said of him. And the bizarre and baseless charge against O'Hare could easily have been refuted. The committee staff and others had still more information with the potential to cause a disastrous backfire if the Dodd forces carried out their plan. This information alleged a series of sociable interludes between a Dodd secretary in her thirties and three of Dodd's young sons. More than that I could not learn from my contacts in the press and in the Dodd camp. But Andrew Glass of the *Washington Post* reported: "It was learned that several affidavits and counter affidavits had been exchanged between the Senate adversaries behind the scenes before Dodd reached his decision to dampen Long's attack in this quarter."

In any event, Long glumly announced to the Senate that the feature attraction had to be canceled. "I have discussed this matter with the chairman of the committee, and we understand each other in this matter," he explained cryptically. He attributed the sudden backdown to Dodd's charity. Dodd asked him not to use the sordid material, he said. "That illustrates the impeccable character of Tom Dodd. He is a man who would be crucified but, for reasons of decency, would spare his crucifiers from the complete exposure they deserve."

Though the speech on which he had based such hope had been gutted, Long nonetheless tried to mount a major oration. He paced up and down the aisles, waving his arms, trying to revive the interest of his disappointed hearers. He cited every authority from Jesus to his old Uncle Earl. Dodd was an "honorable, high-type, lovable man." Boyd was a "rotten apple in the barrel . . . a corrupt, immoral, deceitful scoundrel." Drew Pearson was a "crocodile." Screaming at the top of his voice, Long denounced Michael O'Hare with maniacal fury: "That crook, that thief, that liar, that scoundrel, that bandit—if you can think of another crime, let's put that in there too! That murderer! He is trying to murder Tom Dodd politically!" Senators and newsmen alike were incredulous as the Assistant Majority Leader of the United States Senate wandered ranting through the Senate aisles. The evidence against Dodd was "fruit from a poisoned tree . . . they want us to eat that fruit," he bellowed. "Well, I'm just not going to eat it. Jack Anderson is the serpent on that tree," and he made a slithering motion with his right hand. "He wants us to consume that fruit and destroy a Senator. When Adam ate the fruit he didn't fare well. And neither did the serpent. He had to crawl around on his belly. Even Eve had some problems."

For seven hours, as hope for a final vote that day faded and disappeared, Long rambled on. Sometimes, he seemed to have lost touch with reality. Dodd covered his eyes when his defender lapsed into his old bayou stories to show that Dodd's plight was universal. He quoted the advice of his Uncle Earl, the former governor, to a candidate in the back country: " 'Those country folks out there don't know who you are.' he says. 'All those fine, spotless clothes of yours, you have got to do something about that. Get a little dirt on you. Get down and roll on the ground.'

"And Uncle Earl added, 'Furthermore, while you are at it, take the rubber band off that big wad of green bills you got there, and spread some dough around among those country folks. Otherwise, you're going to get beat.' Mr. President, that man had legitimate campaign expenses."

Despite his antics, he failed to hold the attention of the Senate. A buzz of conversation filled the Chamber and the galleries. One by one, Senators left the floor, some in undisguised disgust. By mid-afternoon only sixteen of the original ninety-six remained.

Long spoke on while shadows lengthened in the Senate courtyard. The dispatches going out on all the news wires taunted him with failure to make good on his pledge. They were saying that Long had annoyed and embarrassed the Senate, that he was doing Dodd more harm than good, that he was displaying an irresponsibility that forever doomed his aspirations to become Majority Leader.

There was pathos in this as well as buffoonery. The Senate Chamber was no stranger to grotesque performances. Usually they served some selfish interest of the performer and little odium was attached to them. But there was no apparent element of self-interest in Long's effort to defend Dodd. From the beginning, that effort had posed the gravest risks for him. What started as a generous impulse to defend a friend who had no defenders had somehow laid hold of Long, overheated his strong emotions, and revived the recklessness and instability of a former day.

He was telling the Senate, "As much as I love my friends, I'm not willing to take the place of anybody on the cross of crucifixion. I might be willing to help him lug that heavy piece of wood down the highway, but. . . ."

As he railed on, it seemed more and more probable that his own Senate career would share in the approaching ruin of Tom Dodd.

*　　*　　*

Dodd had by now begun to crumble visibly.

"As the days wore on, you could see his confidence drain like blood from an open wound," wrote columnist James Kilpatrick. He hunched over his little desk in apparent exhaustion. His face alternately flushed and paled as the verbal fusillades ricocheted around him. At times when he rose to speak, stooped with the weight of a martyr's cloak, he seemed dazed and swayed uncertainly. Russell Long had warned Dodd. "I told him that if he breaks down and cries that I would vote for censure. 'Be a man,' I said. 'The reporters in the gallery want you to cry.'" But Dodd seemed close to a breakdown now. His voice cracked often. He had begun to beg.

His last hope lay in persuading the Senate to take its first vote on the issue he was strongest on—the double-billing charge. On this count, only the testimony of Michael O'Hare backed the Ethics Committee's charge that the double billing was deliberate and not accidental, as Dodd claimed. It was, Dodd and Long continually declared, the word of a Senator against that of a mere employee. The class line was drawn, and the issue gave Senators a chance to register their appalled disapproval of staff members who presumed to rise up and accuse their chief. Dodd might well win on this vote. Then he and Long could delay the vote on the main issue indefinitely, while bargaining to soften the censure into a harmless admonition. His opposition was willing to vote on the secondary issue first, if Dodd and Long would agree to cease tying up the Senate and allow a vote on the main issue immediately thereafter. But to this Dodd and Long would not agree.

Dodd thought he could yet get his vote, on his own terms. He had always believed he knew how to appeal to the raw sympathies of others. Haggard and wan, he would exhibit himself as the victim, rather than the author, of the delay in the proceedings. He rose to plead with the Senate:

"I have been through enough in the last 18 months," he said in a half-sobbing voice, grasping the rails of his desk. "I don't know how much longer I can physically stand the ordeal. . . . Don't drag me through any more," he implored. "You are in a position to destroy me and I know it. My life is at stake. I'm not asking very much . . . if you want to brand me a thief, do it today, before the sun goes down, and let me skulk away, ashamed to face you tomorrow."

Then his trembling voice rose to an angry shout.

"How many times do you want to hang me? You want to do it? Do it!—Be done with me! Do away with me! In the twilight of my life! And that will be the end of me!"

Then his voice sank again. "Give me a night's rest," he pleaded, "either in sorrow or relief."

But the opposition had grown insensitive to the desperate pleas that had for days swept over the Senate and it would not yield. The reality of impending disgrace, the impossibility of escape, the banishment of illusion and hope at last closed in on Tom Dodd.

"Dodd is plainly a broken man," wrote Tom Wicker of the *New York Times.* "On the Senate floor . . . he looked old, shrunken, hapless. His aimless hands were wringing and twisting nervously, occasionally flopping out in supplication. There was a tone of amazed petulance in his words, rather like a child's insistence that a parent's discipline is simply unfair. As he pled his poverty, relating how his wife had 'done her own work, made her own clothes, done our cooking,' he was near to sobbing."

The clogged parliamentary machine ground slowly.

"Have I used the testimonials to enrich myself or live lavishly?" Dodd cried out. It was June 21st, the seventh day of debate. "I don't think the public wants my head!" he shouted. His face was scarlet, clenched fists flailed the air. "What the people want is a clearly defined code of conduct . . . rather than the punishment of a single Senator. . . . What this comes home to is: have I got the dough or not? No. I don't have it. It is shameful that I have to go through all this!" His voice broke and in a whisper he said, "I hope it never happens to any one of you, what has happened to me."

June 22nd: "I don't understand all of this. I don't know whether you're trying to build a gallows or a courtroom."

June 23rd: "Whatever fate befalls me, I am satisfied that history will justify me. You know me well enough to let your consciences be your guide."

With a crushing force, the votes at last had come. Long's motion to soften the censure had been defeated by a vote of 92 to 2. Only Long and Abe Ribicoff of Connecticut stood with Dodd. Other amendments designed to lessen the sting of censure were rejected 87 to 9 and 78 to 18. And now, as the words of Dodd's final plea faded, the climactic moment had come. It was three o'clock on the afternoon of June 23rd. The Clerk read the Censure Resolution prior to the vote:

"Resolved, that it is the judgment of the Senate that the Senator from Connecticut, Thomas J. Dodd . . .

"Deserves the censure of the Senate and he is so censured for his conduct, which is contrary to accepted morals, derogates from the public trust expected of a Senator, and tends to bring the Senate into dishonor and disrepute."

The Clerk called the roll:

"Mr. Aiken?" "Yes."

"Mr. Allott?" "Yes."

"Mr. Anderson?" "Yes."

"Mr. Baker?" "Yes."

Russell Long had thrown an arm around Dodd and led him to the well of the Senate. There Senator Mansfield took his arm and escorted him out of the Chamber. While the roll continued, Dodd waited in the Marble Room just off the Senate floor.

"Mr. Kennedy of Massachusetts?" "Yes."

"Mr. Kennedy of New York?" "Yes."

"Mr. Kuchel?" "Yes."

"Mr. Lausche?" "Yes."

Up in the family gallery, Grace Dodd abandoned the station she had occupied throughout the nine days of debate. As the vote for censure mounted, the Dodd family left one by one, except for Thomas, Jr., who stayed until the end.

When the vote was finished, but before it was announced, an emissary went to Dodd and informed him of the result. Ninety-two of his peers had voted to condemn him, only four had voted "nay"—Long, Ribicoff, Thurmond of South Carolina, and Tower of Texas. Dodd's eyes filled with tears. Then, recovering, he rose and returned to the Senate Chamber. He motioned for recognition.

"The Senator from Connecticut," said the Chair.

"No!" Dodd voted, a ring of defiance in his voice, thus becoming the first Senator to vote for himself in a censure proceeding.

Later, he addressed the Senate: "I think a grave mistake has been made and I am the one who must bear the scar of that mistake all the rest of my life . . . in my heart I have no feeling of wrongdoing. If I did, I do not think I would show up here again. But only time can tell that." As tears crept down his cheeks, he was again led off the floor.

Back in his office, Dodd sat alone for a few minutes in the unreal twilight that so soothed him. Then his family was admitted and for some time remained closeted with the Senator. Outside, the staff was left to deal with the press which was gathering in the hall.

"If he's asked any more questions he may crack," said one tense aide. Two secretaries were weeping unrestrainedly. One of them went out into the hall and asked the reporters to spare Senator Dodd the ordeal of facing them. "Please, he's so tired," she sobbed. "He's been so good. He and Mrs. Dodd just want to go home."

Later in the day the Senate voted 51 to 45 to spare Dodd the humiliation of a second censure on the double-billing charge. But that was now only a footnote to the solitary fact that Thomas Dodd had become the only Senator in the 179-year history of the Senate to be censured for financial misconduct. The judgment of the nation, so long withheld, would not be merciful. In newspaper offices throughout the country that afternoon, editorials were being written demanding that Senator Dodd resign from public life. One had already appeared in the *Washington Post:*

> His selfish exploitation of his friends to enhance his personal wealth, maintain his political place and enrich his private life, as revealed by his own admissions, entitles him to universal contempt. He is a disgrace to the Senate. He is a liability to his state. He is an embarrassment to his colleagues. He is an encumbrance to anything he embraces.
>
> If he stays in the Senate, his endorsement will be the worst misfortune that can befall any legislative measure. Whenever he rises to speak, his reputation will stand beside him, like Banquo's ghost . . .
>
> . . . He stands a veritable monument to many of the frauds, frailties and flaws in our public life. The very sight of him must wound every man of sensibility and patriotism who has the capacity to reflect upon the curious follies of our elective system.

CHAPTER NINE

I N the days before the trouble came, Tom Dodd was fond of an old
Al Smith quote which he used often in his speeches: "I know the
difference between right and wrong," he would say. "If I ever do
wrong you must hold me accountable, for you will know that it was
intentional."

But lately, he had taken to a new motto: "There ought to be a rule,
regulation, or law so a man knows whether he is doing right or
wrong." He had been true, he kept insisting, to the standards he had
encountered along the path to high office.

My first reaction was to think of him as a hypocrite. Yet, underneath
his delusions and self-pity, there was, I had to concede, a trace of
honest bafflement at the chain of events that had brought him down.
During the last days of the censure debate, when the outcome seemed
at last assured and the time for my own unyielding militance was past,
I began again to look on Tom Dodd with, I think, some of the understanding and sympathy I once possessed.

As I watched him in the last act of his ordeal, saw his television interviews and the news pictures of him in the halls of the Capitol, I
could not help recalling the scenes of earlier years. I thought of when
we had first walked those halls together, and at odd moments I saw
the man as I had first known him. Old, unconnected images returned:
the ritual he made out of lighting the logs in the fireplace each evening; his joy in animals; the feasts he would prepare—how he would

wrap the ears of corn in tinfoil and carefully cover the boiling lobsters with seaweed, and cry out in exaggerated pain "Oh, oh, oh" as he pulled the baked potatoes out of the oven, how he would fill everyone's plate over and over, and then insist preposterously on doing the dishes all by himself.

And there were the nights of laughter. So infectious was his humor then that the poorest joke told in a circle was an instant howling success. He would roar and slap his knees in convulsed and helpless mirth. And he would sit by the firelight, entertaining his listeners for hours with outlandish tales he swore were true, told with consummate mimicry, until it was suddenly three A.M.

He was, in those days, a man of inexhaustible energies and interests, with a vast capacity for life, for sentiment, for fellowship, for caring.

So much of his early career had been admirable: his work against crime; his projects to help impoverished youths; his unheralded fight for civil rights when it was an unknown cause; his role at Nuremberg, where, amid the ashes of Nazi depravity, he had represented, not unworthily, the principles of justice, decency, and international law.

In his early years in politics, he had often rejected expediency, defied the party bosses, and battled for idealistic goals. His long fight for nomination and election to the Senate, a fight against wealth, political machines, and the vagaries of fate, had exhibited courage and even nobility. He had the gift to inspire, the power to pull people toward him. And, in the Senate, he often had been drawn to the larger issues. Here was a man with a capacity and an instinct for high public service who seemed destined for a career of illustrious achievement. What had unfolded instead possessed, along with the ignominy, an element of high tragedy, not without its moral on public life in a free society.

When Tom Dodd turned to politics in Connecticut, he entered a milieu in which the run of men confidently expect public office to be an avenue to private enrichment. State legislators held high-salaried sinecures in the state administration to assure their support of the governor's programs. Party functionaries obtained fraudulent agent's commissions, distributed by the party chairman, on the insurance that the State of Connecticut purchased each year. During nomination campaigns, it was commonplace for local leaders with delegates under their control to hire themselves out to the most generous candidate. And that was the small change—the kind of thing that any aspiring politician would learn about. Dodd, never an insider in the state organization, knew relatively little about how well-placed politicians made fortunes in connection with highway contracts, real estate purchases, legal practice before state commissions, and other enterprises connected with government. But he observed that such practices were making wealthy men out of some of his political contemporaries. So he began to learn.

He discovered some of the niceties of campaign finance from Senator Brien McMahon, whom he served as an aide in 1950.

"Brien liked to deal in cash," Dodd once confided to me, with a tinge of admiration. "One day he took me into his room at the house we had rented for the campaign. He opened the drawers of his dresser —they were bulging with money. 'Spend whatever we need,' Brien told me. 'There's plenty more where that came from.'" Where it did come from, and how it was accounted for, Dodd did not know, nor did he inquire. That was the way things were done, he felt, and he often voiced suspicions to me over the years that this or that candidate had "made a fortune on campaign contributions."

The technique of $100-a-plate dinners Dodd learned from John M. Bailey, who held one, sometimes two, every year. The proceeds were supposed to go for the legitimate expenses of running the party. No doubt they did. But just how much money was raised was never announced, nor was any public accounting of its use given or expected. These customs were not lost on Tom Dodd.

Of course, Connecticut had a law governing campaign contributions, but its laxity was so obviously deliberate that politicians had no reason to take it seriously. There was no provision requiring that contributions be deposited in a bank or that rigorous accounting procedures be followed. There was no rule for listing the address of a contributor, or even his state. Since no report had to be made before election day, by the time the report came out it was already irrelevant. There was never an official check into a report. And just in case some busybody began poking around later on, the law permitted the records to be destroyed after fifteen months—and, as we had found, the destruction was carried out with religious punctuality. The inevitable result was that Dodd and other politicians came to regard the matter of political money as a private affair—their own business and no one else's.

When Dodd entered the House of Representatives in the early 1950's, he found that despite its stately veneer of mosaic floors, muraled walls, and high, painted ceilings, the ethical climate was merely an extension of what he had left behind in Connecticut. Covert trimming was a Congressional institution, protected by a network of secrecy. Congress had decreed, for instance, that the public must not be told who was on a Congressman's staff, or what Congressmen did with their government allowance for office supplies, or how much of the taxpayers' money a Congressman spent while junketing in Paris or Rome or Rio. And so more than a hundred Congressmen had quietly placed their wives and relatives on their office payrolls, many members regularly pocketed large portions of their housekeeping allowances and, at the close of each session, the body departed more or less *en masse* for the world's pleasure spots to conduct investigations. Recurring scandals and spectacles eventually forced a reluctant Congress to lift somewhat its veil of secrecy, but most avenues to petty profiteering remained open.

Deceit was also formalized in other, more dangerous, ways. There was the "teller vote," a method of voting on public measures that permitted the individual Congressman to conceal his stance from his constituents. It sometimes occurred that, after a teller vote, a record vote on the same issue would be demanded. In such instances, forty to sixty Congressmen sometimes switched sides, often reversing the outcome of the original ballot. One might think that such studied cynicism at the heart of the legislative process would be a matter of shame to the Congress. But these vote reversals occurred year after year and were regarded merely as occasions for cloakroom jests.

Dodd rose higher, to the Senate of the United States, where practices are more refined. One by one, he discovered its authorized duplicities.

A Senator who is vacationing on a Florida beach or drying out after a binge is invariably listed in the Congressional Record as "present" on quorum calls or "absent on official business." The Congressional Record, assumed by historians and judges to be an accurate transcript of debate, a record on which treatises and judicial decisions are based, is actually in part a work of fiction. Each evening, after the Senate adjourns, the large, round table in the Official Reporter's office is crowded with Senators and aides who are busily rewriting the day's discussions. It is not just the bad grammar that is reworked. The substance is often changed, even reversed. Whole paragraphs are deleted, entire pages are added, and the Record is transformed from an account of what was, to a scenario of what its participants would have liked it to be.

Small matters? Perhaps. But it is the small things as well as the large that set the moral tone of an institution. Once deceit in voting, in debating, in payrolls, in expense allowances becomes enshrined by custom and protected by secrecy, it is a small step to graver abuses.

Dodd learned that the law Congress had written governing campaign financing was even more calculatedly dissembling than the Connecticut statute. A Senator could collect a million dollars and report only $10,000, with no questions asked. Such a law, and its cynical non-inforcement, was an open invitation to fraud. In the forty years of the law's existence, during which some 16,000 reports had been filed, not a single violation had ever been reported to the Justice Department by either the Senate or the House.

Dodd observed that there was big money around and that some legislators knew how to extract it. There were, for instance, the large gifts from lobbyists representing mail-order businesses and postal workers, sums that were presented at "appreciation dinners" to Congressman Thaddeus "Teddy" Dulski and other members of the House Post Office Committee—the committee which determines postal rates and the salaries of postal employees. The respected Senator Willis Robertson, Chairman of the Senate Banking and Currency Committee, which consistently dealt in legislation concerning the nation's banks, permitted himself to accept campaign contributions from the very industry he was supposed to be regulating, as bankers, pleased with Robertson's pro-banking policies, organized fund-raising ventures in his behalf.

The Bobby Baker hearings showed how easily it could be done. When the Senate Finance Committee seemed on the verge of adopting a tax amendment that was highly unfavorable to certain savings and loan associations, the adversely affected businesses promptly presented $90,000 to Baker to spread among influential Senators. The offending amendment was withdrawn soon thereafter. When, during the Baker probe, a finger of guilt was pointed at Senator Robert Kerr and others, had not the chairman of the investigating committee, Senator Everett Jordan, declared, "We are not investigating Senators"? Dodd could confidently expect that it would always be thus.

And so, while Dodd was "investigating" the firearms industry and conducting hearings on the advisability of outlawing the virtually unrestricted mail-order commerce in lethal weapons, he was not without precedent when he accepted both personal financial gifts and campaign contributions from officials of the arms industry, which naturally sought to delay controls and to alter any restrictive legislation to its

advantage. Dodd's crusade against mail-order firearms sputtered spas-
modically and dragged on ineffectually for years, while gifts and contributions poured in from arms-industry officials in 1961, 1963, 1964,
and 1965.

Each year Dodd saw proposals for ethical reform in the Congress
defeated by overwhelming margins.

"A Senator is the judge of his own conduct," Senator Dirksen would
say, and his colleagues would nod approvingly.

And so, the Senate appeared to Dodd not as a harsh and exacting
judge, but as a permissive and protective accomplice. His occasional
inanities in debate would always appear in the Record as words of
wisdom. His absence would be reported as a presence. His vacation
trips would not only be paid for by the Senate, but would be billed as
"official business." His honorariums and legal kickbacks and finder fees
and gifts were excused from the prohibitions that covered all government officials except Congressmen and Senators. His fraudulent campaign reports would always be accepted at face value. Not only could
he keep unsavory contributions, he could route them through the Senate Campaign Committee and thus hide their origin. He could use his
official allowances to buy birthday presents, wedding invitations, and
the like, and no one would know. He had reason to consider himself
immune from investigation.

"We are not investigating Senators," Jordan had said.

And there was the need for money, for the symbols of success, for
some guarantee of security and status at the end. After all the struggle, all the sacrifice, all the victories, there had to be a commensurate
reward. But the monetary rewards of government service are modest.

The child of wealth can play at the game of politics without staking
his total existence on it. He is spared the meaner considerations that
constantly beset his poorer counterpart. For Dodd, like many another,
there was in defeat no family estate to retire to, no inherited fortune
to give solace, no corporate portfolio to assume.

To the man whose very livelihood is tied to the caucus and the
ballot box, politics is a fearsome gamble. Each time he wins on the
way up, he but increases his obligations and enlarges the scope of his
future struggles. Until he at last wins a major office and becomes a
"success," all his campaigns are fought at his own risk. He mortgages
everything; society invests nothing. If he loses any of the recurring
tests of strength, he may be finished, bankrupt, and forgotten. In
American politics there is no place for the loser. Even victory is fleet-

ing and must constantly be reaffirmed. A Senator knows that he may not always be the millionaire's darling, holidaying at the estates of near-strangers. Why, he asks himself, should he be poor, while his deferential hosts are rich?

And so Tom Dodd, a solitary, sanguinary man, hardened by the indignities of politics, disillusioned by its shabbiness, alienated by its brutality and its indifference to his survival, his fears, his needs, at some point began to betray his office for the tangible rewards that public service does not in itself bestow. As late as his third year in the Senate he had resisted temptation. But what he had encountered along the way of his long travail had fed his weaknesses, not his strengths, and, compromise by compromise, he had fallen.

"There is no victory here for anyone, and no victory against anyone," proclaimed John Stennis, in valedictory, after the overwhelming vote for censure.

"I feel that the adoption of this resolution, in a way, is a new start for the Senate." And he promised that the committee would begin work on a new code of ethics.

Certainly the Dodd case had shown some of the reforms that were needed: an absolute ban on any form of outside income for members of Congress that bears a relation to public issues or public business; annual disclosure of all income and assets by members of Congress; public financing of election campaigns, with strict reporting laws and the prohibition of large private contributions; removal of the loopholes from the conflict-of-interest and bribery statutes; tight controls on lobbyists, including itemized reporting of all their expenditures; an end to the secrecy and evasion by which the Congress shields its internal operations from the public. And if present salaries and expense allowances are inadequate, then Congress should increase them so that the proper rewards and costs of office are paid openly by the public, not subsidized secretly by either personal wealth or the favors of lobbyists.

But did the Senate really want, as Stennis proclaimed, "a new start"? Or would it wait confidently, as in times past, for the restoration of public indifference? Tom Dodd had got himself caught; and the Senate had, after a year and a half, reluctantly voted to condemn him. But the system remained. Whether the Senate would go beyond the mere offering of a public sacrifice and reform the system itself would depend, in the end, on the unrelenting insistence of the American people that the temple must be cleansed.

The fight was all over. The Senate Chamber was at last silent. Tom Dodd could assess the extent of his ruin. It was being advertised on all sides as an accomplished fact. Congressman Curtis declared that Dodd should have been expelled, like Powell. According to the press, the Justice Department and the Internal Revenue Service were stepping up their probes of possible criminal violations. The leading newspapers in Connecticut were demanding his resignation.

A less resilient man might have been chastened by such tidings, but Tom Dodd chose them as the occasion for announcing his candidacy for re-election in 1970. Reaction in Connecticut was "all good," he said, "especially in the rural areas where people know I'm no crook. Don't worry, the truth will catch up."

His colleagues had censured him, but he was no fragile flower to be withered by a rebuke from a body that was itself so compromised that it could neither fully investigate nor adequately punish any one of its members for fear of unlocking the secrets of many others. Resign? Nonsense. He might yet ride this thing out. He was still a Senator, with undiminished seniority and two and a half years to go on his second term. He still headed up, unabashedly, Senate investigations into crime and delinquency. He was still acting chairman of the subcommittee charged with probing subversion and "security risks" in government. He remained a member in good standing of the Senate Foreign Relations Committee at a time of deepening national division over the Vietnam war. In his fortress on the Senate Judiciary Committee he continued to pass upon the qualifications of judicial nominees and to sit in judgment on the legislative requests of the Department of Justice, which was nonetheless supposed to be investigating him. The great corporations must still come to him for help. The White House needed his vote more than ever now that a Congressional revolt against the President's program was underway. And the Democratic politicians back in Connecticut were afraid to move against him, or even to criticize him, for he could yet be a spoiler.

And so, in his hour of public disgrace, Tom Dodd announced that henceforth he would carry on in the Senate as if nothing had happened. He aimed to show up on the floor every day, to rise in debate, to pilot legislation through the Senate, to conduct public hearings into the misconduct of others, to carry on his long-interrupted assault on the doves and appeasers who were endangering the country. And he was confident of overwhelming re-election, he said. But, reporters asked, who would support him? Where would he get campaign funds?

"I guess I'll have to do some panhandling around the state," he said softly. "And there won't be any skulking or slinking around by me. That's for the people without a clear conscience. . . . I'll take my case to the people who count, the people in Connecticut."

Surely it appeared on that June morning that Tom Dodd's career was destroyed. And other, more menacing, investigations might lie ahead. But in a sense it would be left to the people of Connecticut to decide his ultimate fate. And in this circumstance he saw a glimmer of hope. There had always been something almost mystical about his faith in his ability to explain things to the folks at home. He was, above all else, a campaigner. He would get back there on the old circuit, starting up around Mystic and Old Saybrook, in the church basements and lodge halls and on the picnic grounds, out where he could talk to people, where he knew all the shortcuts and catwalks, and where, at night, the fog rolls in along the shore. There they would see it all differently.

APPENDIX ONE

April 4, 1967

Honorable John Stennis
Honorable Wallace Bennett
Committee on Standards and Conduct
United States Senate
Washington, D. C.

Gentlemen:

As citizens who have devoted a considerable part of the last two years to bringing the so-called Dodd case before the public, the Senate and the Justice Department, and as witnesses called by the Ethics Committee in its presentation of that case, we ask your indulgence in stating our opinion on the present status of the Senate investigation into the affairs of Senator Thomas J. Dodd.

We are deeply concerned by your announcement that the investigation is over and that the Committee will soon issue its findings. Despite our respect for the Committee and its staff, we feel constrained to express regret that the Committee saw fit to exclude from the hearings more than a score of serious matters on which there was eyewitness testimony and substantiating documentation.

Were it merely an individual episode here and there that the Committee did not feel worthy of public inquiry, we would have assumed that the evidence had proved insufficient or that the Committee, in its superior judgment, considered certain offenses negligible. But since several whole areas of misconduct, about which we had given exhaustive testimony, were not pursued, we are left with the conclusion that there was a policy decision to limit the scope of the hearings. Upon what considerations it was based we do not know. But we feel that the areas not covered in the hearings constitute the heart of the Dodd case.

The Stipulations introduced at the hearings showed that, as we had informed the Committee a year ago, Senator Dodd used hundreds of thousands of dollars in contributions for his personal use. However, it was not shown how he exploited his office as a United States Senator to encourage these donations and to reward benefactors. We feel it is in this latter area that the ethical questions of principal significance to the country lie, and we feel that, as the Senate prepares to enact a code of ethics, the public has a right to know all the major aspects of the Dodd case, so it can bring an informed judgment to bear upon the Senate deliberations promised for later this year.

Therefore, we ask the Committee to reopen its hearings and we presume to cite several areas of the Dodd case as proper subjects.

We understand it to be a serious violation of Senate ethics for a chairman or a member of an investigating committee of the Senate to accept gifts, services or anything of substantial value from persons, corporations or groups whose activities are under investigation by that committee.

We point out to the Committee:

that after having requested in January 1964 Senate appropriations for the purpose of investigating the motion picture industry, Senator Dodd accepted a $500 political contribution from Edward Cooper, the Washington lobbyist for the Motion Picture Association, and that the investigation was never conducted;

that during a period in which Senator Dodd was conducting a general investigation into objectionable programming practices in the television industry, he accepted political and personal contributions from John Kluge, President of Metromedia, whose eight-station television network Dodd had been specifically requested to investigate by his Subcommittee staff, following a staff investigation into its programming practices, and that in addition Senator Dodd accepted valuable gifts from other Metromedia executives, including a television set, and that the probe into Metromedia was never undertaken;

that during the period in which Senator Dodd was chairing investigations into practices of the firearms industry and drafting, with the collaboration of the arms industry, legislation to control the interstate shipment of firearms and other matters of fundamental interest to that industry, he accepted upwards of $4,000 in political and personal donations from arms industry officials;

that during the period in which Senator Dodd was assigned by the Senate Antitrust and Monopoly Subcommittee to head an investigation into practices of the insurance industry, he accepted about $4,000 in testimonial gifts from insurance executives, several thousand dollars in fees for speeches delivered to groups of insurance officials, a $5,000 legal fee for obtaining for the Bankers' Life and Casualty Company a charter to do business in Connecticut, several thousand dollars in "finders' fees" for helping an associate, Manlio Liccione, to obtain business loans from Hartford insurance companies and, in addition, the Senator failed to pay over $3,000 in insurance premiums owed to a Hartford firm covering a three-year period;

that during a period when two committees on which Senator Dodd served, the Antitrust and Monopoly Subcommittee and the Foreign Relations Committee, were occupied in a protracted investigation into the drug industry that involved, among other parties, the McKesson and Robbins Company of New Jersey, Senator Dodd accepted on a regular basis the free use of a private aircraft provided by the McKesson and Robbins Company, a service which over a period of years amounted to a "thing of value" worth several thousands of dollars, and that in addition Senator Dodd accepted a $1,000 campaign contribution from Laurence Ehrhardt, a McKesson and Robbins Vice President;

that during a period when a subcommittee of the Senate Judiciary Committee was conducting its investigation of price-fixing in the electrical industry, Senator Dodd, a member of the Judiciary Committee, accepted the gift of a stereo console from John Lane, the Washington representative of Westinghouse, a company deeply involved in that investigation, and that Senator Dodd also accepted testimonial donations from Mr. Lane and accepted his participation in the organization of the D.C. Testimonial Reception held for Senator Dodd in Washington in 1963.

We understand it to be a serious violation of Senate ethics for a Senator to accept monetary contributions and other personal gifts from businessmen or other groups for whom he has performed official services.

We point out:

that in regard to the stipulated $2,100 cash donation given to Senator Dodd by Robert Blinkin, President of the Mite Corporation, Senator Dodd had made repeated official efforts to obtain government contracts for the Mite Corporation;

that in regard to the stipulated arrangements by which the Dunbar Transfer Company made three automobiles available to Senator Dodd, it is relevant that during this same period, Senator Dodd was intervening with the Atomic Energy Commission and the Government Printing Office to help obtain government contracts for the Dunbar Transfer Company;

that following extensive efforts by Senator Dodd to obtain government contracts for Kaman Aircraft, Senator Dodd accepted a $4,000 contribution in 1964 and a $300 testimonial donation in 1963 from Charles Kaman, President of Kaman Aircraft;

that following efforts to obtain a contract for AVCO, so strenuous as to draw a rebuke from Presidential Aide McGeorge Bundy, Senator Dodd enlisted AVCO official Earl Blaik as Master of Ceremonies of a fund-raising affair in March 1965 and accepted the testimonial donations of several AVCO officials including Blaik, President James Kerr and Vice President Paul Deegan;

that while giving prominent support in and out of the Senate to the proposition that 50% of all wheat shipments to Iron Curtain countries must be carried in American ships, manned by American crews, a position strongly endorsed by the Seafarers International Union, Senator Dodd accepted in August 1964 a $1,000 check from the Seafarers Political Action Department, an arm of the Seafarers International Union, which he did not declare as a political contribution, and that Senator Dodd accepted as personal income another $1,000 check from SPAD, dated October 29, 1965, in conjunction with a speech he made in New York at the annual dinner of the Jewish War Veterans on October 30, 1965, in which he advocated any Congressional action necessary to enforce the 50% rule with respect to all American wheat shipments to Communist countries.

We understand it to be a serious violation of Senate ethics for a Senator to engage in the practice of seeking government appointments for persons who have contributed to him large sums of money, or granted to him non-interest bearing loans in large amounts. Though we recognize that this is not a practice unique to Senator Dodd, we feel that its prevalence makes it all the more an important subject for official scrutiny.

We point out the following pattern:

Edgar A. Parser, a diamond merchant, from whom Senator Dodd accepted a loan of $3,000, a campaign contribution of $1,000 and various testimonial and personal gifts, was recommended to the President by Senator Dodd for appointment as Ambassador to Luxembourg;

Mathew Manes, a New York City lawyer, from whom Senator Dodd accepted loans totalling $27,500 and political and testimonial contributions, was recommended for appointment and reappointment by the President to the Board of Directors of the General Aniline Corporation, at the time when that corporation was under United States Government control;

Joseph Sullivan, a New York lawyer from whom Senator Dodd accepted a political contribution of $2,500, was recommended by Senator Dodd for appointment as Ambassador to Ireland and later as Ambassador to Italy or the Netherlands;

John Mosler, President of the Mosler Safe Company in New York, who contributed $1,000 to the Non-Partisan Committee for Senator Dodd in 1964 and who served as Treasurer for that Committee, was immediately thereafter recommended by Senator Dodd for the post of Assistant Secretary of State for African Affairs;

William Benton, publisher of Encyclopaedia Britannica, from whom Senator Dodd accepted a $2,500 contribution in 1964, similar contributions in previous years and a series of valuable gifts and testimonial donations, was recommended to the President by Senator Dodd for appointment as Ambassador to Great Britain;

James Kelley, from whom Senator Dodd accepted a loan of $5,000, was pushed repeatedly by Senator Dodd for a variety of Federal posts until he was at length appointed to a position in the U. S. Department of Commerce;

George Gildea, from whom Senator Dodd had accepted loans in the amount of $20,000, was appointed by Senator Dodd to the staff of the Juvenile Delinquency Subcommittee, a post which he held for several years, though he was assigned no duties to perform;

Albert Morano, from whom Senator Dodd accepted loans totalling $15,000, was appointed by Senator Dodd to his own staff, though he worked out of no Senate office and had no assigned duties.

We understand it to be a serious violation of Senate ethics for a Senator to press the interests of clients before any agency of the Federal government when he is also acting to advance those same interests in his private capacity as lawyer or agent;

We point out:

that while acting as an agent for Thomas Frouge, President of the Frouge Corporation, in a real estate transaction in Marin County, California, and after billing Mr. Frouge for business expenses incurred in his behalf, Senator Dodd, in his role as a U. S. Senator, urged the interests of that same Marin County real estate development before the U. S. Department of the Interior and the General Services Administration;

that while serving as a "consulting lawyer" to Henry A. Neilsen of Hartford, Connecticut, in (a) an attempt to negotiate a loan from the Hartford National Bank, (b) an attempt to secure the reversal of a decision of the Ford Motor Company to withdraw its Ford franchise from Mr. Neilsen, and (c) an attempt to find a lessor for Mr. Neilsen's business property, Senator Dodd, acting as a United States Senator, successfully pressed the

Small Business Administration to grant a $120,000 loan to the Neilsen Company.

We understand it to be a serious violation of Senate ethics for any Senator to place on the Senate payroll, and to maintain there for a period of several years, persons who perform no public business and who render essentially personal services, and that it is a like violation for the chairman of a committee or subcommittee to misuse his committee payroll to the extent that ⅔ of the committee staff is no wise employed on Committee work.

We point out:

that no less than seven staff members devoted the bulk of their efforts to raising funds for Senator Dodd's personal and political use; that most of these employees had no identifiable Senate duties; that of twenty-one members on the payroll of the Senate Juvenile Delinquency Subcommittee, thirteen were diverted by Chairman Dodd to activities that bore no relation to the Committee work for which they were being paid; that staff members assigned to Senator Dodd by the Internal Security Subcommittee were assigned for a considerable period of time to fund-raising or other campaign activities; that some Senate employees were exploited as personal servants; and that beyond misappropriation of staff funds, Senator Dodd habitually used Federal facilities and allowances for personal and business purposes.

We assume it to be a serious violation of Senate ethics for a Senator to use public funds for what essentially are vacation or personal trips. In addition to the stipulated matters concerning "double billings," we have testified, and other staff members are available to testify, that Senator Dodd repeatedly took vacation trips at public expense to Florida, California, the Caribbean and Europe.

All the factual statements made in this letter are demonstrably true, and have been previously presented to the Committee through testimony and documentation. The significance to be attached to them is a question for each Senator to decide. We feel that these matters are so significant that the public is entitled to hearings and to an authoritative judgment by the Senate Committee established for that purpose.

Almost every instance cited in this letter points to the need for a disclosure bill that would require Members of Congress and their immediate families to disclose all assets and all sources of income, loans, gifts, reimbursements and gratuities of all kinds. Had such a disclosure law been in effect, we doubt that Senator Dodd would have been tempted into the predicament which now confronts him and we, ourselves, would have been spared the many difficulties that have attended our lives in the past two years.

We have hoped all along that this painful business would serve a higher purpose than the discreditation of one Senator and that these many revelations would lead to the passage of reform legislation. We feel that the abbreviation of the Committee inquiry has reduced its great potential for reform and therefore we request further Committee consideration of the many unresolved matters involved in the Dodd case.

Very truly yours,

Terry Golden

Marjorie Carpenter

Michael O'Hare

James Boyd

APPENDIX TWO

Calendar No. 186

90TH CONGRESS 1st Session	SENATE	REPORT No. 193

REPORT

OF THE

SELECT COMMITTEE ON STANDARDS AND CONDUCT

UNITED STATES SENATE

ON THE

INVESTIGATION OF SENATOR THOMAS J. DODD OF CONNECTICUT

TO ACCOMPANY S. RES. 112

Under the Authority of
S. Res. 338
(88th Congress, Second Session)

APRIL 27, 1967.—Ordered to be printed

U.S. GOVERNMENT PRINTING OFFICE
65-008   WASHINGTON : 1967

PART 1

RELATIONSHIP WITH JULIUS KLEIN

I. INTRODUCTION

A. ORIGIN AND DEVELOPMENT

About January 24, 1966, there began appearing in newspapers throughout the country a series of syndicated articles alleging that Senator Dodd engaged in certain activities of an ostensibly unethical character. On February 2, 1966, the Select Committee on Standards and Conduct took note of the charges, which up to that point had been limited to Senator Dodd's association with Julius Klein, a public relations representative of certain German interests. No formal investigation was started, but the Committee staff began accumulating background information on the source and extent of the allegations.

On February 18, 1966, the Committee staff made a preliminary report of the matter to the Chairman. Five days later, Senator Dodd formally requested the Committee to investigate the charges and allegations that had been made against him concerning his relationship with Klein.

Subsequent meetings were held by the Committee for the principal purposes of authorizing further investigation by and receiving reports from the Committee staff. In addition, the Chairman and Vice Chairman met with Senator Dodd on several occasions and requested him to furnish certain information and to answer interrogatories by the Committee. A Subcommittee took sworn testimony from several witnesses in executive sessions in order to determine whether there was sufficient cause for a formal investigation. After consideration of all the facts at hand, the Committee concluded that it would have to obtain complete facts from independent sources. It therefore authorized a continuing staff investigation into all allegations against Senator Dodd and ordered particular hearings on Senator Dodd's relationship with Julius Klein.

Public hearings were accordingly conducted by the Committee on June 22, 23, 24, and 27; and July 19, 1966, on Senator Dodd's relationship with Julius Klein. These hearings have been published as Part 1 of the Investigation of Senator Thomas J. Dodd. The public hearings were preceded by two days of closed hearings to explore preliminary matters which therefore were not made part of the printed hearings upon which the findings and conclusions of the Committee were based.

Further investigation of additional allegations continued and ultimately culminated in public hearings on "Political and Official Finances." These hearings have been published as Part 2 of the Investigation of Senator Thomas J. Dodd and are discussed in Part 2 of this report.

B. Method of Investigation

Following the decision of the Committee to limit the initial hearings to the relationship of Senator Dodd with Julius Klein, the staff investigation was concentrated principally on the several charges concerning this relationship. During March, April, May and June, 1966, the staff conducted about seventeen interviews and reviewed many documents furnished to the Committee by Senator Dodd and through the voluntary offer of various persons and organizations.

II. EVIDENCE AND FINDINGS OF FACT

Julius Klein, owner and managing director of a public relations firm based in Chicago, Illinois, registered with the U.S. Department of Justice under the Foreign Agents Registration Act, for various periods of time including 1964 (pp. 7, 8, 509 Hgs.). His clients included the Society for German-American Cooperation (Foerderkreis fuer Deutsch Amerikanische Zusammenarbeit) of Wiesbaden, Germany (p. 9, Hgs.). Klein's testimony before the Senate Foreign Relations Committee on May 14, 1963, indicated that the Federal Republic of Germany contributed financially to the Society (p. 14, Hgs.). Before the Select Committee on Standards and Conduct, Klein stated that the Society was interested in the political and economic "fate" of Germany and the United States, and acknowledged that he had previously provided Senator Dodd with information that the German Foreign Office subsidized or contributed heavily to the Wiesbaden group, and that there was a "strong likelihood" that the German government gave financial support to the Society (pp. 46, 509, 512, 513, Hgs.). Klein stated he would furnish the Committee with a list of the contributors to his Wiesbaden client, but has failed to do so (p. 516 Hgs.).

As a consequence of the hearings held by the Senate Foreign Relations Committee in 1963 on the activities of nondiplomatic representatives of foreign principals in the United States, Klein began to lose some of his German commercial clients and by February 1964 was especially worried about the most important one, the Foerderkreis (p. 39, Hgs.). Starting in December 1963, Klein began to address to Senator Dodd numerous letters, telephone calls, telegrams, and biographies, as well as visits from his employees, in a concerted effort to convince Senator Dodd to go to Germany to intervene on his behalf with German officials and clients (pp. 29–60, 196, 198, Hgs.). Klein insisted in his testimony that his purpose was to correct what he considered to be an unfair judgment of the Senate Foreign Relations Committee (p. 523, Hgs.).

Senator Dodd did make a trip to Germany in April 1964 (p. 469, Hgs.). He testified that it was not made to assist Julius Klein but was for the Subcommittee on Internal Security of which Senator Dodd was Vice Chairman, it being a subcommittee of the Senate Committee on the Judiciary, for the declared purpose of interviewing one Bogdan Stashynsky. Stashynsky was a Soviet citizen who had been convicted in the Federal Republic of Germany for murder and who was imprisoned at Karlsruhe (pp. 470, 473, 479–481, Hgs.). Senator Dodd testified that it was necessary to interview Stashynsky to expose a practice of murder as a Soviet instrument of international policy (pp. 470, 480, Hgs.). He further stated that the Subcommittee had planned for over a year to interview Stashynsky and that February 1964 was the first opportunity he had to make the trip (p. 470, Hgs.). In Germany, Senator Dodd interviewed Stashynsky (p. 471, Hgs.). With the exception of Senator Dodd's admission that he briefly mentioned Julius Klein to Chancellor Adenauer, there is no direct evidence that Senator Dodd intervened with German officials or clients of Klein in Klein's behalf (pp. 454, 455, Hgs.).

There were other facts adduced of which the Committee took notice. Senator Dodd's report on the Stashynsky case was not made until eleven months after his trip to Germany and contained little information that was not available to him before the trip (pp. 326, 408, 409, 413, 419, 420, Hgs.). Testimony was given that Julius Klein provided Senator Dodd with background material on various German officials whom he asked Senator Dodd to see and suggested what Senator Dodd should say to them in Klein's behalf (pp. 44–54, Hgs.). Testimony was also given that these instructions were taken to Germany by Senator Dodd (pp. 197–199, Hgs.). Senator Dodd denied that he took the documents to Germany (p. 454, Hgs.). Evidence was also introduced that Julius Klein provided to Senator Dodd certain favors, but the Committee could not establish their validity with the exception of the repeated use of the Klein suite in the Essex House hotel in New York City (pp. 67, 211, 212, 228, Hgs.). The Committee heard evidence that Senator Dodd signed and sent two letters to Dr. Ludger Westrick, an official of the Federal Republic of Germany, five and eight months after Senator Dodd's return from Germany. The letters were almost verbatim copies of ones that Klein had provided and contained considerable praise for Klein (pp. 289–297, Hgs.). In addition, many of Klein's letters to Senator Dodd in 1963 and 1964 used presumptive, demanding, and disrespectful language, which should not have been countenanced by the Senator (e.g., pp. 273, 274, 284, 289, 290, Hgs.).

III. CONCLUSIONS

1. Senator Dodd traveled to Germany in April 1964 on Senate business under circumstances that suggest that he was also influenced to go by Julius Klein, owner of a public relations firm based in Chicago, Illinois. Klein sought to improve his image because he was losing his German clients.
2. Because a sovereign foreign Government was involved, the Committee was unable to obtain evidence to reveal whether Senator Dodd made any representations in Germany on behalf of Julius Klein, except in a brief conversation with the late Chancellor Adenauer. In view of these circumstances, the Committee could not pursue this phase of the case further.

IV. RECOMMENDATIONS TO THE SENATE

After drawing its conclusions, the Committee was of the opinion that the relationship of Senator Dodd with Julius Klein was indiscreet and beyond the responsibilities of a Senator to any citizen, but that there was not sufficient evidence of wrongdoing to warrant recommendation of disciplinary action by the Senate.

PART 2

POLITICAL AND OFFICIAL FINANCES

I. INTRODUCTION

A. ORIGIN AND DEVELOPMENT

The Investigation of Senator Dodd by the Select Committee on Standards and Conduct began formally in April 1966, although the interest of the Committee in the allegations that had been made against Senator Dodd had its antecedents in January and February of 1966, as described in more detail in Part 1 of this Report.

By March 1966, the syndicated newspapers articles concerning Senator Dodd's activities had extended beyond his relationship to Julius Klein. The Committee staff began to accumulate evidence relating to alleged financial improprieties and to other allegations. A very complex series of activities involving Senator Dodd was gradually reconstructed.

Before a decision was made to hold hearings, the Committee gave Senator Dodd the opportunity to submit a statement of fact and legal construction of the apparent financial improprieties that had been disclosed by the Committee staff investigation.

After Senator Dodd's refusal to provide such a statement, the Committee unanimously decided on June 9, 1966, that it had no alternative except to conduct hearings on the financial matters, and accordingly notified Senator Dodd on June 15, 1966. The Committee then continued to develop the evidence in detail.

On October 26, 1966, the Committee re-affirmed its intention to hold hearings. Such hearings, Senator Dodd was notified, would additionally inquire into the acceptance of certain Senate travel payments and the loan of automobiles.

Public hearings were conducted by the Committee from March 13 to 17, 1967, on the issues of which Senator Dodd had been given notice. These hearings have been published as Part 2 of the Investigation of Senator Thomas J. Dodd.

B. AUTHORITY OF SELECT COMMITTEE ON STANDARDS AND CONDUCT

The Constitution provides in Article 1 that "Each House may determine the Rules of its Proceedings, punish its Members for disorderly Behaviour, and, with the Concurrence of two thirds, expel a Member." The Supreme Court in interpreting the provision has held that the power to punish necessarily involves the ascertainment of facts and application of appropriate rules of law. *Barry* v. *U.S. ex rel Cunningham*, 279 U.S. 597 (1929).

That Constitutional authority was delegated to the Select Committee on Standards and Conduct by Section 2 (a) (1) of Senate Resolution 338 of the 88th Congress which states:

> It shall be the duty of the Select Committee to—
> receive complaints and investigate allegations of improper conduct which may reflect upon the Senate, violations of rules and regulations of the Senate, relating to the conduct of individuals in the performance of their duties as Members of the Senate, or as officers or employees of the Senate, and to make appropriate findings of fact and conclusions with respect thereto.

The Committee is further authorized by Section 3(a)(2) to "hold such hearings * * * as it deems advisable."

At their first meetings the Members reviewed the legislative history of the resolution which had established the Committee and observed that sufficient power had been conferred by the Senate to enable the Committee to undertake investigations of misconduct. The Committee's interpretation of its powers was enhanced by the fact that its membership included the author of the resolution.

Anticipating that it might someday require the opinion of outside counsel on legal problems that might arise, the Committee retained the services of former Supreme Court Justice Charles E. Whittaker as Consulting Counsel in April 1966.

The Committee faced the first test of its jurisdiction when it contemplated holding public hearings on the financial aspects of the Investigation of Senator Dodd. On May 25, 1966, Senator Dodd's counsel presented an argument to the Chairman and the Vice Chairman that the Committee lacked jurisdiction over Senator Dodd's finances which, counsel maintained, were essentially tax matters. The Senators answered that the Committee had a responsibility to inquire into the ethical implications of Senator Dodd's conduct. Shortly thereafter, Senator Dodd's counsel requested that the Committee give further consideration to the prejudicial effect that hearings on finances might have on the determination by the Internal Revenue Service of Senator Dodd's Federal income tax liability.

On June 9, 1966, the full Committee considered the question of jurisdiction and unanimously agreed to hold hearings on the financial matters. Thereafter, Senator Dodd's counsel renewed his plea on several occasions that the Committee lacked jurisdiction over the finances. On January 30, 1967, the Committee granted a special hearing to Senator Dodd's counsel to receive his formal argument on the question. The Committee then considered the argument and ruled unanimously that the anticipated evidence fell within the Committee's jurisdiction.

Upon completion of hearings, the Committee met on March 21, 1967, and agreed unanimously that the evidence, as presented, related directly to Senator Dodd's conduct as a sitting Senator and was within the jurisdiction of the Committee.

C. METHOD OF INVESTIGATION

Although the Committee began collecting evidence of Senator Dodd's political and official finances in March 1966, the staff intensified its investigation of allegations relating to all apparent improprieties of Senator Dodd in June 1966. Because of the seriousness of the charges relating to the use of funds received by Senator Dodd or by persons and committees acting on his behalf and of the charges relating to the acceptance of payments from both the Senate and other sources for travel expenses, the major portion of the Committee staff's effort was directed to a review of these matters.

The Committee staff was compelled to reconstruct the events and financial transactions relating to the monies raised by the several events during the period 1961 through 1965 and during the 1964 campaign from interviews with the organizers of the events and other participants and from bank account records. The purposes of about 75 percent of the disbursements made from Senator Dodd's bank accounts were independently verified by correspondence with the various payees. In addition, 36 loans made to Senator Dodd by 22 lenders were analyzed.

Approximately eighty trips made by Senator Dodd during the period July 1960 through December 1965, for which reimbursement was received from the United States Senate or from other organizations, were reviewed by the staff for instances of reimbursement from more than one source.

The information and financial data developed by these investigative processes formed the basis for substantially all of the factual matters contained in the stipulations of March 11 and 13, 1967.

During the investigation of this phase by the Committee, 105 interviews were conducted, 106 subpoenas *duces tecum* were served, and documents and statements were received from 174 organizations and persons.

The investigation was conducted in Washington, D.C., New York, New York, Los Angeles, California, and at various locations in the state of Connecticut.

D. ORGANIZATION AND PROCEDURE OF HEARINGS

PROCEDURE

Establishing hearing procedure

The Constitution provides express authority for Congress to punish or to expel members for disorderly behavior, but it does not set forth procedural guidelines for conducting misconduct proceedings. Court decisions have established that the action of a House of Congress in judging the conduct of one of its Members is "judicial in nature," *Kilbourn* v. *Thompson*, 103 U.S. 168 (1880), and must be carried out in proceedings consistent with the due process of law requirement of the Fifth Amendment of the Constitution. *Barry* v. *U.S. ex rel Cunningham*, 279 U.S. at 620.

On February 2, 1966, the Committee adopted rules of procedure which were supplemented when the Committee held its first hearings. In complying with Constitutional requirements of due process of law, the Committee took into account as a general guide the practice and procedures of the Federal courts.

Burden of proceeding

The Committee assumed the burden of proceeding with the evidence and instructed its counsel to present all facts pertinent to the matter under investigation.

EVIDENCE

In general

In general the Committee was guided by the rules of evidence applicable to the Federal courts. All testimony from witnesses was taken under oath and by personal appearance. Hearsay evidence was limited and assigned appropriate probative value. Affidavits in lieu of personal appearance by witnesses were admitted only on restricted matters or where the calling of witnesses was impractical or impossible. All documents and records were properly authenticated before being accepted by the Committee.

Documents taken from Senator Dodd's files

At Senator Dodd's request, in April and May 1966, the Committee obtained copies of several thousand documents taken from Senator Dodd's office by former staff members. (The removal of these documents is discussed in the Supplement to this Report.) Copies of the documents were given to Senator Dodd.

The Committee decided that it would be improper to use documents taken without consent from a Senator's office and therefore obtained all facts through its own independent investigation.

Stipulation

Soon after authorizing investigation into the financial matters, the Committee recognized the difficulty of presenting the facts in an understandable and concise manner. The Chairman and the Vice Chairman thereupon offered Senator Dodd an opportunity to furnish a statement of all financial facts to the Committee. After Senator Dodd advised the Committee that he would not do so, the Committee launched a thorough and independent fact-finding investigation.

By November 1, 1966, when the investigation was substantially complete, the staff offered to stipulate those facts which were apparently incontrovertible with Senator Dodd's counsel. No agreement was reached at that time. On January 30, 1967, the Chairman again suggested that a stipulation of fact would save a great deal of time and effort for all parties involved. The draft stipulation previously prepared by the Committee staff was revised and given in its entirety to Senator Dodd's counsel on February 2, 1967.

On February 23, 1967, Senator Dodd's counsel proposed a revised draft of the Committee stipulation which contained a substantial amount of opinion evidence and conclusions of law and fact. The staff refused to accept such opinion and conclusions and its decision was confirmed by the Committee on March 1, 1967.

On March 3, 1967, Senator Dodd's counsel agreed to accept the Committee stipulation of facts and to eliminate the opinion and conclusions. The stipulation was formally signed March 11, 1967, two days prior to opening hearings, and at the outset of the second phase of hearings was accepted in evidence by the Committee.

Affidavits of contributors

At the hearings, Senator Dodd offered about 400 affidavits as evidence of the intent of contributors to the fund-raising events. The affidavits were form language statements with blank spaces for the affiant to fill in his name and the dates of any fund-raising events he had attended for Senator Dodd. The remaining form language indicated that any contributions were given as a gift to Senator Dodd out of respect and admiration and not as political contributions. According to Senator Dodd's counsel, the language of the affidavit was prepared by his office. The forms were then given to Edward Sullivan, an employee of Senator Dodd, who distributed them to 21 individuals who in turn attempted to obtain the signatures of persons whose names had been taken from printed programs of fund-raising affairs. Contact was made by letter, telephone, and personal visit. In total some 400 signatures were obtained.

At the time the affidavits were offered as evidence, the Committee had ruled out the use of testimony by affidavit; however, because of the unusual nature of the problem of taking the testimony of a large number of persons and the relevance of their testimony, the Committee did accept the documents for the record and did review and consider the documents in reaching its conclusions.

RIGHTS AND PRIVILEGES

Subject of hearing

Senator Dodd, as the subject of the Investigation, was afforded the opportunity to attend all hearings and to be accompanied and represented by counsel. He was given notice of the charges to be investigated and given time to prepare for hearings. He was also given the names of witnesses and a summary of their expected testimony prior to hearings. He and his counsel were permitted to cross-examine witnesses called by the Committee and to call and examine additional witnesses and to present additional evidence.

The Committee did not call Senator Dodd as a witness, respecting his right to remain silent. He was however, offered the opportunity to testify and did, in fact, take the stand. At his request, Senator Dodd was examined by Members of the Committee, rather than by Committee counsel. In addition, Senator Dodd was given opportunity to raise, and be heard on, procedural and jurisdictional questions prior to and during hearings and to object and present argument on the admissibility of evidence.

Witnesses

All witnesses were advised of their right to be accompanied by legal counsel. Witnesses were permitted to examine their testimony following hearings. Any person named in public hearings was afforded opportunity to request to appear as a witness or to file a sworn statement relevant to the evidence. All witnesses were treated with respect.

Posthearing procedures

Following the hearings on Part II of the Investigation, the Committee held regular meetings to review the evidence taken at the hearings. All members participated fully in the Committee meetings and discussions.

The Committee carefully reviewed and exhaustively analyzed the expenditures from funds raised for Senator Dodd. This review and analysis resulted in the Committee's conclusions on amounts of funds expended for personal purposes.

In addition to the expenditures which were found to be clearly personal, the Committee regarded the evidence supporting the purpose of certain additional expenditures as inconclusive. Those expenditures were not included in the personal expenditures listed by the Committee in its conclusions.

II. EVIDENCE AND FINDINGS OF FACT

A. FUND-RAISING EVENTS

1. 1961 DINNER

A fund-raising dinner was held for Senator Thomas J. Dodd in Hartford, Connecticut, on November 20, 1961 (p. 853, Hgs.). The fifteen honorary guests were all prominent members of Senator Dodd's political party, including the then Vice President of the United States, Lyndon B. Johnson (pp. 873–876, Hgs.).

Matthew Moriarty, a businessman of Manchester, Connecticut, was the Chairman (p. 875, Hgs.). Arthur Powers, a businessman and First Selecman of Berlin, Connecticut, was the Treasurer (pp. 633, 875, Hgs.). Edward Sullivan, a member of Senator Dodd's Hartford office staff, was the business manager and handled the details of the dinner (p. 1120, Hgs.). Sullivan kept the funds and the financial accounts of the dinner (p. 854, Hgs.).

A letter of invitation to the dinner accompanied by a return address envelope soliciting contributions was prepared and mailed by Powers (pp. 635, 636, 885, 886, Hgs.). The return envelope was addressed to Senator Dodd's Hartford P.O. Box and all funds were collected by Sullivan (pp. 636, 886, Hgs.). Neither the letter nor the return envelope disclosed the intended use of the dinner proceeds (pp. 885, 886, Hgs.).

Moriarty, Powers and Sullivan testified that the dinner was organized to raise funds for Senator Dodd's personal use (pp. 619, 635, 1120, Hgs.), although Powers was quoted by the press at the time of the dinner as saying the proceeds were to be used to pay off campaign deficits (pp. 635, 892, Hgs.). James Boyd, a former Administrative Assistant to Senator Dodd, testified that Senator Dodd told him that the funds were to be used to retire the previous campaign deficit, and that he stated that purpose in arranging for Vice President Johnson's appearance (p. 601, Hgs.). Recently President Johnson stated publicly that he never knew that any dinner he attended was to raise funds for anyone's personal use (p. 893, Hgs.).

Five newspaper articles in Connecticut at the time of the dinner referred to it as a testimonial event without stating the purpose for the use of the proceeds (pp. 888–890, Hgs.). Two newspapers reported that the proceeds of the dinner were to be used to help clear up a deficit from the 1958 election campaign (pp. 891, 892, Hgs.). Form affidavits from about 123 persons attending the 1961 dinner indicated that they contributed money for Senator Dodd's personal use. Newspaper reports indicate 700 persons attended (pp. 889, 891, Hgs.). Boyd and O'Hare, former members of Senator Dodd's staff, testified that Senator Dodd, Sullivan and two other Senate staff employees, James Gartland and George Gildea, were the primary organizers of the dinner (pp. 601, 731, Hgs.). Moriarty stated he had nothing to do with arrangements for the dinner but tried to sell as many tickets as possible (p. 618, Hgs.). Powers testified that the dinner was organized by several friends of Senator Dodd and several staff members (p. 634, Hgs.). Although he was Treasurer, he testified that he did not handle funds or know how much money was raised (p. 637, Hgs.).

The gross receipts of the 1961 dinner were at least $64,245, and the net receipts, after payment of expenses of the dinner were at least $56,110 (p. 854, Hgs.). The net receipts were deposited in Senator Dodd's personal account in the Riggs National Bank in Washington, D.C., and mingled with his personal funds (p. 854, Hgs.). From these funds, Senator Dodd repaid $23,000 on a loan from the Federation Bank and Trust Company, originally borrowed in December 1958 (p. 854, Hgs.). Senator Dodd stated that this and other loans were for "political-personal" purposes (pp. 835, 836, Hgs.). O'Hare testified that the remaining funds, amounting to $33,110, were used for general, household, and personal expenses (pp. 732, 733, Hgs.). This testimony was not contradicted. Because records detailing the $33,110 were not retained by the bank, the Committee could not trace these payments further.

2. 1963 D.C. RECEPTION

A fund-raising reception was held for Senator Thomas J. Dodd in Washington, D.C., on September 15, 1963 (p. 855, Hgs.). Former Postmaster General J. Edward Day was the Honorary Chairman (p. 648, Hgs.), and James Gartland, Administrative Assistant to Senator Dodd, was the Vice Chairman (pp. 650, 898, 899, Hgs.). Sanford Bomstein, a Washington businessman, was the Treasurer until the reception (p. 855, Hgs.). Michael V. O'Hare, Senator Dodd's bookkeeper, was the Treasurer following the reception (p. 855, Hgs.). Robert Shaine, a professional fund-raiser, from New Hampshire, was hired by Senator Dodd to solicit contributions to the reception (p. 855, Hgs.). Others involved in planning or conducting the reception were George Gildea, a member of the staff of the Subcommittee to Investigate Juvenile Delinquency (pp. 603, 648, Hgs.); James Boyd, Senator Dodd's Administrative Assistant (pp. 602, 669, Hgs.); Elizabeth McGill, a secretary on the staff of the Subcommittee to Investigate Juvenile Delinquency (p. 722, Hgs.); "Mattie" Matthews and Joe Mills, of the staff of the Democratic Senatorial Campaign Committee (pp. 649, 651, Hgs.); Joe Barr, Washington representative of United Aircraft Corporation (pp. 674, 675, Hgs.); and Jack Fleischer, a former member of Senator Dodd's staff (p. 669, Hgs.).

Boyd testified that Gartland was the principal staff man organizing the D.C. reception (p. 603, Hgs.). Boyd also testified that a few weeks before the D.C. reception Senator Dodd asked him to intervene in the organization of the reception to get it moving (p. 602, Hgs.). He stated he worked with Shaine in organizing the reception and provided Shaine with office space and secretarial help (p. 603, Hgs.). He attended a meeting at which Senator Dodd answered questions concerning who might be solicited for funds (p. 603, Hgs.).

Bomstein testified that he participated in the organization of the reception after being invited by George Gildea to attend a meeting (p. 648, Hgs.). Bomstein also stated that he thought the purpose of the reception was to raise funds for Senator Dodd to use in any way he wanted (p. 656, Hgs.). Bomstein acknowledged that two resolutions of the "D.C. Committee for Dodd" were passed by Gartland and Bomstein, acting as the Committee (pp. 655, 656, 898, 899, Hgs.). One of the resolutions, dated September 24, 1963, after the funds had been transferred to O'Hare, authorized payment of Senator Dodd's printing, travel, food and lodging expenses, as well as public relations expenses for Senator Dodd (p. 899, Hgs.). Bomstein stated this resolution was intended to express his own intent that the money could be used by Senator Dodd for any purpose (p. 656, Hgs.). Bomstein acknowledged Shaine worked on the reception and stated Gartland did as much of the organizing as anyone (pp. 650, 652, Hgs.). Form affidavits from about 10 persons attending the reception indicated that they contributed money for Senator Dodd's personal use. Approximately 150 persons attended the reception.

Robert Shaine testified that he worked on the D.C. reception as a trial to obtain a contract for public relations work in the 1964 Connecticut election campaign (pp. 668, 674, Hgs.). Shaine stated that the purpose of the D.C. affair, was to raise money for Senator Dodd but that it was "not necessarily" for campaign purposes (p. 672, Hgs.). He received approximately $900 as compensation for his work on the reception (p. 670, Hgs.). Shaine stated that his principal duty was solicitation of funds (pp. 672, 673, Hgs.).

Marjorie Carpenter and Terry Golden testified that they and other secretaries from Senator Dodd's office attended the reception as hostesses (pp. 641, 722, Hgs.).

O'Hare testified that he was not involved in organizing the D.C. reception and that he became Treasurer of the funds after the reception (p. 733, Hgs.). He stated Senator Dodd told him to use the funds to pay bills which could be related to the forthcoming campaign (p. 734, Hgs.).

Senator Dodd testified that he considered the reception proceeds to be his personal funds but acknowledged that he borrowed $6,000 from the proceeds to pay his personal income tax and treated it as a loan from a campaign fund (pp. 825, 856, Hgs.). He later repaid the loan to another campaign fund and said he did so on his accountant's advice (pp. 825, 826, 858, Hgs.).

O'Hare testified that the proceeds of the reception were expended pursuant to Senator Dodd's direction (p. 734, Hgs.). O'Hare further testified that Senator Dodd did not want a number of bills paid by checks on a political account and therefore at O'Hare's suggestion Senator Dodd approved the purchase of money orders and treasurers checks to avoid disclosing the source of the funds (p. 734, Hgs.). Senator Dodd denied knowledge of the use of money orders (p. 841, Hgs.).

The gross proceeds of the D.C. reception were $13,770 and the net proceeds were $12,805 (p. 855, Hgs.). The use of the proceeds from the D.C. reception is set forth on pages 855, 856, and 897 of the printed hearings.

3. OCTOBER 1963 CONNECTICUT EVENTS

A series of four fund-raising events for Senator Dodd, consisting of a breakfast in Hartford, a luncheon in Woodbridge, a reception in Fairfield and a dinner in Bridgeport, were held in Connecticut on October 26, 1963 (p. 856, Hgs.). The four events were managed by different persons (pp. 605, 620, 681, 1124, 1125, Hgs.). The price of tickets to each event was $100 per person (pp. 856, 909, 919, Hgs.).

Hartford breakfast

The business manager of the Hartford breakfast was Edward Sullivan, of Senator Dodd's Hartford office staff (p. 1120, Hgs.). Matthew Moriarty was the Treasurer of the breakfast (pp. 620, 904, Hgs.). Both Moriarty and Sullivan testified that the funds were raised for Senator Dodd's personal use (pp. 621, 1127, Hgs.). A solicitation letter for the breakfast over Moriarty's signature was mailed with a return address envelope enclosed (pp. 909, 910, Hgs.). Neither the letter nor the envelope stated the intended purpose for which the funds were to be used (pp. 909, 910, Hgs.). The return envelopes were addressed to Senator Dodd's Hartford office Post Office Box (pp. 621, 909, Hgs.). Although Moriarty was the Treasurer, all receipts were received and handled by Sullivan (pp. 621, 857, Hgs.). The honorary guests at the breakfast were all prominent members of Senator Dodd's political party (p. 902, Hgs.). $31,040 from the proceeds of the Hartford breakfast and the Woodbridge luncheon were deposited in the "Testimonial for U.S. Senator Thomas J. Dodd" bank account (p. 857, Hgs.).

The Woodbridge luncheon

The Woodbridge luncheon was held at the home of Connecticut State Senator Gloria Schaeffer (p. 856, Hgs.). James Gartland of Senator Dodd's staff was in charge of arrangements for the luncheon (p. 605, Hgs.). The net proceeds of the luncheon were sent to Sullivan who deposited them in the "Testimonial for U.S. Senator Thomas J. Dodd" account (p. 857, Hgs.).

The Fairfield reception and the Bridgeport dinner

The Fairfield reception was held at the home of Archie Perry, a resident of Fairfield, Connecticut (p. 856, Hgs.). The Bridgeport dinner was held at the Stratfield Motor Inn (pp. 856, 913, Hgs.).

Paul McNamara, a lawyer and 1958 election campaign manager for Senator Dodd, managed both of these events (pp. 681, 682, Hgs.). McNamara did not recall who recruited him to act as manager but stated he was in touch with Senator Dodd's office and Sullivan regularly (p. 681, Hgs.). McNamara testified of his concern for Senator Dodd's personal financial problems and stated that the events were intended to raise funds for Senator Dodd's personal use. McNamara did not know the nature or the extent of Senator Dodd's indebtedness (pp. 676–679, Hgs.). Two letters of solicitation were written by McNamara and both specifically requested contributions for Senator Dodd's 1964 campaign (pp. 911, 912, Hgs.). McNamara acknowledged the letters and stated he made additional solicitations by phone and always spoke of Senator Dodd's dire financial problems (pp. 682, 683, Hgs.). McNamara handled all of the funds for these two affairs and after paying $4,886 for the dinner expenses, forwarded proceeds amounting to $10,069 to Senator Dodd (pp. 682, 857, Hgs.). The proceeds were then deposited in the "Testimonial for U.S. Senator Thomas J. Dodd" account (p. 857, Hgs.). McNamara retained about $750 in cash from the contributions to the dinner at Senator Dodd's direction as repayment, in part, of a loan from McNamara to Senator Dodd in about September 1958 (p. 857, Hgs.).

General

The then Vice President of the United States, Lyndon B. Johnson, was the featured guest at each of the four foregoing events (pp. 903, 913, 917–927, Hgs.). Newspaper reports in Connecticut and New York at the time of the October 1963 Connecticut events uniformly reported that their purpose was to raise funds for Senator Dodd's 1964 reelection campaign (pp. 917–927, Hgs.).

James Boyd testified that he was involved in negotiating Vice President Johnson's appearance at the October 1963 Connecticut events (pp. 604, 605, Hgs.). He testified further that in dealing with Ivan Sinclair on Vice President Johnson's staff, he was asked for the purpose of the dinner and that he therefore asked Senator Dodd for a reply (p. 605, Hgs.). Boyd testified that Senator Dodd was upset with the question but told Boyd to tell Sinclair that the events were to raise money for Senator Dodd's campaign starting the next fall (p. 605, Hgs.). Boyd gave that information to Sinclair and said he believed that a letter confirming the conversation was written for Senator Dodd's signature (p. 605, Hgs.).

Ivan Sinclair testified that he recalled conversations with Boyd concerning then Vice President Johnson's attendance at the October 1963 Connecticut events but did not recall whether the purpose of the fund-raising events was for Senator Dodd's 1964 political campaign (pp. 703, 704, Hgs.). An affidavit of Sinclair, dated February 21, 1967, stated that on the basis of conversations with two members of Senator Dodd's staff and from the circumstances of the events, the "declared purpose of Dodd Day was to raise funds for Senator Dodd's forthcoming 1964 campaign for re-election to the Senate" (p. 1034, Hgs.). Sinclair testified that his affidavit was signed without duress and that it was in his possession for six weeks before he signed it but that he had not studied it as closely as he should have (p. 704, Hgs.). He further stated that he did not deny that he had a conversation with Boyd about the purpose of the fund-raising events, but that his honest present recollection was that he could not recall if he discussed the purpose with Boyd (pp. 704, 706, Hgs.).

President Johnson recently stated publicly that he never knew that any dinner he attended was to raise funds for anyone's personal use (p. 893, Hgs.).

Form affidavits of about 117 persons who attended the 1963 Connecticut events indicated that their contributions were intended for Senator Dodd's personal use. Approximately 600 persons attended the four October 1963 events, according to newspaper reports (pp. 917–927, Hgs.).

The gross receipts of the four October 1963 Connecticut events were at least $46,745 (p. 857, Hgs.). Proceeds of the four October 1963 Connecticut events, amounting to at least $41,109, were deposited by Sullivan in the "Testimonial for U.S. Senator Thomas J. Dodd" account in Hartford and later mingled with campaign contributions and the proceeds of the 1965 dinner (pp. 857, 861, Hgs.). The disposition of these funds is described on pages 22 and 23 below.

4. 1964 POLITICAL CAMPAIGN

Receipts and expenditures

During his 1964 campaign for reelection to the Senate, Senator Dodd and committees working on his behalf received at least $246,290 in campaign contributions as follows (pp. 857–860, Hgs.):

Dodd for Senator Committee.....................................	$124,275
Dollars for Dodd Committee.....................................	9,400
National Non-Partisan Committee for Reelection of U.S. Senator Thomas J. Dodd..	11,935
Citizens Committee for Dodd....................................	2,909
Contributions deposited in "Testimonial for U.S. Senator Thomas J. Dodd" bank account.......................................	85,818
Cash (not deposited)..	11,953

The campaign contributions deposited in the "Testimonial for U.S. Senator Thomas J. Dodd" account, amounting to $85,818, were mingled with the proceeds of the October 1963 Connecticut events and the 1965 dinner (p. 861, Hgs.). The disposition of these funds is described on pages 22 and 23 below. The remaining campaign contributions, amounting to $160,-472, were transferred or disbursed as described in testimony and on pages 857–859, 938, 939, and 951–957 of the printed hearings.

Financial reports

Election campaign financial reports filed with the Secretary of State of Connecticut between November 20, 1964, and December 3, 1964, listed the following campaign receipts:

Matthew Moriarty, Political Agent for Senator Dodd (p. 928, Hgs.).	$11,891.60
Dodd for Senator Committee (pp. 940–950, Hgs.)................	167,497.67
Dollars for Dodd Committee (p. 937, Hgs.)....................	7,953.20
Citizens Committee for Dodd (p. 958, Hgs.)....................	7,559.26

An election campaign financial report, filed with the State of New York, on November 10, 1964, listed the following campaign receipts:

National Non-Partisan Committee for the Reelection of United States Senator Thomas J. Dodd (pp. 959–968, Hgs.)................	$11,934.25

An election campaign financial report filed with the United States Senate on December 4, 1964, listed the following campaign receipts:

Thomas J. Dodd of Connecticut (pp. 929–932, Hgs.)............	$11,891.60

5. 1965 DINNER

A fund-raising dinner was held for Senator Dodd in Hartford, Connecticut, on March 6, 1965 (p. 860, Hgs.). The honored guests were all prominent members of Senator Dodd's political party (p. 981, Hgs.). Arthur Barbieri, Democratic Town Chairman for New Haven was the Chairman (p. 976, Hgs.). Matthew Moriarty, a businessman of Manchester, Connecticut, was the Treasurer (p. 976, Hgs.). Edward Sullivan of Senator Dodd's Hartford office handled all of the finances for the dinner (p. 861, Hgs.). Vice President Hubert H. Humphrey was the featured speaker at the dinner (p. 982, Hgs.). A payment of $7,500 was made to the Democratic National Committee from the dinner proceeds for his appearance (p. 993, Hgs.).

Barbieri testified that the dinner grew out of a conversation between Barbieri and James Gartland, Senator Dodd's Administrative Assistant (p. 689, Hgs.). Barbieri said the idea was conceived in mid-December 1964, and he then invited persons to attend a meeting at the Statler Hilton in Hartford, where he was selected Chairman (p. 689, Hgs.). The meeting to organize the dinner was held on Dec. 19, 1964, at the Statler Hilton, and at that time the decision was made to hold a dinner for Senator Dodd (pp. 689, 1144, 1151, Hgs.).

Sullivan, Moriarty, and Barbieri all testified that the dinner was for the purpose of raising funds for Senator Dodd's personal use (pp. 624, 631, 697, 1137, Hgs.).

Two solicitation letters from Barbieri for funds for the dinner were introduced in evidence (pp. 970, 1118, Hgs.). Another letter, dated December 30, 1964, was sent by Barbieri as a political leader to members of his political party requesting them to serve on the dinner committee (p. 969, Hgs.). The first solicitation letter, dated February 3, 1965, was sent to a "great number" of persons throughout Connecticut requesting their participation in the 1965 dinner and stating that the dinner was to "assist in meeting the campaign deficit" (pp. 691, 970, Hgs.). A return envelope was attached to the letter with the return address of Senator Dodd's Hartford office (p. 972, Hgs.). A follow up solicitation letter from Barbieri was mailed on February 25, 1965, and referred to his earlier letter but did not state the purpose for which the funds were to be used (p. 1118).

Newspapers in Connecticut at the time of the event uniformly reported the purpose of the dinner was to pay off Senator Dodd's 1964 campaign deficit (pp. 990–992, Hgs.).

Form affidavits of about 300 persons who attended the 1965 dinner indicated that they contributed money for Senator Dodd's personal use. Approximately 1,000 persons attended the dinner, according to newspaper reports (pp. 991, 992, Hgs.).

Moriarty, the dinner Treasurer, testified he did not handle funds nor know the amount of money raised nor how it was spent (p. 624, Hgs.). Sullivan received and controlled all funds for the dinner (p. 861, Hgs.).

The proceeds from the 1965 dinner, amounting to $79,223, were de-

posited in the "Testimonial for U.S. Senator Thomas J. Dodd" account and
mingled with the proceeds of the October 1963 Connecticut events and
1964 campaign contributions (p. 861, Hgs.). The disposition of these funds
is described on pages 22 and 23 below.

6. INTERNATIONAL LATEX CORPORATION CONTRIBUTION

During the hearing, three former employees of Senator Dodd testified that
in October 1964 during the Connecticut election campaign, Irving Ferman,
a vice president and Washington representative of International Latex Corporation, visited Connecticut and met with Senator Dodd and with David
Martin, a member of the staff of the Senate Internal Security Subcommittee,
who was working in Senator Dodd's campaign. They further testified that
Martin told them, on the evening of Ferman's visit, that Ferman had agreed
to give $10,000 from International Latex Corporation to Senator Dodd's
campaign in return for Senator Dodd's help in obtaining an ambassadorship
for A. N. Spanel, the chairman of the board of International Latex Corporation (pp. 607, 608, 642, 643, 738, Hgs.).

Ferman testified that in August 1964 he spoke with David Martin, of the
Internal Security Subcommittee staff, who asked him to raise $10,000 for
Senator Dodd's 1964 campaign (p. 709, Hgs.). Ferman told Martin at that
time that he would do his best to raise the money (p. 709, Hgs.). Ferman
later went to Connecticut, about two weeks before the 1964 election, at
Martin's request, and again discussed the possibility of raising $10,000
(pp. 712, 713, Hgs.). Ferman stated to Martin at that time that he would
try to raise the money although he had not yet been able to do so (p. 713,
Hgs.). During his trip to Connecticut, Ferman also saw Senator Dodd for
a short visit during a campaign appearance (pp. 712, 713, Hgs.).

During the campaign Ferman and Spanel contributed a total of $2,150
to Senator Dodd's campaign (pp. 709, 718, Hgs.). The campaign reports
filed with the State of Connecticut list $2,150 in contributions from Spanel
(pp. 948, 958, Hgs.).

Ferman testified further that at the end of November 1964, he learned
of a testimonial dinner for Senator Dodd to be given in Connecticut although he did not recall specifically who informed him (p. 714, Hgs.).
He stated that he then went to W. O. Heinze, the President of International
Latex Corporation, who authorized $8,000 from the corporation funds as a
contribution to the dinner (pp. 714, 715, Hgs.). Ferman received the
$8,000 in cash by executing a petty cash voucher charged to "Industrial
Relations Expense" on December 3, 1964 (pp. 715, 1035, Hgs.). He took
the money to Senator Dodd's office and gave it to the Senator "one or two"
weeks after he got the money (p. 716, Hgs.). He told Senator Dodd that
the money was from his "people" as an expression of support (p. 716, Hgs.).

Ferman testified that he had discussed an ambassadorship for Spanel
with Senator Dodd, probably in 1961 (p. 717, Hgs.). He also stated he may
have also discussed it with David Martin (p. 717, Hgs.). He stated he did
not recall whether he discussed it with Martin during his trip to Connecticut

in late 1964 (p. 717, Hgs.). Ferman stated that the $8,000 contribution was not related to any attempt to obtain an ambassadorship for Spanel (p. 718, Hgs.).

Ferman stated that none of the officials of the corporation nor the corporation itself have any domiciliary ties with Connecticut (p. 716, Hgs.).

Terry Golden, a former employee of Senator Dodd, testified that she typed a letter to the President dictated by Martin recommending Spanel for an ambassadorship to France after the election in 1964 (p. 723, Hgs.). She stated she had no knowledge whether the letter was actually signed by Senator Dodd or sent (p. 723, Hgs.). Another letter, with a memorandum from Ferman, was written by Senator Dodd to the President in January 1965 but was marked "not sent" (pp. 725, 1036, Hgs.). Golden stated the January letter was not the one that she typed but that the memorandum may have been the basis for some of the information in the letter recommending Spanel for an ambassadorship (pp. 725, 726, Hgs.).

Senator Dodd testified that he first heard of Ferman's $8,000 contribution in December 1964 or January 1965 (p. 826, Hgs.). He acknowledged that Ferman gave him the money "from a group of his friends" (p. 827, Hgs.). Senator Dodd said Ferman told him he did not want the contribution made public because "they were in business," but never mentioned International Latex Corporation (pp. 827, 828, Hgs.). Senator Dodd said he accepted the money for the 1965 dinner (p. 827, Hgs.).

Senator Dodd stated that he turned the money over to Sullivan to use for 1965 dinner expenses and that Sullivan returned the remainder to him after the dinner (p. 827, Hgs.). He stated he used $3,500 to pay a loan from McNamara but did not explain the use of the remainder (p. 827, Hgs.).

Sullivan testified that Senator Dodd gave him the $8,000 from Ferman in January 1965 and that he used $1,000 to $1,500 for dinner expenses and returned the remaining sum to Senator Dodd the day after the 1965 dinner (pp. 1133, 1134, Hgs.). Sullivan also testified that the 1965 dinner was not decided upon until December 19, 1964, at a dinner meeting at the Statler Hilton Hotel in Hartford, Connecticut (p. 1144, Hgs.). This statement was corroborated by Barbieri in his testimony (pp. 689, 701, Hgs.).

7. "TESTIMONIAL FOR U.S. SENATOR THOMAS J. DODD" BANK ACCOUNT

The "Testimonial for U.S. Senator Thomas J. Dodd" bank account was opened in about October 1963 by Edward Sullivan. The account was closed in June 1965 (p. 857, Hgs.).

Sullivan testified that he used the Testimonial account for testimonial and campaign money and did not distinguish between deposits of campaign receipts or fund-raising proceeds (pp. 1129, 1136, Hgs.).

Between October 1963 and February 1964, $41,109 from the proceeds of the four October 1963 Connecticut events were deposited in the account (p. 857, Hgs.); between March 1964 and January 1965, $85,818 from

contributions to Senator Dodd's 1964 reelection campaign were deposited
in the account (p. 861, Hgs.); between January 1965 and April 1965,
$79,223 from the contributions to the 1965 dinner were deposited in the
account (p. 861, Hgs.); between October and December 1964, $22,593
in net transfers from campaign funds were deposited in the account (p.
861, Hgs.); and in December 1963, $1,567 from the proceeds of the D.C.
reception were deposited in the account (pp. 856, 861, Hgs.). All of these
funds were mingled in the account and were spent without differentiating
between personal and political expenses (pp. 1129, 1136, Hgs.).

From this composite fund, totaling $230,310, the amount of $94,870
was transferred to Senator Dodd's personal account at the Federation Bank
and Trust Company in New York, New York, and used to repay loans and
for other purposes disclosed by the evidence (pp. 861–863, Hgs.).

It was admitted by Senator Dodd that $9,480 from these funds was used
for improvements to Senator Dodd's home in North Stonington, Connecticut, and $4,900 was transferred to his son, Jeremy (p. 862, Hgs.).

It was further stipulated that $28,588 of loans which were originally
used directly or indirectly to pay personal income tax for Senator Dodd
were repaid from these funds (pp. 862, 863, Hgs.).

Senator Dodd testified that an additional $5,000 from the funds in the
Federation account was used to repay a loan taken out during the 1958
campaign and used for political purposes (p. 821, Hgs.). An additional
loan, originally taken out in 1964, which was repaid from the Federation
account, in the amount of $1,750, was used to pay for work on a political
document (p. 862, Hgs.). Three additional loans taken out by Senator
Dodd during and immediately prior to the 1958 campaign, totaling $18,500,
were used for "personal-political" purposes according to Senator Dodd (pp.
820–824, 862, 863, Hgs.). Repayments amounting to $26,652 on six loans
made from late 1959 through 1962 were also made from the funds in the
Federation account (pp. 862, 863, Hgs.). Senator Dodd did not state the
specific use of these loans but did admit that living expenses and personal
expenses were piling up during this period (pp. 820, 822, Hgs.).

The remaining $135,440 of the mingled funds in the "Testimonial for
U.S. Senator Thomas J. Dodd" account were used for both political and
personal expenses of Senator Dodd. These payments are detailed on pages
993–1002 of the printed hearings.

B. SENATE TRAVEL PAYMENTS

On seven occasions from 1961 through 1965, Senator Dodd, while travelling
on official Senate business, paid for by the Senate, also received substantially equivalent expense reimbursement for the same transportation from
private groups for his appearance as a speaker at various events (pp. 746,
747, 863–865, Hgs.).

The trips were to Philadelphia, Pennsylvania, in March 1961; West Palm
Beach, Florida, in March 1961; San Francisco, California, in June 1961;
Miami, Florida, in August 1962; Seattle, Washington, in June 1963; Tucson,

Arizona, in February 1965; and Los Angeles, California, in March 1965. Senator Dodd received reimbursement of travel expenses from private sources for each trip prior to payment by the Senate for the same expenses. Senator Dodd received travel expense payment from a private source for the 1961 San Francisco trip prior to his travel (pp. 863–865, 1003–1014, Hgs.).

Senator Dodd's former bookkeeper, Michael O'Hare, testified that during his employment it was his responsibility to bill the private groups, before whom Senator Dodd appeared as a speaker, for travel expenses and other fees (pp. 746, 747, 748, Hgs.). He testified that in doing so he acted at the express direction of Senator Dodd (pp. 746, 747, Hgs.). O'Hare also testified that two of the seven trips involving duplicate payments were taken prior to his employment (p. 746). The duplicate payments from private sources were deposited in Senator Dodd's personal checking account in Washington, D.C. O'Hare testified that Senator Dodd's Senate travel vouchers were prepared by the subcommittee staffs (p. 747, Hgs.).

Senator Dodd testified that he did not authorize O'Hare nor anyone else to bill twice and that the double billings were the result of sloppy bookkeeping (pp. 832, 834, Hgs.).

It was stipulated that on at least six other trips, which were non-official, Senator Dodd received and used travel expense payments paid by both his political campaign funds and by private sources (pp. 938, 954, 996, 997, 1015–1018, Hgs.). The trips were to Atlantic City, New Jersey, in August 1964; Los Angeles, California, in February 1964; Bal Harbour, Florida, in December 1964; San Francisco, California, in 1964; Tyler, Texas, in September 1963; and Claremont, California, in February 1964.

C. LOAN OF AUTOMOBILES

Between July 1964 and March 1966, Senator Dodd accepted in succession the continuous and exclusive use of three automobiles registered in Connecticut under the name of Dunbar Associates, Inc., and bearing Connecticut "USS 1" license plates (p. 866, Hgs.). The cars were beneficially owned by David P. Dunbar, the corporation president, who personally made installment payments on the cars. Registration and insurance costs on the vehicles were paid by the corporation, but, subsequent to the Committee investigation, were repaid by Dunbar personally (p. 866, Hgs.).

Senator Dodd testified that David P. Dunbar originally offered the cars to him for the 1964 campaign (p. 844, Hgs.). He stated he accepted the cars because David Dunbar's father was an old friend (p. 844, Hgs.). Dunbar later urged him to keep the car and he did so (p. 844, Hgs.). Senator Dodd stated he did not believe it was improper to do so although in retrospect he would not have accepted the offer (p. 844, Hgs.).

O'Hare testified the cars were originally used during the campaign and later used as family cars by Senator Dodd (p. 750, Hgs.).

III. CONCLUSIONS

From the facts found above, the Committee makes the following conclusions:

A. Senator Dodd and members of his staff acting at his direction, organized and controlled fund-raising events for Senator Dodd, consisting of—

    1. A dinner in Connecticut on November 20, 1961;

    2. A reception in the District of Columbia on September 15, 1963;

    3. A breakfast in Connecticut on October 26, 1963;

    4. A luncheon in Connecticut on October 26, 1963;

    5. A reception in Connecticut on October 26, 1963;

    6. A dinner in Connecticut on October 26, 1963; and

    7. A dinner in Connecticut on March 6, 1965.

B. The sponsors of the 1961 Connecticut dinner represented the event in a solicitation letter as a testimonial dinner for Senator Dodd, without stating any further purpose. The sponsors of the October 1963 Connecticut reception and dinner and the 1965 Connecticut dinner represented those fund-raising events for Senator Dodd in solicitation letters as being for political campaign purposes. Contemporary newspaper accounts in Connecticut and New York represented the 1961 Connecticut dinner, the four October 1963 Connecticut events, and the 1965 Connecticut dinner as being for political campaign purposes.

C. From the circumstances of all the fund-raising events, including the exclusive control of the funds by members of Senator Dodd's staff, the extensive participation by members of Senator Dodd's staff, the close political relationship between Senator Dodd and the sponsors of the fund-raising events, the preoccupation of the organizers with Senator Dodd's apparently political indebtedness, and the partisan political nature of the printed programs, Senator Dodd's knowledge of the political character of these events must be presumed.

D. Senator Dodd or his representatives received the proceeds of not less than $64,245 from the 1961 Connecticut fund-raising dinner, $13,770 from the 1963 D.C. fund-raising reception, $46,745 from the October 1963 Connecticut fund-raising breakfast, luncheon, reception and dinner, and $79,223 from the 1965 Connecticut fund-raising dinner, for a total of not less than $203,983.

E. Senator Dodd and political committees supporting his reelection to the Senate in 1964 received campaign contributions of at least $246,290.

F. From the proceeds of the seven fund-raising events from 1961 through 1965 and the contributions to the 1964 political campaign, Senator Dodd or his representatives received funds totaling at least $450,273. From these funds, Senator Dodd authorized the payment of at least $116,083 for his personal purposes. The payments included Federal income tax, improvements to his Connecticut home, club expenses, transfers to a member of his family, and certain other transportation, hotel, restaurant and other expenses incurred by Senator Dodd outside of Connecticut or by members of his family or his representatives outside of the political campaign period.

Senator Dodd further authorized the payment of an additional amount of at least $45,233 from these proceeds for purposes which are neither clearly personal nor political. These payments were for repayment of his loans in the sum of $41,500 classified by Senator Dodd as "political-personal" and $3,733 for bills for food and beverages.

G. After the 1964 election campaign, Irving Ferman gave Senator Dodd $8,000 in cash from the funds of the International Latex Corporation as the consummation of a promise, made by Ferman during the campaign, to raise $10,000 for Senator Dodd's campaign.

H. On seven trips from 1961 through 1965, Senator Dodd requested and accepted reimbursements from both the Senate and private organizations for the same travel.

I. Senator Dodd accepted as a gift the loans of three automobiles in succession from a constituent and used the automobiles for personal transportation for a period of about twenty-one months between 1964 and 1965.

J. Senator Dodd exercised the influence and power of this office as a United States Senator to directly or indirectly obtain funds from the public through testimonials which were political in character, over a period of five years from 1961 to 1965. The notices of these fund-raising events received by the public either stated that the funds were for campaign expenses or deficits or failed to state for what purposes the funds were to be used. Not one solicitation letter, invitation, ticket, program, or other written communication informed the public that the funds were to be used for personal purposes. Senator Dodd used part of the proceeds from these political testimonials and part of the contributions from his political campaign of 1964 for his personal benefit. These acts, together with his requesting and accepting reimbursements from 1961 through 1965 for expenses from both the Senate and private organizations for the same travel, comprise a course of conduct which deserves the censure of the Senate, is contrary to accepted morals, derogates from the public trust expected of a Senator, and tends to bring the Senate into dishonor and disrepute.

IV. OTHER ALLEGATIONS NOT COVERED IN PUBLIC HEARINGS

In addition to the matters considered in public hearings, other allegations of misconduct by Senator Dodd were published in the press or encountered by the staff in its investigation.

Upon completion of its hearings relating to the political and official finances of Senator Dodd, the Committee again examined the additional allegations and determined it would not hold hearings on these matters.

Some of the allegations involved the subject of campaign donations and their personal use, as developed in the hearings held, and upon which the Committee reached its decision to censure Senator Dodd. The Committee found that certain other allegations did not show any wrongdoing.

The Committee does take note of allegations which, if proven, might possibly constitute violations of existing law. After investigation, the Committee determined that it could not secure substantial findings of fact to sustain the allegations. These allegations are therefore being referred to the Department of Justice.

The Committee, however, retains jurisdiction and authority to consider these allegations, or any others, in the future.

V. REFERENCE OF POSSIBLE VIOLATIONS OF LAW TO FEDERAL AUTHORITIES

In accordance with Section 2(a)(4) of Senate Resolution 338 of the 88th Congress, the Committee has directed the Chairman to refer to the Attorney General of the United States the matters of the contribution by the International Latex Corporation to Senator Dodd and the loan of automobiles to Senator Dodd by David P. Dunbar; and to the Commissioner of Internal Revenue the matters of the contribution by the International Latex Corporation to Senator Dodd, the taxability of campaign funds used by Senator Dodd for personal purposes, and the taxability of the funds received by Senator Dodd from the various fund-raising events, for possible violations of law.

The enumeration of these matters is not intended to preclude proper authorities from inquiring into any possible violations of law that may be disclosed by the printed hearings of this Investigation.

VI. RECOMMENDATIONS TO THE SENATE

On the basis of the evidence admitted at the hearings in the Investigation of Senator Thomas J. Dodd and the conclusions expressed in this Report, the Select Committee on Standards and Conduct unanimously directs that the Chairman of the Committee report the following resolution in the United States Senate and the Committee unanimously recommends that the Senate adopt the resolution:

Resolved, That it is the judgement of the Senate that the Senator from Connecticut, Thomas J. Dodd, for having engaged in a course of conduct over a period of five years from 1961 to 1965 of exercising the influence and power of his office as a United States Senator, as shown by the conclusions in the Investigation by the Select Committee on Standards and Conduct,

(a) to obtain, and use for his personal benefit, funds from the public through political testimonials and a political campaign, and

(b) to request and accept reimbursements for expenses from both the Senate and private organizations for the same travel,

deserves the censure of the Senate; and he is so censured for his conduct, which is contrary to accepted morals, derogates from the public trust expected of a Senator, and tends to bring the Senate into dishonor and disrepute.

SUPPLEMENT

UNAUTHORIZED REMOVAL OF DOCUMENTS FROM
SENATOR DODD'S OFFICE

I. INTRODUCTION

The subject of the Investigation on which this Report is made is Senator
Thomas J. Dodd. But the Committee would not be meeting its full re-
sponsibilities if it did not go beyond the disposition of the charges against
Senator Dodd to the acts of his former employees in removing and using
records from his files without his authority. The evidence of these acts was
developed incidentally to the main subject, but is complete enough for the
Committee, to present this Supplement as a brief report of the facts and
Committee views.

II. FINDINGS OF FACT AND CONCLUSIONS

FINDINGS OF FACT

During his initial appearance before the Committee, James Boyd, Administrative Assistant to Senator Dodd until May 1965, testified at some length
that he and three other former employees, working together from about
May to December 1965, removed about 4,000 documents from the files
of Senator Dodd's office in the Old Senate Office Building, Washington,
D.C., without authority, copied them and then returned the documents
to the files (pp. 122, 123, 170, 171, 177, 184, Hgs.). His testimony was
corroborated by Mr. Michael V. O'Hare, a former bookkeeper for Senator
Dodd, who was one of the participants in the removal of the documents
(p. 243, Hgs.). Both Boyd and O'Hare testified they were aided in the
removal of documents by Marjorie Carpenter and Terry Golden, secretaries
on Senator Dodd's staff until December 1964 and October 1965, respec-
tively (pp. 123, 752, 753, 755, Hgs.). Both witnesses volunteered that they
had removed documents, without permission of Senator Dodd, in order to
substantiate what they believed to be evidence of serious wrongdoing (pp.
122, 752, Hgs.). Three of the participants in the removal of documents
were not in Senator Dodd's employ at the time documents were taken.
O'Hare remained on the staff until January 31, 1966, during which time
he participated in the removal and copying of documents from the Senator's files (pp. 752–755, Hgs.). None of the four former staff members
denied their participation in the removal process.

Boyd stated that the plan to remove documents was agreed upon only
after prolonged consideration of the consequences (p. 170, Hgs.). The
group ultimately provided the documents to newspaper columnists for pub-

lication, on the condition that after the documents were assembled they would be turned over to any legitimate authority upon request (p. 171, Hgs.). Using the documents as source material, the columnists wrote and had published between January 1966 and the present time many articles about Senator Dodd's activities.

Boyd testified that the group decided to have the documents published in the press to assure public disclosure of the facts in the hope that this would ultimately result in some form of official investigation into the conduct of Senator Dodd (pp. 170, 171, Hgs.). Boyd and O'Hare denied that they received any financial benefit in connection with the removal or the publishing of the documents (p. 171, Hgs.).

Senator Dodd testified that the former employees, two of whom he fired, were acting in revenge and because of vindictiveness.

CONCLUSIONS

1. James P. Boyd, Jr., Michael V. O'Hare, Marjorie Carpenter, and Terry Golden, each of whom was employed by Senator Dodd until between December 1964 and January 1966, collaborated in removing about 4,000 papers from Senator Dodd's office from about May to December 1965 without Senator Dodd's permission, copied the papers, and then returned them.
2. Boyd, O'Hare, Carpenter, and Golden gave the copies of Senator Dodd's papers to Washington newspaper columnists, who used the papers as the basis for many published articles about Senator Dodd in 1966 and 1967.

III. RECOMMENDATIONS TO THE SENATE

While the Committee recognizes the duty of every Senator, or officer or employee of the Senate, to report wrongdoing to responsible authorities, the Committee believes that the unauthorized removal of papers from a Senator's office by employees and former employees is reprehensible and constitutes a breach of the relationship of trust between a Senator and his staff, is an invasion of what must be considered privileged communications between a Senator and his correspondents, and is a threat to the orderly conduct of business of a public office.

Since the subject employees are no longer in the employ of the Senate, the Committee notes that any disciplinary action against them by the Senate is not possible.

IV. REFERENCE OF POSSIBLE VIOLATION OF LAW TO FEDERAL AUTHORITIES

In accordance with Section 2(a)(4) of Senate Resolution 338 of the 88th Congress, the Committee has directed the Chairman to refer to the Attorney

General of the United States for his action or recommendation the matter of the unauthorized removal of papers from Senator Dodd's office by his former employees.

Approved:

John C. Stennis.

JOHN C. STENNIS
U.S. Senator, Chairman.

Wallace F. Bennett

WALLACE F. BENNETT
U.S. Senator, Vice Chairman.

Mike Monroney

MIKE MONRONEY
U.S. Senator.

John Sherman Cooper

JOHN SHERMAN COOPER
U.S. Senator.

Eugene J. McCarthy

EUGENE J. MCCARTHY
U.S. Senator.

James B. Pearson

JAMES B. PEARSON
U.S. Senator.

APPENDIX THREE

The Senate debate on the Dodd censure lasted nine days, filled three hundred pages in the *Congressional Record,* and embraced half a million words. The description of it in Chapter Eight is necessarily limited to what the author considered the most significant portions. For those who wish a more detailed treatment, Appendix Three reproduces excerpts from the *Congressional Record* and the Senate hearings that stake out nine basic arguments advanced by Senator Dodd and the responses of various members of the Ethics Committee.

Senate debate seldom proceeds in logical sequence. The attempt to reduce it to order and readable proportion, with the arguments and counter-arguments juxtaposed, is infrequently crowned with more than partial success. A salient point made on a Tuesday might not be answered until the following Monday, or might not be answered at all, or might be best answered by remarks that happened to be made the day before the point was raised.

This extract, therefore, has been assembled with a view to placing the rebuttal next to the claim, irrespective of the chronological point in the debate at which either occurred. A partisan of Senator Dodd might have selected different excerpts, of course, and the truly determined reader is referred to the *Congressional Record* itself, for June 13th through June 23rd, 1967.

On the proposition that the testimonial dinner for the purpose of giving a public official money for his own personal use is a common occurrence— a tradition both legitimate and laudable—to which no odium should attach:

Senator Dodd: "There is nothing more common in the State from which I come than testimonial affairs. Never a week passes in the State of Connecticut but that several of them are held for people in private life, for persons in public life, for persons retired from an active life.

"It is a very common thing.

"The fact is, that there is no law or rule prohibiting testimonials, and that I have been judged completely on the basis of nonexistent standards.

"The fact is, further, that nowhere does the report of the committee explicitly condemn as illegal or unethical the use of testimonial affairs as a method of raising funds intended as gifts for men in public life." (*Congressional Record,* June 14, 1967 p. S 8156.)

* * *

Senator Dodd: "I also want to make the point—I tried to do so yesterday and I shall try before we have concluded these proceedings—that so far as I can learn, and I have made every best effort to learn, funds given to a person at a testimonial dinner are his.

"I think it was in Texas that Representative Thomas was retiring and they gave him a Cadillac. It was well advertised in the newspapers.

"What is the difference in receiving a Cadillac which is worth $6,000 to $7,000 and a friend giving you $6,000 or $7,000?

"I do not see much difference in the principle of the thing at all. I think it is identical.

"Therefore, if it is perfectly all right, what are the limitations? Is it a certain sum of money? Must it be in currency? Can it be in automobiles, airplanes, clothing—we could go on and on. I do not know any rules about this. I do not think any have ever been written. If they have been, I have certainly never been able to find them." (*Congressional Record,* June 15, 1967, p. S 8229.)

* * *

Senator Monroney: "The senior Senator from Connecticut has repeated time and time again the doctrine that there is not and should not be any requirements that funds made as 'gifts' at testimonial dinners honoring men in high political office necessarily be spent for political uses.

"Time and time again it has been repeated on the floor by the senior Senator from Connecticut and advocated in written briefs that funds so given under the banquet title of 'testimonial' are funds for the use of the Senator for any purpose he might choose to make of them.

* * *

"If we accept the right of Senators to sponsor their own testimonial dinners, if we accept the accompanying right to spend as he chooses so strongly insisted upon by the senior Senator from Connecticut and his counsel and our distinguished majority whip and his counsel we will have embarked down a road that will plague this body and all other free legislative bodies for scores of years.

*　*　*

"The dangers of giant corporations with special interests corrupting State legislatures—and even some few in the Congress as happened in the earlier days of our nation—would again be possible under this system, if we adopt an ethical standard that sanctions the raising of any amount of funds, from any source, at any time, for any purpose the honoree of a testimonial wants to use them for.

"Such testimonial funds would be unreportable in the regular accounting of campaign expenditures—particularly if they were used for the betterment of the candidate's personal living. They would, I believe, be nontaxable as income on the basis that such subscriptions are 'gifts.' They would be legal and thus their receipt in any amount, high or low, would put their acceptance by a sitting Member or a candidate beyond the reach of the Corrupt Practices Act.

"If we approve the acceptance of testimonial funds as gifts to be used at the personal discretion and for the personal purposes of the recipient, the future implications should be considered carefully now. What is to prevent these present modest donations of $25 or $100 by the party faithful from growing into outright attempts to use vast sums of money to influence votes in this or other legislative bodies by staging testimonials—the income from which, as gifts, would be outside the reach of present statutes. What would the ante be and how rapidly would it grow into a major scandal of attempted vote buying in legislative bodies.

*　*　*

"We must not open for the future another avenue where men of no principle can corrupt for their special interests any Member of this body. We dare not open such an avenue which would establish this local Connecticut testimonial affair of friends as a precedent that could plague us and our traditions for years to come." (*Congressional Record,* June 19, 1967, p. S 8382.)

*　*　*

On the claim of Senator Dodd that it was universally known by the donors to his testimonial dinners that the proceeds were to be used by him for personal, not political, purposes:

Senator Dodd: "The theory of the proposed censure must be that I misled my friends into thinking they were not contributing to a testimonial dinner at all, but to a campaign fund.

"The Committee report is critical of the solicitation material of the various testimonials which were held in my honor. It complains that nowhere is the invitee informed as to the purpose the proceeds will be put.

". . . In my home state of Connecticut testimonials are exceedingly commonplace affairs, and it is universally known by those who are in the habit of attending political functions that the proceeds of testimonials are intended as personal gifts." (*Congressional Record,* June 13, 1967, p. S 8111.)

* * *

Senator Dodd: ". . . I publicly offered to refund the money to any person who claimed that he had not understood the nature of the various testimonials and that he had really intended his money as a political contribution. This offer was carried prominently on the front page of every Connecticut paper and over every Connecticut radio and TV station.

"To date only one person who attended these affairs had written to ask that his $25 contribution be refunded to him." (*Congressional Record,* June 14, 1967, p. S 8156.)

* * *

Senator Monroney: "The solicitation letters sent out to the public, the newspaper publicity about the events, the exclusive control by members of the Senator's staff of the events and the money raised, the close political relationship between the Senator and the sponsors of the events, the concern over the Senator's political debts, and the partisan political nature of the printed programs leave no other conclusion in my mind but that the money was being raised ostensibly to help the senior Senator from Connecticut pay off past campaign debts and finance future campaigns. There was a holding out to the public that these were political events, no matter what the private intent of the senior Senator from Connecticut and his close private associates might have been.

"I believe it is improper to solicit and accept funds for political purposes and then convert those funds to personal use to the extent and with the consistency practiced by the senior Senator from Connecticut. If funds are to be used for personal benefit, I believe the persons solicited and the public in general are entitled to know. There was no such notice given by the senior Senator from Connecticut or by his staff or his political associates.

"In the heat of a campaign or in the course of a Senator's busy schedule, mistakes can be made and things can transpire about which a Senator may not be aware. But in the case of the senior Senator from Connecticut, there was a consistent course of conduct over a period of 5 years of holding events, ostensibly for political purposes, and the funds which were raised were used in large part for personal purposes." (*Congressional Record,* June 19, 1967, p. S 8381.)

* * *

Senator Stennis: "Consider all the proof about the lack of notice, the lack of understanding, the lack of any announcement before or after or at any time that this was anything but money to be used in connection with carrying out public office, for the people, for the little people. What were they told?

"I am not sophisticated enough to put a 'high-falutin' meaning on what the average fellow does who pays $10 or $25 or $100 to go to a testimonial. But I believe I know what he believes in his heart and mind. He wants that person to take the money for the ticket, with a promise to use it in trust for the strengthening of the office that the person is holding for that fellow, whoever he may be; that it will be used that way in connection with carrying out that office. Certainly, that does not include—I speak with the greatest deference—repairs to a house or alterations to a private home of thousands of dollars to a son, however fine the son may be." (*Congressional Record,* June 15, 1967, p. S 8227.)

* * *

Senator Percy: "I looked very carefully at the memorandum of the Senator from Connecticut, dated May 17, entitled 'Ethics Committee Resolution on Testimonial Funds,' wherein he stated, on page 4:

" 'In my home state of Connecticut testimonials are exceedingly commonplace affairs, and it is universally known by those who are in the habit of attending political functions that the proceeds of testimonials are intended as personal gifts.'

"I think, therefore, it is very important that if this is customary, we look to see whether the press, who should be conversant with what is customary in a State, looked upon these as anything other than political dinners.

"And in looking through the press commentary, I think it would be important to see what they said on that one point.

"The October 20, 1963, edition of the *Hartford Courant* stated:

" 'The various fund-raising events could yield the Dodd campaign treasury up to $65,000 or $75,000.'

"Two days later, the October 22, 1963, edition of the *Hartford Times* stated:

" 'More than 400 persons are expected here Saturday at the $100-a-plate breakfast to hear Vice-President Lyndon Johnson kick off the fund-raising drive for the re-election of U. S. Senator Thomas J. Dodd.'

"The same day the *Hartford Courant* of October 22, 1963, stated:

" 'The breakfast is one of a series of fund-raising events for the renomination and re-election of U. S. Senator Thomas J. Dodd that will be held throughout the state that day.'

"On the same day, October 22, 1963, the Associated Press reported in the New Haven *Journal-Courier:*

" 'The breakfast is one of a series of fund-raising events for the renomination and re-election of U. S. Senator Thomas J. Dodd that will be held throughout the state that day.'

"Three days later, the October 25, 1963, edition of the *Hartford Times* stated:

" 'Vice-President Lyndon B. Johnson and "Lady Bird" will be in Connecticut all day Saturday to help bolster the campaign war chest of U. S. Senator Thomas J. Dodd who will be seeking reelection next year.'

"The October 26, 1963, edition of the *Hartford Courant* stated:

" 'With little more ado, LBJ and Ladybird got into a maroon Cadillac and purred off to the Statler Hilton Hotel, where this morning he'll pay $100 for eggs—a contribution to Sen. Dodd's campaign barrel.'

"The same day, October 26, 1963, the *Hartford Times* stated:

" 'The Vice-President and his wife, Ladybird, are in Connecticut today to help bolster Senator Dodd's campaign fund for re-election to his Senate seat in 1964.'

"The same day, the October 26, 1963, edition of the New Haven *Register-Journal-Courier* stated:

" 'Vice-President Lyndon B. Johnson takes his Texas drawl on a tour of Connecticut today aimed at drumming up some dollars for the 1964 re-election campaign of U.S. Senator Thomas J. Dodd . . . Indications were that the Johnson visit will raise a sizeable sum of cash for the Dodd 1964 electioneering . . . The Vice-President and his wife fly back to Washington late tonight. Dodd supporters hope that behind him he will have left a path that raised $40,000 or more for the senator's campaign.'

"The October 28, 1963, edition of the Willimantic [*Chronicle*] stated:

" 'Senator Thomas J. Dodd's campaign war chest for next year's election was fortified considerably by Saturday's fund-raising tour by Vice-President Lyndon B. Johnson . . . The money raised during Johnson's visit is earmarked for battle with a Republican candidate, not a Democratic insurgent. The unusual feature was that the war chest was raised so early—a full year before the campaign.'

"Then I would like to repeat a story which has been denied in veracity and its correctness by Senator Dodd after I gave it the other day. I quote it again:

"The October 27, 1963, edition of the *Hartford Courant* stated:

" 'Vice-President Lyndon Johnson, campaigning as if he were running for first selectman or constable, barnstormed through Connecticut Saturday in behalf of U. S. Senator Thomas J. Dodd. The Vice-President's fund-raising efforts raised $75,000 for Sen. Dodd's 1964 renomination and re-election campaign.'

"This is the particular section that I was interested in:

" 'Throughout the trip, Senator Dodd expressed his "gratitude" to Vice-President and Mrs. Johnson for coming to the state to help him build up a campaign war chest for 1964.'

"When Senator Dodd indicated that he had not said that and that this was not a true account, I telephoned the political editor, who is a highly respected political editor, to ask him in fairness to Senator Dodd, to look at the story again to see whether or not it was an accurate story. Certainly we were only seeking the truth in this case. He replied the next day as follows:

" 'In response to your inquiry about the story I wrote in 1963 during a visit by President Johnson to help Senator Dodd raise campaign funds, which appears on page 920 and 921 of the committee report, I stand by the story and the quotation I attributed to Senator Dodd. This quotation has never, up to this moment, been questioned by anyone, including Senator Dodd, nor has any other story I wrote about Senator Dodd's campaign dinners either before, during or after the dinners. I attended the Johnson breakfast for Senator Dodd in Hartford, I took notes on what was said and, as I recall, the meal was excellent, the crowd was big and enthusiastic, and I wrote a story that, until this day, has never been challenged.' " (*Congressional Record*, June 19, 1967, p. S 8386.)

* * *

On the significance and percentage ratio of the affidavits presented by Senator Dodd as proof that all those who purchased tickets to his dinners intended their contributions as personal gifts:

Senator Dodd: ". . . between 400 and 500 people who purchased tickets have submitted statements saying that they did, in fact, intend their contribution as gifts.

". . . I believe that these hundreds of affidavits constitute overwhelming proof that those who attended the several testimonial functions understood their nature and did intend their contributions as gifts." (*Congressional Record*, June 14, 1967, pp. S 8156 and S 8157.)

* * *

Senator Russell Long: "It is very important to this case, at least from my point of view, that affidavits from 50 percent of the people, over 400, who attended the dinners stated, subject to prosecution for perjury, that they put this money up with the idea that it was all right for Tom Dodd to use it however he wanted to." (*Congressional Record*, June 16, 1967, p. S 8339.)

* * *

Senator Bennett: "With respect to the 400 affidavits, I am sure that our record will show—although I do not have it at the tip of my tongue—the total number of people who attended these dinners. Therefore, the 400 affidavits represent a very small percentage—well, let us say less than a third of those who attended the dinners. These people were approached by Senator Dodd's representatives, or the representatives of his attorney, with a form. They were not given a choice, 'Will you check off whether this is a political contribution or a personal contribution.'

"They were in a printed, or at least a produced form, and they were asked to sign them. If they signed them, they indicated this was to be personal. In some cases, this was 6 or 7 years after the fact.

"I am also aware that the people who went out to solicit the signatures for the affidavits realized Senator Dodd's problems, and they probably conveyed to the people who were to sign the affidavits the feeling that this was one way that they could help Senator Dodd. So it has been my personal feeling that this affidavit was not an example of a free recollection of the situation. It was a very clever means of trying to persuade the people, at no cost or hurt to themselves, to help their friend Tom Dodd. Those who did not agree with the language of the affidavit, of course, did not sign it.

"We do not know how many affidavits were offered and rejected, or we do not know whether they carefully screened the list of the persons to whom they went to be sure of their signatures." (*Congressional Record,* June 13, 1967, p. S 8102.)

* * *

Senator Stennis: "If I may, I will give these figures as to the way in which the committee tabulated the affidavits. . . .

". . . For the 1961 dinner, the best figure we could get was 700 who attended, and there were 123 affidavits. . . .

"At the District of Columbia reception, there were 10 out of 150. In the 1963 Connecticut events—there were four on the same day—there were 117 out of an estimated 600.

"At the 1965 dinner, there were 300 out of an estimated 1,000 who attended." (*Congressional Record,* June 16, 1967, pp. S 8339 and S 8340.)

* * *

On the uses to which the Dodd testimonial money was put:

Senator Dodd: "I would not consider it proper if a Senator used testimonial funds to enrich himself or to live lavishly. But I do consider it proper for a Senator to use such funds at his discretion to help liquidate campaign deficits, to pay off sundry political debts, to offset his costs of office, and to offset or reimburse himself for any money he may have put out-of-pocket to meet politically connected expense.

"That is what I did." (*Congressional Record,* June 14, 1967, p. S 8157.)

* * *

Senator Bennett: "From the net proceeds of the 1961 fund-raising dinner, all of which were deposited in Senator Dodd's personal bank account, the payment of $33,000 for general household and personal expenses was considered as personal and not disputed; $625 was paid from the 1963 District of Columbia reception for personal purposes and included such items as Congressional Country Club charges, limousine service to a race track, and motel accommodations for some of Senator Dodd's personal friends.

"Payments from the testimonial for U.S. Senator Thomas J. Dodd bank account totaling about $5,700 were similarly determined to be personal and included such items as air transportation to Florida, Chicago, San Francisco, Texas and other places by Senator Dodd and members of his family during 1963 and 1964. Other payments from this account include country club charges and hotel bills for Senator Dodd and members of his family. About $4,000 was expended from campaign bank accounts for such purposes as airline trips to Jamaica, Curaçao, Miami and London by Senator and Mrs. Dodd. Hotel and club bills were also paid out of this account. Propane gas service charges for Senator Dodd's Connecticut residence were charged to this account.

"Over $28,000 in political funds were used by Senator Dodd to retire loans that had been made directly or indirectly to pay his Federal income taxes.

"Another $27,000 of political money was applied to the repayment of loans made from late 1959 through 1962 for personal expenses.

"Senator Dodd diverted over $9,000 in political funds to payments for improvements to his Connecticut home. He gave his son $4,900 out of political campaign funds.

"And so the list goes." (*Congressional Record,* June 13, 1967, p. S 8096.)

* * *

On the contention that a Senator is the judge of his own conduct and should be censured only for the violation of explicit, written law:

Senator Dodd: "I think every Senator has to be his own judge. I think this has to do with affairs like this. Senator Bennett said it is necessary to make a more or less arbitrary decision.

"Well, I do not think a U.S. Senator ought to be condemned on such a basis—on an arbitrary basis. There ought to be a rule, regulation, or law, so a man knows whether he is doing right or wrong, and he should not be held to some arbitrary decision or the thinking of one man, or six or 10, or 20, with respect to an issue like this.

"I think each one of us is entitled to know what the rules are, what the law is, so we can abide strictly by it. I have tried to do that all my lifetime.

"Now I find myself caught in a morass, in this gray area which is sometimes referred to, because there were no rules; and there are not any that I know about." (*Congressional Record,* June 15, 1967, p. S 8229.)

* * *

Senator Monroney: "Are there special standards of conduct which Senators must meet? A Senator must, of course, obey the laws of the land and abide by the rules and regulations of the Senate. Beyond this there are now no specific written standards that have been adopted by the Senate which would apply to the charges made against the senior Senator from Connecticut.

"But I firmly believe there is a higher standard of conduct which must guide us as individuals, as well as in our role as Senators—a standard accepted and expected by society. It exists and, nebulous though it may be, we must pay the price when we breach it.

* * *

"Does the lack of any specific, written standard covering the conduct of the senior Senator from Connecticut mean that the Senate should take no action? I think clearly not. For an affirmative answer to that question would mean that the very persons responsible for writing a code of conduct could evade punishment for clearly unethical actions merely by failing or refusing to adopt rules of ethical conduct. If that were the case, we would be a law unto ourselves. As the lawmakers in our society, we would be above any law, above any mores, above any reproach for our actions. We cannot adopt such an attitude." (*Congressional Record,* June 19, 1967, p. S 8380.)

* * *

On the "basic arithmetic" of Senator Dodd's position:

Senator Dodd: "The implication of the report to the average reader would unquestionably be that I have abused my position to enrich myself. This just is not true.

"I have not enriched myself from public office, and all of those who know me are aware of this.

"Let me present to you what I have called the 'basic arithmetic' of my position, so that you can understand my case better.

"I ran for the Senate in 1956 and was defeated. I then conducted a long and bitter campaign for the nomination in 1958. I won the nomination, and I won the race for the Senate. But I had been running nonstop for more than 2 years, and the expenses just piled up and piled up. When I entered the Senate in 1959, I was burdened by a total debt of some $150,000 which had built up during this period. Of this amount, some $120,000 was politically connected.

* * *

"It has always been part of my defense that at the time I entered the Senate in 1959, I had politically connected debts of about $120,000." (*Congressional Record*, June 14, 1967, p. S 8157.)

* * *

Senator Russell Long: "Mr. President, the first stipulation on page 853 states:

"'1. Senator Dodd first campaigned for election to the U.S. Senate from Connecticut in 1956. He was unsuccessful. He successfully campaigned for election to that post in 1958. Between 1956 and 1959, Senator Dodd borrowed a total of about $211,000. At the end of 1959 his personal indebtedness was about $150,000.'

"Would the Senator be willing to agree that that $211,000 which the Senator borrowed was, for the most part—at least 80 percent of it—borrowed to pay political expenses?"

Senator Bennett: "The Senator cannot agree to that because we have no evidence. On the contrary——"

Senator Russell Long: "Did the Senator try to get it?"

Senator Bennett: "Yes, and somewhere in the background is my memory of the fact that the Senator gave us out of that experience about a $7,000 political——"

Senator Russell Long: "At the end of 1959 his indebtedness was about $150,000."

Senator Bennett: "I am sorry. Would the Senator repeat that statement?"

Senator Russell Long: "The Senator may not have completed his first answer.

"However, I am speaking about the $211,000 which the Senator owed."

Senator Bennett: "He borrowed $211,000 between 1956 and 1959. There is no evidence that that was borrowed for political purposes or to repay political debts."

Senator Russell Long: "Is the Senator aware that in 1956 he owed virtually nothing when he started running for the Senate? He was virtually debt free."

Senator Bennett: "Neither this Senator nor the committee has any knowledge of the financial dealings of Senator Dodd, nor are we concerned with the period before the 1961 dinner."

Senator Russell Long: "Oh, it is enormously important, and that is one of the reasons the committee fell into error. I now begin to understand how the committee could have made this grievous error.

"Is the Senator from Utah telling the Senate that the committee did not know that this $211,000 was an indebtedness that the man incurred in those 2 years while he made two unsuccessful campaigns for the U.S. Senate?

Now, I begin to understand. Is the Senator saying that the committee did not know that these were political obligations?"

Senator Bennett: "The Senator is correct. I wish to point out to the Senator from Louisiana that the Senator from Connecticut had many opportunities to tell that to the committee, to point it out, and to give details. He appeared as a witness. We met him in executive session many times and he did not give us that kind of information. How could we know?"

Senator Russell Long: "Now, I begin to understand how there could be such a complete difference of opinion. To this Senator it has been clear all the time.

"The man started running for the U.S. Senate in 1956 with no indebtedness. He was virtually debt free. Then, after he ran he lost and he then had a substantial debt. Then, he tried again. By the time he had been elected and paid what he could out of his personal income to pay political expenses, the next statement is made in the committee report that at the end of 1959 his personal indebtedness was $150,000.

"Do I understand the Senator to say that the committee did not realize, nor did the Senator realize, that the $150,000 was mostly an indebtedness incurred to become a Senator?"

Senator Bennett: "The Senator is saying that Senator Dodd had ample opportunity to make that clear to the committee and failed to do so. I think the committee cannot be charged with ignorance because we began our investigation with 1961 and he had ample opportunity in our discussions to say to us, "I was $150,000 in debt politically so I had to have a dinner to pay that debt." But there was no such evidence coming from the Senator from Connecticut."

Senator Russell Long: "As I have said, I now begin to understand why we are so completely at odds on the conclusions we would reach in this case. When the Senator from Connecticut speaks, we will understand this. It may be that the Senator did not know that the committee did not understand this; that he took it for granted the committee would understand this.

"We shall now proceed to find out the nature of this indebtedness."

Senator Stennis: "Mr. President, will the Senator yield?"

Senator Bennett: "I am happy to yield."

Senator Stennis: "Mr. President, I wish to refer the Senator to page 835, which refers to the point I made this morning about the examination of Senator Dodd. The Senator from Utah has already referred to it. The point to which I refer is near the top of the page. In order to refresh our recollection, the question was propounded by me:

" 'The CHAIRMAN. Now frankly, that is all the information that we have been able to get as the Chairman understands, with reference to these items.'

"Was not that the beginning of the questioning by the committee on these very loans to which the Senator from Utah and the Senator from Louisiana had been referring?"

Senator Bennett: "The Senator is correct."

Senator Stennis: "I shall continue to read from page 835.

"The chairman said:

" 'Now I think if you possibly can, it would certainly be relevant, and perhaps helpful to you to give more definite information than the date and the amount and the name of the lender.'

"Does not that question refer to the stipulations that had been put in by the Senator from Connecticut, and he gave us only these items that I have related?"

Senator Bennett: "The Senator is correct. I think there are other figures which are interesting and which appear a little below that reference on page 835."

Senator Stennis: "Yes."

Senator Bennett (continuing reading):

" 'The CHAIRMAN. I meant to ask you, to be certain now that you are not misled, these are listed here, and totaled for the years.

" 'For instance, there on appendix 7, it is 1956, that is $14,500 total; 1957 has a $36,000 total. And 1958 has a total here on this list of $90,000; 1959, $70,000.'

"In other words, the loans were going up every year even though there were only two political campaigns."

Senator Stennis: "Those were loans which the committee was trying to get the Senator from Connecticut to explain, to his advantage of course, if he could; is that not correct?"

Senator Bennett: "Yes. Let me read further from page 835:

" 'The CHAIRMAN. And they total $211,000, and we were not able to develop any of the facts with reference to those loans as to what the money was borrowed for and what it was used for. Certainly we could not complete the record, and that is what we want you to help do. It shows an outstanding balance by the way of $149,000 on January 1, 1960.'

"All Senator Dodd would say was: 'I think that has practically all been paid now.' "

Senator Stennis: "Refreshing the recollection of the Senator from Utah further, does not the record show, on the next page, that we went into one loan, my question did, regarding the George Gildea loan and it was developed that that was $3,800 with reference to a tax matter, I believe——"

Senator Bennett: "Income tax."

Senator Stennis: "Yes, and $1,200 for an automobile."

Senator Bennett: "That is right."

Senator Stennis: "And we did not get any other evidence along that line even though we opened it all up; is that not correct?"

Senator Bennett: "Yes. This bears out what I was trying to say to the Senator from Louisiana [Mr. Long], that the committee could not get information as to the reason for, or the source of the $211,000 worth of loans and, therefore, we could not assume that they were political loans." (*Congressional Record*, June 13, 1967, p. S 8101.)

*   *   *

On Senator Dodd's assertion that he had nothing to do with the double billing that was done in his name, and was totally unaware of it:

Senator Dodd: "The first fact that should be made clear is that I myself had nothing to do with the so-called double billings.

"In every case, it was O'Hare who wrote to the private organizations involved requesting payment of my transportation expenses.

"In every case, it was O'Hare who picked up tickets at the Capitol ticket office and billed them to my committee credit cards.

"The vouchers subsequently submitted to the Government, moreover, were never signed by me.

"I myself never saw, let alone signed, any document involved in the billing of a private organization or of a Senate committee." (*Congressional Record*, June 14, 1967, p. S 8149.)

*   *   *

Mr. Fern: "Did Senator Dodd take personal interest in his own books?"

Mr. O'Hare: "He took a great personal interest in his personal finances. As far as the books as such goes, why occasionally he would ask to see them or inquire of me as to whether or not they were up to date, and was I keeping them in good order." (*Transcript of Hearings*, p. 730.)

*   *   *

Mr. Fern: "Mr. O'Hare, you have stated that there were duplications in each one of these trips as detailed. Did you know at the time that these were duplications?"

Mr. O'Hare: "Yes sir; I did."

Mr. Fern: "Did you collect deliberately from the honorarium payers as well as from the two campaign funds in accordance with Senator Dodd's instructions?"

Mr. O'Hare: "Yes, sir; I did."

Mr. Fern: "How did you feel that you were collecting in accordance with Senator Dodd's instructions?"

Mr. O'Hare: "The Senator had told me that I was to forward all his airline travel bills, all of his travel expenses to Ed Sullivan so that they could be paid out of his Hartford account. When the question came up about travel for which he was reimbursed, he said to make sure to bill each of these organizations for the actual travel that was involved, but when the checks came in, to enter it as income. He said that this was the way in which the campaign fund could be used to assist him." (*Transcript of Hearings*, p. 744 and 745.)

* * *

Mr. Fern: "You are familiar with the remaining trips, San Francisco, Miami, Seattle, Tucson and Los Angeles; is that correct?"

Mr. O'Hare: "Yes, sir."

Mr. Fern: "In each of these trips, according to the stipulation, there is a duplicate payment, one by the U.S. Senate and one by an honorarium payer. Did you know at the time that you were billing the honorarium organization that a duplicate payment might be involved?"

Mr. O'Hare: "Yes sir."

Mr. Fern: "Were you acting under Senator Dodd's instructions at the time in billing these honorarium organizations for Senator Dodd's travel expenses?"

Mr. O'Hare: "Yes, sir; I was."

Mr. Fern: "Did you discuss any of these trips specifically with Senator Dodd?"

Mr. O'Hare: "The San Francisco trip I recall discussing with him. The Seattle trip I recall discussing with him."

Mr. Fern: "And did you inform him that you were billing the honorarium organizations?"

Mr. O'Hare: "On the San Francisco trip, the actual invitation I believe was arranged through the Subcommittee to Investigate Juvenile Delinquency. In a letter they stated that they would only be able, to the best of my knowledge, that they would only be able to provide a small honorarium for his appearance. He asked me to speak to the staff director of the subcommittee and find out if the National Council of Juvenile Court Judges——"

Mr. Fern: "Excuse me, Mr. O'Hare. You are referring to the payment in paragraph 98; is that correct?"

Mr. O'Hare: "Yes, sir."

Mr. Fern: "Continue."

Mr. O'Hare: "He asked me to have the staff director of the Subcommittee to Investigate Juvenile Delinquency contact the National Council of Juvenile Court Judges to find out if they also expected to cover his expenses for his travel out there, and the staff director did make a call and came back and said that if necessary, although the organization was a poor one and they had limited funds, if it meant Senator Dodd's presence, they would be willing to cover the cost of his travel."

Mr. Fern: "Continue."

Mr. O'Hare: "The Senator then told me that he would travel on the subcommittee funds, but to get the money from the National Council of Juvenile Court Judges for all his expenses, including the travel, and that, when that check arrived to enter it as income, and show it as an honorarium."

Mr. Fern: "And with reference to the Miami, Seattle, Tucson, and Los Angeles trips, did you also bill in accordance with the Senator's orders."

Mr. O'Hare: "Yes, sir. The Miami trip doesn't stand out in my mind quite as much as some of the others, simply because there were several trips to Miami, but if I billed them, I billed them in accordance with his directions." (*Transcript of Hearings,* pp. 746 and 747.)

* * *

Mr. Fern: "Were you ever told not to bill because it represented a duplication?"

Mr. O'Hare: "No, sir."

Mr. Fern: "And were you told the contrary, that even though the Senator was being paid out of committee funds, to nevertheless bill the honorarium payers?"

Mr. O'Hare: "Every time I billed an honorarium payer, I billed him under direction." (*Transcript of Hearings,* pp. 747 and 748.)

* * *

Senator Dodd: "I think the Senate should know that I did not deal with these private organizations in determining whether or not there would be travel reimbursement, nor did I receive from them checks in payment of the air travel expense. This was all done by O'Hare, since it was his job to keep my personal books of account and checkbook, as well as handle all my travel matters.

"I want to make sure I made that clear. He was the one who handled my books and my personal accounts for my income tax. I never prepared them myself. I assume if he had found any erroneous billings, he would have told me. He never did." (*Congressional Record,* June 15, 1967, p. S 8220.)

* * *

Senator Bennett: "In answer to this, it should be pointed out that obviously Senator Dodd had to be involved, essentially and inescapably. This will become crystal clear as I go along, but let me point out first that it was he—not O'Hare—who was enriched by the scheme. It was into his bank account that the improper double reimbursement went. Not only has he never denied this, but by paying it back only 10 days ago he had acknowledged it." (*Congressional Record,* June 19, 1967, p. S 8398.)

Senator Monroney: "I have to make out my income tax. If I found a considerable amount in my income tax return as receipts I think I would recognize it in due checking of the account. We all have that to do, no matter how busy we are." (*Congressional Record,* June 19, 1967, p. S 8384.)

Senator McCarthy: "There were, I think, at least four points in the process of double billing at which we might have expected the Senator to

320 : : **JAMES BOYD**

have made note of what was happening. I do not say he could not have failed to do so, but at least there were four points, in passing at which the possibility of double billing might come to his attention, and might have been noted:

"First. When he was agreeing to make the speech to the private organization, the question of whether or not they were paying the transportation might well have been brought up.

"Second. At the time of the purchase of tickets with committee credit cards, when that purchase was made or when the committee was billed, if that process was followed.

"Third. At the time that he was making deposits in his own bank account of the receipts in the way of an honorarium or repayment from private sources of transportation costs or if he was being repaid by the committee.

"Fourth. The possibility that it might have been checked when subcommittee expenditures were being checked." (*Congressional Record*, June 20, 1967, p. S 8458.)

* * *

On whether the double billing was extensive enough to constitute a pattern of conduct:

Senator Dodd: "During the period in question, 1961 through 1966, I made more than 80 trips for which I was reimbursed either by the Senate or by private organizations. The Ethics Committee's proposed censure relating to reimbursed expenses is based on seven of these more than 80 trips and involves a total reimbursement to me of $1,767.14." (*Congressional Record*, June 13, 1967, p. S 8109.)

* * *

Senator Dodd: "The question for the Senate to decide in this matter is simple enough: Were the seven double billings a result of a conscious, deliberate, willful attempt on my part to defraud the Government or were they the result of inept or inaccurate bookkeeping?

"Before analyzing this matter in more detail, I am constrained to say that the charge is so inherently implausible that I shall never be able to understand how the members of the Ethics Committee found against me.

"I have been in public life now for more than 30 years in different capacities, and prior to this time, no one has ever accused me of double billing or of chiselling in any other way. Indeed, I simply cannot conceive of any public official jeopardizing his entire future by engaging in the kind of petty larceny that has been imputed to me.

"Seven double billings in 7 years does not by any stretch of the imagination suggest a pattern of willful villainy." (*Congressional Record*, June 14, 1967, p. S 8149.)

* * *

Senator Pearson: "During the period involved, the committee made a study of approximately 80 trips, as the Senator from Connecticut correctly stated this morning. From that point, we sought to determine how many of the trips involved a claim which had been made against the Senate. From the records of the disbursing office, it was determined that of the 80, some 26 trips represented claims against the Senate or a subcommittee.

"The next step was to seek to determine, once the issue of the so-called double billing had been framed, how many of those 26 trips represented an occasion—either through the nature of the trip, in a geographical sense, or the timing involved—a dual performance, so to speak; how many were conducted for Senate business. The committee makes no issue of that whatsoever, as the Senator correctly stated. The committee sought to find out how many of those trips were on Senate business but also involved a personal appearance by the Senator. That was determined to be in the number of 10. The figure that resulted was seven. Seven were represented, by the committee report, as supporting the resolution—seven out of 10, which is a great distinction between seven or a fewer number out of some 80 trips that might have been taken.

"There were seven on which there were double payments representing the Senate and also private organizations.

"In the stipulations I referred to on pages 1015 and 1018 there are six additional trips—they are not in issue—which did represent some evidence of a course of conduct, or a pattern, as the trips were taken, and payment was received not only from the private organizations involved, but also from the campaign funds of the testimonial account.

"So we had seven out of 10, by our estimate, and then the six additional." (*Congressional Record,* June 14, 1967, pp. S 8159 and S 8160.)

* * *

Senator Dodd: "Had I really wanted to cheat the Government, however, the total opportunities for cheating was 80. Several of the continuing investigations in which I have been engaged required hearings in metropolitan centers around the country for the purpose of creating as complete a national picture as possible. Had I really been intent on cheating the Government, it would have been a relatively simple matter to arrange for hearings in those cities I visited on the 54 trips I made in connection with speaking engagements.

"And if I were the incorrigible scrounger the committee apparently believes me to be I could, with a little effort, have contrived speaking engagements in the cities I visited in connection with the 26 trips I made on Government business." (*Congressional Record,* June 20, 1967, p. S 8473.)

* * *

Senator Bennett: "Of these approximately 80 trips, 70 were made for a single purpose, such as responding to an invitation to speak, or conducting some Senate committee business. That left 10 trips, and these were the only ones on which Senator Dodd conducted both private business and public business on the same trip. Therefore it is vital to an understanding of the committee's position that these 10 represented his only opportunities for double reimbursement. Last week Senator Dodd made great point of the fact that if he had wanted to cheat on the other 70 trips he could have done it by inventing spurious business as a basis for double billing. Let us look at that claim for a minute. Actually, he could not invent a private appearance which would provide expenses in addition to an honorarium for those trips which he had taken purely for Senate business, so the only opportunity he would have had to invent a basis for double billing was to invent Senate business on trips where he went primarily to address a public group.

"Of the 80 trips, there were 54 trips for private purposes only, and Senator Dodd in his statement on the floor, suggested that if this were directly a 'course of conduct' he could have invented a Government business in order to create the opportunity for double billing. Actually a course of conduct, to my mind, necessarily relates to something that actually happened, not what might have happened. The word 'conduct' itself implies this.

"If there were 54 trips out of 80 on private business only, this leaves 26 trips on which he went on Government business, and among those, as I have said, were 10 on which he did both private and Government business. It is the committee's contention that these 10 provided him with his only available opportunities for double billing involving the Senate funds.

"The committee has tried to make clear that it found elements of double billing in all of these 10 trips—all of them—but with respect to three of them, the committee did not consider the available facts to be conclusive, and therefore, these three were not adduced in the hearings. This leaves the seven, and the facts including double reimbursement of these are admitted by Senator Dodd in his stipulation. . . .

"The printed hearing records, pages 1015 through 1023 also show that Senator Dodd also received payment from both political funds and from private organizations for his transportation expenses on six additional trips.

"The addition of these trips makes 13 instances of admitted double reimbursement—and nearly doubles the range of activities that can be called the 'course of conduct.'" (*Congressional Record*, June 19, 1967, p. S 8403.)

* * *

On the claim that incompetent bookkeeping was the cause of the double billings:

Senator Dodd: "But O'Hare, having gone through my books systematically in an effort to find anything that might compromise me, apparently came across the several instances of double billing that had resulted from his own slipshod bookkeeping, and he told the committee that the errors were not errors but that they were part of a deliberate effort on my part to defraud the Government.

"Let me tell you what kind of bookkeeper O'Hare really was: On 21 occasions, between 1961 and 1966, I incurred travel expenses on official business to my home state, for which I was entitled to reimbursement but for which no claim was ever submitted. O'Hare was directly responsible for the failure to collect reimbursement in 15 instances between fiscal 1961 and the fiscal year of 1966. He was indirectly responsible for the failure to collect reimbursement in 5 instances between fiscal 1961 and the fiscal year of 1966. He was indirectly responsible for the failure of my office to claim reimbursement for official travel to Connecticut subsequent to his departure, because, in handling the books to my secretary, Miss Moloney, he failed to give her any instruction on the matter." (*Congressional Record*, June 14, 1967, p. S 8150.)

* * *

Mr. Fern: "Mr. O'Hare, why didn't you claim Senator Dodd's home State entitlements, which according to law until 1966, fiscal year 1966, he was entitled at the rate of two trips to his home State each year, and after fiscal year 1966, at the rate of six trips per year?"

Mr. O'Hare: "I simply had been unaware of the law. However, even upon learning about the law, I had previously been under Senator Dodd's direct instructions, sending all of Senator Dodd's travel expenses, from 1963, 1964 and 1965 up to the Senator's campaign committee in Hartford.

"When I first started sending these statements, some of the travel, I believe went back as far as 1962. To have billed the Senate at this point for trips, would have constituted only additional duplicate billings, because the Senator had already been paid for each trip that he had taken by his own campaign committee.

"For the time prior, that is the time before I actually started sending his expenses or paying his expenses out of campaign funds, I was faced with a relatively short period of time from May 1961, not even May 1961, since it wasn't my responsibility when I first came on the Senator's staff, but approximately for the period of about a year. In order to gain reimbursement I would have had to do a complete audit of each trip that the Senator took to his home State for that year or maybe year and a half, to determine whether or not he was traveling on official business, and also whether or not he used commercial airliner or a company plane, which he frequently used, and for the sake of just two or three trips, this was just too arduous a task for me to do at this time. I didn't have the intention of his not being reimbursed for something that was due him. I simply had other duties and I set it aside temporarily. My time in office just ran out before I ever did get reimbursement for the time that he was due reimbursement." (*Transcript of Hearings*, pp. 748 and 749.

* * *

Senator Russell Long: "It might be well also to keep in mind that the Government still owes him for 21 trips—21 trips for which the incompetent Michael O'Hare failed to bill the Government as legitimate travel by Tom Dodd to and from Connecticut." (*Congressional Record,* June 16, 1967, p. S 8322.)

* * *

Senator Lausche: "How many trips could he have charged to the Government under the automatic right given of two return trips a year, up to a certain period, and then six return trips?"

Senator Bennett: "There was an opportunity to charge 10 during O'Hare's period of tenure. The record shows one was charged. If I could get my hands on a list, I could tell the Senator. That one was prior to O'Hare's employment, but it was during that period.

"So there were nine that could have been charged while O'Hare was bookkeeper, and the remaining 12 to make up the 21 became available after O'Hare left."

* * *

Senator Lausche: "Does not that indicate a sort of nonknowledge of what was actually going on with the books? It would seem to me he would definitely have charged it otherwise."

Senator Bennett: "I do not think it has to do with the books. It has to do with his lack of knowledge of his rights as a Senator."

* * *

Senator Stennis: "The question was asked a minute ago why we did not give him credit for those 21 trips for the amounts. The Senator from Utah stated that in his view it was irrelevant, and I think he was correct. That is not any of our business. I do not know whether the Senator ever made the trips or not. There is no proof before us, as I recall, that the trips were ever made. He was just eligible to make those trips, and then, if the trips were made, would have been eligible for reimbursement if he had paid out his money. But until proof is made that he made the trips and paid for them out of his pocket, he is not eligible for any reimbursement. . . ." (*Congressional Record,* June 19, 1967, p. S 8408.)

* * *

Senator Brooke: "The Senator agrees that Senator Dodd had a clear opportunity to bill the Senate for 21 trips for which he was entitled to reimbursement but for which he did not bill the Senate?"

Senator Bennett: "We stipulated that on the theory that Senator Dodd must have traveled back and forth to Connecticut over these years at least 21 times. But we had no listing of the trips, the dates, or the places. And apparently Senator Dodd still has none, because his own statement on the floor of the Senate was that his accountants are still hunting for the trips which he can justify as being reimbursable."

Senator Brooke: "Certainly the Senate is entitled to accept a stipulation."

Senator Bennett: "The Senator is correct." (*Congressional Record,* June 19, 1967, p. S 8409.)

INDEX